Proving the Way

Conflict and Practice in the History of Japanese Nativism

Harvard East Asian Monographs 245

Proving the Way
*Conflict and Practice in the History
of Japanese Nativism*

Mark McNally

Published by the Harvard University Asia Center
and distributed by Harvard University Press
Cambridge (Massachusetts) and London 2005

© 2005 by the President and Fellows of Harvard College

Printed in the United States of America

The Harvard University Asia Center publishes a monograph series and, in coordination with the Fairbank Center for East Asian Research, the Korea Institute, the Reischauer Institute of Japanese Studies, and other faculties and institutes, administers research projects designed to further scholarly understanding of China, Japan, Vietnam, Korea, and other Asian countries. The Center also sponsors projects addressing multidisciplinary and regional issues in Asia.

Library of Congress Cataloging-in-Publication Data

McNally, Mark, 1968–
    Proving the way : conflict and practice in the history of Japanese nativism.
        p. cm. -- (Harvard East Asian monographs ; 245)
    Author: Mark McNally. Cf. ECIP t.p. plus.
    Includes bibliographical references and index.
    ISBN 0-674-01778-1 (cloth : alk. paper)
      1. Hirata, Atsutane, 1776-1843. 2. Kokugaku. 3. Japan--Intellectual life--1600-1868. I. Title. II. Series.
    B5244.H474M47 2005
    952'.0072'052--dc22

                                                              2004029107

Index by the author

♾ Printed on acid-free paper

Last figure below indicates year of this printing
15 14 13 12 11 10 09 08 07 06 05

For

Phoebe and Elaine

Acknowledgments

I made use of various libraries and archives while researching my dissertation and later this book. In the United States, I mostly used the Asian collections of the libraries of UCLA, UC Berkeley, the University of Hawai'i at Mānoa, and Harvard University. While conducting research in Japan in 1996, I used the National Diet Library, the Tokyo Municipal Library in Hirō, Kokugakuin University library, and the National Literature Institute (Kokubungaku Kenkyū Shiryōkan) in Shinagawa. While in Japan, I was based at Tokyo University, where I used its Main Library (Sōgō Toshokan), the library of the Faculty of Literature (Bungaku-bu), the departmental libraries of History, Religion, and Ethics, and the Historiographical Institute (Shiryō Hensanjo). I also made use of the resources housed at the Iyataka Shrine (Akita), the Hirata Shrine (Tokyo), the Motoori Shrine (Matsusaka), and the Jinja Honchō (Tokyo). I would like to thank the staff of each of these institutions for their help and patience.

While researching and writing, I was the recipient of various grants and fellowships for which I am grateful. As a graduate student at UCLA, I received a multiyear recruitment package from the Graduate Division, a writing grant from the Office of the Chancellor, and dissertation research grants from the Department of History and the Center for Japanese Studies. In 1998, I received a Postdoctoral Fellowship from the Reischauer Institute of Japanese Studies at Harvard University that allowed me to begin the process of revising the dissertation into a book. At the University of Hawai'i at Mānoa, I have received research funds from the University

Research Council, the Department of History, and the Center for Japanese Studies (Summer Research Fellowship).

I would like to express my gratitude to all the people who have helped me over the years: Fred Notehelfer, John Duncan, Benjamin Elman, Sharon Traweek, Hal Bolitho, Bernhard Scheid, Sharon Minichiello, Bettina Gramlich-Oka, Shoji Kakuko, Koyasu Nobukuni, Kamata Jun'ichi, Omote Tomoyuki, Maita Harue, Sawai Keiichi, Uechi Akihiko, and Minami Orihara. I would also like to thank the two anonymous readers for the press for their insights and advice. A shorter version of Chapter 4 appeared in the *Japanese Journal of Religious Studies*. I thank the editors of that journal for their permission to reproduce it here. Finally, special thanks to the Hirata Shrine for their permission to reproduce *Muchū taimenzu* for the dust jacket.

Finally, there is a group of people who deserve a special expression of thanks. Herman Ooms was my mentor in graduate school from whom I learned much. Herman has a very keen intellect and analytic mind. He encouraged all of his students to study the material deeply and "make connections." I appreciate the training that he gave me and view him as one of a handful of truly brilliant people whom I have had the privilege to meet. Samuel Yamashita was my undergraduate mentor at Pomona College. I first learned about Tokugawa intellectual history and Kokugaku in his seminar. It was from Sam that I learned that an academic life could be fulfilling; I owe my choice of career to him. Kurozumi Makoto was my mentor at Tokyo University, where he taught me how to do research at Japanese institutions. He also taught me how to read *kanbun* and *sōrōbun* documents, and he helped me to decipher several *komonjo* sources as well. This triumvirate is a group of truly outstanding scholars and teachers. I hope to be able to follow their example with my own students.

The final two people who deserve my special gratitude are my wife, Elaine, and my daughter, Phoebe. I have found strength in their love and support, despite the demands of job and career. It is to them that I dedicate this book.

M.M.

Contents

	Tables and Figures	xi
	Preface	xiii
	Conventions and Abbreviations	xv
1	The Ascendancy of Hirata Atsutane and the Invention of Kokugaku	1
2	The Formation of Rival Nativist Schools: The Edo-ha and the Norinaga School	14
3	The Norinaga School in Edo	65
4	The *Sandaikō* Debate: Mythology, Astronomy, and Eschatology	96
5	On a Dream and a Prayer: Atsutane's Discourse of Succession and a New Nativist Tradition	131
6	Forsaking Textualism: Ancient History and the Supernatural	179
7	Bakumatsu Kokugaku and the Hirata School	209
8	Conclusion: Centrality at the Margins	242

Epilogue: Twentieth-Century Ethnology
and Nationalism   257

Reference Matter

Character List   265

Works Cited   267

Index   277

Tables and Figures

Tables

1	Growth of the Hirata School	210
2	Comparison of the enrollments of nativist academies	211

Figures

1	The philology of Yomi as the moon	109
2	The cosmic triad	111
3	The Santetsu lineage	144
4	The Shiushi lineage	144

Preface

This book is concerned mainly with the relationship of Hirata Atsutane to Kokugaku. My interest in Kokugaku and Tokugawa nativism began during my undergraduate years when I read Harry Harootunian's book *Things Seen and Unseen*. Not only was I impressed with its insights into the nature of Kokugaku discourse, but also its theoretical foundations. After college, I moved to Japan; it was there that I decided to pursue the subject of Kokugaku further in graduate school. As a first-year graduate student, my mentor, Herman Ooms, encouraged me to read Koyasu Nobukuni's *Norinaga to Atsutane no sekai*. This book predated Harootunian's by about a decade, but it was also a theoretically informed study of Kokugaku. One of the themes of both Koyasu's study and Harootunian's was the reconciliation of Atsutane's scholarship with that of his nativist contemporaries and predecessors. Although both scholars found interesting discursive continuities between Atsutane and other nativists, an attempt to argue from the opposite view and assert his difference seemed to me a potentially interesting project to undertake.

Two developments during my first year of graduate school finally encouraged me to take this project on as my dissertation. First, I took a seminar on the thought of the late French sociologist, Pierre Bourdieu. I was especially intrigued with Bourdieu's studies of various cultural institutions (art, literature, the Church, law, academe, etc.) as what he called "fields of cultural production." In each of his case studies, Bourdieu demonstrated how the producers who constitute a particular field are always in a state of competition and struggle with one another for control of the field.

He observed that cultural producers tend to congregate around positions that are the polar opposites of each other, which accounts for the energy and hostility that can arise in fields. I applied these insights to what I knew about Tokugawa nativism at the time, and Atsutane and his career seemed to confirm Bourdieu's theory; however, I still needed to do more research. It was toward the end of my first year of graduate school that I found primary sources that seemed to address these issues. The most important of these was a collection of letters that were published as a single compilation in 1834 called the *Kiyosōhansho*. These letters clearly demonstrated that not only was Atsutane unique among Tokugawa nativists, but this difference was also the main source of friction between Atsutane and his nativist colleagues. These letters were proof of the hostility that Bourdieu had seen in other cultural institutions. I decided that I could apply Bourdieu's field analysis to the study of Atsutane and Kokugaku.

One of the advantages of using Bourdieu's ideas is that it allows one to use "theory" but in a more accessible way than is commonly thought among those who eschew theory. Bourdieu was a sociologist and not a philosopher like Michel Foucault or Jacques Derrida. In fact, Bourdieu was very critical of philosophers and their discipline. Since Bourdieu incorporated social practices into his research rather than abstract ideas, his conclusions strike even the non-theoretically inclined as insightful. A second advantage in the use of Bourdieu is that otherwise obscure scholars associated with Kokugaku become prominent due to the analytic emphasis on social interaction. Many of the key figures in this study are virtually unknown in the Japanese and English literature, including Hattori Nakatsune, Kido Chidate, Fujii Takanao, Uematsu Shigetake, and Oyamada Tomokiyo. A final benefit of this study's Bourdieu-inspired approach is the opportunity to break new ground in Tokugawa intellectual history using the sociology of knowledge. Using the sociological methodologies of Bourdieu and others in the analysis of Kokugaku and other intellectual institutions will, I think, revitalize Tokugawa intellectual history. It represents a new scholarly direction for a field that has receded into the margins of Japanese studies in recent years.

Conventions and Abbreviations

The names of schools and intellectual movements are capitalized and not italicized; for example, Kokugaku, Mitogaku, Daoxue.

Macrons are omitted for modern era names (Taisho and Showa) and familiar places (such as Osaka, Tokyo, Hyogo). Also, Japanese words, such as Shinto, shogun, daimyo, bakufu, and bakumatsu that have become familiar in English are not italicized and macrons are omitted.

The following abbreviations are used in the notes and Works Cited:

DNSZ	*Dai Nihon shisō zenshū*
HJAS	*Harvard Journal of Asiatic Studies*
KKNMZ	*Kōhon Kamo no Mabuchi zenshū*
KZ	*Keichū zenshū*
MNS	*Motoori Norinaga shū*
MNZ	*Motoori Norinaga zenshū*
NNS	*Nihon no shisō*
NST	*Nihon shisō taikei*
NZT	*Nihon zuihitsu taisei*
OSZ	*Orikuchi Shinobu zenshū*
SHAZ	*Shinshū Hirata Atsutane zenshū*

Proving the Way

Conflict and Practice in the History of Japanese Nativism

ONE

The Ascendancy of Hirata Atsutane and the Invention of Kokugaku

Kokugaku was one of the most important intellectual movements of the Tokugawa and early Meiji periods. Put simply, it represented an attempt to study Japanese antiquity and to apply its lessons in the rectification of an epoch that many believed was mired in decline. The interest in Japan's remote past has provoked most Western scholars to translate Kokugaku as "nativism."[1] The fact that scholars of the late Meiji, Taisho, and early Showa periods

---

1. I use the term "Kokugaku" to refer specifically to the scholarship of Atsutane and the members of the Norinaga School during the nineteenth century. I have chosen this usage because the term itself was not widely used prior to 1800 and to emphasize Atsutane's role in its systemization. During the seventeenth and eighteenth centuries, scholars used various terms to signify nativism, such as Wagaku. Norinaga called his scholarship "ancient learning" (Kogaku or *inishie manabi*); Atsutane followed Norinaga's example, but he also used the term Kokugaku. Thus, for classical literary studies prior to 1800, and for the various forms of Shinto scholarship of the nineteenth century other than Kokugaku, I use the term nativism. In the Japanese secondary literature, scholars use the term Kokugaku to signify nativist scholarship of the entire Tokugawa period. One of the themes of this study is the process by which Atsutane and the members of the Ibukinoya narrowly defined their nativist scholarship as Kokugaku, a definition that specifically excluded the Edo Faction and the Mabuchi School. This narrow definition of Kokugaku contributed to its nineteenth-century institutional character, which was absent during the eighteenth century. It is for this reason that I maintain the more specific definition advocated by Atsutane and his students.

used the scholarship of Tokugawa nativists to further their own ideological agendas has inspired some modern researchers to think of Kokugaku as a form of proto-nationalism. Whether as nativism or nationalism, the centrality of Kokugaku in the minds of modern scholars is undeniable.

Nativists of the Tokugawa period turned their attention to the production of authentic interpretations of Japanese antiquity in response to the pervasive influence of Confucianism, and especially its impact on Shinto teachings. The eminent political scientist and intellectual historian Maruyama Masao argued that nativism grew to a point during the eighteenth century that it actually displaced Confucianism as the "hegemonic movement in the intellectual world" of Tokugawa Japan.[2] Although it is clear that Maruyama's interpretation of nativism was somewhat exaggerated, his recognition of its influential position within Tokugawa intellectual history was correct.

For Maruyama, nativism was a predominantly literary phenomenon that emerged from the "private side" of the Confucian school of Ogyū Sorai (1666–1728). Motoori Norinaga and Kamo no Mabuchi (1697–1765) occupy prominent positions in his analysis for this reason. Although he acknowledged the importance of Hirata Atsutane for the nineteenth century, Maruyama viewed Atsutane's[3] scholarship as a radical break with Norinaga and Mabuchi. Maruyama recognized that there were two forms of nativism during the Tokugawa period. Rather than account for this differentiation, he chose only to acknowledge the differences while emphasizing its eighteenth-century literary incarnation.

Atsutane himself, however, was also aware of the different forms. For much of his career, he spent his mental energies in an attempt to reconcile the two in such a way as to validate his own scholarship. In some ways, his efforts were successful; he was able

---

2. See his *Studies in the Intellectual History of Tokugawa Japan*, p. 143. Although this work is dated, it is still one of the best books in English on Tokugawa intellectual history.

3. Throughout this study I use the given names of pre-Meiji and early Meiji figures, in order to avoid confusion over those with the same family name. For modern persons, I use the family names.

to assert the validity of his own teachings while preserving the memory of his classicist predecessors, Norinaga and Mabuchi. Thus, the literary aspect of nativism was maintained by Atsutane and his followers. By the end of the Tokugawa period, however, the nature of Atsutane's scholarship and his role in the development of Kokugaku was misunderstood and even forgotten. Puzzled by much of his research, his modern interpreters have not realized the nature of Atsutane's contributions to the institutional form of Kokugaku, knowing that his scholarship fell short of the scholarly standards of his eighteenth-century predecessors. An important goal of the present study is to re-examine Atsutane's scholarship in an effort to restore historicity to the study of Kokugaku. Atsutane was neither an advocate of classicism, nor was he a nineteenth-century aberration. Instead, he was a central figure in the creation and perpetuation of an intellectual tradition that is still a significant part of Japanese history and culture.

༄

Atsutane is one of the most interesting and influential figures in Tokugawa intellectual history. Since his death more than 160 years ago, his scholarship has signified different aspects of intellectual life in Japan's early modern period. The noted scholar of Tokugawa intellectual history Koyasu Nobukuni argues that Atsutane's concern for practical ethics in an indigenous religious idiom, namely Shinto, was a distinctive and significant contribution to nineteenth-century intellectual history.[4] Koyasu responded to the reluctance of mainstream Japanese academics to evaluate Atsutane's impact on Tokugawa intellectual history seriously. Postwar scholars, especially scholars of Shintoism at Kokugakuin University and Kōgakkan University, wrote sparingly about the proto-nationalists and cultural chauvinists of the Tokugawa period. Thus, Koyasu's scholarship represented an attempt to restore Atsutane to his prewar intellectual stature.

Ideologues of the 1930s and 1940s saw in Atsutane's scholarship an opportunity to resurrect a figure from the Tokugawa period who had formulated ideas useful to their nationalist agendas. Atsu-

---

4. Koyasu, *Norinaga to Atsutane no sekai*, pp. 191–96.

tane wrote voluminously on the notion of Japan's uniqueness and superiority, the fundamental teachings of Kokugaku ideology. This close association between wartime scholarship and his ideas contributed to the postwar reluctance to study Atsutane, a reluctance that continues to be felt, despite Koyasu's efforts.

Folklorists at the turn of the century hailed Atsutane as an early-modern ethnographer for his use of information gathered in interviews with commoners. Thus, he had insights into the essence of a Japanese identity based in the everyday experiences of rural society. At the end of the Tokugawa period, his concern with rural society was a theme advocated by his posthumous followers in what has been called grassroots (*sōmō*) Kokugaku. Instead of considering the entirety of rural society, these scholars stressed the leadership roles of village elites in the benevolent administration of the countryside. Atsutane's scholarship was the main source for an ideology that legitimated the social and political dominance of rural elites.

Atsutane's teachings have been appropriated and reappropriated over the years since the end of the Tokugawa era. His prominence, if not infamy, within Japanese intellectual history is secure. Unfortunately, these uses and abuses of his scholarship have obfuscated important aspects of his scholarly life and career. Chief among these distortions is his place within the Kokugaku movement, which many believe began at the end of the seventeenth century and culminated in the writings of Atsutane and his students at the end of the Tokugawa period. In this study, I will focus on deconstructing two myths associated with Atsutane. First, I will carefully examine the notion of Kokugaku itself. It is clear that its institutional coherence as a scholarly movement (*gakumon*) was the result of Atsutane's efforts in the nineteenth century; it was a coherence he projected onto the past. I will examine his reasons for doing this, arguing that all historical accounts written by scholars of Kokugaku in the modern period have not fully appreciated either Atsutane's role in the shaping of Kokugaku or his sociopolitical context for doing it. They have accepted his version of Kokugaku history as valid. Second, the idea that Kokugaku culminated in Atsutane's scholarship obscures his interactions with nativist scholars who had very different views. Thus, I will highlight those scholars whose work has been overshadowed by treatises of Kokugaku slanted in Atsutane's favor. At the same time, I will look more closely at the nature of his contacts with fellow nativists during the first half of the nineteenth century, arguing that his centrality within historical depictions of Kokugaku ignores the profound resistance to his scholarship from contemporaries within the tradition itself.

Framing the Analysis: Ideas Versus Discourse

While the number of articles and monographs on Kokugaku in Japanese is staggering, the same cannot be said of studies in any other language. Studies of Kokugaku in English collectively rank second in number to those in Japanese, but they occupy a distant second place. Of these studies, there are only two monographs in English that deal with the topic.[5] Both books have advanced the study of Kokugaku in the Western world and have also assumed the role of foundational works upon which other studies—this one included—can build.

Peter Nosco's 1990 monograph, *Remembering Paradise*, dealt with the intellectual beginnings of Kokugaku, especially the scholarship of Norinaga. Nosco's study is important for several reasons. First, it is a highly detailed look at the major Kokugaku figures of the eighteenth century. Nosco's thorough research by itself is a major contribution to the literature, furnishing scholars with the kind of data that many Japanese works lack. Nosco analyzes the development of Kokugaku within the context of nostalgic movements that emerged during the Genroku period (that is, the late

---

5. There is a third monograph published in English, one that predates both Nosco and Harootunian. Sajja A. Prasad published his own study of Kokugaku, *The Japanologists: A History* (Andhra Pradesh, India: Samudraiah Prakashan, 1984). Prasad's work, however, was too polemical and vitriolic to be seriously considered by the academic community in either the United States or Japan. In addition, Matsumoto Shigeru published a book in English entitled *Motoori Norinaga, 1730-1801*. It is an intellectual biography that focuses not only on Norinaga's scholarship but also on the ways in which it was a product of his "sociocultural setting" (Matsumoto, *Motoori Norinaga, 1730-1801*, p. 2).

seventeenth and early eighteenth centuries). Second, Nosco's study is also significant because of his new interpretation of Norinaga, the central figure of his book. He asserts that Norinaga's interests in Japanese antiquity were not simply motivated by scholarly curiosity alone. Norinaga's passion for Kokugaku stemmed from a deep religious faith in Shinto.[6] Nosco argues correctly that interpretations of Norinaga have emphasized the secular nature of his work, since most scholars view Kokugaku in an intellectual continuum with Confucian scholarship. This emphasis, however, ignores the fundamentally religious nature of Kokugaku, linked, as it was, to Shinto and the imperial institution.

Two years prior to Nosco, Harry Harootunian published the other major book on Kokugaku in English. Although there is some overlap between Harootunian's book and Nosco's, Harootunian focuses his study on the nineteenth century, especially the bakumatsu period (1830–67). He offers quite a novel interpretation of Kokugaku, arguing that it was one discourse among a handful of others whose adherents advocated local autonomy and even rural secession from the greater whole of the nation.[7] The early scholars of Kokugaku, most of whom are analyzed in quite a different way in Nosco's book, contributed to this Kokugaku discourse, and their bakumatsu followers tried to transmute the discourse into political action.

While these two monographs have significantly deepened our understanding of Kokugaku and of Tokugawa intellectual history in general, the two books are so unlike that they do not complement each other well. Nosco's study focuses on the foundational ideas of Kokugaku and the scholars who produced them. Thus, his book is more traditional in its approach to Tokugawa intellectual history. Harootunian, on the other hand, is more interested in the same ideas as they constitute an autonomous and disembodied discourse, one that is not necessarily the product of individual thinkers. Harootunian's analysis relies on a kind of Foucaultian episteme, a transcendental mental structure that determines the ideas

---

6. Nosco, *Remembering Paradise*, p. 231.
7. Harootunian, *Things Seen and Unseen*, p. 407.

of a given age.[8] Thus, Harootunian has nothing to say about the formative role of contact and interaction among Tokugawa scholars in the generation of that discourse. Moreover, Nosco ends his study with the death of Norinaga in 1801; Harootunian stresses developments during the nineteenth century. Harootunian, therefore, emphasizes the role of Atsutane and his followers; Nosco virtually ignores Atsutane.

The present study will bridge the conceptual gap between Nosco and Harootunian. First, its scope is broader than that of either scholar; it covers figures from the early seventeenth century through the end of the nineteenth century. Second, this study incorporates theoretical assumptions held by both scholars into a coherent methodological approach. For Nosco, Kokugaku cannot be understood without reference to the historical context within which it developed, which he argues is the Genroku era. Contextualization is important for the present study as well. Instead of a general historical context, a particular kind of context is important; specifically, a grasp of the sociopolitical context is crucial, but more on that later. The primary object of analysis in this study is discourse; this is also the case with Harootunian. Harootunian, however, is not concerned with analyzing the changes in discourse. This study stresses the developmental process of a discourse. Change originates not in the genius of individual thinkers, or in the vicissitudes of a transcendental episteme, but in the interactions of the Kokugaku scholars themselves.

Conflict, Practice, and Intellectual History: A Framework and Methodology

Invariably, interactions among scholars produce antagonism, leading to conflict. The sociologist Randall Collins argues that conflict not only gives scholarship vitality and dynamism but is also the principal force behind the production of ideas;[9] antagonisms among scholars produce intellectual change. In *The Sociology of Philosophies*, Collins opposes the notion that "ideas beget ideas," or

---

8. Foucault, *The Archaeology of Knowledge*, p. 191.
9. Collins, *The Sociology of Philosophies*, p. 1.

that "individuals beget ideas," remarks that could apply to both Harootunian and Nosco, respectively.[10] Social interactions that create conflict, however, do beget ideas.

In order for intellectuals and scholars to assert their differences face to face, they must have the regular opportunity to meet. Collins demonstrates that throughout the world and throughout history scholars and intellectuals have congregated as groups around shared ideas. In any given field of intellectual endeavor, they have formed only a few of these groups;[11] members of a particular group have been aware of the other members of the group, as well as the existence of the other groups in the field. Finally, every intellectual field has had its favorites, those who upheld orthodoxy, and its dissidents,[12] those who challenged it. Collins's observations about intellectuals across time and culture are especially apropos in the study of Atsutane and the historical development of Kokugaku.

Atsutane's prominence in Japanese intellectual history is not only the result of nationalist appropriations during the 1930s and 1940s. His scholarship was popular during his lifetime, and his academy boasted an enrollment of students from throughout Japan. Thus, his ascendancy was closely linked to confrontations with his opponents both within and outside the group of students of Motoori Norinaga, which I call the Norinaga School. Both his scholarship and his behavior toward these opponents reflect these tensions. The process by which Atsutane subdued his intellectual foes cannot, however, be fully explained by exclusive reference to either the contents of his scholarship (a text-centered approach) or the extant data on his life (a context-centered approach).[13] To simply declare his inheritance of the Kokugaku tradition (which he did) did not necessarily guarantee that all members of that tradition would accept it. At the same time, an analysis of Atsutane's

---

10. Ibid., p. 2.
11. Ibid., p. 42.
12. Ibid., p. 4.
13. Pierre Bourdieu argues that an examination of the social conditions of production resolves the gap between these two approaches, "which are traditionally perceived as irreconcilable" (*The Rules of Art*, p. 205).

practice, such as the alliances he formed both with the Yoshida house of Shinto ritualists in Kyoto and with rural elites, must be contextualized. While biographical details can be one useful contextualization of practice, his intellectual production, interpreted as fundamentally ideological in nature, provides the most compelling framework. Practice cannot be understood without ideology, and ideology is only comprehensible when analyzed with practice.[14] In this study, I will analyze Atsutane's ascendancy by relating it to the homologous relationship between his ideology and practice. This study will foreground the fierce resistance to Atsutane during his lifetime as evidence of his objective social and intellectual marginality within the Norinaga School.

Many of Atsutane's contemporaries resisted his scholarship and membership within the Norinaga School because of their inherently opposing views of nativism. The scholar Uchino Gorō conceptualizes these different views as a "narrow definition" and a "broad definition" of Kokugaku.[15] The former, brandished as orthodox by Atsutane's students during the bakumatsu period, emphasized scholarship on the ancient Way (*kodō*). The latter, which emphasized literature and literary analysis, is the more accurate view of Kokugaku history, he argues. Uchino locates Atsutane and Norinaga, perhaps the most famous of all Kokugaku scholars (*kokugakusha*), in the lineage of the ancient Way, while placing Kamo no Mabuchi (1697–1769) and his students in the lineage of classical literary studies. The main source of tensions between Atsutane and his critics within the Norinaga School was his loose approach to classical literature, as well as shortcomings in his textual methodology. Uchino, however, emphasizes the tensions between Atsutane and his contemporaries in the Edo-ha (Edo Faction), most of whom were scholars within Mabuchi's lineage. Despite Uchino's groundbreaking research, he has told only part of the story. Textualism and classical literature were also central to the scholarship of Norinaga and his students. Atsutane's negative atti-

---

14. Roger Chartier, historian of French cultural history, uses the categories of "discursive production" and the "objective social positions and properties external to discourse" within which practice takes place (*On the Edge of the Cliff*, p. 20).

15. Uchino, *Shinkokugakuron no tenkai*, p. 91.

tude toward these subjects was irritating for them as well. Both Atsutane's attitude toward literature and his eschatological interests were recurrent themes in criticisms made against him by scholars among Norinaga's students.

Missing from Uchino's history of Kokugaku is an analysis of Atsutane's position within the Norinaga School, which he formally joined in 1805. The rules for inclusion within the School were never outlined as such by Norinaga or his disciples. Thus, Atsutane's first challenge was to establish his credentials as a member while probing the limits of these unarticulated rules. This challenge was made difficult because of the School's emphasis on philology. At the ideological level, he justified his membership within the Norinaga School by attempting to define its orthodoxy. Instead of classical literature and philology, he advocated eschatology as the School's intellectual priority. At a practical level, he borrowed discursive elements of succession and legitimation from other cultural institutions in order to support his assertions. In the process, he gave the Norinaga School an institutional identity that it did not have prior to his ascendancy. No longer was it merely one group of nativists active during the late Tokugawa period; Atsutane believed that the members of the Norinaga School practiced the only legitimate form of scholarship. He transformed the Norinaga School into Kokugaku.

Atsutane reoriented his own scholarship away from classical texts, breaking from the leading figures of both the Norinaga School and the Edo-ha. He maintained an avid interest in eschatology, even before joining the Norinaga School. He first attempted to ground his views of the afterlife in the Shinto classics, with very little success. Instead, he tried to maintain the Norinaga School's emphasis on evidentialism without referring to the classics. At the same time, he took advantage of Norinaga's assertions that the essence of the ancient Way was not exclusively literary; the ancient Way for Norinaga was much broader than that. In Atsutane's estimation, the ancient Way was indeed not found exclusively in literary sources as Norinaga had argued; instead, the Way as practiced by the ancients was about living in accordance with knowledge of the afterlife. His conceptualization of the ancient Way, as well as his non-textualist methodology, were vehemently rejected by many, if not most, of his colleagues in the Norinaga School. This aspect of Atsutane's scholarship faded into obscurity after his death, proving to be unpopular with many of his successors as well. Yet, at the same time, it was instrumental in making his scholarship distinctive enough for him to claim leadership within the Norinaga School and, eventually, Kokugaku itself. Thus, modern researchers have not analyzed his true position within Kokugaku history. One of the goals of this study is to analyze Atsutane's scholarship within the context of the social conditions of its production and to assess its impact on the history of nativism.

Outline of the Chapters

In Chapter 2, I conceptualize the relationship between two contemporaneous groups of nativists during the early nineteenth century: the Edo-ha and the Norinaga School. I argue that these two schools held divergent views and assumptions regarding nativism, despite superficial similarities. The members of the Norinaga School grew more aware of the distinctive nature of their scholarship vis-à-vis their rivals in Edo, which led to its dominance over the Edo-ha outside Edo, due in part to the latter's looser institutional structure and ambivalence toward ideological matters.

In Chapters 3 through 6, I chart the trajectory of Atsutane's ascendancy within the Norinaga School. In Chapter 3, I explain his relationships to both the Norinaga School and the Edo-ha. I account for the apparent paradox of Atsutane's membership in the Nochi-Suzunoya in Matsusaka, an affiliate academy of the Norinaga School, despite his being a resident of Edo and living in close proximity to many of the leading scholars of the Edo-ha. Their indifference to the idea of an exclusively native approach to Japanese antiquity was a reflection of their preoccupation with the study of poetry, an obsession that many of the members of the Norinaga School did not share. It is for this reason that Atsutane became a member of the Norinaga School and was not an active participant in the Edo-ha.

Chapters 4 and 5 deal with Atsutane's career in the Norinaga School. In Chapter 4, the focus of attention is the formulation of his distinctive scholarship against the backdrop of a debate within the Norinaga School over an astronomical text. Atsutane used this debate as an opportunity to advance his eschatological interests against the primacy of classical literature. His participation in the controversy factionalized the Norinaga School and created an intellectual position within it that was the polar opposite of its leaders. The French sociologist Pierre Bourdieu argues that the creation of opposing poles is a necessary first step in the formation of an autonomous field of cultural production.[16] This is an important insight, as the aftermath was perhaps the most significant development for the institutional identity of Kokugaku.

Chapter 5 illustrates Atsutane's attempts to wrest control of the Norinaga School away from the advocates of classicism. He made claims of legitimacy, and eventually succession, against the energetic objections of these rivals. He gave even more shape to what later became Kokugaku by constructing the first orthodox lineage or *dōtō* for Kokugaku. In the context of Atsutane's creation of the Kokugaku *dōtō*, I focus on the two reputed founders of Kokugaku, Keichū (1640–1701) and Kada no Azumamaro (1669–1736). My argument is that these scholars were, contrary to the standard view, ideologically unremarkable for the history of Kokugaku. In other words, the two scholars were assigned an ideological agenda—the discourse of Kokugaku—that they never actually espoused. Kamo no Mabuchi and Motoori Norinaga were also prominent in Atsutane's lineage. I situate these two scholars within an intellectual milieu of increasing dissatisfaction with the hegemony of Song (Neo-)Confucianism. The intellectual contributions of these scholars to nativism, therefore, cannot be understood without reference to critiques of Song Confucian thought.

Having secured for himself a leading position within the Norinaga School, Atsutane nearly abandoned philology in favor of investigations of the afterlife and the supernatural. This is the topic covered in Chapter 6. This shift had two important elements. First, he attempted, by using informants as sources of empirical data, to be no less evidential in these paranormal investigations than his colleagues were in their use of philology. Second, since urban

---

16. Bourdieu, *Rules of Art*, p. 193.

commoners and especially peasants were eager to share their stories, he began to emphasize their personal experiences over the endeavors of scholars. His esteem for rural society had a significant corollary effect as well. Many peasants were enthusiastic about his work, and Atsutane was eager to recruit them into his academy. They were a crucial part of his desire to become a professional scholar so that he could abandon his medical practice. His rural supporters were essential to the logistical and financial support of his academy, since he was never able to attain the official employment that he sought.

In Chapter 7, I discuss how Atsutane's invention of Kokugaku survived into the early Meiji period. Despite selective changes in his message, informed by the ideological concerns of later generations, scholars even today accept to some degree his idea of Kokugaku as standard. Unfortunately for contemporary researchers, Atsutane's ideological triumph, the projection of intellectual and spiritual coherence onto the past, is a legacy that has obscured the historical development of Kokugaku.

ଔ

The first priority of this study is to restore the historicity that has been suppressed and eventually forgotten since the middle of the nineteenth century. Ultimately such a restoration can undermine the intellectual and epistemological basis for Japanese cultural chauvinism, and all such cultural chauvinisms, by conceptualizing the history of Kokugaku as a competition of conflicting discourses advanced by specific scholars. In the middle of the nineteenth century, this discursive plurality was suppressed for particular sociopolitical reasons, but this suppression was not the result of a *conscious* design as such. Atsutane did not plan the invention of Kokugaku. Instead, it was the culmination of a process in which Atsutane responded to his rivals. Consequently, Kokugaku, as the intellectual basis for Japanese cultural chauvinism, was more the result of his political savvy, his "feel for the game," than a desire to formulate a new intellectual tradition. As a discursive irruption in the nineteenth century, Kokugaku was an accident of history and not the realization of a spiritual destiny.

TWO

The Formation of Rival Nativist Schools: The Edo-ha and the Norinaga School

The early decades of the nineteenth century were a crucial period in the development of Tokugawa Kokugaku. Scholars in Edo, Kyoto, Osaka, Matsusaka, and elsewhere were vigorously engaged in the analysis of classical Japanese texts, and they actively recruited students and expanded the influence of nativism into most of the major regions of Japan. In the *Tamadasuki* of 1832, one of a handful of Hirata Atsutane's most significant works, he reflected on the developments of the first three decades of the nineteenth century. In Book IX, he reconstructed the history of Kokugaku, focusing primarily on the lives of Kada no Azumamaro, Kamo no Mabuchi, and Motoori Norinaga. His account created one of the first nativist lineages, and Atsutane included himself within it. With Atsutane included, these "four great men," or *shiushi* (also *shitaijin*), have been central to the orthodox understanding of Kokugaku history that even some contemporary scholars sustain.

Within this lineage, however, there is no acknowledgment of either the Mabuchi School in Edo, the Edo-ha, or the Norinaga School.[1] Little attention has been given to the study of Atsutane's

---

1. The term "Norinaga School" refers to the network of Norinaga's students and disciples in the period following his death in 1801. I use the term "Suzunoya" to refer to his private academy and its students in Matsusaka during the eighteenth

contemporaries within the broader framework of Kokugaku history in general. Thus, not much is known about how the scholars of the Edo-ha and the Norinaga School interacted, or about how Atsutane related to either group and what the impact of this interaction was in the development of his own ideas.

The Edo-ha formed from the remnants of the private academy Mabuchi had inherited in the 1750s. Two of Mabuchi's prominent students, Katō Enao (1692–1785) and Murata Harumichi (d. 1769), formed the core of the early academy. It reached its intellectual apex with the sons of these two men, Katō Chikage (1735–1808) and Murata Harumi (1746–1811). These scholars and their students continued Mabuchi's studies of the *Man'yōshū*, ancient aesthetics, and poetry. By the early nineteenth century, the scholars of the Edo-ha, many of whom were acquaintances of Atsutane, had forsaken any attempt to elucidate an indigenous Japanese Way via poetics, preferring to study and compose verse for its own sake.

While the cohesion of the Edo-ha deteriorated in the years immediately following Mabuchi's death in 1769, Norinaga and his students pursued their own nativist studies in Matsusaka. Inspired by Mabuchi's work on the *Man'yōshū*, Norinaga sought to apprehend the essence of Japanese antiquity through his research on the *Kojiki*. After his death in 1801, his sons, Haruniwa (1763–1828) and Ōhira (1756–1833), continued his rigorous study of antiquity. Like the Mabuchi students of the Edo-ha, Norinaga students developed their studies in a slightly different direction than their School's founder, and none of them was ever able to match the feat that he had achieved with his *Kojiki-den*. Although the Norinaga School had crucial and fundamental differences with the Edo-ha, its emphasis on classical textualism was a trait that it shared with its Edo counterpart. However, by the early years of the nineteenth century, these differences eclipsed any intellectual commonalities between the two groups of scholars.

---

century. Similarly, I use the term "school" to refer to the network of disciples of other scholars and teachers.

The Edo-ha

The intellectual origins of Kokugaku go back to the nativist scholarship of seventeenth-century Kyoto and Osaka.[2] Azumamaro's teachings focused primarily on ancient Shinto rituals and prayers, and he managed to recruit a modest number of students in Edo chiefly from among the ranks of Shinto priests, with a few samurai as well.[3] When he died in 1736, three of his most prominent students in Edo were his adopted son, Arimaro (1706–51), his brother Nobuna (1685–1751), and Mabuchi.[4] Arimaro was the direct heir of Azumamaro's household, as well as his school in Edo; Mabuchi was a talented student of Azumamaro from Hamamatsu. In 1738 the two disciples clashed over the nature of poetry in a debate commissioned by Arimaro's patron, Tayasu Munetake (1715–71).[5] Munetake, the Confucian-trained head of the newly created Tayasu family and son of Shogun Yoshimune, believed that the nature of verse was normative, making it essential to effective political administration; Mabuchi concurred. Arimaro parted ways with the two, arguing that poetry, especially Japanese verse, was the manifestation of emotion and feeling, thereby neutralizing any practical or ethical utility.[6]

Mabuchi went to Edo shortly after Azumamaro's death in 1736. During his early months in Edo, Arimaro introduced him to a prominent merchant family, the Murata, who took an interest in his welfare and gave him financial support. Murata Harumichi

---

2. Uchino, *Edo kokugaku ronkō*, p. 13.
3. Nosco, *Remembering Paradise*, p. 75.
4. Note that Kada no Azumamaro had returned to Fushimi in 1723, never to return to Edo. His school in Edo, however, continued to flourish, while he remained active in Kansai. The two factions of the Azumamaro School developed in divergent ways, however. This fact will become relevant later, during the discussion of the influence of Edo's thriving cultural atmosphere on the development of the Edo-ha.
5. Munetake was the father of the bakufu's chief senior councilor, Matsudaira Sadanobu. For a detailed study of Sadanobu's career, see Ooms, *Charismatic Bureaucrat*.
6. For a more detailed description of this controversy, see Nosco, "Nature, Invention, and National Learning."

hired him as a tutor to his two sons, Harusato (1739-68) and Harumi. Murata Harumi became one of the most influential Mabuchi students during the early nineteenth century. Harumichi introduced Mabuchi to another influential figure in Katō Enao, who also retained his services as a tutor to his son Chikage, another important scholar in the decades following Mabuchi's death.

Mabuchi's stature among his contemporaries rose significantly during the latter half of the 1730s and throughout the 1740s. In 1751 both Nobuna and Arimaro died, leaving only Mabuchi as the last of the great students of Azumamaro in Edo. While Azumamaro was a learned scholar of the *Man'yōshū*, Mabuchi subjected the text to the kind of rigorous analysis that made him more of an authority on it. His scholarship, coupled with a talent for classical Japanese verse, helped him to establish his own academy in Edo dedicated to studies of the *Man'yōshū*. At the time of his death, his academy had an enrollment of "over three hundred."[7]

Mabuchi's Scholarship: Classical Verse and Philology

Unlike his mentor Azumamaro,[8] Mabuchi believed that poetic anthologies were the most important of all classical texts. Azumamaro instructed his students in the importance of a comprehensive investigation of antiquity, which should include poetry as well as Shinto liturgical texts, imperial histories, and texts that recorded the customs and institutions of ancient courtier society. This last field of antiquarian research was known as Yūsokugaku, and was one favored by Arimaro. Mabuchi was not as interested in researching the full range of classical texts, believing that he could fully apprehend antiquity through the study of verse.[9] Mabuchi privileged classical verse because of its inherent link to human emotion; it was the ultimate expression of sincere feeling. Like Keichū (1640–1701) before him, Mabuchi used the term *magokoro* (sincere heart) to signify these emotions.[10]

---

7. Nosco, *Remembering Paradise*, p. 155.
8. Miyake, *Kada no Azumamaro*, p. 600.
9. Nosco, *Remembering Paradise*, p. 124.
10. Kamo no Mabuchi, *Inishie-buri*, p. 971.

For Mabuchi, the two most important compendia of classical verse were the *Kokinshū* (905) and the *Man'yōshū* (759). He began his scholarly career by focusing exclusively on the latter text; later, under the influence of Katō Enao, he focused at least some of his efforts on the *Kokinshū* as well.[11] Of the two anthologies, the *Man'yōshū* exhibited certain native traits that the *Kokinshū* did not. Mabuchi called these traits *masurao*, or "masculine," and he dedicated his work to a deeper understanding of the masculine style of the *Man'yōshū*.[12] Unsurprisingly, he identified the fundamental style of the *Kokinshū* as *taoyame*, or "feminine." During the early Heian period, the ancients gradually embraced more feminine styles of expression as they also came under the increasing sway of Chinese cultural institutions, forsaking their masculine cultural heritage.[13] It was under these circumstances that the *Kokinshū* was compiled. Despite the taint of Chinese influences, Mabuchi maintained his admiration for the text; in its defense, he even pointed out that some of the verses in the *Man'yōshū* had a feminine flair.[14] His defense of the *Kokinshū* notwithstanding, he clearly privileged the study of Nara and pre-Nara culture.[15]

Under the influence of the new textual approaches of Keichū, Itō Jinsai (1627–1705), and Ogyū Sorai (1666–1728), Mabuchi understood that the scholarly traditions of the medieval period were insufficient for his research into classical verse. In the adoption of the philological methodologies of his predecessors, Mabuchi developed a sophisticated theory of language that articulated the sublime qualities of the classical Japanese language. He concluded that only a thorough knowledge of the language of the *Man'yōshū* could yield insight into the emotions of the ancients. Naturally, their spoken language preceded the creation or adoption of any system of writing. One of the most important goals of his work was the recovery of this archaic, spoken language.

---

11. Inoue, *Kamo no Mabuchi no gyōseki to monryū*, p. 184.
12. Kamo no Mabuchi, *Inishie-buri*, p. 967.
13. Ibid., p. 968.
14. Kamo no Mabuchi, *Ka'ikō*, p. 355.
15. Nosco, *Remembering Paradise*, p. 119.

The Formation of Rival Nativist Schools

Mabuchi observed that language was characterized by the unity of its words (*kotoba*) and their meanings (*kokoro*, or *i*). Put simply, the language of the ancients was perfectly transparent to the reality that it was used to reflect. In the words of the Swiss linguist Ferdinand de Saussure, the ancient language represented a unity of signifier and signified.[16] This unique quality gave this language a magical power endowed by the *kami*, which Mabuchi called the *kotodama*.[17] In contrast, the Chinese language began with arbitrary sounds that the Chinese then matched to written ideographs.[18] Thus Chinese, like all languages, was, in Saussure's terminology, "unmotivated."[19] Ancient Japanese, however, was a "motivated" one because of its *kotodama*. During the Nara period, when the Japanese adoption of Chinese writing was still relatively recent, Mabuchi insisted that the ancients were interested only in using ideographs as signifiers: "[the ancients] used them only as signs (*shirushi*)."[20] This situation proved disastrous for the Japanese language. Chinese writing was not suited to the ancient Japanese signifieds (*kōchō no kokoro*) assigned to them.[21] The result of this forced union of alien signifiers and indigenous signifieds was the introduction of foreign signifieds into the Japanese language, as well as the loss of indigenous concepts that Chinese writing could not accommodate.

As in Keichū's earlier observations, Mabuchi compared both classical Chinese and Sanskrit with the Japanese language of antiquity.

> In the land of the rising sun [Japan], we make words (*koto*) out of the fifty sounds. This is a land where we articulate the myriad things with our own mouths. In the land of the setting sun [China], they draw pictures for the myriad things; theirs is a land of signs (*shirushi*). In the land of the sinking sun [India], they draw pictures only of the fifty sounds. It is

---

16. My understanding of structural linguistics comes from Saussure, *Course on General Linguistics*, pp. 1–124.
17. Kamo no Mabuchi, *Go'ikō*, p. 396.
18. Kamo no Mabuchi, *Niimanabi*, p. 371.
19. Saussure, *Course in General Linguistics*, p. 69.
20. Kamo no Mabuchi, *Niimanabi*, p. 371.
21. Kamo no Mabuchi, *Manabi no agetsurai*, p. 892.

a land that uses these [pictures] for the myriad things. However, only in this land [Japan], did we not use pictures, and people were not yet confused.[22]

Sanskrit presented Mabuchi with a dilemma. Unlike Chinese, it did not have thousands of ideographs. Instead, its fifty letters resembled the symbols of each of the two *kana* syllabaries, both of which were intended to replicate the "fifty sounds of nature."[23] Just as he had argued for a unity between the spoken word and meaning in the ancient language, he also conceived of a transparent relationship between the two *kana* and the sounds of nature. The major shortcoming of Sanskrit was that it lacked the necessary number of written signs to handle the plethora of signifieds in reality. In some ways, Sanskrit suffered from a problem opposite to that of Chinese; the latter had many ideographs, which signified only a small number of natural sounds, while Sanskrit had an abundance of spoken words but not enough written symbols. Unsurprisingly, the ancient Japanese language was superior to both, since it had no writing system in antiquity. In addition, the ancient language maintained the perfect balance between spoken words and their meanings. It had precious few of either signifieds or signifiers.

For the most part, the spoken language of Mabuchi's era retained for him few vestiges of its ancient ancestor, which was the result of the adoption of Chinese ideographs. In certain local dialects, however, there were some glimpses of the ancient language. Of all the regional dialects in Japan, Mabuchi believed that the one spoken in the Kinki region was the only genuine Japanese dialect and was the progenitor of the other dialects that still retained archaic forms.[24] As proof of his contention, he observed that speakers of different dialects could still communicate with one another. He attributed this to the ultimate unity of the disparate dialects in remote antiquity.

Mabuchi sought to resurrect and restore this ancient language in order to bring the Japanese people closer to their cultural roots. He

---

22. Kamo no Mabuchi, *Go'ikō*, p. 395.
23. Ibid.
24. Ibid., p. 398.

called the correct use of the ancient language *gago* (elegant language).²⁵ The unrefined use of the ancient language he called *heigo* (common language). Finally, the use of borrowed words, mostly from Chinese, represented the lowest category of Japanese usage, which he called *zokugo* (vulgar language). Note that this last category included the spoken language of Mabuchi's day. Harry Harootunian argues that Mabuchi was critical only of written Chinese.²⁶ This, of course, was only partially true. In some ways, Mabuchi was even more critical of the spoken language of eighteenth-century Japan.

The Edo-ha After Mabuchi

Murata Harumi and Katō Chikage assumed the mantle of leadership within the Mabuchi School by the end of the eighteenth century. Chikage dedicated his career to deepening his knowledge of ancient aesthetics, following Mabuchi's own researches on the concept of *magokoro*.²⁷ As the confidant of Matsudaira Sadanobu (1758–1829),²⁸ Murata Harumi began his career by focusing on Chinese verse before he shifted to classical *waka* in order to continue Mabuchi's work;²⁹ at the same time, he broadened the scope of his investigations to include the nature of Japanese verse itself. While Chikage and Harumi were the leaders of the Edo-ha, the latter's scholarship and energetic personality made Harumi the natural spokesperson for the school as a whole.

Harumi had strong literary inclinations. Interacting with prominent literati of the day,³⁰ he viewed himself as both a scholar and a poet,³¹ asserting that his teacher, Mabuchi, was the greatest scholar of classical poetry in history.³² Like his mentor, Harumi viewed classical poetry as the key to fathoming the sentiments of

---

25. Ibid., p. 420.
26. Harootunian, *Things Seen and Unseen*, p. 56.
27. Uchino, *Edo-ha kokugaku ronkō*, p. 223.
28. Haga N., *Kokugaku no hitobito*, p. 54.
29. Tanaka K., "Murata Harumi no wagaku-ron," p. 30.
30. Uchino, *Edo-ha kokugaku ronkō*, p. 126.
31. Mori, "Murata Harumi iji," p. 95.
32. Murata Harumi, *Utagatari*, p. 241.

antiquity; it was the highest expression of human emotion.[33] He was critical of contemporary poetry for its preoccupation with flowery expressions at the expense of spontaneous emotional expression: "When the ancients wanted to express their hearts, they selected the words; contemporaries, [however], fabricate words then search for [their] hearts."[34]

The challenge before Harumi was to reconcile the interpretation of classical verse with his own attempts at poetic composition in a contemporary style. For Harumi, simply imitating the ancient style, in an attempt to apprehend the sentiments of the ancients, was ultimately futile.[35] While Mabuchi had instructed his students to diligently compose verse in the style of the *Man'yōshū*, Harumi warned that such an activity was geared toward understanding the ancient style through emulation; scholars should never neglect their study of the *Man'yōshū*. He viewed the study of classical verse and poetic composition as two distinct activities that supported one another, yet were at the same time mutually exclusive. Mabuchi's work provided the method by which scholars could apprehend the psychological and emotional conditions of the past. Hence, the work of the contemporary poet was not to try and replicate ancient feelings in his poetry, but to learn how to manifest his own feelings in his own time.[36] The heart of Mabuchi's teachings was to combine scholastic precision with artistic expression.

The eminent scholar of Tokugawa history Haga Noboru asserts that the Edo-ha underwent a subtle transformation at its core during the early nineteenth century. The rigorous analysis of classical poetry advocated by Mabuchi and the first two generations of his students evolved into an emphasis on the philological method itself.[37] Scholars of the Edo-ha began to apply the principles of Kōshōgaku (evidential learning)[38] to all categories of classical texts,

---

33. Ibid., p. 243.
34. Ibid.
35. Kiyohara, *Kokugaku hattatsu-shi*, p. 146; Watanabe H., "'Michi' to 'miyabi,'" p. 652.
36. Ibid., pp. 652–53.
37. Haga N., "Edo ni okeru Edo kabun-ha to Hirata Atsutane," p. 298.
38. I owe this translation of Kaozhengxue (Kōshōgaku) to Elman (1984).

including legal codes, liturgies, Shinto ritual texts, and histories. One of Harumi's most talented students in Kōshōgaku was Oyamada Tomokiyo (1782–1847). Tomokiyo dedicated himself to the textualism of his predecessors, concentrating his efforts on the categorization of classical texts by genre.[39] He viewed these efforts in a continuum with endeavors undertaken for classical Chinese texts. Like Harumi, he viewed nativism as a part of Confucianism;[40] these scholars often referred to themselves as scholars of *wakan*, ("Yamato" and "Han," that is, Japan and China). Like most nativists of the eighteenth century, Tomokiyo used the term Wagaku for nativism, which he thought was unimaginable without reference to China. For Tomokiyo, scholars who referred to Wagaku as Kokugaku, in an attempt to ignore China, were simply mistaken in their terminology, since "Kokugaku" signified domainal schools and had nothing to do with a genuine scholarly discipline.[41] This is an important issue to which we will return in the next chapter.

Tomokiyo was known as one of Edo's most able scholars of evidential learning during the early decades of the nineteenth century, along with Ban Nobutomo (1775–1846).[42] The literary scholar Hisamatsu Sen'ichi agrees with Haga Noboru that Tomokiyo's emphasis on the philological method was part of a general shift within nativism toward Kōshōgaku.[43] Tomokiyo, however, did not labor in isolation. As a bibliographer of classical Japanese texts, he was an avid collector of native tomes, which he allowed other scholars to borrow and study. As his journal, *Yōshorō nikki*, indicates, he received numerous guests at his home, many of whom were not nativists at all.[44] In fact, literati, poets, and authors of comic fiction (*gesakusha*) frequented his salon, interacting with other *wakan* scholars of the Edo-ha.

The Edo-ha during the late eighteenth and early nineteenth centuries was composed of scholars who traced their intellectual de-

---

39. Yasunishi, *Oyamada Tomokiyo no sōken*, p. 8.
40. Tanaka K., "Murata Harumi no wagakuron," p. 35.
41. Yasunishi, *Oyamada Tomokiyo no sōken*, p. 6.
42. Ibid., p. 5. I will discuss Ban Nobutomo in more detail in the next chapter.
43. Hisamatsu, "Bunkengaku-teki kenkyū to kōshōgaku," p. 230.
44. See it in *Kinsei bungei sōsho*, pp. 208–391.

scent from Mabuchi. Their primary interests were in the philological analysis of classical texts and the study of poetry. While the scholars of the Edo-ha were aware of their common intellectual heritage and institutional identity, they were also very active members of an emerging and energetic intellectual and artistic subculture of Edo. The cultural context of the Edo-ha at the turn of the nineteenth century is an important consideration in the analysis of its intellectual development.

The Culture of the Bunjin

The interaction between Edo-ha scholars and elite literati (*bunjin*) had a profound impact on the development of Edo nativism. While Haga and Hisamatsu have observed a movement away from the analysis of classical poetry and toward the embrace of the philological method itself, the literary scholar, Uchino Gorō, sees an increasing aestheticization of the same Edo-ha scholars of the early decades of the nineteenth century. Edo-ha scholars, while continuing their work on the *Man'yōshū* and other classical collections of verse, saw themselves as poets, a shift away from what had been their primary identities as scholars. While it is not clear from his writings how Harumi hierarchized the *composition* of poetry vis-à-vis its scholarly *analysis*, his associations with Edo writers and poets clearly influenced Harumi's emphasis on the former. Tomokiyo perpetuated these close ties between literati and Edo-ha scholars. The philological nativism of Azumamaro in Fushimi had, by the early nineteenth century in Edo, given way to a literary culture. The emergence of the *bunjin* transformed nativism.[45]

During his tenure in Edo, Azumamaro had established a private academy dedicated to nativism near the Yushima district of modern-day Bunkyō ward. After his death, Mabuchi moved to Yushima, and eventually established his own academy there. During the Edo period, Yushima straddled the neighborhoods between the Yamanote district of daimyo estates and the *shitamachi* districts of ordinary townspeople. During the late eighteenth and early nineteenth centuries, the *shitamachi* districts of Edo became the center

---

45. Uchino, *Edo-ha kokugaku ronkō*, p. 228.

of a thriving literary culture. Thus, the Mabuchi School was from the beginning amidst a sea of literary creativity. Geography and timing, therefore, were important factors in the literary development of the Edo-ha.[46]

As a result of this proximity, Edo-ha scholars formed associations and friendships with literary figures such as Santō Kyōden (d. 1816), Shikitei Sanba (d. 1822), and Takizawa Bakin (d. 1848). These were the personal interactions that Tomokiyo's salon fostered and which he described in his journal. Under the influence of this urban subculture, the aesthetic tastes of these literati turned bourgeois. Haga Noboru observes that this refined cultural taste was incorporated into the poetry of the Edo-ha, obliterating, in the process, any potential link between it and the rest of a mostly rural society during the Tokugawa.[47]

These writers and poets felt detached from the rest of Edo society.[48] This sense of detachment was part of the *bunjin* culture imported from China. In China, the *bunjin* (Ch. *wenren*) sought isolation as a refuge from the turmoil around them, especially the upheaval caused by the collapse of the Ming dynasty during the second half of the seventeenth century. They selected rural and inaccessible locales in which to pursue their writing and reflect on the turbulence of the age. In addition to their literary pursuits, they also painted simple ink works; these paintings, called *nanga*, began to filter into Japan during the second decade of the eighteenth century. The culture of the artist in supreme isolation entered during this period with the importation of these *nanga*.[49] Elite townspeople of Edo consumed these works, and some attempted to emulate the lifestyles of Chinese *bunjin* in their own urban setting. The salons of late eighteenth-century Edo served as havens for urban *bunjin* who felt disconnected from the rest of society, finding comfort in the company of their fellow Edo *bunjin*.

---

46. Uchino, "Hirata-ha to Edo-ha no gakushi-teki tei'i," p. 22.
47. Haga, "Edo ni okeru Edo kabun-ha to Hirata Atsutane," p. 275. Such ties between nativism and rural society are important for Haga's work on "grassroots" nativism, which we will discuss in the Chapter 6.
48. Uchino, *Edo-ha kokugaku ronkō*, p. 119.
49. Ibid., p. 120.

Hence, Edo-ha scholars had ample opportunity to interact with these *bunjin* within the salons operated by scholars like Tomokiyo. The *bunjin* were mostly interested in Chinese verse, while scholars of the Edo-ha preferred *waka*. These contradictory interests actually complemented each other, since the traditional nativist preoccupation with verse had always relied on Chinese poetics as a foil against which to assert Japanese poetry. Therefore, the scholars of the Edo-ha were intimately acquainted with the literary pursuits of these self-styled *bunjin*.[50]

The interaction between *bunjin* and the scholars of the Edo-ha contributed to a stronger literary orientation within Edo nativism than elsewhere. In many cases the ties between the two groups were so strong that differentiating between them was difficult. For some Edo nativists, especially those in the Edo-ha, they were less like scholars and more like the *bunjin* themselves.[51] Ueda Akinari (1734–1809) is an example of a Mabuchi student who was both a scholar and a *bunjin*. Akinari studied Mabuchi School nativism with the first-generation scholar Katō Umaki (1721–77), devoting himself to nativism until the age of thirty.[52] In his thirties, he switched his intellectual focus to medicine, which he practiced until the age of fifty-five. After quitting medicine, Akinari resumed his interests in nativism, even debating Norinaga on linguistic topics. In literature, he began his career composing *haikai* and moved to *gesaku* in the prime of his life. Akinari exemplified the combination of creative expression and scholastic erudition that characterized early nineteenth-century nativism in Edo.

The Edo-ha formed from the remnants of Mabuchi's academy in Edo, which itself had formed from the vestiges of the Azumamaro academy decades earlier. The first and second generations of Mabuchi's students became embroiled in the emerging literary culture of the *bunjin*, especially that of *gesaku* authors. The philological analysis of poetry favored by Mabuchi in the middle of the eighteenth century split into the pursuit of philology itself and the

---

50. Ibid., p. 123.
51. Uchino, "Hirata-ha to Edo-ha no gakushi-teki tei'i," p. 21.
52. Uchino, *Edo-ha kokugaku ronkō*, p. 136.

composition of poetry; the Mabuchi students separated philology from poetry. Azumamaro's academy in Edo had already shifted the nativist center of Japan from Kyoto to Edo. Edo nativism became the dominant form by the end of the eighteenth century, despite having significantly diverged from the original intentions of both Azumamaro and Mabuchi; the highly literary and eclectic Edo-ha was the result of a golden age of Japanese literature.[53] A few scholars in Edo like Ban Nobutomo and especially Hirata Atsutane resisted the literary tide that consumed the Edo-ha.

Motoori Norinaga and the Norinaga School

One of Kamo no Mabuchi's "disciples" was Motoori Norinaga. Norinaga's career as a scholar, however, began several years before he became one of Mabuchi's students in 1765. After returning from Kyoto in 1757,[54] Norinaga finished his first scholarly work, the *Ashiwake obune*. This first text was a discourse on the nature of classical Japanese literature, with an emphasis on verse. He focused much of his early efforts on classical verse, as had his nativist predecessors, especially Keichū and Mabuchi. While he admired the work of both scholars on the *Man'yōshū*, he grew dissatisfied with their exclusive interest in the eighth-century text and developed a fondness for the *Kokinshū* and *Shinkokinshū* instead. His poetic interests were more in the Heian and Kamakura periods than in the Nara period favored by Mabuchi. An emphasis on these latter two poetic compilations, however, was nothing unusual for the time: Kada no Arimaro expressed more of an interest in the *Kokinshū* than in the *Man'yōshū* as well.[55] Like others, Norinaga adopted Keichū's method of comparing the words of classical texts, regardless of genre, against one another in an attempt to garner a sense of their meanings. Two important classical texts used in this way were the *Ise monogatari* and the *Genji monogatari*. In his work on these texts, he discovered the same depth of emotional

---

53. Ibid., p. 228.
54. Under the influence of his mother, Norinaga studied medicine in Kyoto from 1752 to 1757 (Haga N., "Motoori Norinaga no shisō keisei," p. 73).
55. Nosco, "Nature, Invention, and National Learning," p. 85.

expression that Mabuchi had argued was contained only in the *Man'yōshū*. The result of Norinaga's work on narrative tales, especially the *Genji monogatari*, was an increasing emphasis on them at the expense of classical verse. By justifying his work on narrative tales in this way, he formulated a notion of aesthetics that enabled him to portray Japan's indigenous Way in a more complete and comprehensive manner than had his predecessor Mabuchi.

Aesthetics and Ethics: *Mono no aware* and *Kanzen chōaku*

Norinaga agreed with Keichū and other scholars that the original intent and purpose of *waka* was the same as that of Chinese poetry (*shi*).[56] Norinaga viewed the composition of poetry as fundamental to human experience, since human beings naturally responded to moving situations by composing verse.[57] In antiquity, people recorded these feelings in poetry. Japanese verse, especially of the *Man'yōshū*, also shared with Chinese verse a preoccupation with the emotions of love and desire (IS, 420). He was careful to indicate that even though love was a popular theme in both Japanese and Chinese poetry, it was not central to *waka*. Unlike Kada no Azumamaro, who had tried to ignore erotic poetry,[58] Norinaga acknowledged its legitimate place within the range of emotional expression, which supported the views of Kamo no Mabuchi.[59] Moreover, he used the example of erotic poetry to assert a key difference between *waka* and *shi*. Whereas authors of *shi* dealt with the virtues of love, authors of *waka* ignored the moral status of erotic love (IS, 428). This was a theme upon which he constructed his formulation of the relationship between poetics and aesthetics, but more on that later.

Norinaga's interpretation of *waka* was mostly in agreement with scholars who had preceded him. Despite his stated preference

---

56. Motoori Norinaga, *Isonokami no sasamegoto* (hereafter IS), p. 322. Subsequent references to this work are cited in the text.
57. Motoori Norinaga, *Tamakushige*, p. 316.
58. Miyake, *Kada no Azumamaro no kotengaku*, vol. 1, p. 153.
59. Kamo no Mabuchi, *Niimanabi*, p. 370.

for Heian and Kamakura poetry over Nara and pre-Nara poetry, the ancient style of poetry was still important to him. One had to master the various later styles of verse before attempting to learn the ancient style.[60] Moreover, in the process of mastering the various styles of classical verse, the scholar blurred the boundaries between the composition and study of poetry. Such a blurring of distinctions was the essence of scholarship itself, as opposed to the strictly intellectual pursuits of Confucian scholarship.

Norinaga acknowledged Mabuchi's observation that not all the poems in the *Man'yōshū* were superb, despite their ancient origins.[61] He criticized scholars of the ancient compilation for failing to understand how most of its poems "were composed using intentional ornamentation. Thus, they are not simply [reflective of] reality."[62] Unlike Mabuchi, he did not dismiss later styles of poetry. Mabuchi was critical of the later styles for their ornate superficiality and shallow emotional expression.[63] Norinaga, however, placed more faith in the literary and emotional utility of decorative language. Such language, when used in a sincere manner, assumed an elegant (*miyabi*) quality.[64] Mabuchi, by contrast, contended that only the language of the *Man'yōshū* qualified as elegant. Thus, Norinaga sought to understand this elegance in both ancient and medieval verse.

Despite Norinaga's admiration of Mabuchi, he declared that the greatest scholar of *waka* was Keichū, for his recognition of the link between the expression of sincere emotion and verse.[65] Norinaga believed that ancient Shinto had been a political discourse because the ruler could understand the feelings of the people by reading their *waka* (IS, 443). This was the first of two important disagreements with Mabuchi. The other was Norinaga's assertion that verse was not the only literary vehicle suitable to convey profound

---

60. Motoori Norinaga, *Uiyamabumi*, p. 534.
61. Ibid., p. 530.
62. Ibid., p. 531.
63. Kamo no Mabuchi, *Ka'ikō*, p. 349.
64. Motoori Norinaga, *Uiyamabumi*, p. 528.
65. Motoori Norinaga, *Shibun yōryo* (hereafter SY), p. 37. Subsequent references are cited in the text.

emotions. Traditional scholars had overemphasized the analysis of verse. "To know about the heart of antiquity by looking only at poetry is trivial," he declared (SY, 223). Narrative tales (*monogatari*) were also used to convey emotion in antiquity. In this sense, narrative tales and *waka* were fundamentally the same: "The Way of Poetry (*kadō*) and narrative tales are completely identical" (SY, 213). He explained that *monogatari* were merely a type of *waka*: "There are many differences between the words of poems (*uta*) and those of prose. They are different, but recently, [some people have begun] to sing (*utau*) the words of prose [namely, narrative tales].... Even though "narrate" is in their name [i.e., narrative tales], we [can] sing them. For this reason, these are all types (*tagui*) of poems" (IS, 258). Thus, he felt justified in privileging narrative tales over *waka* as receptacles of the elegant expression of sentiment. Poetry, of course, was the original expression of *mono no aware* (IS, 300); narrative tales, however, were its supreme expression. In the mature years of his career, therefore, he turned away from the analysis of verse and focused his energies on developing his research on narrative tales.

In Norinaga's estimation, classical narrative tales provided a glimpse into three basic aspects of antiquity. First, they were important sources of information for what he called the "conditions of the world" (*yo no arisama*) (SY, 46). This function of classical texts was perhaps the most useful one for Tokugawa scholars, who scrutinized classical texts for any and all details about life in antiquity. Mabuchi went so far as to admonish his students to use the ancient language as much as possible.[66] A second category of analysis for Norinaga was the "character" or "personality" of ancient persons (*hito no kokorobae*). He believed that the aesthetic quality of classical literature was a reflection of its author; this, however, was not a new literary insight, as Neo-Confucian scholars had believed in a link between moral rectification and verse. Finally, the third category, and the most important one for Norinaga, was the insight into *mono no aware* that classical narrative tales provided. This third category had been traditionally ignored, but its glimpse

---

66. Sakai, *Voices of the Past*, p. 250.

into the emotional lives of the ancients transcended the importance of information about either ancient conditions or ancient people.

The highest example of the genre of narrative tales for Norinaga was the *Genji monogatari* (SY, 230). Traditional interpreters of the *Genji* viewed the frequent references by its author, Murasaki Shikibu, to Buddhism as a testament to its pervasive influence during the Heian period, as well as to Shikibu's personal endorsement of it. Norinaga acknowledged the potential conflict inherent in a literary genre that both articulated *mono no aware* and seemingly endorsed Buddhism. The former was the spontaneous emotional response to sentimental situations and was uniquely native. He observed that Buddhist monks were trained to steel themselves against emotional outbursts (SY, 134–5). In fact, both Buddhists and Neo-Confucians condemned the expression of human emotion in his estimation. He resolved this apparent contradiction by arguing that Shikibu's references to Buddhism do not signify a personal commitment to it. Shikibu used Buddhism as a means to convey *mono no aware* because she understood the fundamental affinity between the two: "So, regarding this Way [Buddhism], there are numerous [instances] of *mono no aware* [within it]. Thus, [Murasaki Shikibu] composed [the text] with many [references to] Buddhism" (IS, 201). This was especially true in the context of her depiction of romantic love (IS, 136). Thus, Norinaga argued that the potential conflict between *mono no aware* and Buddhism was, in fact, a complementary relationship. Buddhism was the ideal idiom to express Shikibu's views on a complex emotional phenomenon like *mono no aware*.

The influence of Confucian and Buddhist teachings had a largely negative impact on the correct interpretation of the *Genji*, according to Norinaga. This was especially true in the evaluation of the text's moral and ethical implications. Although Shikibu noticed an affinity between *mono no aware* and Buddhism, foreign teachings were ill-equipped to correctly appreciate the numerous instances of eroticism in the *Genji*. In Buddhist and Neo-Confucian teachings, erotic love contradicted virtuous conduct and was seen as "evil." In the Chinese normative view of literature known as *kanzen chōaku*, or "reward good and punish evil," Norinaga observed that one would expect all the participants in erotic love to endure punishment; this, however, is not the case. He cautioned scholars not to deduce that erotic acts were devoid of moral considerations. "In this tale, is eroticism (*iro konomu*) rewarded?" he asked. "Eroticism is not a wondrous thing and is not rewarded. Knowing *mono no aware* is rewarded," he concluded (SY, 159). The conduct of the text's main character, Hikaru Genji, is far from the type of virtuous conduct advocated by Buddhists and especially Confucians, yet he is not met with the kind of retribution that one would anticipate with *kanzen chōaku*. Genji had erotic longings and acted on them in a sincere way. Erotic feelings filled a legitimate niche in the range of human emotions. Hence, Norinaga contended that the *Genji* defied interpretation by foreign literary theories. Instead of the traditional Buddhist-Confucian view of goodness—namely, the suppression of desires and a return to an original nature—Norinaga argued that in the *Genji monogatari* goodness is redefined as knowledge of *mono no aware* (IS, 149). "Good" characters in the text have a deep appreciation of love (*koi suru*) that "evil" characters do not.

Norinaga's ultimate conclusion regarding classical literature was that it provided an alternative worldview to that of Buddhism and Confucianism. His notion of *mono no aware* provided him with the means to describe Japanese antiquity in a manner that eluded foreign conceptualizations. This was a crucial initial step in what became a broader attempt to elucidate the notion of an indigenous Way in Japanese antiquity.[67]

---

67. Harry Harootunian, however, does not see the link between *mono no aware* and Norinaga's denial of Buddhist and Confucian views of good and evil. Harootunian insists that *mono no aware* is strictly a poetic phenomenon, while Norinaga's discussion of it in the *Shibun yōryō* is simply the illustration of its myriad forms in everyday life (*Things Seen and Unseen*, p. 107). Moreover, he conceptualizes Norinaga's views of good and evil as based on "the quality of the [particular] deed itself" (ibid., p. 110). As he argues with Mabuchi, he asserts that Norinaga acknowledged and validated a commoner view of the world; Mabuchi validated commoners via his view of spoken language, while Norinaga's notion of *mono no aware* confirmed the capacity of all Japanese people to feel empathetically (ibid., p. 108). This is a misinterpretation of both Mabuchi and Norinaga, and it fabricates a discursive continuity, the validation of commoner experience, where there

Unlike Mabuchi's, Norinaga's view of Japan's indigenous Way—what he called the ancient Way (*kodō*)—was not premised on the simple denial of Buddhism and Confucianism, a strategy that forced Mabuchi to embrace Daoism. Norinaga's strategy was to formulate a comprehensive view of antiquity that could stand on its own intellectual merits. For this reason, he spent the last two decades of his life dedicated to the clarification of the ancient Way. Using the same philological methodology he had used in his analysis of literature, Norinaga devoted the balance of his life to the analysis of the *Kojiki* in order to investigate the ancient Way. The results of his efforts were the contours of a truly unique nativist discourse.

Norinaga's View of Kodō: From Wagaku to Kokugaku

Commensurate with his views of Confucian and Buddhist teachings, Norinaga began his research into the ancient Way by examining its differences with the two traditions. At the outset, he reversed the medieval contention that conceptualized Shinto as a branch of a larger, central Way, whether an aspect of Buddhism or of the Way of the Sages. Instead, all foreign Ways were facets of the Japanese ancient Way, which he identified as Shinto.[68] Conceived as a larger Way by itself, Shinto was superior to any foreign teachings for Norinaga. Despite his assertion of Japanese superiority, he did not condemn Confucianism and Buddhism to the same degree. Although he was critical of both, his refutation was harsher for Confucianism.

As was common among critics of Shinto, he denounced Ryōbu Shinto as an egregious misinterpretation of ancient Shinto.[69] Norinaga echoed the familiar criticism of Ryōbu as a mixture of Buddhism with Shinto, one that diluted ancient Shinto to the point

---

was none. In the case of *mono no aware*, the emphasis was not only on the capacity to feel, but also on a re-formulation of ethics.

68. Motoori Norinaga, *Tamakushige*, p. 309.

69. Motoori Norinaga, *Tamakatsuma*, p. 50.

that it was indistinguishable from Buddhism.[70] Ancient Shinto was tainted not only with Indian Buddhism but also with Chinese Confucianism. Norinaga made it clear that his notion of *magokoro* was opposed to the *karagokoro* of China. While Mabuchi had used the term *magokoro* (true heart) to signify the unity of the ancient Japanese heart with nature, his usage of the term was slightly different from Norinaga's because Mabuchi had argued that ancient Shinto and nature were the same.[71] Norinaga used the term *karagokoro*[72] (Chinese mind) to signify intellection and abstract thinking, as opposed to the natural materiality of the *magokoro*. Scholars who fell under the sway of *karagokoro* placed more faith in principles (*mono no kotowari*) and theories, denouncing the human heart and the emotions as pernicious influences that obstructed the search for principles in nature. In the study of literature, the *karagokoro* manifested itself as the search for good and evil, right and wrong. "Things considered good and right are not actually so," he argued, "Things thought to be evil and wrong are not actually so. . . . [Thus], we cannot say that there are not two [standards of] good and evil, right and wrong."[73] Confucian ethics were not applicable to the ancient Japanese people, who embraced an alternative form of ethics. This was the reason why traditional scholars of the *Genji monogatari* could not fathom the significance of Murasaki Shikibu's illustrations of *mono no aware*.

---

70. Ibid., 124. Watanabe Shōichi argues for an affinity between Norinaga's notion of *magokoro* and the Buddhist idea of *anshin* (relief) ("Motoori Norinaga no 'kami no michi' to 'hito no michi,'" p. 90). Similarly, Matsumoto Shigeru sees a strong relationship between Norinaga's thought and Pure Land Buddhism (*Motoori Norinaga*, p. 188).

71. Inoue, *Kamo no Mabuchi no gyōseki to monryū*, p. 193.

72. The term *karagokoro* had two related meanings. Norinaga rendered the *kara* with the ideograph either for Han or for Tang, in what were specific references to China. The term *kara* also had the meaning of foreign. The exact origin of this meaning is uncertain, but it may derive from the name of the sixth-century Korean state of Kaya, what the Japanese called Mimana. The relationship between Kaya and the early Yamato court was very close, either as a tributary state or as a colony.

73. Motoori Norinaga, *Tamakatsuma*, p. 26.

Norinaga was annoyed by the supposed expertise in Japanese antiquity that many Confucians (*jusha*) only claimed to possess.[74] These scholars privileged the study of Chinese antiquity over that of Japan, which was even more disconcerting. In developing an expertise in the Confucian canon, they were convinced that they had mastered classical Japanese texts as well, he asserted. They were unaware of their corrupting influence in the interpretation of classical Japanese texts, and their *karagokoro* barred them from the truth of Japanese antiquity. He did not, however, issue a complete condemnation of Confucian studies. Perhaps as a result of his own Confucian education as a youth, he acknowledged the utility of Confucian studies: "In order to understand Chinese characters and such, one should study Chinese texts, if one has spare time. If one is firm in one's Japanese spirit (*mikuni damashii*), then there will be no harm done."[75] Confucian studies could be undertaken with a firm resolve and after the proper "purification" of one's acquired *karagokoro*.[76]

The arrogance of Confucians in matters of Japanese antiquity was a result of the low status of nativism within the intellectual world. Scholarship (*gakumon*), Norinaga observed, was always associated exclusively with Confucian studies (*karabumi no manabi*, Kanbungaku); Confucian scholars did not acknowledge a significant theoretical distinction between nativism and Confucianism. The necessity to distinguish the two separated the Norinaga School ideologically from the Edo-ha. While Norinaga lamented that Confucianism, as a foreign body of knowledge, was universalized as scholarship itself, nativism was particularized as Wagaku. In Japan, the situation should be reversed: "Chinese learning is called Kangaku and Jugaku. [Learning focused on] this imperial land should simply be called scholarship (*gakumon*)."[77]

It is interesting to note that Norinaga was aware of a distinction between Kangaku and Jugaku, even though he did not elaborate on it. Generally, he chose not to distinguish between forms of Confu-

---

74. Ibid., p. 17.
75. Motoori Norinaga, *Naobi no mitama*, p. 303.
76. Ibid., p. 25.
77. Motoori Norinaga, *Tamakatsuma*, p. 25.

cian studies (whether Neo-Confucianism, the Sorai School, etc.) and other forms of Chinese scholarship, Daoism included. The idea of the *karagokoro* infused all of these, which relieved him of the necessity to acknowledge their differences. The virtues that were held in such high regard by Neo-Confucians were known intuitively by the ancient Japanese, which eliminated the need for lifelong moral rectification.[78] He also attacked the Duke of Zhou, who was admired by Confucius, for instigating the chaos that plagued the end of the Zhou dynasty and for initiating the pernicious use of the *karagokoro* that characterized the Warring States Period.[79] Norinaga's critique extended to Ogyū Sorai and his followers as well. He condemned the Sages and Early Kings, whom

---

78. Motoori Norinaga, *Naobi no mitama*, p. 305.

79. Motoori Norinaga, *Tamakatsuma*, p. 470. Norinaga had a number of critiques of the Duke of Zhou. For example, he denounced the Duke of Zhou for deceiving people into thinking that teachings made them behave properly. It was also the Duke of Zhou, according to Norinaga, who was responsible for the false practice of divination (ibid., p. 464). The latter example is curious and is probably historically inaccurate. In any case, the Duke of Zhou was not a moral paragon for him. The attacks against the Duke of Zhou were not unique to Norinaga, and Mabuchi had made similar critiques, especially in the *Kokuikō*. As Benjamin Elman tells us, the Duke of Zhou was also assailed in China during the nineteenth century among scholars of Han Learning. Han Learning scholars in China argued that the "Old Text" version of the Duke of Zhou's regency was incorrect and based on flawed Han commentaries. While most scholars of Han Learning clung to this Old Text version, certain Han Learning scholars and those of the New Text School in Changzhou asserted that the Duke of Zhou had *seized* power, thereby bringing his status as a moral exemplar into question. In place of the Duke of Zhou, these scholars favored Confucius as a sage (Elman, "Ming Politics and Confucian Classicism," p. 138). Unlike the Chinese scholars of the nineteenth century, nativists during the eighteenth century did not formulate their views of the Duke of Zhou based on textual issues. Their arguments, such as Mabuchi's criticism of the Duke of Zhou for slaughtering Shang nobles, were less textual and more *logical* refutations. Moreover, the rejection of the Duke of Zhou and the endorsement of Confucius as a sage by nineteenth-century scholars in China seem also to have parallels with the Japanese nineteenth century. In a letter to a friend, Hirata Atsutane explained that Norinaga had rejected the reverence of Confucius as a sage not because of any hostility toward Confucius, but because of Norinaga's admiration for him. Atsutane observed how Norinaga's wholesale condemnation of the ancient Chinese sages did *not* include Confucius, since Norinaga had argued that Confucius was not a sage (Hirata Atsutane, *Shokan* [no. 132], in *Hirata Atsutane kenkyū*, pp. 893–94).

Sorai had so highly esteemed for their creation of the Way. "Those who are unsuccessful at planning and seizing a country are despised as brigands. Those who are successful are called Sages and respected. But even these so-called Sages were merely successful brigands."[80] In addition, he specifically identified Sorai's disciples as particularly skilled at the use of their *karagokoro*.[81]

Despite Norinaga's reluctance to acknowledge differences among various Confucian schools, his remarks seem to be especially critical of the Neo-Confucians, perhaps because of their profound influence on Shinto scholarship during the first half of the Tokugawa period. Occasionally, he briefly discussed near-contemporary developments in Chinese Confucianism that paralleled intellectual developments in the Sorai School. Specifically, he cited the achievements of late Ming dynasty scholars. He observed that Chinese scholars who advocated Han Learning[82] (Kangaku) were opposed to the scholars of Song Learning, especially with regard to the interpretation of the Six Classics.[83] The critiques that Ming Confucians leveled at the Neo-Confucians had merit, and any critique of Neo-Confucianism, he thought, was a good thing. In the final analysis, not even the Ming Confucians had elucidated the one, true Way, clarification of

---

80. Motoori Norinaga, *Naobi no mitama*, p. 296.
81. Motoori Norinaga, *Tamakatsuma*, p. 475.
82. The roots of the Han Learning of the Qing were in the Ming dynasty. Scholars of the Ming knew that success in the examination system, even at the level of the highest degree-holders, the *jinshi*, was not a guarantee of personal moral conduct. Knowledge of the Four Books, essential for success on the exams, did not result in the kind of ethical behavior in which the Neo-Confucians had believed. Scholars of the Ming and Qing dynasties became disillusioned with the utility of Neo-Confucianism as effective political theory, and they actively disputed the teachings of Song scholars like Zhu Xi and his glosses of the Confucian canon, including the Six Classics. In an effort to reverse the damage wrought by Song Confucians and their Neo-Confucianism or "Dao Learning" (Daoxue, Jp. Dōgaku), scholars of the Qing dynasty revived a Han dynasty debate dedicated to the search for authentic versions of the Classics. Qing scholars developed a rigorous philological method designed to facilitate their textual research of the Classics. In acknowledgment of their debt to the Han dynasty, scholars referred to their new brand of Confucianism as Han Learning (Hanxue, Jp. Kangaku), as opposed to Neo-Confucianism, which they called Song Learning. Han Learning was associated with Confucian philology in China.
83. Motoori Norinaga, *Tamakatsuma*, pp. 122–23.

which was the aim of Norinaga's career. Ming Confucians, despite their erudite criticisms of Neo-Confucianism, could never know the Way because they were not Japanese.[84] One cannot help but hear echoes of his famous claim that Japan was superior to China simply because it was Japan.[85]

Despite Norinaga's admiration for some Ming scholars, which he extended to the Sorai School as well, his ultimate condemnation of them was a crucial aspect of his interpretation of the ancient Way. Scholars have argued that Norinaga wrote his *Naobi no mitama* as a response to Dazai Shundai's *Bendōsho*, as Mabuchi had done with the *Kokuikō*.[86]

Dazai Shundai (1680–1747) was one of Ogyū Sorai's most talented disciples,[87] along with Hattori Nankaku (1683–1728).[88] Shundai's *Bendōsho* was a critique of both Neo-Confucianism and Shinto. He especially refuted the work of Shinto scholars who used Neo-Confucian teachings, like the adherents of Suika, Yoshida,

---

84. Ibid., p. 473.
85. Koyasu, *Norinaga mondai to wa nani ka*, p. 81.
86. Ogasawara, *Kokuju ronsō no kenkyū*, p. 2.
87. Along with Itō Jinsai, these scholars formed the core of what later historians have called the School of Ancient Learning. John Tucker and others have criticized this interpretation because it does not emphasize the profound differences between the two primary scholars of Ancient Learning, Sorai and Jinsai. Tucker has found one significant link between the two, however. Both Sorai and Jinsai were heavily influenced by the *Ziyi*, a Song text written by Chen Beixi (1159–1223) in the genre of what Tucker calls "philosophical lexicography." Chen's critique of Cheng-Zhu metaphysics was also influenced by Lu Xiangshan (1139–93), one of Zhu Xi's most important rivals (Tucker, "Chen Beixi, Lu Xiangshan, and Early Tokugawa [1600–1867] Philosophical Lexicography," p. 695).
88. Maruyama Masao has argued that the two scholars represented the main faction of the Sorai School after Sorai's death. Nankaku inherited the "private side" of the school because of his strong interests in Chinese verse. In Sorai's critique of Neo-Confucianism, he dismissed the practice of moral rectification as irrelevant to effective political administration, which was the real essence of the Way of the Sages. Neo-Confucians had viewed poetry composition as part of their moral rectification regimen. Thus, without its moral dimension, poetry composition became a pursuit simply for its own sake. On the other hand, Shundai became the leading figure of the "public side" of the Sorai School. Unlike Nankaku, Shundai interpreted Sorai's teachings on the Way as completely dismissive of poetry. Scholars, Shundai believed, should devote themselves to political and economic matters (Maruyama, *Studies in the Intellectual History of Tokugawa Japan*, p. 138).

and Ise Shinto. For centuries, Shinto theologians had argued that Shinto was the Way of Japan, just as Buddhism and Confucianism were for India and China, respectively. Shundai ridiculed this notion by asserting that there was only one universal Way, the one created by the Chinese Sages and Early Kings of antiquity. Shinto, therefore, did not exist apart from the Way of the Sages, but was one aspect of it. Prior to the importation of Chinese cultural institutions, he observed that the Japanese had no single word or idea that approximated the concept of "Way."[89] Japanese scholars were perhaps understandably confused by a reference in the *Book of Changes* to the term *shendao*, or "Shinto" in Japanese. The confusion was the result of a fundamental misunderstanding of Chinese antiquity. The Sages understood that one of the most effective means of controlling the people was via their superstitious beliefs in spirits (*kijin*).[90] Shinto, therefore, could not possibly exist without the more comprehensive and important Way of the Sages.[91]

Kamo no Mabuchi's best-known critique of Confucianism is the *Kokuikō* of 1765. In part, it was a refutation of Shundai's *Bendōsho*, even if Shundai had already been dead for almost twenty years when it first appeared.[92] Mabuchi actually agreed with Sorai's and Shundai's observations about the Way of the Sages,[93] especially as regards its fundamentally artificial nature.[94] For Sorai and Shundai,

---

89. Dazai Shundai, *Bendōsho*, DNSZ 7: 203.
90. Ibid., p. 172.
91. Ibid., p. 171.
92. Ogasawara, *Kokuju ronsō no kenkyū*, p. 10.
93. Neo-Confucianism achieved the status of orthodoxy in Japan during the seventeenth century. The significant difference with China, of course, was that Japan never had the accompanying civil service examination system. Orthodoxy in Japan, therefore, had a less significant meaning than in China. Robert Backus has shown that the effort to establish a Cheng-Zhu orthodoxy in Japan by Matsudaira Sadanobu at the end of the eighteenth century was primarily geared toward reversing the increasing popularity of heterodox schools, such as the Eclectics and the Sorai School. In the absence of a national examination system and the relative autonomy of domainal schools (*hankō*), such an overt prohibition of heterodoxy had little or no impact in the "realm of scholarship," and Backus argues that the effect of the prohibition was felt most keenly in the area of "samurai education," or the curricula of the domainal schools dedicated to educating samurai officials (Backus, "The Kansei Prohibition of Heterodoxy and Its Effects on Education," p. 103).
94. Nosco, *Remembering Paradise*, p. 141.

however, the artificiality of the Way did not detract from its absoluteness and universality.[95] Mabuchi used this interpretation to refute the Way of the Sages as unnatural. Shinto was more attuned to nature itself, which made it superior to all other foreign teachings. Mabuchi viewed his interests in archaic Shinto, *waka*, the ancient Japanese language, and nature as existing in a continuum. In Saussurian language it would be thus: nature is the referent; Shinto is its signified; the ancient language of *waka* is Shinto's signifier.[96]

Mabuchi's identification of Shinto with Daoism[97] was so strong that he seemed to confirm at times that they were the same.[98] Moreover, he did not hesitate to express his admiration for Laozi, claiming that Laozi had even anticipated Japan's superiority over both China and India.[99] Mabuchi also admired Emperor Wen of the Former Han for implementing a form of Daoist government.[100] After Emperor Wen's brief experiment with Daoism, the Confucians exerted their influence in government and the Way of nature went into decline.[101] The big difference between Daoism and

---

95. Both Sorai and Shundai believed that knowledge contained in the Six Classics collectively represented the Way of the Sages. On the other hand, the Four Books dealt with moral issues and were subsequently irrelevant for the two scholars. Neo-Confucianism was enshrined as exam orthodoxy during the Ming dynasty.

96. It is clear that Mabuchi saw a close relationship between archaic Shinto and classical *waka*. Some of his successors, like Murata Harumi, argued that this relationship was so close that the two were actually identical. If one thinks that their relationship was the same as that of signified to signifier, this argument is not unreasonable. It would be like saying that the word "book" (or poetry) and the idea of "book" (or Shinto) are identical. Motoori Norinaga did not agree with Murata Harumi on this interpretation. As expected, Mabuchi's own words are somewhat vague: "Poetry is something that one composes in one's spare time; without any teachings, it is [an expression of] the sincere heart (*magokoro*). This is the Way of our sublime Gods" (*Niimanabi*, pp. 361–62).

97. Nosco, *Remembering Paradise*, p. 142–43.

98. Kamo no Mabuchi, *Shokan*, KKNMZ, pp. 1292, 1332–33.

99. Kamo no Mabuchi, *Go'ikō*, p. 419.

100. Kamo no Mabuchi, *Manabi no agetsurai*, p. 895.

101. Kamo no Mabuchi, *Kokuikō*, p. 376. Other than this reference to Emperor Wen, Mabuchi did not specifically mention Daoism in the *Kokuikō*. In the translated excerpt from it in *Sources of Japanese Tradition*, vol. 2 (first edition), the translator specifically mentions Laozi. This reference is absent from the version of the text found in the NST.

Shinto was that the latter was the creation of the *kami*, which China lacked. Mabuchi praised the advent of Daoism in Chinese history, specifically during the Former Han, when Emperor Wen's support for it managed to temporarily halt the steady decline of the Way brought on by the various other schools of thought, especially Confucianism.[102] Where the Chinese ultimately failed in their recognition of the merits of Daoism, the Japanese had to implement the true form of Shinto in order to reverse the damage visited on Japan by Buddhism and Confucianism.

Motoori Norinaga was not satisfied with Mabuchi's simple identification of Shinto with nature and Daoism. He agreed that Shinto did not exist in antiquity, but was a more recent fabrication of Buddhism and Confucianism.[103] Ironically, Norinaga shared with Shundai this goal of undermining contemporary Shinto scholarship. As expected, the two scholars diverged over the nature of the term *shintō*. Shundai had argued that references to Shinto were derived from the Chinese term *shendao*, which first appeared in the *Book of Changes*; thus, *shendao* and Shinto were synonymous. Norinaga disagreed, arguing that Japanese Shinto was not based on *shendao*.[104] Japanese Shinto was a reference to the *kami no michi*, or Way of the Gods, to which there were references in classical texts. While he did not deny Shundai's contention that *shendao* had a political instrumentality for the ancient Chinese Sages, the Way of the Gods was a reference to an "immeasurably mysterious Way" that transcended politics and administration.

Norinaga denied that the Way of the Sages was the universal Way that encompassed Japan. At best, it was a "branch Way" (*edamichi*) of the superior Way of the Gods. Unlike Mabuchi, he did not completely deny any political significance and relevance for the Way of the Gods. The notion of a "Way," namely a set of institutional innovations invented for efficient political administration (in Sorai's view), was indeed an alien concept to the ancient Japanese. The closest word to the notion of "Way" was the Japanese word *michi*, but this word signified only a simple road or

---

102. Kamo no Mabuchi, *Kokuikō*, p. 376.
103. Ogasawara, *Kokuju ronsō no kenkyū*, p. 39.
104. Motoori Norinaga, *Naobi no mitama*, p. 301.

path,[105] and not the much more grand notion of the Way of the Sages (IS, 400–401). He noted that despite the invention of the Way of the Sages, Chinese history was rife with violence and turmoil; China was far from a well-administered country. Ancient Japan, on the other hand, was and had always been a peaceful country even without the Way of the Sages.[106] Thus, he concluded that while the Way of the Sages was not practiced by the ancient Japanese, they still had the Way of the Gods. In fact, because the ancients had never spoken of a political Way, this must be proof that such a Way had actually existed. The Chinese had spoken of the Way of the Sages because they never really had it.[107]

Norinaga believed that the ancient Japanese naturally followed the Way by living in harmony with the *kami*.[108] Part of the formula for the implementation of the Way of the Gods was to follow one's *magokoro*, which he argued was naturally consistent with the will of the Gods. This was an internal form of practice that resembled Neo-Confucian teachings regarding moral rectification. Moreover, he made it clear that the emperor, as a divine representative and living *kami*, was the supreme political ruler of Japan.[109] The emperors had ruled Japan since remote antiquity in an unbroken line of descent. The fact that the imperial line was unbroken was significant proof that political reform was both unnecessary and even harmful,[110] and was further proof that the imperial family had never lost its divine mandate to rule because emperors were themselves divine. The idea of the emperor was analogous to Sorai's concept of the Confucian king, namely, as the one who implements the Way. Scholars investigated the ancient Way and advised the ruler, but it was not the scholar's role to implement it.[111]

---

105. According to John Tucker, the Song scholar Chen Beixi (1159–1223) made the same observation that the Way "is like a road," a formula that probably influenced Sorai and, via Sorai, Motoori Norinaga (Tucker, "Chen Beixi, Lu Xiangshan, and Early Tokugawa [1600–1867] Philosophical Lexicography," p. 691).
106. Motoori Norinaga, *Naobi no mitama*, pp. 288–89.
107. Ibid., p. 289.
108. Ibid., p. 283.
109. Ibid.
110. Motoori Norinaga, *Tamakushige*, p. 322.
111. Motoori Norinaga, *Tamakatsuma*, p. 51.

The Suzunoya and the Norinaga School

Between 1770 and 1800, Norinaga's Suzunoya academy grew in national renown with a concomitant increase in its enrollment. With Norinaga's death in 1801, the first generation of his students was contemporary with the first and second generations of the Mabuchi School in Edo. The two groups, ostensibly intellectual cousins through Norinaga's ties with Mabuchi, had an uneasy relationship during the first decades of the nineteenth century, and they often disagreed over issues like the nature of *waka* and the larger purpose of nativist scholarship.

During the first two decades of the nineteenth century, there were four leading scholars among the hundreds of Norinaga's disciples: his son, Haruniwa; his adopted son, Ōhira; Kido Chidate (1778–1845), a Kyoto book merchant; and Fujii Takanao (1764–1840) of Osaka. All these scholars began their careers as students enrolled at Norinaga's Suzunoya academy in Matsusaka.

The Suzunoya as a Private Academy

The Suzunoya began as a gathering of Norinaga's friends at his home for the purpose of composing and reciting *waka*. For much of its early history, most of the students who attended meetings and lectures were from the immediate area around Matsusaka.[112] As Norinaga's fame grew, the Suzunoya's enrollment came increasingly from outside Matsusaka and the province of Ise. At his academy Norinaga lectured on the *Man'yōshū*, the *Engishiki, Kokinshū, Shinkokinshū, Ise monogatari, Genji monogatari, Kojiki*, and other native classics. Students generally attended only those lectures that interested them.[113] He arranged his lectures in the evenings, so that people who worked during the day, like himself, could attend. In addition, he employed a system of evaluation for his students and collected nominal fees. Richard Rubinger indicates that the spread of Kokugaku private academies contributed to a general upgrading

---

112. Rubinger, *Private Academies of Tokugawa Japan*, p. 162.
113. Ibid., pp. 166–67.

of rural education.[114] Rubinger emphasizes the significance of the ruralization of Norinaga nativism in the late eighteenth and early nineteenth centuries. He, however, treats the various private academies affiliated with the Norinaga School as intellectual clones of the Suzunoya. This was not entirely the case. Each of the various academies, except Atsutane's in Edo, developed previously unexplored areas of nativism while remaining within the intellectual scope of Norinaga's scholarship.

Haruniwa and Ōhira: Succession Within the Suzunoya

Motoori Haruniwa was Norinaga's talented biological son, who from an early age displayed an aptitude for scholarship.[115] While Norinaga labored on his magnum opus, the *Kojiki-den*, Haruniwa assisted his father with the various tasks associated with such a monumental undertaking, including the composition of commentaries on various parts of the *Kojiki* for his father's use. Part of the task before Norinaga was the deciphering of the text's difficult written style, assigning Japanese readings (*kundoku*) to its Chinese characters. At times he had to assign readings on the slimmest of textual evidence, and Haruniwa sometimes challenged his father's interpretations.[116] Thus, Haruniwa demonstrated the kind of talent for linguistic analysis that became his calling later in life.

For all of Haruniwa's intellectual abilities, he was not blessed with a robust constitution. As a child he suffered from bouts of illness,[117] eventually succumbing to one that gradually deprived him of sight. His eyesight began to deteriorate around 1790, prompting Norinaga to take him to an eye specialist in Nagoya in 1792.

---

114. Ibid., p. 173. The influence of Kokugaku on the quality of rural education is commonly associated with the Hirata School, decades after Norinaga's death. Rubinger's association of the Suzunoya with rural education, therefore, is not correct and perhaps indicates his conflation of the Norinaga School in Matsusaka with the Hirata School.

115. Yamada, *Motoori Haruniwa*, p. 7. For the discussion of Haruniwa's life, I have relied mostly on this work.

116. Ibid., p. 18.

117. Ibid., p. 21.

Haruniwa underwent treatment for a little over a month, before returning to Matsusaka with scarcely any hope of ever recovering his sight.[118] By 1794, he was completely blind.

Witnessing his son's ordeal proved quite traumatic for Norinaga.[119] By 1796, he began to grow infirm from age, and his thoughts turned to concern over his son's ability to inherit the Motoori household. He decided to adopt Inagake Shigeo, his close disciple in the Suzunoya, and charged him with the proprietorship of the family estate. Shigeo took the name Motoori Ōhira, and the two were inseparable until Norinaga's death.

Norinaga knew that it would be too difficult for Haruniwa, as a blind man, to direct the daily affairs of the household. Perhaps more significantly, Norinaga lacked confidence in his son's ability to run the Suzunoya. Because Haruniwa had demonstrated great talent since childhood, Norinaga had no doubts about his son's intellectual capacity. Ultimately, he decided that Haruniwa would make his living as a physician, just as he himself had done. He sent Haruniwa to Kyoto to receive his medical training. While in Kyoto, Haruniwa met Fujitani Mitsue (1768–1823), the son of the Mabuchi School linguist Fujitani Nariakira (1738–79). Mitsue introduced him to the studies of his father, especially with regard to Nariakira's views of verbs and their conjugations.[120] This encounter, coupled with his previous interests in language studies, profoundly influenced the two linguistic treatises that he wrote, the only texts that Haruniwa ever authored.

Following his father's discussion of poetry in the *Isonokami no sazamegoto*, Haruniwa identified language studies as the key to unlocking the meaning of classical verse. Norinaga, in accordance with Mabuchi, had argued that the meaning of *waka* could be grasped via a precise analysis of its language, rather than relying on the transmission of secret teachings (SY, 39). An influential cadre of scholars in Kyoto, the Nijō School, relied on these secret transmissions, but they, too, acknowledged that the inherent quality of a classical poem could be determined through the close analysis of

---

118. Ibid., p. 29.
119. Ibid., p. 30.
120. Ibid., p. 60.

its language. Nijō scholars did not believe that all *waka* were superb examples of refinement. The difference between good and bad poetry was in the use of elegant language; good poetry, they argued, was sparing in its use of overly decorative language.[121] Norinaga took the Nijō School view a step further, arguing that bad poetry was also the result of poor particle (*teniwoha*) usage. Using the philology of Keichū and Mabuchi, he criticized poor classical poetry from a *linguistic* perspective. In view of the more conservative Nijō School, his pronouncement was quite revolutionary.

Haruniwa completed his own analysis of poetry in 1806, the *Kotoba no yachimata*. The *teniwoha* method for interpreting *waka*, favored by both his father and Mabuchi, was essential in understanding how words within a poem *functioned* relative to one another. Thus, if one understood classical *teniwoha*, as well as the meanings of ancient words, then one had a nearly complete hermeneutic picture of a particular classical verse. However, as Norinaga observed, certain words, especially the *hataraki no kotoba* (words that conjugate: verbs and adjectives), functioned according to rules of their own, distinct from those of *teniwoha*. Haruniwa identified those categories and described them as verb conjugations, many of which are still acknowledged today. He transformed Norinaga's linguistic sensibilities into a full-fledged grammatical approach to the analysis of *waka*.

In response to the influential linguist Tōjō Gimon (1786–1843), Haruniwa wrote his second grammatical treatise, the *Kotoba no kayoichi*, which he finished in 1828. In this work, he expanded his work on verbs by identifying transitive (*tadōshi*) and intransitive (*jidōshi*) categories.[122] Interspersed among the numerous examples he used to support his argument are two themes that dominate this work. The first theme, one he had articulated in his earlier work, was that a knowledge of *teniwoha* was an important element in the study of *waka*, but not the only one. Scholars had to pay close attention to the various verb conjugations that he and his father had already identified if they were to apprehend the meaning of *waka*.

---

121. Nakamura, *Motoori-ha kokugaku no tenkai*, p. 111.
122. Yamada, *Motoori Haruniwa*, p. 95.

According to Haruniwa, contemporary scholars of poetry were misled into pursuing the traditional method of textual interpretation based simply on the meanings of words.[123] These scholars could not apprehend how the *sounds* and *forms* of classical words themselves were closely related to the feelings and emotions of ancient people.[124] A simple knowledge of the meanings of words did not take into account the conditions under which the ancients had produced their language: "For both poetry and prose composition, one must endeavor to understand well the conditions of antiquity."[125] The close analysis of verb conjugations was the most accessible route to recapturing this ancient linguistic codification, since it provided a glimpse into ancient sentiment—the scholastic holy grail coveted by both Azumamaro and Mabuchi.

The second theme of the text concerns the relationship between the scholar and the poet. In much the same way as his nativist predecessors, Haruniwa viewed the recovery of ancient sentiment as a significant component of nativism. Like his father, he viewed the *Kokinshū* and the *Shinkokinshū* as the collections of classical verse that best exhibited these traits, not the *Man'yōshū*.[126] Despite the plethora of excellent *waka* contained in these texts, he cautioned the scholar of poetry against equating the careful analysis of verse with the ability to skillfully compose it. The two practices were not necessarily congruent. Good poets, he argued, had an innate sense of what constituted good poetry without knowing exactly *why*. Scholars, for their part, understood the mechanics of good verse, but oftentimes could not put that knowledge into practice. "Learning and the composition of verse . . . are not the same. No matter how well [a scholar] analyzes classical verse, understanding the words and particles (*teniwoha*), they cannot learn to compose it. Good verse is not the result [of scholarship]."[127] His Edo colleague, Murata Harumi, also recognized the distinction between poetic scholarship and skillful composition. Harumi, how-

---

123. Motoori Haruniwa, *Kotoba no kayoichi*, p. 57.
124. Ibid.
125. Ibid., p. 58.
126. Ibid., p. 111.
127. Ibid., pp. 113–14.

ever, argued that a poet should focus his attention on emulating, in a contemporary poetic style, the ability of the ancients to capture their sentiments in verse. Haruniwa also argued that ancient models were useful for emulation, in his case the two later compilations instead of the *Man'yōshū* favored by Harumi. Moreover, he also advocated the reproduction of ancient feelings. Unlike Harumi, he provided a precise *methodological* approach to the emulation of classical *waka*. The key for Haruniwa was knowledge of classical grammar, specifically verb conjugations. Thus, the implication was that scholars armed with the grammatical knowledge advocated by Haruniwa could finally eliminate the barrier between scholar and poet. His idea of scholarly brilliance also included skillful poetic composition.

Despite Norinaga's wishes to the contrary, Haruniwa established himself as a scholar in his own right with the completion of *Kotoba no yachimata* in 1806. He christened his academy "The Later Suzunoya" (Nochi Suzunoya) and began to recruit a sizable following that rivaled that of his father's academy at the height of its popularity. Two of Norinaga's most prominent students, Uematsu Arinobu (1754–1813) and Suzuki Akira (1764–1837), joined Haruniwa's academy, forming the core of this reconstituted Suzunoya.[128]

Motoori Ōhira

Ōhira was Norinaga's designated successor, and he established his own Matsusaka residence in 1800. While Haruniwa proved to be a keen scholar and popular teacher, his activities served to remind scholars that there were two de facto successors; in reality, Haruniwa's presence in the Norinaga School only underscored Ōhira's leadership role within it. Ōhira felt constrained to preserve the memory of Norinaga, a responsibility that effectively prevented him from pursuing innovative scholarship. He presided over the expansion of the Norinaga School beyond Matsusaka, however, which amounted to his greatest accomplishment. While his contemporaries in the Mabuchi School socialized in the salons of Edo,

---

128. Nakamura, *Motoori-ha kokugaku no tenkai*, pp. 20–21.

he and his disciples were actively recruiting students and spreading the influence of Norinaga's scholarship.

Even before his adoption by Norinaga, Ōhira was very close to his mentor, often accompanying Norinaga and Haruniwa (before the onset of blindness) on various lectures that Norinaga gave outside Matsusaka—in Nagoya, for example.[129] Norinaga was especially impressed with Ōhira's grasp of classical *waka*, and he tried to develop Ōhira's talents. After Norinaga decided to select him as his legal heir, the two grew even closer; Ōhira, for instance, assisted Norinaga in selecting his gravesite at the summit of a small mountain overlooking Matsusaka called Yamamuro.[130]

The lord of Kii-Wakayama, Tokugawa Harutomi (1771–1852), took an interest in nativism sometime during the early 1790s, and he was especially fond of Norinaga's scholarship. Norinaga became Harutomi's physician and tutor in 1791. Following Norinaga's death, Harutomi invited Ōhira to Wakayama to give lectures, as he had done with Norinaga. Upon receiving Ōhira in 1803, he formally recognized Ōhira's succession of Norinaga and asked him to leave Matsusaka and establish a residence and academy in Wakayama. Having secured such a coveted position, Ōhira readily assented, and he relocated there in 1809. With his departure, the former membership of the Suzunoya disbanded, breaking a circle of scholars that had been meeting for the previous two generations.[131] From 1809 until Haruniwa's death in 1828, the two scholars maintained a regular correspondence.

By and large, the relationship between Haruniwa and Ōhira was a friendly one. Haruniwa respected Ōhira's administrative responsibilities, and Ōhira had a deep admiration for Haruniwa's intellectual talents. In his letters to Haruniwa, Ōhira often inquired about

---

129. Yamada, *Motoori Haruniwa*, p. 23.

130. It was Norinaga's wish that he be interred alone at the Myōraku-ji atop Yamamuroyama. During the Meiji period, a shrine was built on a landing nearby and was called Yamamuroyama Shrine. Later the shrine, along with Norinaga's home, was moved to within the walls of Matsusaka Castle, and Norinaga's home was converted into a museum. The shrine was also renamed the Motoori no Miya. Haruniwa, however, was buried on the family plot in Jukyō-ji in Matsusaka, not far from the castle.

131. Yamada, *Motoori Haruniwa*, p. 66.

the affairs of the Motoori family, and about Haruniwa's academy. The two scholars, however, had their disagreements, especially with regard to succession within the Norinaga School. This disagreement culminated in a brief falling out, during which the two had little contact with each other. This dispute between Ōhira and Haruniwa is important because it highlights their preoccupation with legitimate succession.

Haruniwa had a biological son whom he deemed incapable of succeeding to the head of his academy in Matsusaka. He therefore asked Ōhira for permission to adopt the eldest of his three sons. Ōhira agreed, but in 1820, his son died a premature death at the age of 32.[132] Meanwhile, Ōhira had designated his second son as his own heir. After the death of the adopted successor, Haruniwa requested permission to adopt his third son, not knowing that Tokugawa Harutomi also had designs on Ōhira's third son for adoption. Annoyed with Haruniwa's request, Ōhira suggested either that he designate his own son as heir or that he adopt another of Norinaga's grandsons. For Ōhira, this was the natural solution, since the preservation of bloodlines was more important to him than the perpetuation of the "scholarly lineage" (*gakutō*).[133]

Haruniwa was not pleased with Ōhira's suggestion. The rift between the two, however, resolved itself in a rather tragic way. The following year, in 1821, Ōhira's second son suddenly died at the age of 33, forcing him to adopt an heir. He sent his newly adopted son to Matsusaka to study with Haruniwa. Later that year, this adopted son returned to Wakayama and quit the Motoori family entirely, later returning to Matsusaka as one of Haruniwa's assistants. In the meantime, Haruniwa had taken Ōhira's advice and designated his own son, Motoori Arisato (1804-1852), as his heir. Ōhira, coping with the loss of two sons and the resignation of his adopted son, decided to adopt his sister's son as his own heir, who later became Motoori Uchitō (1792-1855).[134]

For Ōhira, the problem of succession was made even more painful by the premature deaths of his sons. His tragedy, however, did

---

132. Ibid., p. 75.
133. Ibid., p. 76.
134. Ibid., p. 78.

The Formation of Rival Nativist Schools 51

not end there. During his lifetime, he lost three wives to premature death. Moreover, the rising prominence of Atsutane in Edo added to Ōhira's problems as the leader of the Norinaga School.[135] The cumulative pressure of these three events, all occurring within the three years from 1819 to 1822, contributed to his personal anguish and despair. Haruniwa's blindness and Ōhira's personal losses made the lives of Norinaga's two successors often difficult and bitter.

Despite the hardships that Ōhira faced, he was committed to perpetuating and defending the scholarship of Norinaga. He took a special interest in *kagura*, or Shinto ritual dance and verse, believing that he had received the mandate to pursue his work from Norinaga himself.[136] Just as Norinaga had devoted his career to the *Kojiki*, Ōhira focused his energies on interpreting and analyzing *kagura*, which culminated in his own magnum opus, the *Kagura shinshaku*.[137] Not coincidentally, Harutomi took an interest in Ōhira because he himself esteemed *kagura*. Ōhira's work not only perpetuated Norinaga's legacy for classical Japanese texts, but it also served notice that in spite of Norinaga's death, his disciples formed a vibrant and thriving group.[138] This was particularly important given the activities of Atsutane and the scholars of the Edo-ha.

As previously mentioned, Oyamada Tomokiyo was known as one of the premier scholars of evidential learning in the Edo-ha. One area of his research was, as with Ōhira's, ancient *kagura*. Ōhira's friend and disciple, Ban Nobutomo, a *kōshōgakusha* himself, closely monitored Tomokiyo's progress, and he relayed periodic reports to Ōhira. In the early 1820s, Ōhira sent Nobutomo a draft of *Kagura shinshaku*. Nobutomo knew that Tomokiyo had already published his own work on the same subject in 1819. Fearing that Tomokiyo had already rendered Ōhira's work obsolete, he sent Ōhira's manuscript back to him in 1822, warning him of Tomokiyo's work.[139] Ōhira ignored his friend's admonitions and published his text anyway. Ōhira was defiant because he may have con-

---

135. Nakamura, *Motoori-ha kokugaku no tenkai*, p. 114.
136. Ibid., p. 116.
137. Ibid., p. 115.
138. Ibid., pp. 121–22.
139. Ibid., p. 127.

sidered Nobutomo a rival, especially in view of Nobutomo's considerable skill in Kōshōgaku.[140] For his part, Nobutomo feared that a comparison between the evidential research of Tomokiyo and that of Ōhira would potentially reveal the mutual strengths and weaknesses of the Edo-ha and the Norinaga School.[141] Perhaps Nobutomo wanted to avoid any comparison that would lead to another confrontation between the two groups, following the *Meidōsho* debate earlier in the century (which is the subject of the next chapter).

In 1809 Ōhira reflected on the nature of Norinaga's learning and the intellectual goals of nativism in general in his *Kogakuyō*.[142] In addition to reiterating Norinaga's positions on classical literature, he stated that the mission of the Norinaga School was to explicate the ancient Way in support of institutional Shinto. As was the case in much of his scholarly career, Ōhira avoided innovation in favor of supporting Norinaga's scholarship.

Ōhira complained that contemporary Shinto scholarship ignored the debilitating influences of both Buddhism and Confucianism.[143] Shinto scholars had forgotten that Buddhism and Confucianism were "branch Ways" (*edamichi*) of Shinto. One must first ground oneself in the fundamentals of Shinto before embarking on a study of foreign teachings. As a first step, one had to understand that Shinto had existed in a more pristine condition before the importation of either foreign doctrine.[144] Hence, the study of remote Japanese antiquity was essential to nativism. Interestingly, he did not advocate a complete rejection of the two.[145] Knowledge of

---

140. Ibid., p. 130.
141. Ibid., p. 126.
142. Despite Harry Harootunian's claim that the *Kogakuyō* was written in order "to counter Atsutane's charges and provide a coherent defense of the Suzunoya" (*Things Seen and Unseen*, p. 122), it is clear that Atsutane did not write his first influential work, the *Tama no mihashira*, until 1812. Instead, one can interpret Ōhira's arguments as a response to Hattori Nakatsune's *Sandaikō*. However, an addendum to the *Kogakuyō*, written about twenty years later, does include statements that seem to contradict the *Tama no mihashira*, without naming Atsutane specifically.
143. Motoori Ōhira, *Kogakuyō*, *Nihon kokusui zensho*, vol. 13, p. 2.
144. Ibid., p. 5.
145. Ibid., p. 3.

Confucianism and Buddhism was not pernicious by itself; the privileging of the two over Shinto was the source of their malignancy. Nativists had to recover the ideological purity of the previous era, which he identified as 1764–80, and which was forgotten by his contemporaries.[146] He may have reserved this last observation for the Edo-ha.

Pristine Shinto, practiced by the ancients before the coming of Buddhism and Confucianism, left its legacy in the form of *waka*. The ancient Way, therefore, had been transmitted to the present in the form of *kadō*, or the "Way of Poetry."[147] The task of the nativist was to extract this ancient Way from classical *waka*, and for this he advocated the philology of Norinaga. In recent years, however, nativists had expanded their intellectual horizons to include research beyond *waka*. "Among the old man Suzunoya's [Norinaga] students, [no one] focuses solely on verse," he observed, going on to say that "they broadly peruse Chinese texts, and, among Japanese texts, focus on histories, legal codes, rituals, and so forth."[148] For Ōhira this development was beneficial for nativism as a whole. Regardless of specialization, the methodology remained unchanged and united all nativists: the close, precise analysis of language.[149]

Ultimately, Ōhira wanted to fashion a scholarly tradition for Shinto that he knew had made Buddhism and Confucianism so enduring.[150] Not only did he seek to divorce Shinto from its foreign influences, but he also wanted to use philology to elevate it to the same intellectual level as the two. He envisioned a form of Shinto that would rival foreign teachings intellectually, yet exceed them culturally. In addition to the tautological argument advocated by Norinaga (Japan is great because it is Japan), he also asserted that Shinto did not need the corrupting influence of professional scholars.[151] The corrupted nature of foreign teachings, especially Confucianism, was due to a class of professional elites who did nothing

---

146. Ibid., p. 31.
147. Ibid., p. 13.
148. Motoori Ōhira, *Kogakuyō*, Kokumin dōtoku sōsho, vol.2, p. 213.
149. Motoori Ōhira, *Kogakuyō*, Nihon kokusui zensho, p. 30.
150. Ibid., p. 25.
151. Ibid.

more than exercise their subjective intellects. Shinto scholars, he argued, derived no personal benefit from their work, and their intellectual labor was always directed at the greater glory of the ancient Way.

The Expansion of the Norinaga School

An essential aspect of glorifying Shinto was the adherence to the tenets of nativism established by Norinaga, a responsibility that Ōhira solemnly assumed. Moreover, as the leader and spokesperson for the Norinaga School, he was also responsible for the recruitment of Norinaga disciples outside Matsusaka and Wakayama. To this end, he established branch academies of the Suzunoya. The most important of these were in the major urban centers of Japan: Osaka, Edo, Kyoto, and Nagoya. In addition, he and his students made significant progress toward the installation of nativist curricula in domainal schools. Ōhira oversaw the institutional propagation of the Norinaga School during the first half of the nineteenth century; during the latter half of the century, it would grow into the most significant school of Kokugaku.

Ōhira recognized the prestige that the installation of his curriculum within domainal schools would bring to the Norinaga School. In 1794 Norinaga himself sought such recognition. That year, he petitioned the Matsusaka authorities to establish an academy dedicated to nativism.[152] He understood, however, that an exclusively nativist curriculum was unreasonable and would not provide for the educational needs of the domain's samurai. Therefore, in addition to nativist topics, Norinaga promised to teach Confucian subjects, especially those that dealt with military science and civil administration. His request was denied. Years later, after his death, his student, Hattori Nakatsune (1756–1824), petitioned the domain on his behalf once again, eventually resulting in the establishment of an official academy in 1804.[153] The curriculum was still primarily dedicated to Kangaku, but nativist subjects were also taught. Thus, for most of the first three decades of the nineteenth century,

---

152. Matsumoto, *Motoori Norinaga, 1730–1801*, p. 130.
153. Nakamura, *Motoori-ha kokugaku no tenkai*, p. 20.

The Formation of Rival Nativist Schools

Ōhira and his students succeeded in establishing nativism within the curricula of domainal schools in Kii-Wakayama and elsewhere, but the actual academy devoted exclusively to nativism would have to wait until the bakumatsu period.[154]

Domainal lords were an integral part of this expansion in the bakumatsu period. In 1851, Shimazu Nariakira (1809–58), the *tozama* lord of Satsuma, took an interest in Kokugaku, adding it to the curriculum of his domainal school;[155] the vast majority of daimyo interested in nativism, however, came from the ranks of the *shinpan* and *fudai*.[156] In addition to making nativist additions to their curricula, these daimyo invited nativists, many of whom were from the Norinaga School, to lecture and teach, which provided a source of employment for scholars who were otherwise engaged in scholarship as a private interest. Commonly, daimyo studied nativism for personal reasons, perhaps as an alternative to the ubiquitous Neo-Confucian curriculum already installed in their schools. In any case, their patronage was a crucial element in the expansion of nativism during the nineteenth century, and especially of the Norinaga School led by Ōhira.

Much of the expansion orchestrated by Norinaga and Ōhira relied on the proliferation of *shijuku*, or "private academies."[157] By 1810, Haruniwa had revived the Suzunoya of Matsusaka into a thriving academy. As Norinaga's successor, Ōhira had established his own academy in Wakayama. Hence, the Norinaga School comprised two distinct centers of activity. This was not the end of its expansion, however. In 1816 a Kyoto merchant, Kido Chidate, founded his own academy, the Nudenoya, which he affiliated with the Norinaga School. A few years later, a prominent student of Norinaga, Fujii Takanao, was instrumental in establishing an academy in Osaka. Suzuki Akira (1764–1837) and Uematsu Shigetake (1793–1876) helped to establish a private academy in Nagoya with much of its curriculum dedicated to Norinaga's scholarship. Finally, in 1803 Hirata Atsutane established his own academy, the

---

154. Ibid., p. 18.
155. Ibid., p. 56.
156. Ibid., p. 61.
157. Rubinger, *Private Academies of Tokugawa Japan*, p. 159.

Ibukinoya, in the urban heart of the Mabuchi School in Edo, which he a few years later formally linked to the Norinaga School. Each cell of the Norinaga School crafted its own distinctive character, which was a testament to the School's versatile approach to the investigation of the ancient Way.

Kido Chidate and the Nudenoya

Kido Chidate was a merchant who ran a publishing business in Kyoto; even before founding his academy, he had published some of Norinaga's works at Ōhira's request. Despite his financial interests in the Norinaga School, he considered himself to be a serious scholar, and his academy reflected this dedication. The origins of the Nudenoya, unlike those of the original Suzunoya, were not as informal. Chidate viewed his academy and its students as a bona fide institution committed to the clarification of the ancient Way.[158]

The Nudenoya was primarily oriented toward the analysis of classical *waka*.[159] Chidate invited prominent nativists, like Ōhira and Murata Harukado (1765–1836) of Osaka, to lecture on *waka*, and solicited Fujii Takanao, also of Osaka, to lecture on classical prose.[160] His interest in classical poetry had its origins in the work of the first-generation Mabuchi student Arakida Hisaoyu (1746–1804). Therefore, in addition to members of the Norinaga School, he maintained ties with scholars of the Edo-ha as well. In his *Shimimuro zakki*, he recorded a visit to the Nudenoya by Ōhira in 1819, followed by an appearance in 1820 by Shimizu Hamaomi, a disciple of Murata Harumi.[161] Chidate observed how the activities of the Edo-ha were similar to those of the Nudenoya, noting how both schools revered Mabuchi.[162]

Notwithstanding the Nudenoya's ties to influential scholars of the Norinaga School and the Edo-ha, the academy never achieved

---

158. Motohashi, "Kasei Tenpō-ki ni okeru Keihan no kokugaku no ichidanmen," p. 93.
159. Ibid., p. 95.
160. Ibid., p. 91.
161. Kido Chidate, *Shimimuro zakki*, p. 5.
162. Ibid., pp. 231–32.

the kind of national recognition that Chidate sought.[163] Chidate's emphasis on *waka*, to the exclusion of other sanctioned subjects like Shinto theology, forced the Nudenoya into the margins of the Norinaga School.[164] Moreover, as we will discuss later, his embrace of the Edo-ha as a kindred nativist school was actually a controversial position within the Norinaga School. Ōhira and especially Atsutane emphasized differences with the Edo-ha, most notably with regard to the interpretation of Mabuchi's scholarship.

Classical Verse and the Emperor

We have seen that while the scholars of the Edo-ha grew more bohemian, those of the Norinaga School conducted a steady institutional expansion, and the ranks of its enrolled students swelled. While the Norinaga School engaged in the same kind of philological analysis of *waka* favored by the Edo-ha, they did not rely *exclusively* on such scholarship. Ōhira, as the designated leader of the School, countenanced a pluralistic approach to what he viewed as the goal of nativist scholarship, namely, the investigation of the ancient Way. Kido Chidate, however, represented an even more fundamentalist wing within the School. He disagreed with Ōhira, insisting that *waka* studies were the only legitimate form of nativism. His insistence on an intellectually intolerant form of scholarship relegated him to an extremist position among Norinaga's disciples. It is not surprising, therefore, that he cultivated such friendly ties with the Edo-ha, because the latter shared his narrow view of scholarship.

In the same year that Chidate founded the Nudenoya, he authored an outline of the Norinaga School's orthodoxy, the *Manabi no hiromichi*. Repeating the same caveats against Buddhism and Confucianism previously articulated by Norinaga and Ōhira, he also was critical of Rangaku (Dutch Learning). As Ōhira had argued years earlier, the analysis of classical Japanese texts was the key to healing the wounds inflicted on Japan by an indulgence in

---

163. Motohashi, "Kasei Tenpō-ki ni okeru Keihan no kokugaku no ichidanmen," p. 101.
164. Ibid.

foreign teachings. While Ōhira exhibited a tolerance for varied approaches to the study of antiquity, Chidate relied exclusively on classical poetics. Chidate, perhaps more than Ōhira, linked philology to classical *waka*, even to the point of ignoring the links obtaining between elegance (*miyabi*) and *mono no aware*, issues that were central to Norinaga.[165]

Poetry embodied the feelings and emotions of the ancients. The nativist, according to Chidate, had to recover and restore those feelings, using the precise techniques of textual analysis perfected by Mabuchi and Norinaga. Such careful scholarship eliminated the kind of subjective interpretations for which Confucian scholars were renowned.[166] Reiterating the views espoused by Norinaga, he criticized Confucians for their inclination to analyze Japanese antiquity using Chinese theoretical categories like Yin and Yang and the Five Phases.[167] Analysis of this kind imputed intentions into the words of the ancient Japanese that distorted their original meanings. Moreover, these Confucian categories were highly analytic, abstract, and ill-suited to the highly emotional nature of native verse.

At the heart of Confucian Shinto was the search for universal virtues in Japanese antiquity, exemplified primarily by the work of Yamazaki Ansai (1618–82). Although Chidate believed that the effort to discern examples of good and evil in antiquity was tied to the Mandate of Heaven, rendering it flawed, he did acknowledge the universality of Confucian virtues.[168] The virtues of filial piety, benevolence, and so forth had already existed in antiquity *before* the importation of Confucianism and *without* the rigid framework of teachings.[169] As Norinaga had argued, the ancient Japanese were superior and worthy of emulation, since they exhibited these universal virtues without the need for teachings.

---

165. Watanabe H., " 'Michi' to 'miyabi,' " p. 249.
166. Kido Chidate, *Manabi no hiromichi*, p. 281.
167. Wai-ming Ng argues that these categories form the basis for Neo-Confucian metaphysics and come primarily from the *Book of Changes* (*The 'I Ching' in Tokugawa Thought and Culture*, p. 204).
168. Kido Chidate, *Manabi no hiromichi*, p. 291.
169. Ibid., pp. 299–305.

The Formation of Rival Nativist Schools

Most of the textual examples of these indigenous virtues came from the *Nihongi* and the *Kojiki*. Neither text, however, truly captured the feelings of the ancients like *waka*, which is why Chidate privileged poetry over all other forms of literature. Agreeing with Mabuchi, he asserted that emulation of the ancient style was a key ingredient in the analysis of classical verse.[170] Scholars who emulated the ancient style could apprehend the emotional complexity of antiquity and perceive the essence of the ancient heart in the process. This essence was the spiritual devotion of the Japanese people to the emperor. "The ancients respected and worshipped the emperor in their hearts," he observed.[171] The idea of *kadō* (the Way of Poetry) forms the essential core of nativism because it was the only means of understanding the relationship between the emperor and his people. A reliance on Buddhism, Confucianism, and Rangaku threatened to undermine this mission by forsaking the role of the emperor. Nativism was dedicated to the emperor, and the study of *waka* was essential for his glorification. It is important to note that Chidate's assertion gave poetry a political significance that Norinaga had explicitly denied it. Such an insistence on the political function of verse was consistent with the views of Mabuchi.

In 1823, another academy affiliated with the Norinaga School opened in Osaka. It was called the Koshibaya, and like the Nudenoya, its scholars concentrated on the study of classical poetry. In contrast to the devoted scholars with whom Chidate surrounded himself in Kyoto, those of the Koshibaya were mostly merchants who were new to scholarship.[172] Perhaps for this reason, its membership was also not as committed to *waka* as its Kyoto brethren. Many of its members demonstrated an inclination toward Shinto theology as well.[173] Not much is known about the Koshibaya because it never achieved anything beyond a regional

---

170. Ibid., p. 284. This position was not the same as Norinaga's, who privileged Heian poetry over that of Nara. Chidate's view of classical *waka* was another indication of his esteem for the Edo-ha and Mabuchi.

171. Ibid., p. 287.

172. Motohashi, "Kasei Tenpō-ki ni okeru Keihan no kokugaku no ichidanmen," pp. 103–4.

173. Fujii F., "Fujii Takanao to Nudenoya," p. 15.

following.[174] However, one of the pivotal figures in its formation was the prominent Norinaga disciple Fujii Takanao. In fact, the Koshibaya's less dogmatic approach to poetry reflected Takanao's own views. His more diverse view of nativism was more faithful to Norinaga's vision than was Chidate's.[175]

Fujii Takanao: Prose over Poetry

The scholars we have examined thus far each had a particular focus within the Norinaga School. Ōhira concentrated his efforts for the most part on ancient Shinto *kagura*. Haruniwa, Norinaga's biological son, devoted his two published treatises to the language of the Shinto classics. Kido Chidate emphasized the role of classical verse. Fujii Takanao represented yet another facet of nativist scholarship. Like his contemporaries, however, Takanao confined his scholarship largely to literature.

Takanao joined the Suzunoya in 1793, taking the pen name Matsunoya in 1795.[176] Norinaga was especially fond of Takanao, recognizing his considerable scholarly talents in classical literature, especially with regard to the *Genji monogatari*.[177] Takanao spent most of his life in Kansai, making occasional appearances in Kyoto at Chidate's academy; as Chidate's friend, he spent much of his time at the Nudenoya. He also maintained an interest in the nativist activities of his contemporaries in Edo. Although he was critical of Mabuchi's views of the *Ise monogatari*,[178] he was on friendly terms with at least two scholars of the Mabuchi School, Katō Chikage and Shimizu Hamaomi.[179] Takanao traveled to Edo at least twice during the first decades of the nineteenth century. The first

---

174. Ibid., p. 16.
175. Motohashi, "Kasei Tenpō-ki ni okeru Keihan no kokugaku no ichidanmen," p. 104.
176. Oyamada Tomokiyo also referred to himself as Matsunoya. In a parody of Edo nativists, including Norinaga and Atsutane, an anonymous scholar, poking fun at Tomokiyo and nativists in general, inquired, "Fujii Takanao also calls himself the Matsunoya—what's that about?" *Shiryūgoto*, p. 426.
177. Kudō, *Fujii Takanao to Matsunoya-ha*, p. 13.
178. Ibid., p. 79.
179. Fujii, "Fujii Takanao to Nudenoya," p. 10.

time, perhaps in 1803 or 1804, he met Atsutane.[180] On a second trip in 1821, he stayed with Atsutane as a guest, and the two became friends. His associations with certain scholars of the Edo-ha are not difficult to imagine given his friendship with Chidate; but his friendship with Atsutane made him unpopular with the scholars of the Nudenoya, including Chidate. Although Takanao's view of *waka* had a religious dimension that came close to Atsutane's theological views,[181] it is perhaps safe to assume that Takanao's esteem for Atsutane was personal and not necessarily commensurate with the considerable intellectual differences that separated the two.

Takanao divided nativism into four distinct categories, in the following order: poetry (*kagaku*), prose (*bunshōgaku*), history (*kiroku gakumon*), and Shinto.[182] These four divisions resonated with those that Norinaga had created: theology (*shingaku*), antiquarianism (*yūsokugaku*), history (*kiroku*), and poetry. Takanao transposed the position of poetry with that of theology in Norinaga's hierarchy and replaced *yūsokugaku* with prose. Clearly, however, Takanao emphasized poetry and prose as the most significant areas of nativism. He argued that poetry must come before prose because one had to study poetry in order to compose effective prose. Hence, prose composition was the ultimate goal and not the study of *waka*.[183]

Takanao discussed the relationships among the Way, poetry, and prose. Agreeing with his colleagues in both Matsusaka and Edo, he claimed that the essential function of *waka* was the expression of emotion.[184] He parted company, however, with the Edo-ha by reiterating Norinaga's teaching that the *Kokinshū* exhibited the qualities of good poetry more consistently than the *Man'yōshū*. He insisted that the goal of Norinaga's *waka* studies was the investigation of ancient emotion and *not* its replication in poetic composition.[185] In order to unlock the emotional qualities of classical verse,

---

180. Ibid.
181. Watanabe H., "'Michi to 'miyabi,'" p. 258.
182. Kudō, *Fujii Takanao to Matsunoya-ha*, p. 69.
183. Ibid., p. 71.
184. Fujii Takanao, *Mitsu no shirube*, p. 21.
185. Ibid., p. 26.

a scholar had to pay close attention to its language; mimicking poetic words without understanding their meanings did not produce good *waka*. To put it another way, a thorough knowledge of poetic words did not guarantee the composition of good *waka*, let alone poetry that captured the emotional depth of the ancients.[186] Thus, nativists should abandon their efforts to compose poetry in the ancient style. They should instead orient their study of classical verse toward the composition of beautiful prose.

Takanao privileged prose over poetry because of its inherent clarity, unfettered by the conventions of elegant language that could obscure its meaning.[187] He was especially fond of the *Ise monogatari* and the *Genji monogatari*, texts that he believed were excellent examples of the clarity that he sought to recover.[188] Both texts were composed in what he called a "middle-antiquity style" (*chūkotai*), as opposed to the ancient style (*jōkotai*) of the *Man'yōshū*. Scholars had to master the "middle-antiquity style" in order to compose effective prose, reserving the ancient style only for Shinto liturgies (*norito*). His faith in this style was in sharp contrast to the views of Mabuchi and his student Tachibana Moribe (1780–1849), both of whom advocated the odd use of the ancient style for *norito* and for prose.[189]

In addition to Takanao's admonitions regarding prose, he studied classical manuscripts in an attempt to reconstruct their definitive versions by correcting the flawed glosses of previous scholars.[190] Like many of his contemporaries, he relied on Kōshōgaku in his research. Takanao, however, viewed this effort as an effective use of Kōshōgaku, and not a self-indulgent exercise, a remark that was perhaps a criticism of the Edo-ha.[191] Despite Takanao's views to the contrary, his analysis of classical texts completely ignored Norinaga's notion of *mono no aware*.[192] His emphasis on Kōshōgaku overlooked its significant role in the formation of the intel-

---

186. Ibid., p. 31.
187. Ibid., p. 38.
188. Ibid., p. 40.
189. Kudō, *Fujii Takanao to Matsunoya-ha*, p. 72.
190. Ibid., p. 80.
191. Ibid., p. 74.
192. Ibid., p. 80.

lectual foundation for the Suzunoya. However, his stature in the Norinaga School and his ties to Matsusaka, Osaka, and Kyoto gained recognition for his scholarship and academy, and his new approach to nativism contributed to the pluralism of the School.

Conclusion

Takanao represented a distinct intellectual position within the Norinaga School. Like his colleagues Haruniwa, Ōhira, and Chidate, he focused on an important facet of Norinaga's scholarship, namely, the genre of narrative tales. The scholars of the Norinaga School were united in their commitment to Norinaga's scholarship, as well as their emphasis on the precise examination of native texts. These commonalities were important because it allowed them to recognize one another as members of the same collective school, despite differences in intellectual focus, scholastic interest, and geographic location. It is for this reason that the Norinaga School had a broad-minded approach to the investigation of the ancient Way.

The ancient Way was an issue that distinguished the Norinaga School from its counterpart, the Edo-ha. The Edo-ha was a group of scholars who formed a coherent school, although it was not as well organized institutionally as the Norinaga School. The Edo-ha's senior members and its most influential scholars were individuals who had either studied with Mabuchi or were the sons of scholars who had. Mabuchi's disciples did not have the same ideological commitment as Norinaga and his disciples, since Mabuchi simply viewed ancient Shinto as nature. Like their colleagues in the Norinaga School, they placed great emphasis on the philological examination of Japan's classical canon. Whereas Norinaga and his disciples were engaged in a scholastic examination of antiquity, many scholars of the Edo-ha, such as Murata Harumi, viewed nativist scholarship as harboring a significant artistic component as well. While scholars of the Norinaga School attempted to recover a lost ancient Way through their efforts, those of the Edo-ha emphasized the importance of poetic elegance and artistic flair. The Edo-ha's preoccupation with creative expression was related to its proximity to an emerging literati culture of the *bunjin* in early nineteenth-century Edo. The intellectual agendas of the

Norinaga School and the Edo-ha were fundamentally opposed at this time.

The major centers of the expanding Norinaga School in the early decades of the nineteenth century were Matsusaka, Wakayama, Kyoto, and to a lesser degree, Osaka. Tokugawa Japan's most populous urban center, Edo, however, was not one of the School's larger outposts. A few intrepid scholars in Edo did join the School in this period, despite the popularity of its rival school, the Edo-ha. Hirata Atsutane, the focus of this study, was part of this contingent in Edo.

THREE

The Norinaga School in Edo

Sociologists observe that fields of cultural production operate by a distinct set of rules regarding membership.[1] Both the Edo-ha and the Norinaga School functioned as fields of this kind. The qualifications for membership in either field varied from scholar to scholar. Generally speaking, close proximity to either Kamo no Mabuchi or Motoori Norinaga translated into automatic membership. For those without such links, such as Hirata Atsutane, establishing a set of legitimate scholarly credentials was more of a challenge. Atsutane, as an outsider, had to gain the attention of scholars in either of the two fields.[2] Such attention could be either positive or negative; active rejection could signify membership in the field just as well as unqualified acceptance.[3] The worst situation for scholars seeking entrance into the field was to incur the collective indifference of its members. This chapter deals with Atsutane's relationship to the two fields of nativism during the early years of the nineteenth century.

The members of both the Edo-ha and the Norinaga School undertook their studies in active scholarly communities during the first half of the nineteenth century. Atsutane, a resident of Edo, was never acknowledged as a member of the Edo-ha. For this rea-

---

1. Collins, *The Sociology of Philosophies*, pp. 22–28.
2. Ibid., pp. 38–40.
3. For Bourdieu, the primary criterion for membership in the field is the ability "to produce effects," which can either mean rejection or acceptance (Bourdieu and Wacquant, *An Invitation to Reflexive Sociology*, p. 107).

son, he formally joined Haruniwa's academy in Matsusaka in 1806. As a member of the Norinaga School living among scholars of the Edo-ha, he was torn between these two very distinct social and intellectual spheres. During the early 1800s, he was a virtual outsider to the Edo-ha, and had yet to establish himself in the Norinaga School. The analysis of the social and intellectual dynamics of both the Edo-ha and the Norinaga School will help to explain his rejection of the former and his uneasy embrace of the latter.

Izumi Makuni and Ban Nobutomo

Despite the success of the Norinaga School's expansion, Motoori Ōhira had difficulty spreading its influence to Edo. The scholars of the Edo-ha had a longer history there, and they cultivated ties with *bunjin* that enhanced their cultural standing and social reputation. Although the Edo-ha was dominant, the Norinaga School did have a small contingent of affiliated scholars in Edo. At the beginning of the nineteenth century, the three most important of these were Izumi Makuni (?–1805), Ban Nobutomo (1773–1846), and Hirata Atsutane. Of the three, Atsutane and Nobutomo eventually became important members of the Norinaga School; Izumi Makuni made a name for himself in a debate with Murata Harumi. Nobutomo was especially prominent in the School because of his commitment to Norinaga's methodological legacy. In fact, his devotion to Norinaga made him one of the most respected scholars of evidential learning in Edo, on a par with the Edo-ha scholar Oyamada Tomokiyo. While Nobutomo perpetuated Norinaga's attitude toward *waka*, treating it as one, albeit essential, aspect of the ancient Way, his scholarship resisted the literary influences of the *bunjin*. Unlike his colleagues Motoori Ōhira, Kido Chidate, and Fujii Takanao, Nobutomo avoided ideological discussions, preferring to devote his energy solely to research on antiquity. Makuni, by contrast, was concerned with nativist ideology, which was the reason for his debate with Harumi. Atsutane was caught between the two scholars. Ultimately, Atsutane distanced himself from Makuni and tried to deny Nobutomo a place in the orthodox history of Kokugaku; his relationship with Ōhira deteriorated as well.

Ban Nobutomo

Nobutomo was a serious scholar who was generally oblivious to the larger intellectual controversies that raged around him.[4] Nobutomo's achievements with Kōshōgaku placed him in an intellectual continuum with Mabuchi and Norinaga. As mentioned in the last chapter, scholars of the Edo-ha separated Kōshōgaku from *waka* studies. They viewed the composition of poetry and the textual analysis of classical literature as two distinct activities, as opposed to those scholars of the Norinaga School who viewed the two activities as interrelated. The pursuit of Kōshōgaku was one of the Edo-ha's most distinctive features.[5] Their counterparts in the Norinaga School, like Nobutomo, used Kōshōgaku as a methodological tool in a larger nativist project. While both groups were composed of skilled *kōshōgakusha*, those in the Norinaga School were motivated by an ultimate, intellectual goal: the ancient Way.

Nobutomo was very concerned with the accurate replication of Norinaga's work.[6] Nobutomo believed that he followed Norinaga's exact instructions regarding the study of antiquity.[7] His careful approach gave him the courage to challenge long-held views of classical texts. In one instance, he argued that the accepted view of the three imperial regalia was mistaken. Citing the relevant passage from the *Nihongi*, he observed that it did not indicate that there were three objects—the sword, the mirror, and the jewel—but instead signified that the sword and the mirror were themselves jewels: "The reality is that the sources mention the mirror and the sword. The jewel referred to the divine symbols (*shinji*) [collectively]."[8] Mabuchi had argued that the jewel was especially prized over both the sword and the mirror. Nobutomo agreed with Mabuchi's emphasis on the jewel, but he insisted that both the sword and the mirror exhibited the same divine qualities sym-

---

4. Hisamatsu, "Bunkengaku-teki kenkyū to kōshōgaku," p. 228.
5. Ibid., p. 229.
6. Morita, *Ban Nobutomo no shisō*, p. 79. Morita is my main source of information on Ban Nobutomo.
7. Ibid., p. 64.
8. Ban Nobutomo, *Shinji sanben*, p. 600.

bolized by the concept of "jewel," namely, the spirit of the *kami*. Using the same etymological argument formulated by Norinaga, he cited the similarity between the word for jewel, *tama*, and the word for spirit, *tamashii*.[9]

The example of the three imperial regalia highlights Nobutomo's interests in the spirituality of antiquity. He viewed Norinaga's method as the means to enter the past without the epistemological baggage of the present. Nobutomo used textual research to apprehend the ancient consciousness by thoroughly investigating the meanings of words, in an effort to reconstruct the conditions of the past.[10] Through these endeavors, he recognized a divine will at work in history. The scholar's mission was to understand this historical essence; he felt obligated to experience the very emotions of the ancients. The encounter with ancient emotionality was the central focus of his historiography. Unlike the Kōshōgaku of his Edo contemporaries, Nobutomo's goal was the articulation of a "spiritual history" (*seishinshi*; Morita's term).[11] In a letter to Murata Harukado, he criticized scholars who strove for historical accuracy without first comprehending ancient spirituality: "Of course, even in their dreams, [they] will [never] understand the ancient Way."[12]

There are two additional themes in Nobutomo's scholarship. First, he was an avid scholar of the native classics who believed that his research method could reveal the ancient Way. His emphasis on the use of classical texts for this purpose linked him to his Norinaga School colleagues Ōhira, Haruniwa, Chidate, and Takanao; his skill in Kōshōgaku, however, distinguished him even within this elite group. Second, it was this same skill that made him a potential candidate to succeed Norinaga as the leading intellect of the Norinaga School during the nineteenth century. Although the School's presence in Edo was minimal, he was one of its most renowned members.

While both Atsutane and Nobutomo lived and worked on the geographic margins of the Norinaga School, they were also active

---

9. Morita, *Ban Nobutomo no shisō*, p. 205.
10. Ibid., p. 158.
11. Ibid., p. 183.
12. Quoted in ibid., p. 184.

in the territorial heart of their school's rival, the Edo-ha. For much of the eighteenth century, Edo was the center of nativist activity in Japan, having displaced Kyoto. With the dynamic development of the Norinaga School, Matsusaka and Wakayama threatened to displace Edo as the new centers of nativism. Perhaps sensing this change, Murata Harumi became more vocal in his criticism of Norinaga, especially after the latter's death.[13] During the early years of the nineteenth century, neither Nobutomo nor Atsutane were formal members of the Norinaga School. Izumi Makuni was one of the few members of the Norinaga School living in Edo at the time. Makuni challenged Murata Harumi to a debate over the latter's critique of Norinaga. This debate culminated in the publication of the *Meidōsho* shortly before Makuni's death. The issues raised in the exchanges between Makuni and Harumi demonstrate the intellectually opposed approaches of the two schools and their fundamental assumptions regarding the ideological nature of nativism. Other than Atsutane's *Tamadasuki*, it is one of the few texts from the first half of the nineteenth century that directly articulates the differences between the Edo-ha and the Norinaga School.

The Edo-ha Versus the Norinaga School: Murata Harumi and Izumi Makuni

Makuni saw himself as Norinaga's proxy in the debate with Harumi. This was not the first time that Harumi confronted Norinaga via one of the latter's disciples. At the end of the eighteenth century, Harumi shared his growing doubts about Norinaga with other members of the Edo-ha, which led to a heated exchange with Motoori Ōhira in 1800.[14] Harumi had previously perused Norinaga's work on narrative tales, especially the *Ise monogatari* and the *Genji monogatari*, and found that Norinaga's conclusions significantly diverged from those of Mabuchi. Implicit in Harumi's critique was the idea that Norinaga was not a true disciple of Mabuchi. Several years later, Harumi authored the *Utagatari*, in

---

13. Tanaka K., "Edo-ha to iu genshō," p. 37.
14. Ibid., p. 34.

which he made, as a retort to Ōhira, oblique references to some of his doubts about Norinaga.[15]

Unlike the earlier controversy with Ōhira, Izumi Makuni and Murata Harumi directly debated the various merits of their nativist schools from 1803 to 1804. Their discussions focused on the interpretation of the *Ryōnogige* (compiled in 833) and, through it, the nature of the indigenous Way.[16] The text of the *Meidōsho* is divided into three sections. In the first part, Makuni enumerated Harumi's myriad mistakes and misinterpretations. He recalled a specific occasion when he voiced these objections to Harumi personally, perhaps with Harumi's students in attendance. The second part records Harumi's reply to Makuni, which includes Harumi's refutation of Norinaga as well. In the third part, Makuni had the last word, declaring that Harumi was a traitor to the nativist cause.[17] Building his own observations of the Edo-ha on those of Makuni, Atsutane wrote a commentary on this debate in the *Tamadasuki*. In contrast to Makuni, he focused on the nativist preoccupation with *waka*, a criticism of certain members of both the Edo-ha and the Norinaga School.

Makuni repeated the Norinaga School's tenet that the investigation of *waka* was merely one aspect of nativism. The elegant expression of feeling that characterized classical texts resided in what Makuni called ancient *teburi*, or "form." He criticized Harumi for claiming that poetry alone exhibited sublime *teburi*; consequently, nativists were compelled to devote themselves to the study of classical *waka*. As we have seen, Harumi emphasized such investigation as the prerequisite for the composition of beautiful poetry in a *contemporary* form, instead of the ancient form favored by his mentor Mabuchi. Moreover, the Edo-ha as a whole was more concerned with poetry than the Norinaga School because of the former's connections with the most famous writers and poets of the time. Makuni, however, asserted that even works of classical prose exhibited the elegance of *teburi* (130). Thus, he advocated the same

---

15. Ibid., p. 37.
16. Nakamura, *Motoori-ha kokugaku no tenkai*, p. 65.
17. Izumi Makuni, *Meidōsho*, p. 136. Subsequent references are cited in the text.

pluralistic approach to the study of antiquity that characterized the Norinaga School under the leadership of Ōhira.

For Makuni, Harumi's emphasis on *waka* over the large corpus of classical prose was symptomatic of Harumi's generally flawed scholarship. Recalling his meeting with Harumi, he recounted a specific example of the Edo-ha scholar's questionable interpretations. Harumi argued that a difficult phrase from the *Ryōnogige* must be the title of an otherwise little known classical work because he could not make sense of it any other way. Makuni informed him that this obscure phrase was in fact a passage taken from a Chinese text dating to the Former Han (130). Embarrassed, Harumi "strikes the tatami" (*tatami uchitataki*), declaring that Makuni must be mistaken. For Makuni, Harumi's obvious mistake only indicated much larger problems with his research on antiquity. In his own defense, Harumi claimed that he did not have sufficient time to prepare an answer, insisting that in his normal setting, he discussed his work with his students and colleagues before formulating interpretations. In other words, Makuni had caught him off-guard. If anything, Harumi proclaimed, the study of antiquity was too daunting a task for a scholar to pursue alone (146).

Perhaps Harumi's initial response to Makuni's accusation of incompetence originated in the pride that he took in his knowledge of classical Chinese texts. He insisted that the ancient Japanese people could not compare with their Chinese counterparts in literary composition (149), and that they merely copied the works of their Chinese predecessors. Scholars could not understand either the *Kojiki* or the *Nihongi* without reference to classical Chinese texts (157). For Harumi, Kōshōgaku was not the methodological key to a thorough knowledge of native, classical texts as much as it signified a potential mastery of Chinese sources, in what may have been a reference to Ming and Qing Kaozhengxue.[18] Thus, any investigation of Japanese antiquity must begin with Chinese texts. Native textual analysis was unimaginable without Chinese scholarship: "Scholars who attempt to fathom textual principles by learn-

---

18. Wai-ming Ng observes that Tokugawa scholars were aware of both Ming and Qing scholarship, holding a low opinion especially of the latter (*The 'I Ching' in Tokugawa Thought and Culture*, p. 32).

ing [even] a few Chinese texts will not be misguided" (143). Harumi noted that Confucians (*jusei*) in antiquity did not even acknowledge the validity of Japanese history as a discipline. "The responsibility of Confucians, as they understood it, was to master Chinese texts," he contended; "they viewed matters [regarding] our land as outside their profession; [hence,] they had lost sight of the [true] essence of scholarship."[19] The term for nativism, Wagaku, was not created until the early twelfth century, Harumi asserted, when its scholarly validity was finally recognized. Even at this time, however, it was considered an aspect of Confucian learning. He maintained that nativism was never viewed as a separate discipline in all of Japanese history.

Makuni admitted his heavy reliance on Japanese texts in his research on antiquity. He was adamant, however, that such reliance rendered his scholarship no more "immature" (*osanashi*) than Harumi's preference for Chinese sources (165). In fact, he claimed that Harumi's use of Chinese sources was a profound weakness; this was especially true for a scholar of Kōshōgaku. A defining activity for all nativists, Makuni asserted, was the correction of flaws in extant versions of texts (142). Makuni doubted the efficacy of Harumi's method, since much of this kind of work involved comparisons of words from various Japanese works. Using Chinese sources introduced subjective conjecture and obfuscated the original, ancient meanings (173). He asserted that Harumi's use of Chinese sources was a thinly disguised attempt to privilege China over Japan: "Since I have heard what you [Harumi] have said, [I have concluded that] you are opposed to all [of Mabuchi's teachings]. You privilege a foreign land, [while] rejecting our [own]" (209–10).

Norinaga, Mabuchi, and the Way

While Harumi confessed his occasional oversights in the analysis of Japanese antiquity, he was much less forgiving of errors that he perceived in Norinaga's work. He recognized that Norinaga and Mabuchi had their differences, which certainly did not compromise the latter's teachings. Scholars of the Norinaga School, how-

---

19. Murata Harumi, *Wagaku taigai*, p. 448.

ever, used these differences to attack Mabuchi, and for this he felt compelled to attack Norinaga.[20] Although Harumi conceded that Norinaga was a gifted scholar, he refused to recognize Norinaga's skill in either prose or *waka* composition, skills for which Harumi praised Mabuchi.[21] Norinaga was a capable scholar of classical poetry, but he was no poet.[22] In the *Meidōsho*, Harumi overcame his earlier reluctance to criticize Norinaga's scholarship and launched into a comprehensive refutation of the latter's work, even the vaunted *Kojiki-den*.

Reminiscent of Makuni's humiliating remarks, Harumi indicated a similar misinterpretation that Norinaga had made. Norinaga had claimed that a difficult term he encountered in a certain classical text was incomprehensible, concluding, therefore, that it was a mistake. He took the liberty of replacing it with a similar, more logical alternative. Harumi, drawing on his knowledge of Chinese sources, claimed that the original term was indeed correct:

> When [composing] commentaries, everyone makes mistakes. Of these, some are grave and others are trivial. I must provide an example. In the *Montoku jitsuroku* (879), there is the phrase, "I just received some poems (*shihitsu*) by Yuan Bao which I humbly present." In Norinaga's *Tamakatsuma*, he says, "The term 'some poems' is used in the classical sources. However, since it [the *Montoku jitsuroku*] refers to Yuan Bao and to 'the emperor's supreme joy,' etc., the term 'poetic anthology' was mistakenly copied as 'some poems.'" This is a terrible mistake. Replacing 'some poems' with 'poetic anthology' is a very harmful [interpretation]. This is because the term 'some poems' was a common term during the Tang. Since that was a time of [cultural exchange], it became a common word at our imperial court, and which is why it was used in the text. (147)

The term that Norinaga had failed to understand correctly originated in the Tang dynasty and was subsequently transmitted from China to Japan sometime during the Nara period. Norinaga's proposed substitution, he added, did not even exist in the Tang dynasty; consequently, it could not possibly be the correct term. Harumi concluded that this example illustrated that Norinaga "was

---

20. Mori, "Murata Harumi iji," p. 106.
21. Ibid.
22. Watanabe H., "'Michi' to 'miyabi,'" p. 651.

uneducated and ignorant" (147). Apparently aware of the similarity between his critique of Norinaga and Makuni's critique of himself, he claimed that his own lapses originated in an "overreading"; Norinaga was just a bad scholar.

Despite the venom in Harumi's critique of Norinaga, he denied that he merely indicated Norinaga's errors out of spite (148), a complaint lodged against him by Makuni. Petty criticism, he argued, was the chief characteristic of the Japanese heart (*yamatogokoro*) that Makuni and Norinaga held in such high regard. The two were perfect examples of "vulgar men" (*shōnin*), the Confucian antithesis to the "gentleman" (*kunshi*). Harumi refused to reduce himself morally to the level of his opponents.

Makuni replied to Harumi's refusal to engage in ad hominem attacks by noting how Harumi had previously praised Norinaga's work (211). Harumi's sudden about-face amounted to an ethical betrayal. Makuni noted that Norinaga had never attacked Harumi and, in death, was powerless to defend himself. Makuni assumed the role of defending his mentor's scholarship, proclaiming that Norinaga's learning was the only true source of teachings for Japan (182-83). He felt only contempt for Harumi's repudiation of such a great scholar (174).

Harumi not only viewed Norinaga's Kōshōgaku as careless, but also argued that Norinaga's scholarship was based on a blatant misreading of Mabuchi's works. He asserted that Mabuchi's famous text, the *Kokuikō*, was *not* an ideological manifesto for nativism. It was a manual for the composition of *waka* and the interpretation of classical texts—and nothing more (160). He recalled the evening in Matsusaka when Norinaga had met Mabuchi for the first time, claiming that he had accompanied Mabuchi on the journey (158). Through the influence of his father, Harumichi, he joined Mabuchi's school at the age of thirteen, decades before Norinaga. Harumi implied that his credentials as a close disciple of Mabuchi speak for themselves; he better than anyone else, and especially better than Norinaga, understood the true intent of Mabuchi's teachings.

Makuni was unimpressed with Harumi's intellectual pedigree. The *Kokuikō*, he maintained, *was* a proclamation for the existence of an indigenous Way, perpetuating notions first articulated by Kada no Azumamaro (134). The idea that nativists had to resurrect and defend the Way against the pervasive and pernicious influence of foreign teachings, especially Buddhism and Confucianism, was transmitted from Azumamaro to Mabuchi, Makuni asserted, and Norinaga ultimately incorporated it into his teachings. This nativist project was what Norinaga meant by the term "Japanese spirit" (*Nihon damashii* or *Yamato damashii*) (134). Mabuchi had known that the study of classical *waka* served a much broader purpose (212). By failing to comprehend Mabuchi's larger ideological goals, Harumi's scholarship fundamentally contravened Mabuchi (214).

Makuni circumvented Harumi's contention that Norinaga had misread Mabuchi by broadening the scope of the discussion to include Azumamaro. He was aware that both Norinaga and Harumi were first-generation Mabuchi students, and that Harumi had closer ties to Mabuchi than Norinaga. He attacked Harumi's commitment to a greater nativist cause, and steered clear of an assault on Harumi's pedigree. Since Harumi was not a true nativist, he could not be a faithful disciple of Mabuchi either. "The Way of our land is high, far, and deep, such that the inability of you [Harumi] and others like you to understand this is grave. Even among the Old Man's [Mabuchi's] disciples whom he carefully instructed, such as yourself, those who negligently misunderstand the Way are pitiful and even odd" (187). While Harumi tried to stand aloof from a self-serving critique of Norinaga, Makuni contended that his own evaluation of Harumi was "simply for the good of Japan" and "for the good of the Way" (162).

Harumi was unconvinced by Makuni's assertions that Mabuchi had viewed the study of classical *waka* as part of a broader investigation of an indigenous Way. Even though the various Confucian schools of Chinese antiquity had their doctrinal differences, he argued, they all agreed that there was only one Way in the world; on this point even the historical Buddha, Shakyamuni, was in agreement (151). "Our land did not have a Way because the ancients never made references to the Way of our land. Moreover, in the classical sources of our land, there are none that deal with the Way of our land, so it is clear that our land had no Way."[23] Norinaga's vision of a separate Japanese Way contradicted this fundamental axiom. Harumi's teacher, Mabuchi, would never have made such an egregious error. Although he was not entirely hostile toward Buddhism, Harumi clearly privileged the Confucian concept of the Way, specifically the Way of the Sages (*seijin no oshie*, literally "teachings of the Sages"), over it. He perceived the hostility toward Confucianism exhibited by Norinaga and his followers as a threat to purge Japan of the Way of the Sages: "The followers of Norinaga recklessly seek to reject the teachings of the Sages. . . . Do they want to rid [Japan] of [the Way]? This is very difficult to comprehend" (153). His concern was further exacerbated by his insistence that the Way of the Sages was very successful in Japan: Why, he asks, would Norinaga try to rid Japan of something that was clearly effective in governing the realm? Not following the Way of the Sages was like "trying to form circles and rectangles without a compass and a square" (153).

Repeating his earlier repudiation, Harumi observed that Norinaga's confusion regarding Mabuchi's references to the Way stemmed from the ancient usage of the term "Shinto" in the *Nihongi*. "Shinto," he insisted, was a reference to religious rituals and had nothing to do with politics: "In the *Nihongi*, we see [the word] *shendao*. This meant reverence for the *kami*. It did not mean the Way to pacify the people and administer the realm."[24] Thus, Japan could not have had an indigenous concept of the Way to rival that of the Way of the Sages (153–54). Any references to Shinto in Mabuchi's writings signified this ancient religion and not an indigenous and autonomous Way. In response to Makuni's charge that he was unfaithful to Mabuchi, he replied that though he respected Mabuchi as his mentor, the sages of Chinese antiquity were his true teachers (160). He insisted that, far from making him an unfaithful disciple, his defense of the Way of the Sages actually demonstrated his level of commitment to a higher cause.

Makuni, however, refused to capitulate. In his estimation, Harumi simply mimicked the argument made two generations earlier

---

23. Murata Harumi, quoted in Tanaka K., "Edo-ha to iu genshō," p. 41.
24. Ibid.

by Dazai Shundai, namely, that Japan has no Way of its own. He referred specifically to Shundai's *Bendōsho*. Agreeing with Shundai's mentor, Ogyū Sorai, Makuni argued that the Way of the Sages was a human fabrication and not "nature" (*shizen no michi*) (185). The Japanese Way incorporated both the concept of nature and a set of administrative institutions that resembled the Way of the Sages (200–201). The Japanese Way was truly unique in the world, and this distinctiveness had eluded Harumi's grasp.

According to Makuni, Harumi's contention regarding Norinaga's intolerance of Confucian scholarship was not accurate. Confucian studies were an integral component of the educational backgrounds of both Mabuchi and Norinaga. "[Harumi] should understand that we are not [trying] to rid [Japan] of Confucianism (*jukyō*)," he stated (192). In fact, many prominent Japanese Confucians had indeed recognized an indigenous Japanese Way (163). Both Hayashi Razan (1583–1657) and Kumazawa Banzan (1619–91) had known of Japan's indigenous Way. They were "true" Confucians (196).

The debate between Makuni and Harumi over the issue of an indigenous Way demonstrated profound differences between the Edo-ha and the Norinaga School. As Harumi's response to Makuni suggests, he did not perceive himself as a nativist to the exclusion of Confucian learning. By contrast, it is clear from Makuni's faithful recapitulation of Norinaga's teachings that members of the Norinaga School saw themselves as nativists first, and their antiforeign rhetoric indicated an intolerant attitude toward Confucianism. Indeed, early in his response to Makuni, Harumi declared that he was a Confucian (*onore wa jusha nari*), and expressed his astonishment at the zeal of Makuni's ideological position (139).[25] Harumi's negative stance regarding the idea of a Japanese Way, coupled with his insistence on a Confucian identity, indicated the considerable ideological disparity between the two schools. In a letter to his Edo-ha colleague, Shimizu Hamaomi, dated 1801, Harumi observed, "The idea of an ancient Way for this land, in what

---

25. Harumi's ambivalence toward ideology was typical of nativists, according to Teeuwen. Norinaga's ideological concerns, and those of his students like Izumi Makuni, were the exception (Teeuwen, "Poetry, Sake, and Acrimony," p. 324).

sources (*fumi*) do [we] see this? I have read many of them and have yet to see any such references in the ancient sources."[26] The Edo-ha scholars considered themselves to be Confucians engaged in the study of Japanese antiquity; they saw their work as consistent with the Wagaku of their Muromachi predecessors. On the other hand, Makuni's response to Harumi appears to be a complete repudiation of Confucianism, a statement that he was a nativist to the exclusion of all other foreign teachings. Surprisingly, he stopped short of such a repudiation, a reluctance that was not shared by Norinaga. Makuni could not declare that nativism was completely autonomous, yet he could not countenance a tolerance of Confucianism either. Makuni's interpretation of archaic Shinto as Japan's Way was consistent with the views of prominent Neo-Confucians and not exactly congruent with Norinaga's teachings. Harumi's interpretation supported those of the Sorai School. By shying away from a nativist "declaration of independence," Makuni left its intellectual status, as a coherent tradition unto itself, unclear and in need of further elaboration.

Between Two Schools: Atsutane in Edo

As a resident of Edo, Atsutane could have joined the Edo-ha, but instead became a member of the Norinaga School in 1806. Before entering the Norinaga School, however, he did attempt to become a regular member of the Edo-ha. In 1803 he published his own explanation of the Japanese Way in the *Kamōsho*, the same year as the *Meidōsho* came out. Atsutane's text was his first published work, composed fully three years before joining the Norinaga School. It was a response to the *Bendōsho*, and like his colleague Makuni, he argued against Shundai's view of Shinto. Atsutane condemned Shundai less harshly than either Makuni or Norinaga, arguing that Shundai's views were the result of a pervasive and malevolent Chinese worldview that held unwitting yet talented scholars under its sway. With the publication of the *Kamōsho*, Atsutane succeeded in declaring his interests in nativism, but he failed to elicit any significant response from scholars in the Edo-ha. Thus, he eventually

---

26. Murata Harumi, quoted in Tanaka K., "Edo-ha to iu genshō," p. 39.

abandoned the effort to gain acceptance into its fold. In 1805 he drafted the *Shinkishinron* in an effort to impress Motoori Ōhira, the leader of the Norinaga School. This effort, too, proved unsuccessful. Although it was unknown to him at the time, his stance with regard to Makuni's debate with Harumi persuaded Ōhira to ignore Atsutane and the *Shinkishinron*, which forced Atsutane to join Haruniwa's academy instead. Both his attempt to gain acceptance in the Edo-ha and his subsequent enrollment in the Norinaga School were intended to secure an institutional sanction for his scholarship. Although he was never formally rejected by the Edo-ha, he thought that his growing skeptical attitude toward textualism would receive a more tolerant hearing in the Norinaga School. As we will see, this expectation was only partially realized.

The Response to Dazai Shundai

While Makuni focused his critiques of both Shundai and Harumi on the interpretation of archaic Shinto, as it was recorded in classical Japanese sources, Atsutane began his analysis with the *kami*. Shundai had stated that the ideograph for *kami*, *shin* (Ch. *shen*), was a frequently recurring word in the *Book of Changes*, so the ancients borrowed it in order to denote the *kami* in texts like the *Nihongi*; thus, the ancients thought that the *kami* were fundamentally the same as the Chinese *shen*. For this reason, Shundai had felt justified in drawing conclusions about the Japanese *kami* from Chinese sources.

According to Atsutane, Shundai had drawn two basic conclusions. First, since the ancient Chinese people recognized the significance of the *shen* when composing the Confucian classics, *shendao* (or Shinto) must be a branch of the Way of the Sages.[27] Second, since the Chinese concept of *shen* signified a power that was natural, yet beyond human ken, the same must be true of the *kami* as well. Atsutane, like Makuni, rejected the first conclusion—that Shinto was part of the Way of the Sages. Both he and Makuni wanted Confucians to acknowledge that the two Ways were separate and distinct. Contrary to Makuni, Atsutane agreed with Shundai's under-

---

27. Hirata Atsutane, *Kamōsho*, p. 145.

standing of *shen* as signifying the suprahuman, although he rejected Shundai's extension of this interpretation to include the *kami*. The *kami* were more than just suprahuman; Shundai could not recognize their "mysterious quality" (*myō naru tokoro*). The implication here is that the Japanese *kami* possessed a mystical aura about them that inspired religious devotion; the Chinese *shen* did not.

Chinese "theories" (*setsu*), Atsutane contended, were full of references to gods and the divine. These references, however, portrayed the suprahuman and supernatural without the religious qualities that characterized the *kami*. Both Sorai and Shundai were wrong about the Chinese Sages; they were actually ignorant of "spirits" (*kishin*), and their idea of the Mandate of Heaven was not particularly inspirational either.[28] The Sages, he concluded, were not interested in the kind of religious practice that was necessary to fully comprehend the divinity of the *kami*. He cautioned Confucian scholars not to make the kind of false conclusions about the *kami* as Shundai. In Atsutane's mind, Shundai had failed to see the inherent subtleties of Shinto.

Confucians of Shundai's ilk were not fit to study Japanese antiquity, Atsutane continued. They did not understand that the same Chinese ideographs could have different meanings in different contexts; Atsutane, it seems, recognized that one signifier can denote more than one signified. Shinto and *shendao* were not identical. He was careful, however, to indicate that not all Confucians had committed this error. Some of them learned to privilege Japan over China, he insisted, specifically citing Yamazaki Ansai and Asami Keisai (1652–1711) as examples.[29]

In the *Kamōsho*, Atsutane was not clear as to what the exact relationship was between Shinto and the Way of the Sages: whether he viewed Shinto in the same manner as the Ansai School, concluding that the two were the same, or if he viewed it like Norinaga, namely, that the two were different and that Shinto was superior. He succeeded in arguing against Shundai's interpretation of Shinto without offering a coherent account of his own. It was perhaps this lacuna that inspired the general ambivalence toward the

---

28. Ibid., p. 149.
29. Ibid., pp. 180–81.

text exhibited by members of both the Edo-ha and the Norinaga School. Moreover, his critique of Shundai contradicted Murata Harumi's position as well. Before Makuni published the *Meidōsho*, Atsutane claimed that he actively discouraged Makuni from doing so.[30] Apparently, he did not want to encourage enmity between the two schools, preferring to ignore differences in an effort to cultivate harmony between them. Perhaps this was Atsutane's way of earning Harumi's esteem, since he had his intellectual disagreements with him. Makuni ignored his advice.[31] The *Kamōsho*, written before joining the Norinaga School, demonstrated his inability to commit to the Edo-ha. Atsutane seemed hesitant to enter the Norinaga School as well at that time; he was caught between two intellectual fields in Edo represented by Harumi and Makuni. His enrollment in the Norinaga School indicated the intellectual and even social isolation that he most likely felt vis-à-vis his colleagues in the Edo-ha. Thus, the *Shinkishinron*, written two years after the *Kamōsho*, was his first attempt to impress the members of the Norinaga School, and it ushered in a period of uneasy social relations with the members of the Edo-ha that culminated in his complete denunciation of it during the 1820s.

Atsutane on Poetry

After joining Haruniwa's academy, Atsutane began his research into classical literature. However, for the next two decades, he gradually lost interest in it, especially *waka* studies. He set these views down in various texts during the 1820s. His general disdain for *waka* led him to criticize both the Edo-ha and most members of the Norinaga School. Atsutane finally provided his own description of the *Meidōsho* debate in the *Tamadasuki* (1832). The debate served as a focal point in his narrative history of Kokugaku in Book IX of the text. By the time of its publication, he had established himself as one of the most prominent nativists of the Norinaga School. With no need to demonstrate his credentials any longer, he chose to side with neither Makuni nor Harumi. Instead,

---

30. Haga, "Edo ni okeru Edo kabun-ha to Hirata Atsutane," p. 279.
31. Nakamura, *Motoori-ha kokugaku no tenkai*, p. 70.

he used their debate as an opportunity to discuss the Norinaga School and the Edo-ha within the broader framework of literary studies. Following Makuni's lead, he emphasized the role of Mabuchi in helping to shape the ideology of Kokugaku. The Edo-ha's preoccupation with poetry, he contended, represented a misreading of Mabuchi's work. Atsutane outlined his view of poetry and its relationship to nativism, completing ideas that he had begun in his earlier treatises on poetry, especially the *Kadō tai'i* and the *Ibukinoya hisso*.

Atsutane viewed classical *waka* as an important vehicle for studying the conditions of antiquity. The study of ancient words revealed the "hearts" (*kokoro*) and "deeds" (*waza*) of the ancients.[32] Man'yōgaku, pioneered by Keichū, was the methodology for the investigation of the classical language. Scholars used Man'yōgaku in the analysis of words (*kotoba*) in order to understand the *kokoro* of the ancients. It was also an efficacious methodology for the investigation of other texts, most notably histories like the *Kojiki*.[33] Histories were not intended to convey emotion; rather, they were instrumental in the transmission of ancient facts. Following the Norinaga School's doctrine, he argued that there were two fundamental genres of classical texts, poetry and history, and *both* were instrumental in completing a portrait of conditions in antiquity (*yo no arisama*). For Atsutane, scholars used the philology of Mabuchi and Keichū in order to investigate both types of classical texts.

Scholars who privileged the analysis of classical *waka* did so with the belief that the methodology of Mabuchi and Keichū was intended solely for that purpose. Many members of the Norinaga School devoted themselves to *waka* exclusively with the goal of illuminating the ancient Way. Since they investigated verse instead of classical histories, their efforts were in vain. Moreover, in their zeal to study *waka*, many nativists became poets themselves. *Waka* studies, he lamented, had degenerated into an effort to compose contemporary-style poetry.[34] His colleagues called themselves scholars of ancient learning, but they were actually poets in dis-

---

32. Hirata Atsutane, *Kadō tai'i*, p. 6.
33. Ibid.
34. Ibid., p. 7.

guise: "Although [these] poets say [they practice] Kogaku, [they] do not [understand] the meaning of true ancient learning (*inishie manabi*)."[35]

Atsutane condemned the evolution of his fellow nativists into poets. The composition of *waka* had become their primary concern, instead of inquiries into the ancient Way.[36] To make matters worse, scholars forgot that contemporary poetry was not the equivalent of its classical counterpart. As Mabuchi had taught, scholars had to emulate the style of the *Man'yōshū* in an effort to comprehend the subtleties of ancient *waka*, a doctrine that Atsutane believed most nativists had neglected.[37] He argued that this fundamental misunderstanding of Mabuchi led to the unwarranted criticism of Norinaga, especially by his Edo-ha colleagues.[38] Agreeing with Makuni, he insisted that not only was Mabuchi misunderstood but Norinaga as well. Neither scholar had emphasized the study of verse without the larger framework of investigation into the ancient Way.[39] He was especially critical of the Edo-ha, likening its members to aesthetes who admire a tree's blossoms without noticing the beauty of the tree itself.[40] Mabuchi had privileged the *waka* of the *Man'yōshū* while Norinaga had favored the Heian compilation of the *Kokinshū*; both scholars, however, had recognized that the investigation of poetic language should be undertaken only in the context of the ancient Way. Clearly, his insistence on intellectual flexibility within nativism supported Ōhira's position, and ultimately served to justify his own neglect of verse.

Spirits and Nativism

Atsutane composed two texts before finally joining Haruniwa's academy in 1806: first, the *Kamōsho* (1803), then the *Shinkishinron* (1805) (renamed *Kishinshinron* in 1820). In the *Kamōsho*, Atsutane argued that a close analysis of classical Japanese and Chinese texts

---

35. Ibid.
36. Ibid., p. 8.
37. Ibid., p. 7.
38. Hirata Atsutane, *Ibukinoya hisso*, p. 472.
39. Ibid., p. 474.
40. Ibid.

yielded the same insights into both Shinto and the Way of the Sages, respectively. Hence, he defended the efforts of earlier nativists while avoiding a direct condemnation of Confucians. As Murata Harumi's comments suggested, nativists, especially those in Edo, did not clearly distinguish between their own scholarship and that of Confucians. "In antiquity, Wagaku was not a separate field of scholarship," he observed, "all Confucians studied it."[41] Harumi viewed himself in this way, as a Confucian who studied nativism. Atsutane exhibited this same attitude in the *Kamōsho*.

Two years later, Atsutane completed the manuscript of the *Shinkishinron*, his first foray into the topic of spirits that later dominated his scholarship. His subsequent discussions of spirits, especially the *Tama no mihashira*, radically diverged from the *Shinkishinron*. With this earlier text, he still refused to completely distinguish between nativism and Confucianism. In fact, he subscribed to the arguments of several influential Confucians from the previous century. Nevertheless, he was quite proud of his work, which led him to send copies of the manuscript to both Nobutomo and Ōhira, perhaps in an effort to gain admission to Ōhira's academy (as Nobutomo had done several months earlier). However, just as his views in the *Kamōsho* contradicted those of the leading scholar of the Edo-ha—a critical miscalculation—Atsutane used a largely Confucian-oriented text in the hope of impressing the adopted son of perhaps Japan's most influential nativist.

The key issue in Atsutane's treatise on *kishin* was whether Confucius ever acknowledged their existence. Atsutane did not explain his reasons for citing the authority of Confucius, but the implication is clear: if Confucius had acknowledged the existence of spirits, then this would buttress Atsutane's own claim for their significance in Japanese antiquity. Spirits were a universal phenomenon for him; they were not, strictly speaking, particular to China or Japan. He hierarchized Japan over China, however, by arguing that evidence for the existence of spirits in China was only circumstantial and the result of considerable scholarly inquiry, while more direct evidence existed in classical Japanese sources. Foreign

---

41. Murata Harumi, *Wagaku taigai*, p. 448.

countries like India and China at one time possessed the "true ancient transmissions" but lost them over the centuries,[42] while the Japanese maintained their supernatural knowledge from the beginning of time. This wisdom escaped all nativists except Atsutane.

There were two reasons for Confucius's failure to discuss spirits in any detail. First, the Chinese had lost their detailed knowledge of spirits long before the time of Confucius, and so he was precluded from knowing about them. Second, Confucius had understood that knowledge of the divine was impossible via the human intellect alone. Consequently, he had never speculated on the existence of spirits, opting for a more practical ethical agenda focused on human benevolence and wisdom.[43]

Despite these impediments, Atsutane asserted that if one examined the *Analects* carefully, one could glean elements of Confucius's attitude toward spirits. Confucius had focused his attention on human behavior, realizing that virtuous conduct was highly influenced by the divine. Comprehension of this relationship between mortals and the divine was difficult, Atsutane conceded, yet Confucius had come very close to realizing this fundamental truth. Moreover, China, as Norinaga had observed, was characterized by empty speculation and was culturally handicapped in the realization of divine wisdom. Confucius's reverence for the divine was proof of his enlightenment on the subject: "He comprehended the mysterious principle of the divine (*kami*), surpassing most ordinary people."[44]

Atsutane ultimately declared that Confucius had understood the significance of a genuine eschatology in the observance of ancestor worship rituals. According to Atsutane, most Confucians insisted that Confucius was completely silent on the issue of spirits despite the existence of Chinese theories regarding the soul, especially the idea that the soul had two components, the *hun* and the *po*.[45]

---

42. Hirata Atsutane, *Kishinshinron*, p. 17.
43. Ibid., p. 45.
44. Ibid., p. 27.
45. Ibid., p. 47. The *hun* (Jp. *kon*) was the material aspect of the soul, while the *po* (Jp. *paku*) was its ethereal form.

The Confucian Debate on Kishin

Atsutane drew two significant conclusions about spirits in the *Kishinshinron*. First, the existence of spirits was essential for the observance of ancestor worship. Confucius must have made the connection between the existence of spirits and the afterlife. Without such a connection, Atsutane reasoned, ancestor worship became an empty practice. If one had to observe rituals for the dead, then the dead must have a "real" existence as spirits in the afterlife. For Atsutane, the meaning of filial piety encompassed knowledge of spirits and the afterlife. Those who declared that Confucius did not acknowledge the existence of spirits in his admonitions to observe ancestor rituals were themselves unfilial.[46] Second, a reverence for the everyday influence of spirits was an essential aspect of faith in the power of the *kami*. He claimed to follow Confucius's lead by avoiding the search for concrete knowledge of the divine that Confucians sought, especially Neo-Confucians who practiced *kakubutsu kyūri* (the investigation of things and the exhaustion of principle). His proclamation that Confucius had acknowledged the existence of spirits supported the views of earlier Confucian scholars who had debated the same issue. He joined the growing chorus of scholars who agreed with Sorai's refutation of Zhu Xi's denial of spirits.

Atsutane's text was a nativist contribution to what was originally a Confucian debate. Both Atsutane and his contemporary, Yamagata Bantō (1748–1821), grappled with the issue of spirits, the two relying heavily on the earlier work of Arai Hakuseki (1657–1725). Hakuseki authored his own treatise, the *Kishinron*, arguing that despite a paucity of direct textual evidence, Confucius had believed in the existence of spirits. Hakuseki wanted to offer a Confucian alternative to the prevailing Shinto-Buddhist views of *kishin*.[47] Both Atsutane and Bantō used nearly the same Chinese sources in their work on spirits. Atsutane sided with Hakuseki against Bantō. Moreover, neither Atsutane nor Bantō cited the views of Zhu Xi. Atsutane, however, did not completely ignore

---

46. Ibid., p. 45.
47. Nakai, *Shogunal Politics*, p. 295.

Song interpretations, and he cited the Cheng brothers of the Northern Song in his analysis.[48]

Atsutane's views were consistent with those of prominent Confucians like Yamazaki Ansai and Muro Kyūsō (1658–1734); his most significant Confucian forerunners, however, were Sorai and Shundai, scholars whose views he had previously refuted. Their beliefs in spirits, however, were ironically based on some views held by Zhu Xi. Zhu Xi had never overtly acknowledged the issue of spirits in his formal writings, but he did believe in the existence of a physical and a spiritual *qi* (Jp: *ki*). Upon death, he believed, the spiritual *ki* was obliterated along with the destruction of the physical *ki* of the body. Two questions, however, intrigued him. Zhu Xi believed that the spiritual *ki* was not destroyed at precisely the same moment as the physical body: how long, then, was the interval between the destruction of the spiritual *ki* after that of the body? The second question: during this interval, where was the spiritual *ki*?[49] Although he had speculated that the interval between the death of the body and the extinction of the soul was short, he did not offer an answer to the second question. His critics attacked him for basing his own views of the spiritual *ki* upon Buddhist theories of the soul. The significance of Zhu Xi's ideas for Confucian scholars of Tokugawa Japan lay in his tacit conviction regarding the existence of "ghosts" (*yūrei*), even if he had denied the existence of *kishin* as such.[50]

Sorai had refuted Zhu Xi's observations of *kishin*, accusing him of disloyalty to the ancient Sages: "To say that there are no spirits is to deny the Sages."[51] He also repudiated the argument prevalent in his own day asserting that the *kishin* did not actually exist since they were invisible. This view, he had reasoned, could be used to deny the existence of Heaven as well. For Sorai, the belief in *kishin* was more than a symbolic admonition to the people by the ancient Sages. The *kishin* were an integral part of the ancient institutions and customs established by the Sages in antiquity.

---

48. Nakamura, *Motoori-ha kokugaku no tenkai*, p. 273.
49. Ibid., p. 275.
50. Ibid., p. 278.
51. Ogyū Sorai, quoted in ibid., p. 292.

Sorai's predecessor, Itō Jinsai, had a stronger faith in the truth of classical texts. He had argued that since there was little, if any, substantive textual evidence to support the contention that Confucius had believed in *kishin*, the conclusion one way or the other could never be established with certainty.[52] The point was moot for Jinsai. Instead of dabbling in matters of the unknown, he preferred to devote his scholarship to issues relating to ethical behavior. Jinsai avoided drawing conclusions based on textual ambiguities exemplified by issues such as the afterlife and *kishin*.[53]

Yamagata Bantō supported Jinsai. In the absence of concrete evidence, he believed, the existence of mysterious phenomena could never be proven. Bantō, therefore, embraced a more "scientific" attitude toward spirits than his counterpart Atsutane, or his Confucian predecessors Shundai, Sorai, and Hakuseki. In a reply to Atsutane's contention that without some belief in the afterlife ancestor worship would be an empty ritual, he responded that because ancestor worship was a *ritual* observance, it emphasized the sincerity of the observer and not the existence of *kishin*.[54]

A Lukewarm Reception for Atsutane: Motoori Ōhira and Ban Nobutomo

Like his colleague Atsutane, Nobutomo viewed literary studies as only one aspect of his research.[55] As fellow members of the Norinaga School after 1806, he and Atsutane were close friends until sometime in the 1820s. The more textually inclined Nobutomo grew increasingly annoyed with Atsutane's cavalier approach to classical texts. His appreciation of textual accuracy and Atsutane's increasing disregard for it were symptomatic of the general personality differences between the two.[56] Their relationship had an important impact on the history of nativism in the nineteenth cen-

---

52. John Tucker argues that Jinsai did believe in *kishin*, and his views were close to those of the Neo-Confucians ("Ghosts and Spirits in Tokugawa Japan," p. 242).
53. Nakamura, *Motoori-ha kokugaku no tenkai*, p. 291.
54. Ibid., p. 281.
55. Hisamatsu, "Bunkengaku-teki kenkyū to kōshōgaku," p. 232.
56. Ibid., p. 231.

tury. Ōhira, Nobutomo's teacher, introduced him to Atsutane sometime in early 1806. Shortly after this meeting, Atsutane joined the Norinaga School, opting for Haruniwa's academy instead of Ōhira's. For the next twenty years or so, Atsutane and Nobutomo had a tumultuous friendship, becoming rivals before they finally parted ways. The rift that developed between the two was, perhaps, inevitable.

The most significant intellectual divide between the two nativists concerned the status of language in antiquity. Atsutane asserted that the ancient Japanese had a writing system of their own, known as the *jindai moji*, even before the importation of written Chinese.[57] Nobutomo disagreed, arguing that Atsutane had no textual evidence for this view and therefore was forced to make the classical sources conform to his mistaken ideas.[58] Atsutane was not the first scholar to make this claim for a pre-Chinese writing system; it had precedents in the thirteenth and fourteenth centuries.[59] In spite of these, Nobutomo was adamant; without textual substantiation, any such claims were without merit. These interpretations underscored what was, in Nobutomo's mind, Atsutane's fundamentally flawed understanding of antiquity.

Atsutane's views of the classical language disturbed Nobutomo because they threatened to undermine his own idealized view of the ancient Japanese people. According to Nobutomo, they had no need for a writing system before the importation of Chinese. Instead of writing, they exercised their powers of memorization, nurturing, in the process, superior intellects.[60] At the appropriate time, he argued, the ancients adopted the Chinese writing system. This development did not impugn the hierarchy of memorization over writing. The ancients adopted writing because it was the will of the *kami*.[61] Thus, he cautioned scholars against pursuing this line of inquiry any further, since attempts to fathom the inscrutable were inspired by foreign teachings.

---

57. Morita, *Ban Nobutomo no shisō*, p. 37.
58. Ibid., p. 51.
59. Ibid., p. 57.
60. Ibid., p. 61.
61. Ibid., p. 62.

Membership in the Norinaga School required a foundation in classical literature. Nobutomo's credentials made him a leading scholar, perhaps even of the same stature as Norinaga. Atsutane later made his own case for this status based on intellectual innovation rather than through the replication of Norinaga's methodology. From 1806 to 1820, Atsutane began to interpret the essence of Norinaga's teachings as focused on the investigation of the ancient Way, though Nobutomo contended that this investigation had to conform to strict methodological principles. Atsutane acknowledged Nobutomo's successful application of Norinaga's textual methodology, but denied for him the true apprehension of Norinaga's teachings. In Atsutane's eyes, Nobutomo was a slave to Kōshōgaku like Oyamada Tomokiyo of the Edo-ha.

Soon after their first meeting in 1806, Atsutane sent his *Shinkishinron* to Ōhira in Matsusaka that same year and lent a copy of the manuscript to Nobutomo as well. Nobutomo was initially impressed with the work, observing that some of Atsutane's views meshed with his own, including Atsutane's insistence that faith in the *kami* was as legitimate as faith in the Buddha. Thus, Nobutomo encouraged him to send his manuscript to Ōhira and request the latter's comments. Nobutomo suggested that Atsutane use these remarks as a preface to the eventual publication of the *Shinkishinron*.

Ōhira received Atsutane's manuscript, and his initial reaction was, like Nobutomo's, positive. He apparently intended to grant Atsutane's request and compose some remarks that could be used as a preface. Perhaps constrained by time, he delayed forwarding his comments. In 1807 he finally heard from his student Uematsu Arinobu[62] about the debate between Murata Harumi and Izumi Makuni in Edo. Ōhira expressed his profound gratitude to Makuni for defending Norinaga's memory against Harumi's attacks. He was also saddened that he had not learned of Makuni's deed until two years after his death and could not thank Makuni in person. Hearing that Atsutane had condemned Makuni's debate with

---

62. Arinobu was a woodblock carver from Nagoya who had assisted Norinaga in the publication of some of his works.

Harumi, Ōhira concluded that Makuni had spent his final years in Edo isolated and without the support of his fellow nativists. Ōhira's feelings toward Atsutane changed profoundly after hearing the details regarding the debate of 1803.[63] Ōhira, therefore, decided not to comply with Atsutane's request, and Atsutane was not able to publish his text until 1820, by which time he had changed the title to *Kishinshinron*. Atsutane's lack of support for Makuni was a portent of the friction that later developed between Ōhira and himself.

Another potential factor in Ōhira's change of heart may have been Nobutomo's own criticism of Atsutane's text. In 1819 Nobutomo wrote a treatise on Buddhism, the *Busshinron*, in which he discussed the relationship between Shinto and Buddhism. He contended that Buddhism was an Indian expression of Shinto.[64] In Nobutomo's estimation, foreign cultures failed to grasp the profound spirituality of the *kami*, despite the originality of some religious traditions like Buddhism. For Atsutane, however, foreign cultures succeeded in fathoming the mysteries of the Japanese gods. Nobutomo viewed this contention as textually unsubstantiated.[65] Moreover, he was annoyed with Atsutane's preoccupation with matters that did little to rectify the "Chinese mind," a mission he viewed as central to Norinaga's teachings.[66] In support of Nobutomo's assessment and irritated with Atsutane's handling of Makuni, Ōhira never sanctioned Atsutane's text, a sanction that Atsutane had earnestly sought.[67]

Atsutane's Early Years

Both the *Kamōsho* and the *Shinkishinron* were texts that Atsutane wrote prior to his formal enrollment in Haruniwa's academy. Scholars have developed various interpretations of these early years. The historian Nakamura Kazumoto ignores the question of the Edo-ha and suggests that Atsutane enrolled in Haruniwa's academy

---

63. Nakamura, *Motoori-ha kokugaku no tenkai*, p. 77.
64. Morita, *Ban Nobutomo no shisō*, p. 55.
65. Ibid., p. 54.
66. Nakamura, *Motoori-ha kokugaku no tenkai*, p. 90.
67. Ibid., p. 85.

because of Ōhira's social disapproval of him. Uchino Gorō asserts that he chose to side with the Norinaga School because of his unsuccessful efforts to establish ties with the Edo-ha.[68] Atsutane's brand of cosmological and religious Kokugaku was distinct from the Edo-ha's emphasis on *waka*. Uchino, however, grapples with an even more puzzling question. He tries to find the reason, other than the lack of attention generated by the *Kamōsho*, why Atsutane, as a resident of Edo, did not become a regular member of the Edo-ha.

The Edo-ha assumed a literary character beginning in the late decades of the eighteenth century. The scholars of the Edo-ha lived and interacted with many of the most famous literary figures of the day within the confines of the *shitamachi* districts in Edo. The physical proximity between the two groups, therefore, was the central factor in the transformation of the Edo-ha.

For much of Atsutane's tenure in Edo, he lived in districts either close to or within the same *shitamachi* neighborhoods of the Edo-ha, such as Nihonbashi, Kyōbashi, and Asakusa.[69] Despite the close associations that were made between Edo-ha scholars and literary figures, Atsutane did not socialize closely with anyone in either group.[70] There is evidence that he may actually have met both Katō Chikage and Murata Harumi, but no social or scholarly association ensued.[71] During the years when he composed the *Kamōsho* and *Shinkishinron*, he served as a physician to the Itakura family, spending his days on their estate and his evenings at his academy pursuing scholarly matters.[72] This period, however, was a difficult one in his life; the Hirata family, his adoptive family, suffered from profound poverty. Moreover, this period was also one in which he and his family moved frequently between marginal locations that bordered both the *shitamachi* and Yamanote areas of Edo. Atsutane's own personal despair combined with his inability to attract the attention of scholars in the Edo-ha influenced the development

---

68. Uchino, *Edo-ha kokugaku ronkō*, p. 92.
69. Ibid., p. 87.
70. Ibid.
71. Uchino, "Hirata-ha to Edo-ha no gakushi-teki tei'i," p. 20.
72. Uchino, *Edo-ha kokugaku ronkō*, p. 162.

of his scholarship. He spurned the literary version of nativism favored by the scholars of the Edo-ha because they never recognized his literary talents.

Atsutane's despair turned to grief with the death of his first wife in 1812, the same year that he published his first innovative work, the *Tama no mihashira*. He eventually remarried, however. In 1821 he moved, with his new wife and daughter, into the Yushima district of Edo (located near the Hayashi academy as well as modern-day Tokyo University).[73] The upheaval and instability of his early adulthood, when he lived with his adoptive family, gave way to an independent life with his own family. These years seem to have been his happiest, and during this time he made great strides in his intellectual career as well. Yushima,[74] despite its Yamanote identity, had a strikingly *shitamachi* flavor.[75] Many of the Edo-ha scholars lived in this area where Azumamaro and Mabuchi had lived and worked. Atsutane, however, seems to have had little contact with them, outside of his occasional appearances at Oyamada Tomokiyo's salon. The nature of these visits is not entirely clear, and some scholars speculate that he went to Tomokiyo's salon simply to borrow books. Consequently, his relationship with the Edo-ha was uneasy, and even bordered on hostile. Modern scholars, however, have had little direct evidence to study this relationship since both Atsutane and the members of the Edo-ha seemed to have mutually ignored one another.

It is clear that there was a link between Atsutane's scholarship and his ambiguous relationship with the Edo-ha. It is not a coincidence that he strenuously rejected the notion of a poetry-based vision of nativism that the Edo-ha embraced. Uchino argues that the literary character of the Edo-ha was a radical departure from the nativism of Azumamaro and even Mabuchi. As the discussion of Murata Harumi has shown, many of the Edo-ha scholars privileged poetry and philology as legitimate pursuits in themselves, and not

---

73. Ibid., p. 166.
74. Seidensticker notes that it had become an unlicensed pleasure quarter by the end of the Tokugawa period because of its proximity to the Tokugawa family mausoleums in Ueno (*Low City, High City*, p. 243).
75. Uchino, *Edo-ha kokugaku ronkō*, p. 166.

as integral parts of the articulation of a larger goal—the ancient Way. Atsutane, however, resisted this trend within the Edo-ha. By joining the Norinaga School, he formulated a view of nativism that was less elite and more grounded in the experiences of rural folk.[76] His ties to the Norinaga School were the logical result of his efforts to maintain what he believed was the nativism of Azumamaro that the Edo-ha had abandoned.

Conclusion

In the *Kamōsho* and the *Shinkishinron*, Atsutane addressed Confucian issues in an effort to garner attention for his emerging career as a scholar. His insistence on maintaining the idea of a valid, indigenous Way clashed with the views of Murata Harumi, who maintained his identity as a Confucian first. His interest in spirits was completely alien to the Edo-ha. These early texts, therefore, established Atsutane's fundamental differences with his colleagues in the Edo-ha.

The events surrounding the composition of the *Shinkishinron* indicate that Atsutane sought entry into the Norinaga School perhaps as a result of his own rejection by the Edo-ha. This attempt, however, demonstrated that there was a growing contempt for him among established nativists such as Motoori Ōhira and Ban Nobutomo. He eventually joined Haruniwa's academy, but the enmity that he had incurred lingered for several decades thereafter.

Atsutane, although a member of the Norinaga School after 1806, found himself on the social and intellectual periphery of two distinct nativist schools. His views of cosmology and history clashed with the aesthetics and philology of the Edo-ha. At the same time, his scholarship irritated members of the Norinaga School because of his loose approach to textualism. Although he was rejected in different ways by the membership of both schools, he joined the Norinaga School because he knew that its diverse approaches to antiquity offered a more amenable environment for his own research. What he did not realize, however, was that this scholastic tolerance was grounded in the classics. Unlike scholars of the Edo-

---

76. Uchino, "Hirata-ha to Edo-ha no gakushi-teki tei'i," p. 22.

ha, who separated artistic composition from the pursuit of philology, those of the Norinaga School linked the two as part of the investigation of the ancient Way. Edo-ha scholars denied the existence of such a Way. For Atsutane, the pursuit of the ancient Way was paramount, even if that meant having to abandon philology. Thus, he denied the textualist foundation upon which the rest of the members of the Norinaga School stood.

FOUR

The Sandaikō *Debate: Mythology, Astronomy, and Eschatology*

Throughout the final decades of the eighteenth century, Motoori Norinaga taught and lectured on a host of classical texts at his home in Matsusaka. Because of his methodological approach—a careful and exact examination of the classical language of antiquity—he attracted a substantial following. In fact, his research and methodology became so popular that, by the early decades of the nineteenth century, earnest students (*monjin*) and disciples had established academies devoted to his scholarship in most of the major urban centers in Japan. The philological image associated with Kokugaku, therefore, was Norinaga's handiwork, as well as that of his predecessor Mabuchi. The relationship between Kokugaku and religious practice, however, is more commonly associated with Hirata Atsutane, who generated controversy among the scholars of the Norinaga School[1] with his interests in spirits and the afterlife, represented by the *Shinkishinron*. Kokugaku scholars at the time could see that his interests in these areas threatened to undermine their "faith" in philology.

---

1. To this point, I have used the term "Norinaga School" to signify affiliated academies in Matsusaka, Haruniwa's Nochi-Suzunoya, the Nudenoya in Kyoto, the Koshibaya in Osaka, the Meirindō in Nagoya, the Fuji-no-kakitsu in Wakayama, and Atsutane's Ibukinoya in Edo.

Atsutane attempted to initiate a transition within the Norinaga School, from the philological investigation of literature to an eschatological approach, by resurrecting an older debate surrounding a cosmological text attached to Norinaga's *Kojiki-den*. This was Hattori Nakatsune's *Sandaikō*, a controversial treatise on the creation chapters of the *Kojiki*. Atsutane supported many of the central assertions of the *Sandaikō*, and when Motoori Ōhira criticized Nakatsune, he drafted a scathing attack on Ōhira. His support for Nakatsune instigated a much larger dispute among members of the Norinaga School, prompting modern scholars to call it the "*Sandaikō* debate" (*Sandaikō no ronsō*). This debate drove a wedge into the Norinaga School, and the antagonism of the two opposing sides that it spawned grew in the years leading up to 1830. The energy that fueled these hostilities stemmed from a struggle to define the intellectual foundations of the Norinaga School. This debate over the merits of Nakatsune's work developed into a contestation over the nature of the Norinaga School's mission; it represented an opportunity to clearly formulate, for the first time, its intellectual orthodoxy. Atsutane's pre-eminence within the School by the end of the 1820s is an indication of his success in creating there a new intellectual position.

Modern interpreters of the *Sandaikō* debate emphasize its intellectual implications for bakumatsu Kokugaku. All these researchers are Japanese, and no studies of the debate exist in English. A brief discussion of the Japanese secondary literature, therefore, is in order, since the interpretation offered in this study is significantly different. Japanese intellectual historians of Kokugaku generally do not focus on the disagreements among Tokugawa nativists. They do, however, admit that the early decades of the nineteenth century were not without friction and conflict among the members of the Norinaga School, arguing that peace was ultimately restored, and that the new hybrid Kokugaku of the 1830s grew into a significant intellectual and social movement during the late Tokugawa and early Meiji periods. These historians have provided us with the general context within which this debate developed, and have clarified the role that it served in the general scheme of Atsutane's thought. These insights, however, are products of traditional forms of intellectual history, such as the history of ideas. For many modern scholars, Atsutane's status as heir to Norinaga's teachings was purely intellectual and the culmination of an evolving, autonomous discourse.[2] We will consider an alternative view: the *Sandaikō* debate was the occasion in which Atsutane began to claim a legitimate position within the Norinaga School. It was only after his rejection by leading members of the School that his claims of orthodoxy emerged.[3] What appeared to be the autonomous development of a Kokugaku discourse was actually the result of strategy, good timing, and luck. The debate was played out on an intellectual level, as well as at the social level of internecine struggle. Ultimately, a contestation over the dominant position within the Norinaga School developed, and the result was a higher degree of ideological articulation for the School and for Kokugaku.

Norinaga and Nakatsune: Continuity or Discontinuity?

In addition to their focus on the general intellectual context of the debate, modern studies have stressed the issue of continuity between Norinaga and Nakatsune (and, by extension, Atsutane). Scholars concerned with the context argue that the significance of the *Sandaikō* lies in its novel approach to cosmology in the face of

---

2. For an excellent example of the discourse-analysis approach to Kokugaku history in general, see Koyasu, *Norinaga to Atsutane no sekai*.

3. Maruyama Masao has identified two categories of orthodoxy in his study of the Kimon School. The first is what he called "L-orthodoxy," which referred to efforts by Kimon scholars to establish their legitimate positions by linking themselves to their school's founder, Yamazaki Ansai. Prior to the *Sandaikō* debate, the Suzunoya had such an "L-orthodoxy": Norinaga's evidential methodology, which was never articulated as such until the nineteenth century, as a direct result of the intramural dispute. The second kind of orthodoxy to which Maruyama referred was "O-orthodoxy." This signified the perpetuation of the teachings of Zhu Xi and the Daoxue tradition. The argument in this chapter is that the Norinaga School did not have an "O-orthodoxy" until Atsutane formulated one in response to his critics. See Maruyama, "Orthodoxy and Legitimacy in the Kimon School (Part I)," p. 30. It is possible that Atsutane's concern with these issues was a result of the Kimon School's influence on his thought, especially via Asami Keisai; see ibid., p. 19.

competing Chinese and Buddhist theories. Examining the intellectual continuity issue, others see the text as evidence of a clear break with Norinaga, or they assert that it was proof of the seamless development of Kokugaku intellectual history.

Omote Tomoyuki, a scholar of early modern intellectual history, looks at the *Sandaikō* as a nativist contribution to a cosmological discussion that took place at the end of the eighteenth century. Agreeing with the scholar Ozawa Masao, he locates the novelty of Nakatsune's approach in his use of Western "scientific" models. Singling out Rangaku specifically, Ozawa argued that the criticism leveled against Nakatsune by his contemporaries—that he was too Western in his approach—was an accurate appraisal of the text.[4] Both scholars conclude that the use of these Western astronomical models by other nativists, including Nakatsune, is proof of the pervasive influence of Western "science" in the late eighteenth century.[5]

Omote argues that Nakatsune's use of Rangaku represented an attempt to rationalize Japanese mythology with Western astronomy. Ozawa went even further in his analysis, asserting that such a rationalization was a project initiated not by Nakatsune but by Norinaga himself. While Omote sees Nakatsune's use of Western knowledge as a watershed in Japanese intellectual history, he does not argue for an incipient development of this trend in Norinaga. Ozawa, however, demonstrated that Norinaga had developed an interest in Rangaku at an early point in his career—as early as 1782, fully a decade before the publication of Nakatsune's *Sandaikō*.[6] Of more significance is Ozawa's claim that this use of Rangaku not only began with Norinaga and was perpetuated in the work of Nakatsune but was inherited by Atsutane as well. Consequently, an interest in Rangaku was something all three nativists shared.

Contrary to Omote and Ozawa, the scholar Nishikawa Masatami sees an important intellectual break between Nakatsune and Norinaga. Like Omote, he argues that Nakatsune approached clas-

---

4. Ozawa Masao, "*Sandaikō* wo meguru ronsō," p. 465.
5. Omote, "Hito no kangaete shirubeki wa tada me no mae oyobu kagiri," p. 12.
6. Ozawa, "*Sandaikō* wo meguru ronsō," p. 467.

sical texts with a certain "scientific" rigor.[7] The only clear intellectual link between the two was Norinaga's suggestion to Nakatsune that Takama-no-hara was the sun, an idea that was central to the *Sandaikō*, as we will see.[8]

The intellectual historian Miki Shōtarō, however, disagrees with Nishikawa, insisting that the issue of Takama-no-hara was but one aspect of a broader set of intellectual continuities between Norinaga and Nakatsune. The ultimate goal of Norinaga's work was the execution of accurate Kōshōgaku. Interpretive precision was his aim, and he avoided speculation in an effort to preserve it. The hermeneutic lacunae in his analysis of the *Kojiki* were the result of gaps in the text itself; he did not want to speculate on matters that lacked textual evidence.[9] Thus, Nakatsune tried to apply this method to the classical texts in an effort to somehow overcome these gaps.[10] The conspicuous similarities between Nakatsune and Atsutane, he argues, represent the faithful perpetuation of Norinaga's teachings by Nakatsune; consequently, Atsutane also successfully fulfilled Norinaga's philological objectives. The only difference between Nakatsune and Atsutane was the latter's emphasis on the afterlife;[11] this, however, was less a sign of an intellectual break than it was Atsutane's clarification of issues that had eluded the grasp of both Nakatsune and Norinaga. For Miki, interests in the afterlife were not a threat to the bonds of intellectual kinship among the three scholars.

Modern scholars have analyzed the *Sandaikō* debate in an effort either to situate it within the broader history of its time or to assess its significance within the intellectual history of Kokugaku. Understandably, they have exclusively addressed intellectual themes, viewing the nativists as polemicists, and the development of Kokugaku as autonomous from historical forces outside discourse. What is missing in these assessments is an account of the interests of the nativists themselves, especially with regard to key

---

7. Nishikawa, "*Sandaikō* no seiritsu ni tsuite," p. 194.
8. Ibid., p. 200.
9. Miki S., "Hirata Atsutane no tenchi kaibyaku-setsu," p. 145.
10. Ibid., p. 141.
11. Ibid., p. 157.

developments within the Norinaga School. The analysis of purely intellectual and discursive developments cannot penetrate to the level of strategy that occurred behind the scenes during the years of the controversy; this social context of cultural production seems elusive because it is not immediately manifested within the written texts themselves. Viewing the debate as both an intellectual phenomenon *and* a social struggle for dominance, we will see that it served as the vehicle by which Atsutane tried to demonstrate his rightful position within the field.

The *Kojiki-den*: Language and the Ancient Way

Norinaga's pioneering work, the *Kojiki-den*, was an authoritative study of Japanese antiquity revered by all Norinaga School members. As the pre-eminent scholar of the *Kojiki*, he examined the text in its entirety, including the important chapters on the Age of the Gods (*kamiyo*). In some ways, his analysis yielded only cautious results, leaving a few important questions unanswered. Although these omissions provided ample opportunities for argumentation in the generation following his death, his own goal in the *Kojiki-den* was quite conservative; Norinaga did not seek the kind of comprehensive analysis that his rigorous methodology may have implied. He simply sought to "cleanse" interpretations of antiquity of their Chinese impurities. For this reason, the conclusions reached were not as important as his strict adherence to a philological framework.

The two most important extant records of ancient Japanese history are the *Kojiki* and the *Nihongi*. Both texts were compiled in the early decades of the eighth century, and they largely cover the same material—from the creation of the universe through the reign of the first emperor Jimmu (beginning in 660 BCE) to the events of the late seventh century. The two texts, however, diverge radically in their written style. The *Kojiki* was written in a potentially confusing combination of archaic Japanese and classical Chinese; the difficulty of its written form was mostly due to its use of Chinese ideographs chosen for either their phonetic or semantic functions.¹² As the primary author of the *Kojiki*, Ō no Yasumaro (?-723), himself explained:

> In antiquity words and meanings were unsophisticated, and it was difficult to represent sentences and phrases in writing. If written entirely in characters used for their meanings, the words do not correspond to sense; if written completely in characters used for their sound value, the text becomes much longer. For this reason, in some cases passages have been written by means of characters employed sometimes for their sound value and sometimes for their meaning, while in other cases the meanings only have been employed.¹³

The *Nihongi*, on the other hand, was written almost entirely in classical Chinese. Consequently, it did not pose the same linguistic challenges to comprehensibility as did the *Kojiki*. For this reason, Norinaga chose to focus on the *Kojiki* and not the *Nihongi*, and he attempted to make the former as accessible as the latter. He complained that the perception of the *Nihongi*'s lucidity was associated with its written form—clarity was equated with classical Chinese. The *Kojiki*, he believed, was difficult because it used a foreign writing system in order to express the spoken language of the ancient Japanese. Through careful study and analysis, he thought that he could recover that ancient language and demonstrate how the apparent intelligibility of the *Nihongi* was the result of the *karagokoro*, which was incapable of articulating the emotional depth and richness of the ancient Japanese language as captured in the *Kojiki*.¹⁴ The *Kojiki* posed greater challenges for scholars than the

---

12. This *Kojiki* and *Man'yōshū*-style of written Japanese was a de rigueur form of literary expression for many *kokugakusha* during the nineteenth century.

13. Ō no Yasumaro, *Kojiki*, as quoted in Seeley, *A History of Writing in Japan*, pp. 43–44. Ironically, the style of the *Kojiki* was chosen in order to make it as accessible as possible (ibid., p. 44).

14. Using Jacques Derrida's insights regarding Jean-Jacques Rousseau, one could argue that Norinaga (like Rousseau) recognized how speech (that is, ancient Japanese) was less linguistically mediated than writing, so that the former was a closer approximation of "presence" than the latter. Privileging speech, therefore, was an attempt to undo the primacy of writing. See Derrida, *Of Grammatology*, p. 241. Norinaga attempted to overcome the dominance of writing in the abstract, which he equated with the Chinese language, by attacking what he perceived to be its artificiality. The intellectual historian Sawai Keiichi observes that Norinaga privileged the *kana* syllabary over Chinese ideographs in his emphasis on speech over writing,

Nihongi, but the potential reward—the resurrection of the ancient language—was too attractive for him to ignore.

Besides the use of classical Chinese, the authors of the *Nihongi* employed many Chinese concepts in their descriptions of antiquity. They used notions like Yin and Yang and the Five Phases that, to Norinaga, made the text Chinese not only in form but also in content. Thus, the *Kojiki* seemed less tainted by the pervasive influence of Chinese culture, rendering it more suitable for philological analysis. Norinaga, however, was reluctant to condemn the *Nihongi* wholesale for its use of Chinese concepts and terms; it was still a valuable historical record of antiquity. Instead, he criticized his contemporaries for using these Chinese categories to interpret the two classical histories. He was especially critical of scholars who analyzed the *Kojiki* with a Confucian interpretive framework as if it was universally valid. He associated this framework with the search for *ri* (or *kotowari*, "principle"), which was linked to the interpretation of texts in terms of Confucian ethical values like "benevolence" (*jin*). The *Kojiki-den* was his answer to scholars who used Neo-Confucian ideas in their studies of Japanese antiquity.[15]

Norinaga and Philology

Norinaga viewed Confucian hermeneutics as problematic not only because of their alien origins but also because of their irredeemable flaws. Equating Confucianism with Chinese culture in general, he claimed that the chief characteristic of the *karagokoro* was its *sakashira* (artifice). He condemned the search for *ri* and *jin* in the classical texts, since these concepts were unknown in the eighth century; Japanese scholars projected these subjective categories onto the texts, obfuscating their true meanings in the process. As a result,

---

which amounted to a renewed reliance on writing ("Jūhasseiki Nihon ni okeru 'ninshikiron' no tankyū," p. 227). In Derrida's analysis of Rousseau, the logic of Rousseau's critique of writing, namely, its supplemental nature, could also be applied to speech. Thus, speech was no less supplemental or mediated than writing. In this way, Rousseau's analysis seems more sophisticated than Norinaga's. This was because Norinaga professed more faith in the divine nature of the ancient language, like Mabuchi. Rousseau, however, was more secular in his outlook.

15. Omote, "Katareru 'kamiyo' to 'utsushi,'" p. 75.

Confucian interpretations of Japanese antiquity were inaccurate, the result of an overly developed intellect that had lost any vestige of its humanity.

To combat Confucian intellectual artifice, Norinaga emphasized the completely *unbiased* analysis of texts; to accomplish this, he relied on the precision of the Kōshōgaku developed by his Confucian predecessors Jinsai and Sorai, as well as his nativist forebears Mabuchi and Keichū:

> Someone said that ancient learning [namely, the philological methodology] emerged from the Confucian adherents of *kobunji* [that is, students of Ogyū Sorai]. This is false. Our ancient learning [nativist philology] was begun by Keichū prior [to Sorai and Jinsai]. Itō [Jinsai] and others started Confucian Ancient Learning at about the same time as Keichū, but Keichū was first. Itō came later. Ogyū was later still. How could [Keichū] learn from [Jinsai]?[16]

Norinaga believed that he could analyze the *Kojiki* in a completely transparent way. As Hattori Nakatsune put it, "According to the august words of the Great Man [Norinaga], 'I have not added artifice to the ancient transmissions as they are and have not exceeded them by even one matter or one ideograph.'"[17] Norinaga used Kōshōgaku as an instrument to produce the kind of objectivity that had eluded Confucian interpreters of antiquity.[18]

As Miki Shōtarō has observed, the fruits of Norinaga's textual labors were limited. Norinaga found himself incapable of commenting on issues that he felt defied precise documentation.[19] His foremost concern in the analysis of *kamiyo* was to clarify the ori-

---

16. Motoori Norinaga, *Tamakatsuma*, p. 264. Members of the Suzunoya officially denied any influence from Sorai, but Ōhira did acknowledge the influence of Jinsai via his son Tōgai (Maruyama, *Studies in the Intellectual History of Tokugawa Japan*, p. 144n17).

17. Hattori Nakatsune, *Minoda Suigetsu Hattori Nakatsune-ō norito*, p. 458. Note that the expression used to convey the unbiased nature of their research was not the same as the term "impartial" (Ch. *pingxin*, Jp. *heishin*) used by Qing evidential scholars.

18. His use of Kōshōgaku resulted in a denial of Confucian ethical norms in antiquity and a denial of those ethics in general. In a similar way, "evidential learning" developed during the late Ming dynasty as a response to the Neo-Confucian dominance of the examination-system curriculum.

19. Miki S., "Hirata Atsutane no tenchi kaibyaku setsu," p. 140.

gins of the various *kami*.²⁰ He managed, however, to make three fundamental conclusions about the origins of the cosmos (*ametsuchi no some*). First, the notion of *ame* (heaven) was not the same as *ten* (Ch. *tian*), even though it was written with the same ideograph. Instead, *ame* was a physical place with no mind and thus had no ties to ethical principles.²¹ At the same time, he claimed that it was also not simply the "sky" (*ōzora*) either; this was his second major point. He confidently concluded that *ōzora* and *ame* were two distinct concepts in the *Kojiki*; yet he did not proceed beyond this assertion to explain how they were potentially related. Finally, he described Yomi as a foul and polluted place where the souls of the dead reside.²² Although he offered no insight as to its precise spatial location,²³ he did argue that the two locales Yoru-no-osu-kuni and Yomi-no-kuni were identical.²⁴

Norinaga's reluctance to comment further about the origins of the cosmos came out of a desire to avoid the sort of speculation that he associated with Confucian scholarship. This led many of his disciples to conclude that further research into the origins of the cosmos, using the *Kojiki*, was superfluous. One disciple, Nakatsune, thought otherwise. He attempted to create a more comprehensive interpretation of *kamiyo* with the *Kojiki*, while claiming to use the same methodology that Norinaga had employed in the *Kojiki-den*. The result was the completion of his *Sandaikō* in 1791; with Norinaga's approval, it was published as part of the *Kojiki-den* the following year. Nakatsune's clear contradiction of Norinaga's conclusions in this text was the genesis of the considerable controversy that followed.

Hattori Nakatsune and the *Sandaikō*

Nakatsune enrolled in Norinaga's Suzunoya in 1785. He was particularly interested in the relationship between classical Japanese works and the Confucian and Buddhist cosmologies that had circu-

---

20. Nishikawa, "*Sandaikō* no seiritsu ni tsuite," p. 197.
21. Motoori Norinaga, *Michi to iu koto no ron*, p. 110.
22. Motoori Norinaga, *Kojiki-den*, p. 238.
23. Miki, "Hirata Atsutane no tenchi kaibyaku setsu," p. 141.
24. Motoori Norinaga, *Kojiki-den*, p. 238.

lated in Japan during the latter half of the eighteenth century. Thus, he viewed the close analysis of the *Kojiki* as an opportunity to develop a new cosmological scheme based on Japanese antiquity in response to these competing foreign theories.[25]

In particular, Nakatsune was critical of Buddhist cosmologies that contradicted not only the *Kojiki* but also what he thought was common sense. He was quite skeptical of the Buddhist view that the cosmos was a complex series of hierarchical levels,[26] preferring a simpler model that was confirmed by human observation: "Theories using principles are unacceptable. What people can think and know is limited by the reach of the eye, the reach of the heart, and the reach of measurement. As for those unreachable places, even after much consideration, they will remain unknowable."[27] His first foray into cosmology came in 1789, in a text that he wrote in close consultation with Norinaga,[28] such that his conclusions were nearly identical to those of the *Kojiki-den*. He revised this work over the next year, which resulted in the first draft of the *Sandaikō*. In 1791, however, he read another cosmological text written by a colleague in the Suzunoya; under the inspiration of this text, he revised his work again and completed the final draft.

Norinaga assumed an important role in the development of Nakatsune's ideas in the *Sandaikō*. When Norinaga included the text as part of his *Kojiki-den*, he signified at least cautious approval for it, since many of its conclusions were direct contradictions of his own. In the epilogue of the *Sandaikō*, Norinaga wrote, "[Knowledge of] Takama-no-hara and Yoru-no-osu-kuni is very uncertain. This is lamentable. However, the transmissions of antiquity are more and more dignified [by Nakatsune], as is Japan."[29] It is also possible that its inclusion signified a more sincere recognition of Nakatsune's views. Omote even asserts that Nakatsune's text was true to the "hermeneutic discourse" of the *Kojiki-den*; that is to say, Norinaga

---

25. Nishikawa, "*Sandaikō* no seiritsu ni tsuite," p. 197; Ozawa, "*Sandaikō* wo meguru ronsō," p. 466.

26. He was especially critical of the interpretations offered in the Qing cosmological text *Tianjing huowen* (*Tenkei wakumon*) of 1675.

27. Hattori Nakatsune, *Sandaikō*, p. 255.

28. Ozawa, "*Sandaikō* wo meguru ronsō," p. 466.

29. Motoori Norinaga, *Sandaikō wo yomite shirie ni shiruseru*, p. 270.

recognized the merits of Nakatsune's methodology even if the latter's conclusions were different.[30] Other modern scholars, however, believe that the reason for its inclusion is even more straightforward, since many of the controversial conclusions reached by Nakatsune were actually suggested by Norinaga himself.[31]

Norinaga had demonstrated that references to *ame* (heaven) were also references to Takama-no-hara (High Heavenly Plain). In the *Sandaikō*, Nakatsune took this formulation a step further: *ame* signified Takama-no-hara, and the latter was none other than the sun.[32] The *Kojiki* states that the sun goddess, Amaterasu, lives in Takama-no-hara, leading Nakatsune to conclude that Amaterasu resides within the sun. Norinaga had claimed that *ame* was a "place" and not an ethical idea, even though scholars rendered it with the ideograph for "heaven"; it was a *kuni* (realm).[33] Nakatsune, however, thought that because one cannot see a *kuni* in the sky, it must have a special, archaic meaning. Thus, if Takama-no-hara was the sun, and Amaterasu lived in the heavenly *kuni* of Takama-no-hara, then Amaterasu must reside *inside* the sun.[34]

Armed with this conclusion, Nakatsune approached the related interpretation of two elusive concepts, *uwabe no kuni* and *uchibe no kuni*, both of which were crucial in the determination of this archaic meaning. Norinaga had explained that the authors of the *Kojiki* carefully distinguished between the two terms. He, however, did not provide any further details regarding the two terms. Thus, Nakatsune filled this void: "Takama-no-hara is [the sun]. Just as it says in the *Kojiki-den*, even in heaven there is a realm, like [that of] our own land. Thus, the realms on the earth are all [called] earthly *uwabe*; those in heaven are [called] *uchibe*. . . . The nature (*shitsu*) of heaven is not that of our land; it is pure and diffuse."[35] Nakatsune observed that the term *uwabe* was written with the ideograph for "surface" or "front" (*omote*), so that *uwabe no kuni* was a reference

---

30. Omote, "Katareru 'kamiyo' to 'utsushi,'" p. 73.
31. Miki S., "Hirata Atsutane no tenchi kaibyaku-setsu," p. 153.
32. Hattori Nakatsune, *Sandaikō*, p. 262.
33. Omote, "Katareru 'kamiyo' to 'utsushi,'" p. 72.
34. Omote, "Hito no kangaete shirubeki wa tada me no mae no oyobu kagiri," p. 10.
35. Hattori Nakatsune, *Sandaikō*, p. 263.

to the surface of the earth, namely, the various countries of the world. Conversely, the *uchibe no kuni* must refer to a kind of "interior realm," since it had the ideograph for "inside" (*uchi*). Thus, it must describe Amaterasu's relationship to the sun.[36]

Another *uchibe no kuni* was Yoru-no-osu-kuni. The god of the moon, Tsuki-yomi-no-mikoto, was one of its denizens. Consequently, the moon god, like Amaterasu with the sun, must also reside *inside* the moon, which Nakatsune identified with Yoru-no-osu-kuni. He also equated it with Yomi-no-kuni, as well as with Ne-no-kuni.[37] As a result, he determined that Yomi-no-kuni was another name for the moon. In this way, he linked the moon to the hereafter; at the same time, he determined the precise location of the afterlife, something that his mentor Norinaga had not done. In a philological move reminiscent of Norinaga, he supported his claim: "The Land of Yomi is the Land of the Night, so that Tsuki-yomi-no-mikoto [i.e., the moon god] is its god. The name Yomi is the same as [the] *yomi* [of the moon god's name]."[38] Compare this interpretation with Norinaga's own in the *Kojiki-den*: "The deity of Yomi is one of the heavenly and earthly deities. [The name] should be read Yomotsukami. What sort of deity is he? There are no transmissions [regarding this matter]; so we cannot know [for certain]. We only know that he is one of the deities who dwells in Yomi."[39]

Nakatsune extended his argument even further: Tsuki-yomi-no-mikoto was another name for Susanō-no-mikoto, the god of the sea.[40] As the *Kojiki* relates, Izanami-no-mikoto, the mother of Susanō, journeyed to Yomi after her earthly demise; thus, the *Kojiki* refers to Yomi as the land of Susanō's mother, and this link between Susanō and Yomi justified his conclusion that Susanō and the moon god were identical (see Fig. 1).

---

36. Omote, "Hito no kangaete shirubeki wa tada me no mae no oyobu kagiri," p. 10.
37. Hattori Nakatsune, *Sandaikō*, p. 263.
38. Ibid.
39. Motoori Norinaga, *Kojiki-den*, p. 243.
40. Hattori Nakatsune, *Sandaikō*, p. 264.

> A   Susanō = the moon god
>   Tsuki-yomi = the moon god
>   ∴ Susanō = Tsuki-yomi
>
> B   Susanō = the god of Yomi
>   Susanō = the moon god
>   ∴ Yomi = the moon
>
> Fig. 1   The philology of Yomi as the moon

Izanami resides in Yomi-no-kuni. . . . As for the reason that Ne-no-kuni is Yoru-no-osu-kuni, in the ninth fascicle of [our] teacher's *Kojiki-den*, it says that there are numerous indications that perhaps Tsuki-yomi-no-mikoto and Susanō-no-mikoto are one. . . . The fact that the tides follow the movements of the moon [indicates that] Susanō-no-mikoto is the august name of Tsuki-yomi-no-mikoto, and that the two [*kami*] must be one.[41]

Nishikawa explains the apparent weakness of Nakatsune's argument by citing the cosmological goals of Nakatsune's scholarship. Whereas Norinaga had researched the divine origins of the *kami*, Nakatsune sought to create an astronomical account of the stories of *kamiyo*. Thus, he had no choice but to conflate Susanō with Tsuki-yomi because the former would have had no direct cosmological function otherwise.[42] However tenuous the logic, Nakatsune relied on a series of philological formulations that led him to conclude that Yomi and the moon were the same. Not only did he successfully resolve a lacuna left behind by Norinaga, but he also formulated what became the central concept upon which Atsutane based his *Tama no mihashira*, but more on that later.

Continuing his discussion of the sun and moon, Nakatsune reconstructed the creation of the solar system using evidence culled from the *Kojiki*. Like Norinaga, he argued that *ōzora* (the "sky," i.e., the universe) and *ame* were two distinct phenomena. The latter rose to its present position in the cosmos because of its light and airy elemental character. The earth and Yomi (the moon) were

---

41. Ibid.
42. Nishikawa, "*Sandaikō* no seiritsu ni tsuite," p. 197.

formed from much heavier materials; thus, they "sank" to their present positions beneath *ame*. From these facts, he deduced that heaven (the sun), the earth, and the moon (the "cosmic triad" of the text's title) formed from the same primordial body. In addition, he concluded that the distinctions among these three spheres originated in their respective material compositions.

In a series of schematic diagrams, Nakatsune described how a process of primordial cosmic division produced three heavenly bodies (see Fig. 2). As the lighter material rose to form heaven and the heavier elements that composed the moon sank, the stuff that became the earth settled in the middle. Heaven, as the sun, formed "above" the earth, while Yomi, as the moon, formed "beneath" it. Before the separation of the sun and moon from the earth, both realms were connected to the earth by threads of primordial material. For Nakatsune, the connection between the earth and heaven was the Heavenly Floating Bridge (*ame no ukihashi*) from which Izanagi and Izanami had formed the islands of Japan. A second important function for the Heavenly Floating Bridge was its transmission of Amaterasu's descendant to the earth. On the other side of the earth, there was a similar bridge to Yomi. After the imperial august grandchild, Sumemima (i.e., Ninigi-no-mikoto), had descended to the earth, the Heavenly Floating Bridge disappeared, and the link between the earth and Yomi also vanished. Knowing that the earth was to be ruled by Amaterasu's descendants, Ōkuninushi-no-kami left the earth and journeyed to Yomi. In Norinaga's view of Yomi, the soul finds its way there in the absence of this earthly link; while corpses remain on the earthly plane, their souls travel to Yomi because they were no longer confined to the body. "Most people die and go to Yomi, [while] their bodies remain on the earth. It is the soul that journeys [to Yomi]; even though there is no longer a path that connects it to the earth, it [still manages to] journey [to Yomi]. However, the traveling of the corporeal form (*utsushimi*), without a connecting path [to Yomi], is impossible."[43] Nakatsune's view of the soul was a recapitulation of Norinaga's: "Someone asked me, '"to die and go to

---

43. Hattori Nakatsune, *Sandaikō*, p. 266.

The Sandaikō Debate

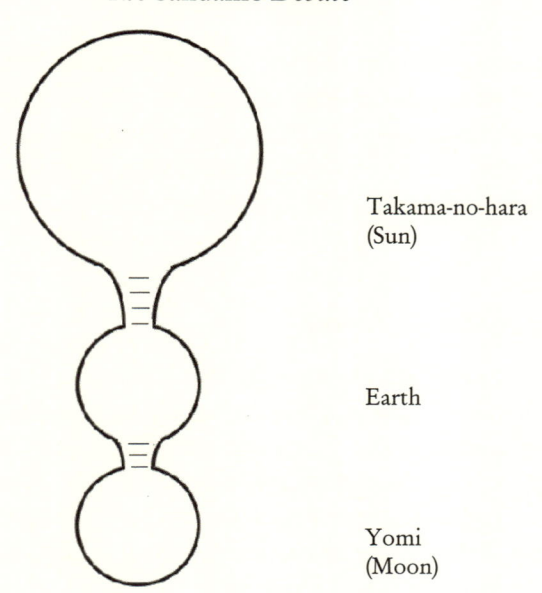

Takama-no-hara (Sun)

Earth

Yomi (Moon)

Fig. 2 The cosmic triad (based on drawings in NST 50)

Yomi"—does it mean that the body goes to Yomi or the soul?' I replied: 'The body becomes a corpse. Since it remains in the manifest realm (*utsushi kuni*), it is the soul that must go to Yomi-no-kuni.'"[44]

Although much of Nakatsune's interpretation of *kamiyo* was rational, he made allowances for phenomena that defied explanation. The miraculous nature of the soul's journey to the afterlife was one such matter. A second was his assessment of the divine origin of sunlight. The essence of the moon is like water, which is why the moon influences the tides. On the other hand, the essence of the sun is merely similar to fire, but it is *not* fire itself. If the essence of the sun were fire, then it might lead one to conclude that the sun shines because of the light emitted by its internal flame. The sun shines, Nakatsune argued, not because of some cosmic inferno, but because it is Amaterasu's blessing for the earth.[45] Thus, despite his search for an astronomical explanation of the *Kojiki*'s

---

44. Motoori Norinaga, *Kojiki-den*, p. 238.
45. Hattori Nakatsune, *Sandaikō*, pp. 268–69.

account of *kamiyo*, he did so without compromising Amaterasu's divinity. Although he emphasized the role of observation in the analysis of nature, he, like Norinaga, admitted that some aspects of classical texts were ultimately inscrutable; both scholars concluded that there were limits to human knowledge.

Nakatsune's Critics: Suzuki Akira and Motoori Ōhira

Despite Nakatsune's efforts to be faithful to his mentor's teachings, he was harshly criticized for his analysis of *kamiyo*, especially in the years following Norinaga's death. The first critiques came from two prominent members of the Suzunoya: Suzuki Akira and Motoori Ōhira. Their critiques focused on the core interpretations of heaven, Yomi, and the earth. The most crucial aspect of their assessments, however, was their insistence that Nakatsune's research was based on flawed Kōshōgaku. Both Akira and Ōhira were compelled to make the first authoritative statement of the Norinaga's School's intellectual mission, in what became its first declaration of orthodoxy.

After Norinaga's death, Akira and Ōhira were two senior members of the Norinaga School, along with Nakatsune. Nakatsune's *Sandaikō* had long annoyed Akira, which prompted him to author a critique that he never published. It was a text later circulated among members of the Suzunoya under the title *Sandaikō Suzuki Akira setsu*.[46] In fact, Akira approached Ōhira at some point during the decade following Norinaga's death and asked him if he was interested in writing a refutation of Nakatsune. Ōhira readily agreed, and he composed the *Sandaikō-ben* largely with Akira's help.[47] Although Ōhira's inspiration came mostly from Akira, his *Sandaikō-ben* was the first blow struck against Nakatsune's cosmology in what developed into a larger intramural conflict. At this

---

46. Because this text was never published, its precise date of composition is unknown. Some modern scholars claim that it was written in 1816. Since Akira had collaborated with Ōhira in the composition of the *Sandaikō-ben* in 1811, it is fairly certain that even if his text was not written or circulated until 1816, he had already developed the fundamental aspects of his critique several years earlier.

47. Uematsu Shigeru, *Uematsu Shigetake*, p. 58.

early stage in the debate, Ōhira (as the leader of the Norinaga School) and Akira spearheaded these attacks.

Two themes dominated the critiques leveled at Nakatsune by Akira and Ōhira. First, they asserted that his use of Western knowledge, most notably in the form of Rangaku, was inappropriate to the task of studying Japanese antiquity. Part of the reason for Norinaga's attack on Buddhism and Confucianism was that they were inadequate for the analysis of native texts, precisely because of their foreign origins; replacing Buddhism and Confucianism with Rangaku contradicted this fundamental axiom. Nakatsune, however, freely confessed his admiration for the Europeans:

> Recently, the peoples of countries in the far west have mastered navigation and sailed around [the world]. They have surveyed the world and [learned that] it is round. They have been able to determine that the world floats in the sky, and [to determine] the movements of the sun and moon. [By contrast], the ancient Chinese explanations are full of errors. These were determined with principle (*ri*) and are difficult to accept.... [Ancient Japanese explanations], when viewed with [the European ones] do not depart from [the latter] even a little. Thus, one can realize the truth of the ancient transmissions.[48]

Despite Nakatsune's insistence on the accuracy of Rangaku, it was still poor Kōshōgaku in the minds of Ōhira and Akira. It was this latter critique that shaped the major points made by the two in their attempt to dismantle the philological basis of the *Sandaikō*.

Akira's first priority was to refute Nakatsune's interpretation of *uchibe no kuni*. For Akira, the term simply signified realms not of this earth. Thus, Takama-no-hara was still a *kuni*, even if it was not visible to earthbound observers. He argued that Nakatsune's formulation equating Takama-no-hara with the sun was also incorrect: "There is not even one [reference] to the sun as *ame*."[49] Ōhira agreed with Akira that Takama-no-hara was a *kuni*, and both scholars invoked Norinaga's *Kojiki-den* in support of their arguments. Ōhira, however, *agreed* with Nakatsune on the issue of the sun. Although he disagreed with Nakatsune over Takama-no-hara's ontological status, the idea that Takama-no-hara was the sun

---

48. Hattori Nakatsune, *Sandaikō*, pp. 255–56.
49. Suzuki Akira, *Sandaikō Suzuki Akira setsu*, n.p.

seemed plausible to him: "In the *Sandaikō*, it says that the sun is *ame*. To say that Takama-no-hara is the sun truly hits the mark."[50] Ōhira's qualified support for Nakatsune on this matter disappointed Akira, leading him to lobby one of Ōhira's students, Uematsu Shigetake, to compose a critical evaluation of Nakatsune that was more consistent with his own.

Ōhira and Akira agreed on one major point: Nakatsune's interpretation of Yomi was unacceptable. Following his own definition of *uchibe no kuni* in the interpretation of Takama-no-hara, Akira acknowledged that Yoru-no-osu-kuni was the *kuni* within the moon; it was not, however, the same realm as Yomi-no-kuni.[51] Yomi-no-kuni was not an *amatsukuni* (heavenly realm) like Takama-no-hara and Yoru-no-osu-kuni. Thus, this confusion led to Nakatsune's incorrect formulations. His conclusions were textually unsubstantiated. As Akira stated: "[The interpretation that] Yoru-no-osu-kuni is Yomi-no-kuni [relies on] evidence that does not exist. Looking at these views, [I see] no beauty. . . . These are all speculations and new theories. Such is the case with [the interpretation of] Yomi-no-kuni."[52] Instead, Yomi was *inside* the earth. As the destination of the soul, it had to be inside the earth, he reasoned. In this way, he claimed that Yomi was an *uchibe no kuni*, but not in the manner conceived by Nakatsune.

Next, Akira attacked Nakatsune's interpretation of the moon god: "Tsuki-yomi-no-mikoto, like the great goddess of the sun, is a beautiful, great, and august god. [However, to associate him with] the foul Yomi-no-kuni, is this reverential? . . . These explanations are speculations and are not at all [consistent with] the ancient meanings."[53] If Yoru-no-osu-kuni and Yomi-no-kuni were separate realms, then Tsuki-yomi-no-mikoto could *not* be the same *kami* as Susanō.[54] Hence, the moon could not possibly be Yomi. This specific assertion was intended to undermine Nakatsune's philology. Nakatsune never challenged Norinaga's view that Yomi was the

---

50. Motoori Ōhira, *Sandaikō-ben*, n.p.
51. Suzuki Akira, *Sandaikō Suzuki Akira setsu*, n.p.
52. Ibid.
53. Ibid.
54. Ibid.

destination of the soul; he merely made a pronouncement regarding its exact cosmological location. Hence, he suppressed elements of the *Kojiki* that did not conform to his astronomical interpretations. He could not reconcile the existence of Yomi within the earth, as advocated by Akira, with the solar and lunar formations at the beginning of cosmic time. Ironically, Nakatsune and Akira agreed on *what* Yomi was but not on *where* it was. The difference between the two interpretations originated in methodology. Akira, as well as Nakatsune's other detractors, relied on the use of philology to produce literal interpretations of the classics. Nakatsune, despite claiming the mantle of that same philological method, based his views more on logic in the production of metaphorical interpretations. Yomi presented him with a difficult problem. If he were to interpret the ancient creation myths from an astronomical perspective, Yomi would have to become a heavenly body. Since there were no substantive details about the moon in the myths, he deduced that Yomi and the moon must be related. For Akira, Nakatsune's interpretation of Yomi was based on the application of flawed philological techniques.

Although Ōhira wrote his *Sandaikō-ben* with Akira's support, he withheld such a harsh attack on Nakatsune's philology. In Ōhira's view, the mission of the Norinaga School was to furnish Shinto with the kind of precise scholarship that both Buddhism and Confucianism possessed.[55] Philological precision was the sine qua non necessary to accomplish this goal, and he cautioned that it was an extremely demanding requirement. Classical texts lacked the level of detail, in many instances, to draw conclusions with any degree of certainty. The nativist, therefore, must confine himself only to those interpretations that can be supported with evidence.[56] For Ōhira, Nakatsune's error was in crossing the line into evidential uncertainty; Nakatsune employed subjective speculation, using his *karagokoro*.[57] Ōhira admired Nakatsune's enthusiasm in the *Sandaikō*, but it was that same zeal that had ultimately led the latter's scholarship astray. At the end of his life, Nakatsune admit-

---

55. Motoori Ōhira, *Kogakuyō*, in *Nihon kokusui zensho*, p. 25.
56. Motoori Ōhira, *Sandaikō-ben*, n.p.
57. Motoori Ōhira, *Kogakuyō*, p. 2.

ted that some of his conclusions lacked a foundation of hard evidence, but he still maintained that they were valid: "The *Sandaikō* interprets the sun as heaven, the moon as Yomi, Susanō as Tsukiyomi, and so on. Even though none of these are stated in the ancient transmissions, they are all taken from them."[58]

Ōhira rejected Nakatsune's admiration of Rangaku:

> Suzuki Jōsuke Akira's view of the *Sandaikō* is that [Nakatsune] seems to have carefully studied knowledge of heaven and earth, the moon, the sun, and the stars from foreign countries [like] Holland. [Akira] despises this, and [Nakatsune's views] are not consistent with the ancient meanings. They are contrary to the Japanese heart. These matters were argued by [Akira] and are exactly the same [views] as Ōhira's.[59]

In an attempt to analyze the *kamiyo* chapters of the *Kojiki*, Nakatsune had borrowed Western ideas, and in so doing, drew erroneous conclusions that contradicted the careful scholarship of Norinaga. Ōhira viewed the *Sandaikō*'s inclusion in the *Kojiki-den* as merely Norinaga's approval of Nakatsune's ingenuity—*not* his conclusions. As the custodian of Norinaga's intellectual legacy, he had to insist on strict adherence to Norinaga's rigorous standards. Nakatsune's hybrid scholarship of Rangaku and Kōshōgaku was not authentic Kōshōgaku at all for Ōhira.

Atsutane Joins the Fray

Soon after Ōhira's critique of Nakatsune, Atsutane composed the *Tama no mihashira*, which he published in 1812.[60] This work functioned as both a defense of Nakatsune's scholarship and a platform from which he could declare that eschatology took precedence over philology. His strategy, however, was to avoid a direct attack on philology and textualism. Throughout the text, he claimed to adhere to strict methodological principles. Thus, he recognized the significance of a rigorous philology for the members of the Norinaga School. Nevertheless, in an effort to emphasize knowledge of the afterlife, he made subtle remarks that were critical of textual-

---

58. Hattori Nakatsune, *Minoda Suigetsu Hattori Nakatsune-ō norito*, p. 460.
59. Motoori Ōhira, *Sandaikō-ben*, n.p.
60. Citations from the version of the text found in NST 50.

ism, even as he declared his commitment to it. The year of the text's publication represented an early stage in his career. Nakatsune's text and the controversy that it generated created the ideal conditions for Atsutane to make a noticeable impact in the field of the Norinaga School for the first time.[61]

Atsutane agreed with the fundamental conclusions of the *Sandaikō* and erected his own argument on Nakatsune's foundation. Heaven (*ame*) was another name for the sun, and it was the home of Amaterasu.[62] As far as Nakatsune's opponents were concerned, this assertion proved to be less controversial than others made by Atsutane; Ōhira agreed with it in the *Sandaikō-ben*, despite Akira's opposition. Like Nakatsune before him, Atsutane claimed that prior to the formation of heaven, Yomi, and the earth, the universe (*ōzora*) was filled with a massive sphere of undifferentiated matter.[63] Out of this sphere, the lighter elements rose and formed heaven (the sun), while the heavier elements congealed into the earth and Yomi (the moon). Akira and Ōhira had agreed that this view was mistaken. For Ōhira, even if heaven was another term for the sun, it did *not* form from the same material as the earth and the polluted realm of Yomi. Both scholars thought that this formulation, offered by Nakatsune and supported by Atsutane, threatened the sacredness of Takama-no-hara and, by extension, Amaterasu. Nevertheless, Atsutane made this assertion because it was necessary for his overall objective: a justification for the investigation of spirits and the afterlife.

Moreover, Atsutane concurred with Nakatsune that Yoru-no-osu-kuni was the moon and that its god, Tsuki-yomi-no-mikoto, was also Susanō.[64] Despite this agreement, the identification of Yomi with the moon held a special significance for Atsutane, and it ultimately distinguished his scholarship from Nakatsune's. He did not simply mimic the views of his senior colleague in the *Tama no mihashira*.

---

61. Uchino, "Norinaga gakutō no keishō," p. 14.
62. Hirata Atsutane, *Tama no mihashira*, p. 22.
63. Ibid., p. 18.
64. Ibid., p. 63.

In addition to the text's more substantial length, it diverged from Nakatsune's in several respects. For example, Nakatsune had contended that the essence of the sun was like fire, while that of the moon was like water. Atsutane reversed this: water was more like the elemental composition of the sun, and fire that of the moon. While Nakatsune had argued that fire was linked to the sun because its illumination was similar to sunlight, and the moon was like water because of its tidal influences, Atsutane argued that fire was ritually polluted so that it could not be associated with the sun. Water in its most elemental form, clear and clean, was a more appropriate metaphor for the solar element.[65] As another example, Nakatsune had viewed the Heavenly Floating Bridge as the link between heaven and earth before their physical separation upon Ninigi-no-mikoto's descent from Takama-no-hara. Atsutane did not deny that it was the path by which Ninigi-no-mikoto had descended to the earth. However, through a convoluted series of philological arguments, he proved that the word *hashi* did not mean "bridge" in antiquity; its meaning was actually closer to "boat." He observed that "the floating bridge is a present-day boat. After embarking, one arrives at the desired place. Thus, it is also called the *iwafune* [stone boat]."[66] Consequently, Ninigi-no-mikoto had descended to the earth in a boat-like vehicle and not via a bridge; after all, he reasoned, if Ninigi-no-mikoto came to the earth across a bridge, then how come other *kami* did not follow him? "If something like Nakatsune's interpretation [were true]," he argued, "then after the descent of the imperial august grandchild from Takama-no-hara, other *kami* would have ascended and descended."[67]

Atsutane also parted company with Nakatsune in more important ways that made his own interpretations distinctive. These differences were based on his redefinition of Yomi. As stated above, Nakatsune had claimed that the authors of the *Kojiki* left clues pertaining to the precise location of Yomi, which he argued was the moon, and Atsutane supported this formulation in the *Tama no mihashira*. Norinaga had viewed Yomi as the polluted realm of

---

65. Ibid., p. 26.
66. Ibid., p. 86.
67. Ibid., p. 88.

the dead; thus, Nakatsune saw the moon as the destination of the soul. Atsutane claimed that Norinaga's view of Yomi, and by extension Nakatsune's as well, was predicated on a fundamental misunderstanding of the *Kojiki*.[68] Norinaga had assumed, he argued, that because Izanami journeyed to Yomi, she must have died; the compilers of the *Kojiki* had used the ideograph for "spring" to signify Yomi (rendered in ideographs as "yellow springs") as the hereafter. Consequently, he concluded that the ancients had used a concept taken from Chinese mythology. Norinaga had derived his view of Yomi as the dank, forbidding resting place of the soul from the traditional Chinese view of the afterlife. Atsutane cited many reasons that negated Yomi as the Yellow Springs, but his general theme was that the idea of the Yellow Springs was not a native one. Hence, the idea itself *had to be* false; the ancients knew this, he reasoned, but had no alternative other than to use the term as a metaphor to describe the afterlife. Yomi and the moon were the same for him, but neither of them was the destination of the soul. Not even Norinaga, whose views of Yomi Atsutane rejected, was doomed to an eternity of despair in the afterlife: "[Concerning the idea that] all souls journey to that realm [Yomi], there are no transmissions or examples [of it]. Even the old man, [our] teacher [Norinaga], made this mistake and said that the destination of the soul (*tama no yukue*) was that place. However, not even the august soul of the venerable old man journeyed to Yomi-no-kuni."[69]

Having disproved the interpretation of Yomi offered by Norinaga and Nakatsune, Atsutane was free to abandon the *Kojiki* and search for textual evidence elsewhere. He used the *Sandaikō* debate as an opportunity to introduce his ideas on the afterlife and its significance for the living. The justifications for his views, however, were philologically tenuous. He claimed, for example, that it was possible for the soul to ascend to heaven, citing a brief reference in the *Nihongi* to the phrase *ame ni noboru*.[70] He admitted that this evidence was thin, and he refrained from basing his entire view of

---

68. Ibid., p. 98.
69. Ibid., pp. 118–19.
70. Ibid., p. 105.

the afterlife on it, but it illustrated the kind of textual evidence that he used.[71]

Nakatsune had grounded his interpretation of Yomi in the formation of the universe; thus, he explained the creation stories of the *Kojiki* in an astronomical way. In the *Sandaikō* he had focused on the origins of the sun, the earth, and the moon. Shortly before his death, he penned a new manuscript, the *Shichidaikō*, which expanded his astronomical interpretation of *kamiyo* to include the major planets of the solar system.[72] Without the same interests in astronomy, Atsutane was not a prisoner of Nakatsune's framework. His concept of the hereafter, which he called either the *yūmei* or *kami no mikado*, was an alternative to Yomi as the afterlife: "To say that the souls of people journey to Yomi is mistaken."[73] In his view, the afterlife was not a particular place; it was, instead, a spiritual realm. Unlike the Yellow Springs, it was not a particularly inhospitable realm either. In addition, he contended that this spiritual realm spatially coexisted with that of the living: "This spirit realm exists in this manifest realm and is not [in] a separate location. It is within the manifest realm simultaneously and is invisible; from the manifest world, it cannot be seen."[74] Attempts to precisely locate it were futile, he observed,

---

71. Richard Devine, echoing a position articulated previously by Muraoka Tsunetsugu in his *Nihon shisōshi kenkyū*, claims that Atsutane's views of the afterlife were derived from Christianity. Citing sixteenth- and seventeenth-century Jesuit texts from China, Devine portrays Atsutane's thought as completely derivative of these texts, which circulated illegally in Japan ("Hirata Atsutane and Christian Sources," p. 42). Although the Christian influence on Atsutane's thought is unmistakable, the extent to which his thought was either derivative or original is debatable. Miki Shōtarō, for instance, has argued that the creator deity of Amenominakanushi-no-kami did not come from Christianity and that this particular deity had a small role even in Atsutane's *Tama no mihashira* ("Hirata Atsutane no tenchi kaibyaku-setsu," p. 161). In any case, Atsutane's view of the afterlife would have been impossible without his reinterpretation of Yomi.

72. Nishikawa, "*Sandaikō* no seiritsu ni tsuite," pp. 206–7. In this work, Nakatsune changed his interpretation of Yomi, arguing that it was the planet Mars instead.

73. Hirata Atsutane, *Tama no mihashira*, p. 97.

74. Ibid., p. 109.

because it is everywhere. Citing the story of Ōkuninushi-no-kami, he argued that the soul did not journey to the spiritual realm after death. Instead, it disappeared into this realm, much like Ōkuninushi-no-kami had done after the descent to the earth of Ninigi-no-mikoto.[75] According to Atsutane, the key terms in the *Kojiki* regarding Ōkuninushi were *kakuru* (to disappear) and *yasokumade*, from the passage, "He disappeared into *yasokumade*." Norinaga had argued that the passage simply meant that Ōkuninushi went to Yomi: "The phrase *yasokumade* means the same thing as Katasu-kuni, Soko-no-kuni, etc. . . . [The word] *kakurite* [meant that] he left the manifest realm and [went] to Yomi-no-kuni."[76] Citing evidence from the *Man'yōshū*, Atsutane argued that Norinaga was mistaken. The passage did not signify that Ōkuninushi had journeyed to Yomi; instead, it indicated his state of invisibility.[77] Gravesites served as the portals into the spirit realm.[78] Once the soul entered this realm, it thereafter protected its living descendants from the afterlife. In this way, he believed that his own recently deceased wife had guided him through the composition of the *Tama no mihashira*.[79]

During the Age of the Gods, Ōkuninushi-no-kami passed into the *yūmei* so as not to challenge the earthly rule of Amaterasu's descendants. In the afterlife, Ōkuninushi-no-kami ruled over the souls of the dead in a manner similar to that of the emperor's reign in the world of the living.[80] In Norinaga's view, Susanō was banished to Yomi because of his mischievous conduct on earth. As we have seen, Nakatsune, equating the moon with Yomi, had concluded that Susanō was the moon god who reigned over Yomi. For Atsutane, since Yomi was not the destination of the soul, its overlord could not be Susanō. On the contrary, the afterlife was administered by the benign figure of Ōkuninushi-no-kami. Moreover, the spatial coexistence of the spirit realm and that of the living

---

75. Ibid., p. 73.
76. Motoori Norinaga, *Kojiki-den*, p. 118.
77. Hirata Atsutane, *Tama no mihashira*, pp. 74–75.
78. Ibid., p. 120.
79. Ibid., pp. 112, 121.
80. Ibid., p. 77.

made the former relevant to the latter. Thus, his notion of the spirit realm was fundamentally more optimistic than those of previous nativists who clung to the idea that Yomi was the afterlife.

Although Atsutane admitted that any *direct* contact between the two realms was difficult and rare, it was possible to affect one from the other. Activities among the living could affect deceased loved ones in the hereafter; through profound religious devotion combined with pious *conduct*, one could potentially influence affairs in the spirit realm. In this way, he emphasized the daily performance of religious *practices*, such as ancestor worship, in the observance of Shinto. In the *Kishinshinron* (1820), he observed: "I usually say that people who think there is nothing to know [about] the afterlife (*hito shinite*) are absolutely unfilial. This is because they worship their [deceased] parents and ancestors without a sincere heart. It is simply decoration and does not truly attain the [proper] sincerity and devotion. It is a lie."[81] Unlike Ōhira, who saw the mission of the Norinaga School to introduce scholasticism into Shinto,[82] he wanted to generate religious devotion among its followers. He imagined himself hefting a spear, bow, and sword and "ascending into the sky and joining the ranks of a divine army," which he would lead in order to defend the teachings of Norinaga against his enemies.[83]

Atsutane's religious vision was his specific contribution to the discourse of the Norinaga School, and the occasion of the *Sandaikō* debate was the ideal opportunity to voice his ideas. He used Nakatsune's scholarship and maneuvered it into a discussion of the nature of the soul, the afterlife, and religious faith itself.[84] He completed a transition in his own scholarship from classical philology to eschatology via Nakatsune's cosmological views. Nakatsune's influence on his ideas was actually quite minimal, despite Nakatsune's later assertions that the two were in complete agreement:

---

81. Hirata Atsutane, *Kishinshinron*, p. 45.
82. Motoori Ōhira, *Kogakuyō, Nihon kokusui zensho*, p. 25.
83. Hirata Atsutane, *Tama no mihashira*, p. 122. Note how Atsutane saw *himself*, literally, as the Norinaga School's defender-of-the-faith. Ōhira, of course, viewed himself in the same way. The dispute between the two, therefore, was inevitable.
84. Uchino, "Norinaga gakutō no keishō," p. 16.

In the tenth year of Bunka [1813], in Great Edo, a person named Taira no Atsutane wrote a text called *Tama no mihashira*. He sent copies of it to Fuji-no-kakitsu [Motoori Ōhira] and to Nakatsune. He had completely received the teachings of the Great Man [Norinaga] and perpetuated his august mind in complete agreement with the *Sandaikō*. His devotion is truly profound. However, Fuji-no-kakitsu had not yet concurred with the text, and he argued against it. Atsutane responded to him three times; he researched the august heart of the Great Man and his interpretations were not even slightly different from my own.[85]

By demonstrating that Yomi and the moon were identical, Nakatsune had opened the door for Atsutane to assert his views of the afterlife. None of these ideas, however, came from Nakatsune's interpretations. Atsutane's use of Nakatsune's ideas, and his invocation of Nakatsune's name, was part of a larger *sociopolitical* strategy geared toward the advancement of his position vis-à-vis his contemporaries in the Norinaga School.

The intellectual historian Tanaka Yoshito has assessed the relationship between the two as that of a *kyōdai no yaku* (fraternal agreement).[86] Atsutane established this relationship since Nakatsune was a senior member of the Norinaga School.[87] Uchino Gorō asserts that Atsutane's belief in Nakatsune's high regard within the School was badly misguided. As the only scholar of *kodōgaku* (ancient Way learning), Nakatsune was actually a marginal figure within the School.[88] Atsutane allied himself with Nakatsune because neither one of them had the proper background in *bungeigaku* (literature), the intellectual foundation of the Norinaga School.[89] Atsutane's advocacy of supernatural and eschatological knowledge ensured his marginality within the Norinaga School, yet it made his research distinctive. He created a clear position for himself by advancing his eschatological scholarship, while asserting the merits of philology in order to maintain his membership within the Norinaga School. An alliance with Nakatsune could serve to bolster his legitimacy in the eyes of his critics.

---

85. Hattori Nakatsune, *Minoda Suigetsu Hattori Nakatsune-ō norito*, pp. 461–62.
86. Tanaka Y., *Hirata Atsutane no tetsugaku*, p. 102.
87. Okino, *Hirata Atsutane to sono jidai*, p. 173.
88. Uchino, "Norinaga gakutō no keishō," p. 16.
89. Uchino, "Norinaga to Atsutane," p. 5.

Naturally, Atsutane claimed that the raison d'être of nativism (which he called Kogaku) was to understand the destination of the soul (*tama no yukue*): "The idea of supporting pillars is also the basis of the Japanese spirit for those who practice ancient learning. . . . By adhering to [the idea of] the destination of the soul, they establish these pillars. . . . Seeking to fortify and solidify their Japanese spirit, they begin with knowledge of the destination of the soul."[90] To achieve this goal, he redefined the concept of Yomi, using Nakatsune's ideas from the *Sandaikō*. Prior to the publication of the *Tama no mihashira*, the critiques written by Ōhira and Akira guaranteed that his conclusions would not go unchallenged. Once Atsutane's opponents realized that he claimed a place for himself at the intellectual center of the Norinaga School, they responded to these declarations in an attempt to reassert their own dominance. His text transformed the *Sandaikō* debate into a struggle for orthodoxy, and his opponents energetically reclaimed the legitimacy of proper Kōshōgaku.

Atsutane's Critics

Uematsu Shigetake responded to the *Tama no mihashira* with the composition of the *Tensetsu-ben* (1816). Shigetake was a disciple of Ōhira, who highly esteemed his young protégé.[91] When Ōhira read Atsutane's *Tama no mihashira*, he asked Shigetake to write a response in his stead; Shigetake completed a draft that received the approval of both Ōhira and Akira.[92] While Shigetake's critique focused primarily on Atsutane, it included Nakatsune as well.

Agreeing with Akira's previous observations, Shigetake attacked Nakatsune's assertions regarding the nature of heaven (*ame*). The classical texts, he argued, left few clues as to how the cosmos formed; so it was impossible to draw conclusions with any certainty. One thing was certain: heaven, as the abode of the gods, cannot have formed from the same primordial matter as the

---

90. Hirata Atsutane, *Tama no mihashira*, pp. 12–13.
91. Uematsu, *Uematsu Shigetake*, p. 60.
92. Shigetake's descendant Uematsu Shigeru argues that Ōhira approved of the text so enthusiastically that it became a kind of *sotsugyō ronbun* (graduation thesis) for Shigetake (ibid., p. 64).

earth.⁹³ Thus, heaven was not the sun. Moreover, Amaterasu was not merely the goddess of the sun: "If we say [only] that the Sun Goddess [Amaterasu] reigns over the sun, then there should be [references to her as] Hiterasu. Although there are [various references to light and heaven], there are no references to a Hiterasu. Why is this so?"⁹⁴ The answer is that Amaterasu was a central *kami* whose significance, and even divinity, was threatened by the reduction of heaven to the sun. Shigetake viewed heaven as existing *before* creation; so there was no generative process for it. Thus, Nakatsune's interpretation of creation was actually an investigation of the divine origins of the *kami*.⁹⁵ Amaterasu was supreme among all the various deities because she was charged with reigning over heaven, and it was her earthly descendants, the imperial line, who reigned over "all under heaven."

The most important critique that Shigetake leveled at Atsutane specifically concerned Yomi. Yomi was not the moon, as Nakatsune had earlier asserted, with Atsutane's concurrence. Commensurate with its place in heaven, the moon could not be the foul and defiled realm of the dead.⁹⁶ As Shigetake argued:

Thus, for the claim that heaven is something which rose [from a primordial sphere], there should be transmissions that it [in fact] separated [from it]. For the claim that it is the sun, there would certainly be transmissions that it began to move about [that is, revolve, etc.]. The fact that there are no transmissions is as I have stated previously: the [interpretation] that heaven is something which has risen is a mistake, and that heaven is the sun is also a mistake. Of transmissions [regarding] the beginning and ending of heaven, there are none. As for the issue of a risen [heaven], it is as Suzuki Akira explained: it is [an explanation of] the source (*ryō*) of the *kami*.⁹⁷

He accepted the interpretations of the *Kojiki-den* unquestioningly, including Norinaga's observations concerning Yomi. Like Akira and Ōhira, he asserted that Yomi was in fact *inside* the earth,

---

93. Uematsu Shigetake, *Tensetsu-ben*, p. 339.
94. Ibid., p. 338.
95. Ibid., p. 339.
96. Ibid., p. 340.
97. Ibid., p. 339.

where only the most polluted elements of terrestrial matter had congealed.[98]

The most striking feature of Shigetake's critique of Atsutane is that he confined it mostly to the latter's interpretation of Yomi. Atsutane, however, had adopted Nakatsune's view of Yomi in order to deny its link with the afterlife, which gave him the reason to outline his own eschatological discourse. Shigetake made no direct attack on the content of Atsutane's assertions concerning the afterlife. By attacking the *Tama no mihashira* at its weakest evidential link, namely Yomi, and by exhibiting faith in Norinaga's teachings, Shigetake re-asserted the validity of nativist philology. Shigetake demonstrated that there were discrepancies in Atsutane's work, which eliminated the necessity to invalidate Atsutane's larger conclusions. Poor philology alone nullified Atsutane's interpretations.

Under the influence of Akira, Shigetake served as the new leader in the rhetorical war against Nakatsune and Atsutane.[99] The *Sandaikō-ben* represented a first volley in the debate; after Shigetake's *Tensetsu-ben*, Ōhira, as the leader of the Norinaga School, chose to remain in the background. Akira also made no subsequent contribution to the discussion. By the early 1820s, the controversy centered around the two figures of Atsutane and Shigetake. After studying the refutations of his critics, Atsutane penned responses to both Ōhira and Shigetake. While insisting on the merits of his philology, he emphasized his *spiritual* continuity with Norinaga. Without religious devotion and faith, the intellectual achievements of the Norinaga School were insignificant, and he answered their attacks by arguing that they were overly obsessed with philology. Their passion for a rigorous methodology blinded them to the true goal of nativism: the realization that eschatology was the ancient Way.

---

98. This is one reason why he had to separate heaven from the earth. If the two formed from the same material, as Atsutane had contended, then heaven would be composed of the same stuff as the earth and, by extension, Yomi. Nakatsune and Atsutane had circumvented this predicament by claiming that lighter elements formed heaven and heavier ones formed the earth and Yomi.

99. Ozawa, "*Sandaikō* wo meguru ronsō," p. 475.

Atsutane's *Sandaikō-benben* (1814) was a defense of Nakatsune against what he perceived to be Ōhira's unfair criticisms. Dismissing the views of the *Sandaikō-ben* as particularly "immature" (*osanashi*),[100] he repeated the arguments that he had made in the *Tama no mihashira*.[101] In response to Ōhira's charge that Nakatsune was too Western in his intellectual orientation, he argued that this was not true. To this refutation, however, he added an interesting twist. He claimed that neither he nor Nakatsune used their study of Rangaku in order to prove the validity of their claims about Japanese antiquity. The situation was reversed: he and Nakatsune found independent verification of Western forms of knowledge in Japanese antiquity. Classical Japanese texts confirmed the validity of Western knowledge, not vice versa. The fact that Westerners could fathom the truths of Japanese antiquity, he reasoned, meant that Western knowledge *itself* was not particularly harmful:

> Although there are many things in the artificial explanations [namely, Rangaku] that we should not believe, there are others with which we can agree. Among these, explanations of the heavens (*tenmon*) and such, and the various situations that have [been] investigated and such, illuminate the ancient transmissions. When we truly understand that this is evidence, it is evidence of the ancient transmissions of the imperial realm and is replete with honor and sublimity.[102]

This type of cultural intolerance, exhibited by Ōhira and others, was more the defining attribute of the Chinese than it was of those who followed true Shinto: "Chinese people, thinking that only their own country is genuine, despise foreign things.... It is typical of an obstinate mind."[103] In addition to denying being pro-Western, he also defended Nakatsune's philology. The evidence to

---

100. Hirata Atsutane, *Sandaikō-benben*, p. 256.
101. In fact, Atsutane could not believe that Ōhira had written the *Sandaikō-ben*, even when told that this was the case (Uchino, "Norinaga gakutō no keishō," p. 16). His harsh criticism of the *Sandaikō-ben* was probably due to the belief that some other scholar had authored it. Ban Nobutomo, however, later informed him that Ōhira was the one responsible. Atsutane, even after learning the truth, decided not to recant his critique.
102. Hirata Atsutane, *Sandaikō-benben*, p. 259.
103. Ibid.

support Nakatsune's claims was voluminous, he argued. Ōhira simply refused to understand that the ancients used different names to designate the same thing;[104] the task of the scholar, which Norinaga had understood well, was to decipher the classical texts and determine these semiotic formulations. This was the reason why Nakatsune's philology was, in fact, exemplary.[105]

Ōhira was hurt by the severity of Atsutane's critique. In a letter to one of his disciples, he confessed, "Atsutane repeatedly said to [Natsume] Mikamaro gentle things [about me]. However, he [continued] to speak ill [of me], for which [I] took offense. The [whole situation] is unfortunate."[106] Ōhira refused to respond in kind, even though he continued to correspond with his students concerning his outrage over Atsutane's lack of decorum.[107] In his stead, he directed his student, Shigetake, to retaliate. In 1817 Atsutane defended both himself and Nakatsune from these attacks. As in the *Sandaikō-benben* of three years earlier, in his *Tensetsu-benben* he claimed philological validity for his and Nakatsune's conclusions. He even accused Shigetake of having intellectual limitations: "To think that heaven and earth did not form from one [primordial] sphere is the result of a lack of scholarly prowess (*gakumon no chikara*)."[108] In addition, he cited the inclusion of the *Sandaikō* in the *Kojiki-den* as proof that Norinaga had given his full endorsement.[109] Shigetake's obvious contempt for Nakatsune was tantamount to besmirching Norinaga himself.[110] Norinaga, viewing the activities of his students from the afterlife, must have been saddened by the whole affair: "They do not deeply appreciate the monumental undertaking of his *Kojiki-den*. They despise its inclusion of the *Sandaikō*, and they are unfaithful (*mamenaranu*) to the Master [Norinaga]. From the spirit realm (*yūmei*), he has [surely] seen [what has happened]. It makes me weep [for him]."[111]

---

104. Ibid., p. 257.
105. Ibid., p. 247.
106. Motoori Ōhira, *Fuji-no-kakitsu shōsoku* (letter dated 1817), p. 8.
107. Motoori Ōhira, *Fuji-no-kakitsu-ō chinjōbun* (1825), p. 502.
108. Hirata Atsutane, *Tensetsu-benben*, p. 275.
109. Ibid., p. 269.
110. Ibid.
111. Ibid., p. 270.

In the *Tensetsu-benben*, Atsutane began to move away from the tired bickering over whose conclusions were more philologically sound. Instead, he proclaimed that he and his students were guided by a religious mission. Under the protective gaze of Norinaga's spirit, he declared his own scholarship to be infallible and not subject to the same weaknesses that had plagued Ōhira and his other critics. By 1817, he found a new device to undermine his opponents: by linking himself to Norinaga spiritually, he could essentially lay claim to the status of Norinaga's sole, legitimate successor. As the only true heir to Norinaga's teachings, he could designate his own scholarship as orthodox. Naturally, Ōhira and his supporters attempted to counter this new move; the controversy over succession culminated in Atsutane's journey to Kyoto in 1823 and his first face-to-face encounter with his detractors.

Conclusion

The Norinaga School had extended its influence throughout Japan by the early nineteenth century. Shortly before his death, Norinaga had more than five hundred students and dozens of close disciples in his academy, which created the foundation for the success of the Norinaga School.[112] The various private academies of the School were united in their commitment to the analysis of classical Japanese texts, both prose and poetry. Norinaga had a great interest in both, and his work on the *Kojiki* and Japanese aesthetics is well documented. The unifying principle of Norinaga's research was his methodology: a precise philology informed by the principles of Kōshōgaku. Norinaga and his students used Kōshōgaku in their approach to classical texts, and it was this combination of intellectual content with methodological form that defined the Norinaga School.

After Norinaga's death, his students carried on his classical research. They recognized one another as fellow members of the same school not by any particular emphasis within the large corpus of native texts, but by their common usage of Norinaga's textual approach. For this reason, the attacks launched by Akira,

---

112. Matsumoto, *Motoori Norinaga, 1730–1801*, p. 125.

Ōhira, Shigetake, and others focused on the quality of Nakatsune's and Atsutane's philology. The former group attempted to dismiss the latter two scholars from the ranks of the School's membership because their conclusions threatened to undermine the School's rigorous standards.

Conversely, Atsutane defended himself and Nakatsune by advocating the merits of their textual methodology in an attempt to avoid *exclusion* from the field. Atsutane understood that membership in the Norinaga School was contingent upon philological precision. He tried, therefore, to justify his eschatological research while maintaining his textualist credentials. For many of the School's prominent scholars, Atsutane's claims were specious.

Despite Atsutane's recognition of the significance of philology, it was not the means by which he could propel himself to prominence within the Norinaga School. Faced with potential obscurity, he turned to eschatology and composed the *Shinkishinron*, followed shortly thereafter by the *Tama no mihashira*. The latter work was significant because he introduced his hybrid of philology and eschatology, and he composed the *Sandaikō-benben* (1814) to defend it. Afterward, he abandoned these efforts, perhaps realizing their futility. The *Tensetsu-benben* (1817) marked the beginning of a new strategy that linked his teachings to the will of Norinaga.

The debate surrounding the correct interpretation of *kamiyo* initiated the struggle within the Norinaga School over its orthodoxy. The assertion of philological rigor by Ōhira and others forced Atsutane into a defense of his own scholarship. The fact that he ceased to defend his work indicates that he had in fact *lost* the debate to Ōhira.[113] Losing the debate forced him to maneuver onto more hospitable intellectual terrain. His inability to convince his critics that he belonged in the Norinaga School resulted in the discourse of succession that he later asserted.

---

113. Nevertheless, note that Nakatsune claimed victory for Atsutane: "The august spirit of the Great Man assisted [Atsutane]. In the end, Atsutane defeated Ōhira" (*Minoda Suigetsu Hattori Nakatsune-ō norito*, p. 462).

FIVE

On a Dream and a Prayer: Atsutane's Discourse of Succession and a New Nativist Tradition

With his legitimacy as a member of the Norinaga School threatened as a result of the *Sandaikō* debate, Atsutane initiated an effort to claim the reins of orthodoxy. As the furor over Nakatsune's interpretation of *kamiyo* subsided, Atsutane began the campaign to establish his dominance. There were two phases in this effort. The first was his articulation of the orthodox lineage of Kokugaku, which he outlined in the *Tamadasuki* (1832). He did not, however, address the crucial issue of his status as the heir to Norinaga's teachings. Thus, his role as Norinaga's successor was only by implication and was without substantiation in this work. The second was the attempt to rectify this shortcoming, the result of which was the publication of the *Kiyosōhansho* (1834). Atsutane employed various strategies to increase his influence within the Norinaga School during the 1820s. Of particular importance were a dream that he claimed to have had in which he allegedly met Norinaga and a Shinto *norito* (prayer) composed by Hattori Nakatsune, one of his key supporters, following the *Sandaikō* debate. Both the dream and the *norito* were central elements of the *Kiyosōhansho* and instrumental in the solidification of not only his position within the Norinaga School but also his claim to be Norinaga's sole, orthodox successor. Both symbols derived their efficacy as proof of orthodoxy from older, more established traditions that had clearly defined succession schemes of their own. In particular, both Zen Buddhism and Neo-Confucianism furnished Atsutane with useful tools for the establishment of a Kokugaku lineage in which teachers and disciples had transmitted their teachings over time.

Fortunately for Atsutane, the Norinaga School had no orthodoxy to claim, beyond the study of classical literature using the methodology of evidential learning. The lineage of the *Tamadasuki* symbolized the fabrication of a broader orthodoxy, one that transcended the scholarly lineage of the Norinaga School. The dream and the *norito* gave Atsutane the opportunity to claim this larger orthodoxy for himself.

Discourses of Orthodox Succession

The efficacy of Atsutane's dream as proof of the transmission of orthodoxy relies on similar discourses of succession in other cultural traditions. The dream and the *norito* derived their potency as symbols of orthodoxy from these older, more established cultural institutions. This nativist discourse of orthodoxy was a hybrid of succession schemes taken directly from the Ansai School of Neo-Confucianism and Shinto and indirectly from Chinese Song Confucianism and Zen Buddhism.

Song Confucianism and Zen

We can locate the origins of Japanese discourses of succession in the Chinese master-disciple genealogies formulated during the Tang and Song dynasties. The structural similarities between Buddhist and Confucian lineages stem from a shared developmental history. Unlike the Buddhists, the Confucians had to overcome centuries of history when asserting that the *daotong* (the transmission of the *dao*; Jp. *dōtō*), which began with the sages and early kings, was eventually repossessed by Confucius and Mencius; subsequently, the propagation of the *dao* was lost from the end of the Warring States period to the Song dynasty, a span of more than twelve centuries. While Chan Buddhists of the Tang and Song used the concept of "mind to mind" transfer of the dharma in the formation of their lineages, Neo-Confucians relied on the textual nature of the *dao* in order to overcome centuries of its nontransmission.[1] The "mind to mind" transmission of the dharma in Chan was predicated on close master-disciple relationships characterized by face-to-face contact. For Song Confucians, face-to-face contact with Mencius was obviously out of the question. Thus, they argued that Mencius had left his wisdom concerning the *dao* in the *Mencius* as a legacy for later generations. Confucians of the Han and Tang, they believed, had misinterpreted his words and misappropriated the *Mencius* for their own subjective agendas. It was only through careful study conducted within a framework of self-rectification that a scholar could apprehend the *dao* and revive the *daotong*. Careful internal discipline and rigorous scholarship were the keys to the recovery of the transmission of the *dao* lost since Mencius. In the twelfth century, Zhu Xi believed that his predecessor Zhou Dunyi (1017–73) had accomplished this feat. Zhou then transmitted this knowledge to the Cheng brothers, Hao (1032–85) and Yi (1033–1107); eventually, Zhu Xi himself received the wisdom of the *dao*, along with the moral authority that accompanied it,[2] either via his teacher Li Tong (1093–1163)[3] or through the study of the writings of the Cheng brothers.[4]

Atsutane's discussion of the nativist *dōtō* closely followed Zhu Xi's account. Just as the wisdom of the *dao* was lost for a number of centuries after Mencius in the third century BCE, so, too, was knowledge of Japan's ancient Way lost after Sugawara no Michizane (845–903):

> The *kami* Sugawara is called Tenman Daijizai Tenjin. The reason why we worship him as the *kami* of scholarship is articulated in the *Tenmangū godenki ryaku* in which Takahashi Masao and others recorded the previously mentioned explanation.... The revered and awesome Tōshōgū [i.e., Tokugawa Ieyasu] [re]opened scholarship on the ancient Way and transmitted it to the world by perpetuating the august minds of the son, Keikō of Owari [Tokugawa Yoshinao (1600–1650)] and of the grandson, Gikō of Mito [Tokugawa Mitsukuni (1628–1700)]. I have recorded further details

---

1. For genealogical tables of Chinese Neo-Confucianism, see Appendix B of Wilson, *Genealogy of the Way*.
2. Bol, *"This Culture of Ours,"* p. 28.
3. Tillman, *Confucian Discourse and Chu Hsi's Ascendancy*, p. 138.
4. Ibid., p. 83.

in my *Nyūgaku montō*. That outline resembles the beginning of this document. The first step on the path of scholarship is for many people to emerge in the world who will elucidate this idea. . . . However, most followers [of nativism], with the intention to articulate the ancient meanings of [classical] verse, consult Keikō's *Jingi hōten* and the *Ruishū Nihongi* and consult Gikō's *Shintō shūsei* and *Dai Nihonshi*. Although there was the intention to elucidate the righteousness of the ancient Way. . . . [The one] who deeply immersed his heart in its righteousness was, originally, the Great Man, Kada no Azumamaro.[5]

For Atsutane, Azumamaro was comparable to Zhou Dunyi, the scholar who had successfully repossessed the Way. In a key departure from Zhu Xi, however, Atsutane identified three prominent political figures who made Azumamaro's achievement possible. He gave credit to the Tokugawa bakufu for the revival of nativism, perhaps in an attempt to placate the authorities and convince them that he was not a political subversive.

According to the logic of the *dōtō*, the achievements of both Zhou Dunyi (and perhaps Zhu Xi) and Azumamaro were tributes to their brilliance in comprehending the classical works of their respective traditions. Unfortunately for those who followed them, possession of the Way depended on the creation of a lineage for its transmission over time. The fundamental relationship in lineage formation was that of master and disciple, which itself developed through the competition between Tiantai Buddhism and Chan during the Tang and Song dynasties. The resultant discourse on the transmission of knowledge from master to disciple was one of the chief Buddhist influences on Neo-Confucianism.

The Transmission of Orthodoxy in Tiantai and Chan

The reliance on textualism created opportunities for the kind of subjective interpretations that the Neo-Confucians had hoped to suppress, leading to factionalization within the Confucian traditions of the later Song, Yuan, and Ming dynasties. This inherent flaw of exegesis did not plague the Buddhism of the early Tang,

---

5. Hirata Atsutane, *Tamadasuki*, pp. 480–81.

however; Buddhists had traditionally tolerated a plurality of techniques to perpetuate the dharma, which itself fundamentally resisted textual articulation. Conflict within Chinese Buddhism in this period, however, did emerge from the confrontation between Tiantai and Chan over how and with whom the dharma had been transmitted to China. The conflict between these two Tang Buddhist institutions generated the basic discourse of lineage formation and succession that prevailed during the Tokugawa period.

Thomas Wilson observes that Han and Tang Buddhists stressed the effectiveness of their teachings without consideration for the "authenticity or accuracy" of a particular sutra.[6] Buddhist theologians had ignored issues of genealogical exclusion, at least in this early phase. There was, as yet, no need to assert orthodoxy. Beginning in the eighth century, conflict erupted over the issue of the dharma's transmission to China from India. Tiantai and Chan Buddhists clashed over which tradition had received the authentic teachings of the Buddha first. Tiantai Buddhists relied on scriptural authority in asserting their legitimacy; Chan Buddhists, however, rejected the primacy of scripture in favor of an autonomous Buddha mind that masters transmitted to their disciples. In order to bolster their assertions of primacy, Chan Buddhists demonstrated how their patriarchs had received the original transmission of the dharma from Sakyamuni. Specifically, they argued that their sixth patriarch was directly linked to the historical Buddha and formulated a genealogical lineage to prove this. More so than the Neo-Confucian lineage formulated during the Song, the Chan lineage was based on the personal links between masters and their disciples since antiquity. If the Chan could successfully demonstrate such a direct lineage, Tiantai Buddhists would be consigned to the propagation of an illegitimate tradition—or, at the very least, a tradition overshadowed by the Chan.

During the Southern Song, this doctrinal controversy culminated in a genealogical debate between the two Buddhist schools, in which Tiantai scholars responded to the Chan by constructing a lineage of their own. By compiling the *Orthodox Lineage of the*

---

6. Wilson, *Genealogy of the Way*, p. 125.

Buddhist Schools, Tiantai scholars recorded the genealogies of the Indian patriarchs since Sakyamuni, and tied them to those of their own patriarchs. In sum, Tiantai scholars of the Tang had emphasized scriptural evidence as the basis for their legitimacy; circumventing scripture, Chan Buddhists of the Song asserted the inarticulatable nature of the dharma that required its transmission via face-to-face contact. Finally, this debate culminated with Tiantai genealogists of the Song carefully crafting lineages in order to exclude the Chan patriarchs entirely.

The Ansai School

The most important discursive source of legitimacy and orthodoxy during the Tokugawa period came from the Confucian and Shinto schools of Yamazaki Ansai. There are two main reasons for the significance of Ansai and his school for Atsutane. First, Atsutane's boyhood tutor in Akita was a student of the Ansai School, also known as the Kimon School. As was the case for most educated samurai of the Tokugawa period, Atsutane's education was built on a Neo-Confucian foundation, and he often praised Ansai for his erudition. Second, by the early nineteenth century, Ansai's Suika Shinto was a dominant presence in the world of doctrinal Shinto, in addition to the Shinto traditions of Yoshida and Ise. Suika theology, therefore, was an important source of knowledge for Tokugawa nativists.

Ansai's followers incorporated Neo-Confucian metaphysics into Shinto as they purged it of Buddhist influences embodied most notably by Ryōbu Shinto. The result of their efforts was Suika Shinto. While it was more intolerant of Buddhism than either Yoshida or Ise Shinto, Ansai sought the support of both of these more established traditions by accepting secret teachings from Kikkawa Koretaru and Watarai Nobuyoshi, the Shinto leaders of Yoshida and Ise, respectively.[7] Ritualists of the two traditions engaged in the practice of transmitting secret teachings from teacher to selected disciples in an effort to perpetuate their traditions and guarantee legitimacy. Scholars of both forms of Shinto were aware of the sig-

---

7. Ooms, *Tokugawa Ideology*, p. 222.

nificance of legitimacy and orthodoxy, and Ansai was especially attuned to these issues.

Suika Shinto, however, was not Ansai's only legacy. After his death, those students who believed that Neo-Confucianism took precedence over Shinto formed the Kimon School. Like their Suika Shinto counterparts, Kimon scholars were also deeply concerned with issues of legitimacy and orthodoxy.[8] Kimon scholars, following their teacher Ansai, believed that it was their mission to perpetuate the Daoxue of Zhu Xi in Japan. Thus, they viewed orthodoxy more reverently than their peers in other Confucian academies. They attempted to demonstrate their possession of the Way by dismissing the claims to orthodoxy of their rivals. Just as Zhu Xi had claimed that the Way was lost after Mencius, Ansai argued that it was lost after Zhu Xi. By identifying himself with Zhu Xi, Ansai believed that he had inherited the Neo-Confucian *dōtō* from him in Japan.[9]

Nativism and the Transmission of Teachings

The practice of formulating orthodox genealogies was eventually brought to medieval Japan. By the end of the sixteenth century, Zen monks and Confucian scholars were not the only ones who were absorbed by it. Teachers and students in other areas of cultural production had begun to engage in their own forms of lineage formation, which scholars have since called the *iemoto* system.[10] The *iemoto* specifically refers to the head of a school of cultural production who controls its highly specialized knowledge and practices (such as those of the tea ceremony, cuisine, or Noh theater), and supervises not only the recruitment of students but their instruction as well.[11] Leadership within the school is the sole possession of the *iemoto*; the future success of the school, however, depends on the selection of a successor. The *iemoto* chooses one or more of his disciples and endows them with all the knowledge

---

8. Maruyama, "Orthodoxy and Legitimacy in the Kimon School," p. 14.
9. Ooms, *Tokugawa Ideology*, p. 207.
10. Nishiyama, *Iemoto no kenkyū*, p. 3.
11. Nishiyama, *Edo Culture*, pp. 4-5.

needed to perpetuate the school. This leads to the central practice of *hiden*, whereby the *iemoto* secretly transmits the school's knowledge to his successor.¹² As in the case of Zen Buddhism, this interaction must be via the direct, face-to-face contact between master and disciple.

Despite the dominance of *dōtō* lineages in schools of Neo-Confucianism during the Tokugawa period, the *iemoto* system was prevalent in most of the other schools of cultural production, including nativism.¹³ It was for this reason that Motoori Norinaga chose his adopted son, Ōhira, to succeed him as head of the Motoori household and the Suzunoya academy. Since Atsutane was left out of Norinaga's *iemoto* system of succession, the discourse of the *dōtō* better suited his effort to lay claim to the leadership of nativism.

Scholars of the eighteenth and early nineteenth centuries acknowledged two basic views of the history of nativism. In one account, Keichū was asserted to be the first scholar to use the method that Kamo no Mabuchi and Motoori Norinaga would later perfect. In the other account, one that became important during the nineteenth century, Kada no Azumamaro's *Sōgakkōkei* was viewed as the first articulation of a unique nativist discourse. The contention of the present study is that while the two scholars were certainly nativists, their status as founders of an ideological form of nativism—namely, Kokugaku—is a matter of retrospective projection and not historical development. The success of the latter view, which privileged Azumamaro as the founder, is due to two factors. The first was the myth of Azumamaro's authorship of the *Sōgakkōkei*. The second was his mentorship of Kamo no Mabuchi. As the notion of an orthodox lineage became more prevalent among nativists during the nineteenth century, the need to clearly establish teacher-disciple relationships also grew, which may explain the fabricated story of Azumamaro's meeting with Keichū on the latter's deathbed.¹⁴ In the absence of ties between Keichū and Mabuchi (even apocryphal ones), an emphasis on Azumamaro became unavoidable.

---

12. Nishiyama, *Iemoto no kenkyū*, p. 25.
13. Ibid., p. 105.
14. Abe, "Keichū, Azumamaro, Mabuchi," p. 564.

Narrating the Kokugaku *Dōtō*: The *Tamadasuki* (1832)

Hirata Atsutane was faced with choosing between Keichū and Azumamaro when discussing the "father" (*oya*) of Tokugawa nativism. There were others besides Azumamaro and Keichū; yet none of them figured prominently enough in Atsutane's estimation. Thus, it was Atsutane who narrowed the field of candidates to Keichū and Azumamaro.

Atsutane focused attention on Keichū because Norinaga and his students had revered him as their scholarly inspiration. A central concern for Atsutane was the status of poetry. Norinaga had respected Keichū because of the latter's scholarship on the *Man'yōshū*. In addition, members of the Edo-ha held Keichū's scholarship in high regard as well. Thus, Keichū was the key to Atsutane's effort to exclude his rivals in both the Norinaga School and the Edo-ha from the orthodox lineage of nativism.

Keichū

For Keichū, Japanese verse (*waka*) was fundamentally the same as Chinese verse (*shi*).[15] This was an important assumption because he used it as a license to interpret *waka* in the same way as Chinese verse. He felt no hesitation in using the categories of Confucianism and, of course, Buddhism, in his analysis of classical verse. In fact, he admonished the reader not to forsake either Confucianism or Buddhism when studying classical verse; an exclusive focus on Shinto, he argued, was not up to the task:

> Shinto has been changed by Buddhism and Confucianism. We can see this in the *Nihongi* and other texts. In the time of Emperor Ōjin, Confucian teachings came, and in the time of Emperor Kinmei, Buddhism reached [Japan]. Thereafter, the Court combined the two and ruled. Thus, it [Shinto] ensued. People who try to read verse and make Shinto the basis [of their interpretation] must be mindful of Buddhism and Confucianism and not neglect them.[16]

---

15. Keichū, *Man'yō daishoki no sōshaku*, p. 194.
16. Ibid., pp. 161–62.

Most of his interpretations of the classical verses of the *Man'yōshū*, however, were decidedly Buddhist in tone.[17]

In addition to their hermeneutic utility, ancient Buddhist and Confucian texts served another important role for Keichū. These works were useful in the effort to decipher or reinterpret some of the more impenetrable poems of the anthology.[18] Words, he believed, had gradually lost their original meanings over time. Hence, scholars had to use texts that were either contemporaneous with or had preceded the poem.[19] Thus, Keichū focused most of his attention on Confucian texts from the Tang dynasty and Buddhist texts from the Tang, Sui, and earlier eras.

Keichū not only attempted to decipher classical Japanese poetry, he also sought to reconstruct the sounds[20] of its ancient recitation.[21] Through the recovery of ancient pronunciations and meanings, Keichū thought that he could provide definitive glosses of classical poems that had previously defied interpretation.

Keichū's erudition was not limited to either the Confucian or Buddhist canon, however. While these texts were crucial in his work, he did not neglect native texts written at or about the same time as the *Man'yōshū*. Classical Japanese texts were essential in his research on the anthology. Research on native texts allowed Keichū to compare various historical references in the *Man'yōshū* to similar references in other classical texts. As Peter Nosco tells us, the texts that were the most useful to him included the *Kaifūsō* (751), the *Kanke man'yōshū* (893), the *Wamyōsho* (938), the *Kogo shūi* (807), the *Kojiki* (712), and the *Nihongi* (720).[22]

---

17. Hisamatsu, *Keichū*, pp. 131–32.
18. Nosco, "Keichū," p. 243.
19. Keichū, *Man'yō daishoki no sōshaku*, p. 162.
20. Naoki Sakai explores the importance of phoneticism in his *Voices of the Past*. He argues that Tokugawa scholars understood the dilemma posed by the nature of language itself, between the meanings of utterances (what he calls the enunciated) and the performative aspect of the utterance (the enunciation). As a Tokugawa scholar, Keichū was part of this intellectual trend, even though Sakai does not discuss him specifically.
21. Hisamatsu, "*Man'yō daishoki* no seikaku to ichi," p. 614.
22. Nosco, *Remembering Paradise*, p. 58.

Keichū used his philological research on the *Man'yōshū* to make a number of observations concerning Japanese antiquity. First of all, the "divine language" of the *Man'yōshū* was *not* impenetrable. It was the spoken language of antiquity: "The ancients [talked about] difficult matters (*kataki koto*). They did not intend to confuse people by making easy matters difficult."[23] He argued that previous scholars of the *Man'yōshū* attributed the difficulty of its language to its relative proximity to the Age of the Gods; its difficulty was the result of its divine origins. The classical language was virtually opaque to Tokugawa readers simply because the Japanese language had changed over the centuries; this was the primary reason why Tokugawa texts were useless in the effort to understand classical words. Specifically, Keichū cited changes in the usage of *kana* as a source of difficulty. Thus, he supported the efforts of his fellow scholars in researching ancient *kana* usage (*kanazukai*).

Keichū believed that the poets of antiquity composed beautiful verse without resorting to the use of overly ornate language. In his eyes, this was a sublime achievement made possible by the efforts of the ancients to capture their feelings in ordinary words. Thus, the true purpose of versification was the articulation of genuine emotion; the depth of expression in a poem determined its aesthetic value. Poets in antiquity were concerned with articulating their own personal feelings in their verse, which Keichū called *magokoro* (true heart). "Sincerity without a deceptive heart," he asserted, "is called truth. Truth (*makoto*) is language without deception."[24] Keichū's views of the *magokoro* in classical verse influenced the scholarship of later figures, including Mabuchi and Norinaga.

Although Chinese Confucian texts were important in Keichū's research, he reserved a special place in it for Indian culture. Before attempting his analysis of the *Man'yōshū*, Keichū had studied Sanskrit for his work on ancient Buddhist texts. His methodology for the analysis of the *Man'yōshū* was mostly the same one that he had used for ancient Sanskrit texts.[25] In fact, he made an interesting observation about the relationship between the Japanese language and

---

23. Keichū, *Man'yō daishoki no sōshaku*, p. 200.
24. Ibid., p. 194.
25. Hisamatsu, *Keichū*, p. 117.

Sanskrit. In antiquity, Japan had received Buddhism via China from India, which made China a cultural intermediary between India and Japan. Early Buddhist missionaries had attempted to translate their teachings into the Chinese language. These early scholars, he observed, sought to preserve the pronunciation of the original Sanskrit while simultaneously conveying the correct meaning of the teachings in Chinese. Since there were two basic pronunciations for these teachings in classical Chinese—a Wu pronunciation and a Han pronunciation—he concluded that these teachings must have come to China at different times and even from different regions within India. The Wu pronunciation originated in "southern India" (*minami Tenjiku*), and the Han pronunciation came from "middle India" (*naka Indo*).[26] Both Chinese pronunciations were legitimate, and those of the Tang were based on them. The Japanese pronunciations of these words were based on these Tang pronunciations; so the Japanese readings were legitimate as well.

The Chinese people of antiquity, however, had to incorporate the translated Sanskrit terminology into their language. They did this by reversing the original Sanskrit word order in order to make it conform to Chinese grammar. Keichū argued that the ancient Indians placed "things" (*koto*) before "principles" (*kotowari*) in Sanskrit grammar. Thus, the former functioned as nouns, especially as the direct objects of a sentence. On the other hand, the latter acted on these *koto*, functioning, therefore, as verbs. Thus, Sanskrit grammar placed direct objects before verbs. The Chinese, however, had reversed this order, which compromised the sanctity of the original Sanskrit. Ultimately, the ancient Japanese people reversed the Chinese, giving precedence to *koto* over *kotowari*. Consequently, the Japanese language was, at a fundamental level, the same as Sanskrit: "Japanese *koto* are not the only correct things; the pronunciations transmitted from the Tang are as well. During the Tang, the Chinese stated *kotowari* first and *koto* second. In Tenjiku [India], they stated *koto* first and *kotowari* second. The norms (*nori*) of our land are the same as those of Tenjiku."[27] Despite Japan's tertiary status in

---

26. Keichū, *Man'yō daishoki no sōshaku*, p. 213.
27. Ibid.

the propagation of Buddhist teachings, it bore a closer identity to the original teachings than did those of China, which had a temporal and geographical proximity that Japan lacked. Although later nativists hailed Keichū as an intellectual inspiration, it is clear that he privileged India over Japan. While his contribution to Tokugawa nativism is without question, it was methodological rather than ideological, an issue that Atsutane understood well.

The Santetsu

The most significant legacy of the *Tamadasuki*, according to Uchino Gorō, is its articulation of Atsutane's orthodox lineage, which evolved into the *shiushi* (four great men) paradigm that many scholars still acknowledge today (see Fig. 4).[28] This lineage supplanted an earlier one described by Murata Harumi in the *Utagatari* (1809), known as the *santetsu* (three learned men) lineage (see Fig. 3). Generally speaking, it was predominant during the 1820s.[29] In addition to Harumi's description, as well as that of Atsutane in the *Tamadasuki*, there are at least two other accounts of the *santetsu*. Perhaps not surprisingly, Harumi's prominent disciple Shimizu Hamaomi had briefly commented on the lineage in the *Sazanami hitsuwa* (1808). Finally, in a text entitled the *Santetsu shōden* (1818), the monk Ryūkō[30] (1763-1824) composed short biographies of each of the *santetsu* scholars: "In the present age, [scholars] study the noble and base [aspects] of antiquity. They read the ancient classics and make themselves a bit more knowledgeable about the Japanese heart (*shikishima no yamatogokoro*). The *azari* Enshuan [Keichū], the Great Man Agatai [Mabuchi], and the venerable Suzunoya [Norinaga] are the three men who achieved this."[31]

---

28. Uchino, "Hirata-ha to Edo-ha no gakushi-teki tei'i," p. 13.
29. Matsuura, "Ōkuni Takamasa ni okeru kokugaku shitaijin-kan no keisei katei," p. 54.
30. In the *Tamadasuki*, however, Atsutane attributed the *Santetsu shōden* to another Edo nativist, Saitō Hikomaro (1768-1854), who may have assisted Ryūkō (*Tamadasuki*, p. 522). This may indicate that Atsutane did not actually read the text.
31. Ryūkō, *Santetsu shōden, jobun* 1b.

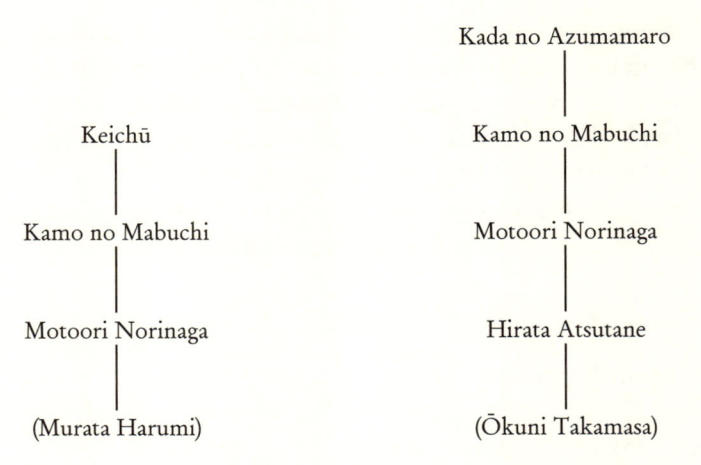

```
         Keichū                    Kada no Azumamaro
           |                              |
     Kamo no Mabuchi              Kamo no Mabuchi
           |                              |
     Motoori Norinaga             Motoori Norinaga
           |                              |
     (Murata Harumi)               Hirata Atsutane
                                          |
                                   (Ōkuni Takamasa)
```

Fig. 3   The Santetsu lineage (ca. 1809)   Fig. 4   The Shiushi lineage (ca. 1857)

This text is important because Atsutane referred to it specifically in the *Tamadasuki*. Atsutane agreed with the hagiographical treatment of Mabuchi and Norinaga, but his assessment of Keichū was more critical and he replaced him with Azumamaro. Uchino asserts that replacing the ostensible founder of Kokugaku is a significant issue that scholars have not fully appreciated.[32] The *santetsu* was the historical view of nativism for many members of the Edo-ha. Thus, the acceptance of Atsutane's lineage led to the decline of the *santetsu*, as well as of the centrality of the Edo-ha in Kokugaku history.

In the *santetsu* lineage, Keichū was the first scholar to offer an interpretation of native verse to challenge the Dōjō School of Kyoto, which espoused the medieval model of poetics during the seventeenth century.[33] His groundbreaking textual analysis of the *Man'yōshū*, Uchino contends, made him the natural figure to serve as the first major nativist of the Tokugawa period in the eyes of Edo-ha scholars.[34] Murata Harumi acknowledged Keichū's vital role as Mabuchi's primary methodological influence:

---

32. Uchino, "Hirata-ha to Edo-ha no gakushi-teki tei'i," p. 13.
33. Hisamatsu, *Keichū*, p. 28. The members of the Dōjō School based their versification on the style of Fujiwara no Sadaie (1162–1241), and they enjoyed the patronage of the imperial court.
34. Uchino, "Hirata-ha to Edo-ha no gakushi-teki tei'i," p. 15.

If I were to think about the greatest minds of classical verse, I would have to start with our venerable Agatai [Mabuchi]. Beginning with the Great Man Kada no Azumamaro, he embarked on the Way of the learning of antiquity, but he never dismissed verse [as Azumamaro had done]. Then, [Kada no] Arimaro seemed to reconsider things in the [*Kokka*] *hachiron*. However, he only esteemed the verse of the *Shinkokin*[*shū*], [a conclusion] with which I cannot concur. The Buddhist priest Keichū of Naniwa was an extremely talented person. He was the first to be able to grasp the correct interpretations of classical verse. . . . The person who wants [to compose verse] in the refined style of antiquity should refer to the teachings of our venerable Agatai.[35]

Harumi distinguished between Keichū and Mabuchi by observing that the former was a great *scholar* of classical poetry, but he was not the great scholar and superb *poet* that Mabuchi had been.[36] Harumi knew that Mabuchi had left Hamamatsu in order to become one of Azumamaro's disciples in Fushimi. Although Azumamaro was a superlative nativist, he was not a specialist in the study of classical verse. Mabuchi did not acquire his redoubtable skills from his mentor. Arimaro, Azumamaro's adopted son and contemporary of Mabuchi, was such a specialist but he had mistakenly emphasized the *Shinkokinshū* over the *Man'yōshū* (a view that Norinaga later shared). Uchino observes that Harumi privileged Keichū over both of the Kada scholars because Keichū had never met either of them; thus Keichū was never able to transmit his knowledge of classical verse to them.[37] Harumi clearly privileged Mabuchi over all others, including Keichū.

In contrast to Harumi, who perhaps only reluctantly acknowledged Keichū's influence on Mabuchi, Atsutane did not withhold praise for Keichū and his devotion to native texts. He observed that Keichū's notoriety was founded mostly on his philological analysis of the *Man'yōshū*. Although he claimed that Keichū had harbored an interest in classical Shinto histories like the *Nihongi*, he never made a significant contribution in that crucial area. Despite Keichū's accomplishments, Atsutane ultimately excluded him

---

35. Murata Harumi, *Utagatari*, pp. 241–42.
36. Ibid., p. 241.
37. Uchino, "Hirata-ha to Edo-ha no gakushi-teki tei'i," p. 15.

from the lineage. On the other hand, Harumi, despite his reservations about Keichū, did grant him a position in the *santetsu*. Contrary to what one might expect, Atsutane did not invoke Keichū's status as a Shingon priest to exclude him from the lineage of great nativists. Neither did he resort to Harumi's strategy, which portrayed Keichū as a good scholar, but lacking in skills of versification. Instead, Atsutane simply observed: "In Naniwa, there was Shimokōbe Chōryū and the Buddhist priest Keichū, both of whom propagated the ancient learning [philology] of the Way of poetry."[38] Missing from the scholarship of Chōryū and Keichū was a greater purpose for their philological efforts. The first scholar who understood this purpose, he claimed, was Kada no Azumamaro.

At nearly the same time that Harumi composed the *Utagatari*, his student, Shimizu Hamaomi, commented on the *santetsu* in the *Sazanami hitsuwa*. He recalled that Harumi had once told him of the illustrious achievements of Keichū, Mabuchi, and Norinaga: "People think that these three men never left their desks."[39] Hamaomi likened the scholars of the *santetsu* to the great minds of the Sorai School: "We can compare Kōtsu Ajari [Keichū] to Master Jinsai. The venerable Agatai had many similarities with Master Sorai. Motoori [Norinaga] had the dignity of Master Shundai. Does Hagizono [Katō Chikage (1735–1808)] compare with Master Nankaku?"[40] Hamaomi recognized Keichū as the intellectual equal of Jinsai, one of the most celebrated scholars of the Tokugawa period. His assessment of Norinaga was not quite as reverent, even though Shundai was one of the foremost scholars of political economy. Ultimately, Hamaomi agreed with Harumi's insistence that Mabuchi was the most prominent nativist by invoking the comparison with Sorai, the greatest Confucian scholar of the Tokugawa period.

As Mabuchi's disciple, Harumi's support for the *santetsu* lineage served to enhance his own prestige within the Edo-ha. Uchino suggests that Harumi saw himself as a fourth addition to the *santetsu*.[41]

---

38. Hirata Atsutane, *Tamadasuki*, p. 481.
39. Shimizu Hamaomi, *Sazanami hitsuwa*, p. 246.
40. Ibid., p. 250.
41. Uchino, "Hirata-ha to Edo-ha no gakushi-teki tei'i," p. 16.

Hamaomi recalled the words of Harumi that seem to support this contention:

> My teacher [Murata Harumi] often says that people nowadays view Ajari Keichū and the venerable Agatai as if they each had four eyes and two mouths. "They were no different than people of today," he said. "They were human just as I am. I am not praising myself. Keichū, the venerable Agatai, and recently, Motoori [Norinaga], and their ilk, if I were to compare myself to them, I do not think that I am inferior."[42]

Although Harumi may have wanted to claim a position in the lineage following Norinaga,[43] he was never one of Norinaga's disciples. In fact, he had virtually no ties to Norinaga whatsoever. Consequently, face-to-face contact between master and disciple did not apply to the *santetsu*. Mabuchi was not Keichū's disciple and Norinaga's relationship to Mabuchi was not that of a direct disciple either. In none of the sources that mention the *santetsu* is there any mention of such connections among its three scholars.

The Kokugaku *Dōtō*

Since the master-disciple relationship was important to Atsutane's lineage, he devoted much of his discussion to the issue of Norinaga's intellectual link to Mabuchi. He knew that the large number of Mabuchi's disciples in Edo had more direct ties to him than had Norinaga, and he acknowledged their status as such. In order to assert that Norinaga was the true successor to Mabuchi, he had to dispense with the *iemoto* orthodoxy of Mabuchi's Edo-ha disciples. He accomplished this by borrowing the discourse of the *dōtō* from Neo-Confucianism. The *dōtō* allowed him to privilege the perpetuation of a divine spirit through history and to repudiate the simple replication of an *iemoto*'s teachings.

Having excluded Keichū from the lineage, Atsutane emphasized Azumamaro's achievements. He asserted that Azumamaro was the first to comprehend the ancient Way, the knowledge of which he transmitted to Mabuchi. Keichū, the first figure in the *santetsu*, had impressive scholarly credentials, but he never grasped this spirit in

---

42. Shimizu Hamaomi, *Sazanami hitsuwa*, p. 245.
43. Uchino, *Edo-ha kokugaku ronkō*, p. 195.

his work on antiquity. In Atsutane's view, of all of Azumamaro's disciples, Mabuchi was the only one to understand the ancient Way. Such wisdom had eluded Kada no Arimaro, Azumamaro's chosen successor. Not surprisingly, Mabuchi transmitted his knowledge of the ancient Way to only one of his disciples, Norinaga.

The Shiushi

Atsutane's advocacy of Azumamaro, Mabuchi, and Norinaga as the three great nativists of the age was not an especially controversial position within the Norinaga School. Outside the *Tamadasuki*, there are at least two other instances in which members of the Norinaga School voiced their support for this view without any influence from Atsutane. During the early decades of the nineteenth century, Kido Chidate[44] and Izumi Makuni commented on this lineage. Makuni's account is especially significant because of his more substantive treatment of the issue, which Chidate did not provide. Makuni circumvented Harumi's contention that Norinaga had misread Mabuchi by broadening the scope of the discussion to include Azumamaro. Like Atsutane, he was aware that both Norinaga and Harumi were first-generation Mabuchi students and that Harumi had the closer relationship of the two. Makuni, therefore, decided to attack Harumi's commitment to a greater nativist cause, and he steered clear of any discussion of Harumi's scholarly pedigree. Harumi, he simply claimed, was not a true nativist. He was too obsessed with classical verse to understand that it was but one aspect of the native Way. Mabuchi had understood this fundamental truth; since Harumi failed to absorb this teaching, he was not a true disciple of Mabuchi, unlike Norinaga.[45]

At the outset of Book IX of the *Tamadasuki*, there is a *norito* composed by Atsutane in which he recounted the deeds of the major nativists who had preceded him:

The following should be recited before the *kami* of scholarship: "There are the *kami* whom we worship for their blessings upon ancient learning: Yagokoro-omoikane-no-kami [a *kami* of wisdom and knowledge], Imibe-

---

44. See Kido Chidate, *Shimimuro zakki*, p. 245.
45. Izumi Makuni, *Meidōsho*, p. 187.

no-kami [Imibe no Hironari, author of the *Kogo shūi*], and Sugawara-no-kami [Sugawara no Michizane]. In addition, there are the Great Men Kada [Azumamaro], Okabe [Kamo no Mabuchi], and Motoori [Norinaga], whom we also worship. Before Kuebiko-no-mikoto, we respectfully request help in our scholarship. . . . With the deepest respect, we pray for Kuebiko-no-mikoto's reign over all under Heaven."[46]

Of the six figures mentioned in Atsutane's lineage, only one was not an actual historical person, the deity Yagokoro-omoikane-no-kami. As mentioned earlier, Atsutane also credited three key political leaders of the Tokugawa family, Ieyasu, Yoshinao, and Mitsukuni, with making the restoration of nativism possible. The basic structure of this lineage is strikingly similar to the Neo-Confucian *daotong*: there were divine and semi-divine figures like the ancient Sages of China; there were significant figures from antiquity analogous to the Duke of Zhou, Confucius, and Mencius; and there were illustrious scholars from the previous century, comparable to Zhou Dunyi and the Cheng brothers. Above all, Atsutane stood in the same position as Zhu Xi.

Kada no Azumamaro

According to Atsutane, Azumamaro had apprehended the "great righteousness" (*taigi*) of nativism, as evidenced by the *Sōgakkōkei*.[47] Thus, Azumamaro was the founder of Tokugawa nativism. Atsutane was unimpressed with Keichū's methodological achievements, but he praised Azumamaro for his recognition of the ancient Way. Thus, in addition to an analysis of the *Sōgakkōkei*, it is necessary to look at the general character of Azumamaro's scholarship as well. Ultimately, neither could sustain Atsutane's claims about Azumamaro, a fact that highlights Atsutane's own ideological role in the development of Kokugaku.

Azumamaro's scholarship and ideas exhibited important continuities with Neo-Confucianism and Neo-Confucian Shinto, rather than hailing the radical break with these traditions as advocated by Atsutane. Unlike later nativists who refused to acknowledge any

---

46. Hirata Atsutane, *Tamadasuki*, p. 479.
47. Ibid., p. 481.

normative aspect to the native literary canon, Azumamaro looked at these classical works as indigenous sources of Confucian moral values.[48] The study of classical verse was important as a method for regulating the emotions. Erotic verse, which Norinaga later praised for its sincerity, troubled Azumamaro, and he admonished his followers to avoid its corrupting influences. In addition to poetry, classical histories were also important to his scholarship. Azumamaro appreciated the *Nihongi* especially, since it demonstrated Neo-Confucian values and ideas better than any other classical history.[49] Norinaga later argued that the *Nihongi* was perhaps the most tainted of the classical histories due to these influences that Azumamaro had praised. Finally, Azumamaro's attitude toward philology was closer to that of the Neo-Confucians than it was to either later nativists or his contemporaries, who were followers of Itō Jinsai and Ogyū Sorai. Rather than challenge Neo-Confucian ideas and interpretations with philology, in the manner of Jinsai and Sorai, Azumamaro used it to confirm his moral views of classical literature.[50]

Azumamaro retained the Neo-Confucian categories of *ri* and *ki* and applied them to a cosmology that he fashioned from classical sources. He believed that a human being had a body that served as the source of moral impurities. At the same time, humans also possessed a soul that functioned as the ultimate source of goodness. Humans, therefore, had to overcome the moral turpitude of their bodies and return to the probity of their souls.[51] Clearly, there was almost no difference between Azumamaro's cosmology and the Neo-Confucian ideas of "original nature" (*honzen no sei*) and "physical nature" (*kishitsu no sei*).[52]

Aside from these intellectual similarities, Azumamaro believed that Shinto and Confucianism were fundamentally identical and opposed the idea of completely divorcing one from the other.[53]

---

48. Miyake, *Kada no Azumamaro no kotengaku*, vol. 1, p. 161.
49. Ueda, "Kada no Azumamaro no shingaku," p. 2.
50. Nosco, "Keichū," p. 238.
51. Miyake, *Kada no Azumamaro no kotengaku*, vol. 1, p. 143.
52. Ueda, "Kada no Azumamaro no shingaku," p. 58.
53. Miyake, *Kada no Azumamaro*, p. 588.

The notion that Shinto could not exist without Confucianism was the basic assumption of Neo-Confucian Shinto. One of the leading figures of Shinto during the seventeenth century was Watarai Nobuyoshi (1615–90), who compared archaic Shinto to the Way of Yao and Shun.[54] Another leading Shinto figure of the same era, Kikkawa (Yoshikawa) Koretaru (1616–94), argued that the two traditions naturally complemented each other because of the importance of the lord-vassal relationship in antiquity, one of the Five Relationships of Confucianism.[55] Perhaps more strongly than either of these two Shinto scholars, Yamazaki Ansai asserted that the Shinto of antiquity was equivalent to Neo-Confucianism; thus, he believed that he could inherit the Neo-Confucian *dōtō* through Shinto.[56] Other figures outside of Neo-Confucian Shinto also advocated the notion of an essential unity of Shinto and Confucianism, most notably Hayashi Razan (1583–1657). Shinto scholars of the Tokugawa period were generally unaware of Razan's views on Shinto because Hayashi scholars guarded them as secret transmissions,[57] which indicates the importance of Shinto to Razan. Razan likened Shinto to principle[58] and to the Way of Humanity (*jindō*).[59] Because of the links between Shinto cosmology and the imperial line, he also identified it with the Way of Kings (*ōdō*):

The three [horizontal lines] of [the ideograph for] king are the triad of heaven, earth, and humanity. . . . That which encompasses heaven, earth, and humanity is Shinto. Thus, according to the Way of Kings, the highest person is the ruler (*kimi*) of all under heaven; this is the king. [The ideograph for] master (*shu*) is [the same as] king with a stroke at the top, which [signifies a] flame. . . . In the beginning, Amaterasu Ōkami was the sun. The august grandchild of the sun deity became the master of Japan; so it was called "the realm of the source of the sun" (*nihonkoku*).[60]

---

54. Watarai Nobuyoshi, *Yōfukuki*, p. 89.
55. Taira, "Kinsei no shintō shisō," p. 526.
56. Ooms, *Tokugawa Ideology*, p. 221.
57. Ibid., p. 81.
58. Hayashi Razan, *Shintō denju*, p. 45.
59. Ibid., p. 14.
60. Ibid., p. 21.

The Sōgakkōkei

Atsutane's claim that Azumamaro was the first scholar of the Tokugawa period to repossess the ancient Way contradicted the general character of Azumamaro's scholarship and ideas. Atsutane based his conclusions about Azumamaro on the *Sōgakkōkei* only; outside this one text, it is unlikely that Atsutane actually read his other writings.[61] While the text does seem to confirm some of Atsutane's assertions regarding Azumamaro's apprehension of the ancient Way, its authenticity is far from certain. Since it is the only evidence Atsutane used to prove his assertions, a brief discussion of both its contents and its provenance is warranted.

The *Sōgakkōkei* is thought by many to be the first ideological articulation of Kokugaku.[62] Supporters of this view believe that Azumamaro dispatched his adopted son, Arimaro, to Edo in 1728 in order to deliver the petition to Shogun Yoshimune, who allegedly refused it. In the document, Azumamaro argued that Japan had an indigenous Way that was as legitimate as either Confucianism or Buddhism—as the indigenous Ways of China and India, respectively. Articulating a major theme of what became a familiar Kokugaku argument, he lamented that the importation of Buddhism and Confucianism had gradually eroded the memory of Japan's ancient Way.[63] The decline of Kokugaku accompanied the ascendancy of foreign forms of knowledge, especially Confucianism. Unfortunately, Confucians were not interested in the accurate explication of the ancient Way, and their ignorance served only to distort the truth of Japanese antiquity. In a second important theme, therefore, Azumamaro condemned Confucianism for its pernicious influence on Kokugaku. The key to reversing this trend, he asserted, was to employ careful philological methods when examining the classical texts, thereby returning to the original intentions of the ancient Japanese people:

---

61. Miyake, *Kada no Azumamaro*, p. 471.

62. The proponents of this interpretation include William Theodore de Bary, Peter Nosco, Abe Akio, Maita Katsuyasu, and Yamada Yoshio.

63. *Sōgakkōkei*, pp. 332–33.

If we do not understand ancient words, we cannot illuminate ancient meanings. If we do not illuminate ancient meanings, we will not revive ancient learning. The customs of the former kings are fading and the intentions of the ancient wise men are nearly forgotten. This is all due to a neglect of the study of ancient words. Thus, I have devoted my life's efforts to ancient words. I firmly believe that whether this scholarship will be established or not depends on if this action is undertaken.[64]

Despite the significance of Azumamaro's text, its validity is not universally recognized. Miyake Kiyoshi, a scholar of Tokugawa intellectual history, has researched the origins of the *Sōgakkōkei*. Miyake's work casts serious doubts on the authenticity of what is a crucial document in the history of Kokugaku.

Miyake demonstrates that most versions of the text fall into one of two categories. The version that most scholars are familiar with, he notes, is the version of 1798 that appeared in the publication of Azumamaro's collected writings. There is, however, another version, in the possession of the Hagura family, that has several significant differences with the circulated text. This latter text, Miyake argues, is most likely the older version.[65] Contrary to the views of many contemporary scholars, Miyake demonstrates that in the original manuscript the term Kokugaku never appears; instead, one sees the terms Wagaku and Kogaku.[66] The belief that Azumamaro had used the term Kokugaku was a result of its use in the circulated version of the text, which was published seventy years after its alleged submission.

There are, however, problems with the original manuscript as well. It was thought that Azumamaro submitted the petition in 1728, yet there are references to physical frailties that did not develop until after 1730.[67] In addition, there are many other features of the manuscript that indicate its doubtful origins. The most notable

---

64. Ibid., p. 336.
65. Miyake, *Kada no Azumamaro no kotengaku*, vol. 1, p. 250.
66. Ibid., p. 254.
67. Ibid., p. 260. Azumamaro suffered from two serious ailments: angina and palsy. He began to feel the effects of the former in 1726 and the latter in 1730. The preface to the *Sōgakkōkei* refers to difficulty with speaking and moving, both of which are most likely references to the palsy, which did not arise until two years after the alleged submission of the petition.

of these is the written style of the text. In several instances, the circulated text does not have the proper mix of polite and humble expressions appropriate to the genre of bakufu petitions. In many ways, the manuscript is too direct in its language, which an educated individual such as Azumamaro would have known to avoid.[68]

Miyake concludes that neither version of the text was a work of Azumamaro. Moreover, he argues that while contemporary scholars have viewed the document as a request to establish a school, the language of the text indicates otherwise. More precisely, the petition was a request to create a library.[69] Ultimately, he concludes that Azumamaro never actually composed the text, since his age and health at the time would have precluded him from serving as the head of either a school or library.[70] Instead, the text was most likely composed by one of Azumamaro's students at the end of the eighteenth century. If such a document was ever submitted to the bakufu, there would have been some record of its existence, even if it was denied. No such record has ever emerged.

Atsutane emphasized the significance of the *Sōgakkōkei*, even though this text was barely known even in his time.[71] He believed that it was authentic and that Azumamaro had submitted it to Yoshimune. In fact, his memory seems to have failed him when he suggested that Azumamaro's petition was in fact approved; illness and old age, he maintained, had prevented Azumamaro from fulfilling his goal.[72] His motivation behind this portrayal of Azumamaro is clear: he tried to establish Azumamaro as the first scholar to apprehend the ancient Way.[73] Having proved Azumamaro's role

---

68. Ibid., p. 264.
69. Ibid., p. 260.
70. Ibid., p. 269.
71. Uchino, "Hirata-ha to Edo-ha no gakushi-teki tei'i," p. 16.
72. Hirata Atsutane, *Tamadasuki*, p. 483.
73. The ideological link between Atsutane and Azumamaro is important and has not gone unnoticed within the Shinto community in modern Japan. In a roundtable (*zadankai*) discussion sponsored by the Jinja Honchō, Maita Katsuyasu, a descendant of Atsutane, along with Hagura Nobuya, a descendant of Azumamaro, emphasized the intellectual and spiritual link between their forebears in the context of a discussion of the *shiushi* lineage (see Hagura, Maita, and Sakurai, *Shintō kokugaku to Shōwa jidai*, pp. 12–13).

as the founder of Kokugaku, he cleared a path to argue that Mabuchi received knowledge of the ancient Way from Azumamaro.

Before Atsutane was able to begin the discussion of Mabuchi, he had to account for Azumamaro's heir, Arimaro. First of all, as he observed, Arimaro was not Azumamaro's biological son, but merely his adopted son. More than a decade after his father's passing, Arimaro succumbed quite suddenly to illness; he and Azumamaro's younger brother, Nobuna, both died unexpectedly in 1751. With the unfortunate demise of these two scholars, Mabuchi was poised to assume control of their academy in Edo. However, Atsutane was adamant that Mabuchi's succession of Azumamaro was not simply a matter of default. Azumamaro had transmitted the wisdom of the ancient Way to Mabuchi before he died, and this was the crucial function that he performed in his capacity as the founder of Kokugaku: "It is known that the Great Man [Mabuchi] perpetuated (*tsugareshi*) the main intention (*honshi*) of the old man Kada [Azumamaro]."[74]

Beginning in 1733, Mabuchi had studied with Azumamaro for at least four years, Atsutane recounted. During these crucial years, he distinguished himself as the most talented scholar of the Fushimi academy, surpassing Arimaro and Nobuna.[75] Mabuchi was a scholar without peer: "We know that there was no one who surpassed the Master."[76] Scholars, especially Mabuchi's own students, had forgotten the significant contributions made by Azumamaro to Mabuchi's thought. While Harumi had dismissed Azumamaro's scholarship as trivial and irrelevant to the study of classical verse, Atsutane asserted that such a false view of Azumamaro stemmed from the paucity of his extant writings.[77] Azumamaro, in fact, had produced innovative work on the nature of the classical language and for this Mabuchi owed him a great debt.[78] By validating Azumamaro as a superb scholar in his own right, Atsutane undermined the Edo-ha

---

74. Hirata Atsutane, *Tamadasuki*, p. 495.
75. Ibid., pp. 494–95.
76. Ibid.
77. Ibid., p. 488. Azumamaro is believed to have burned most of his works before his death.
78. Ibid., p. 495.

emphasis on Keichū as the premier forerunner of Mabuchi. Thus, Azumamaro's legacy was that of a rigorous textual analysis for the explication of the ancient Way; such a textual methodology must not, however, be an end unto itself. Mabuchi had grasped the true nature of Azumamaro's teachings: "The Great Man Okabe inherited in his scholarship the muscle and bone of righteousness," which was best exemplified by his *Man'yōshū* studies.[79] Of all of the Edo scholars of poetry, who were as "numerous as ants" (*ari no gotoku ōkaru ni*),[80] only Mabuchi had properly apprehended the function of poetic studies. "Although he [Mabuchi] composed poetry in order to study antiquity (*keiko*)," Atsutane observed, "it was not truly central [to his scholarship]."[81]

Despite Atsutane's assertions, the differences between Azumamaro and Mabuchi were significant. Perhaps the most notable difference concerned their respective views of verse, particularly classical verse. Mabuchi viewed classical verse as the receptacle of human emotion; its critical analysis was the key to the recovery of ancient Shinto. For Azumamaro, however, poetry had little to do with Japan's indigenous Way.[82] He had not broken with traditional Shinto scholarship that equated ancient Shinto with the Way of the Sages. Despite this attitude toward poetry, he was interested in classical verse, but only as a confirmation of his moral views of antiquity. Thus, even as the recognized heir to Azumamaro's teachings, Mabuchi's scholarship was not a complete replication of his mentor's teachings.

Just as Atsutane had to justify his exclusion of Arimaro from the orthodox lineage, he had an even greater challenge explaining his negative assessment of the Edo-ha. As in his discussion of Keichū, he specifically focused on the role of poetic scholarship and versification within Kokugaku. Since Mabuchi's research on the *Man'yōshū* was part of a larger investigation of the ancient Way, poetry was merely one aspect of it.[83] Mabuchi's students, however,

---

79. Ibid., p. 488.
80. Ibid.
81. Ibid., p. 505.
82. Miyake, *Kada no Azumamaro no kotengaku*, vol. 1, p. 301.
83. Hirata Atsutane, *Ibukinoya hissō*, p. 474; Hirata Atsutane, *Kadō tai'i*, p. 7.

had resisted following this tenet: "Skill in versification was nothing special to the Great Man [Mabuchi]. However, his slow-witted followers, who fathom the trivial and not the significant, needlessly praise the Great Man's verse."[84] He was especially critical of Murata Harumi in his debate with Izumi Makuni. Harumi's argument in favor of Mabuchi's exclusive preoccupation with poetry was proof that the Edo-ha had deviated from Mabuchi's true teachings. At the same time, Atsutane could not condone Makuni's behavior either. He claimed to have warned Makuni not to engage in useless argumentation, implying that Makuni had initiated the debate with Harumi out of personal vanity and pride:

> The controversy developed when Harumi made his absurd argument (*guron*), but the cause of the debate was the result of Makuni's headstrong ways. At that time, I was a friend of both Harumi and Makuni; so I knew the situation [between them]. I expressed my views to Makuni, but he ignored them. As a result, my friendship with Makuni ended.[85]

Haga Noboru suggests that although Atsutane ultimately supported Makuni's position with respect to Harumi, he could not approve of his "attitude."[86] He avoided the sort of personal attacks against Harumi that Makuni had voiced in the *Meidōsho*. As we have already seen, his lack of support for Makuni earned him Ōhira's enmity a few years after Makuni's death.[87]

Classical poetry, though not absolutely central to the study of the ancient Way, was useful for understanding the conditions of antiquity.[88] Mabuchi, Atsutane maintained, had recognized the utility of the study of classical verse in establishing the *masuraogokoro* (masculine heart). Also known as the *yamatogokoro* (Japanese heart), it was the key to rectifying the malevolent influences of the *karagokoro* (Chinese mind). The close investigation of the classical language of verse was a practice that gradually purified the hearts of scholars and transformed them into true nativists.

---

84. Hirata Atsutane, *Tamadasuki*, p. 512.
85. Ibid., p. 507.
86. Haga N., "Edo ni okeru Edo kabun-ha to Hirata Atsutane," p. 279.
87. Nakamura, *Motoori-ha kokugaku no tenkai*, p. 81.
88. Hirata Atsutane, *Tamadasuki*, p. 508.

Mabuchi's antiquarian methodology represented an essential first step in the elucidation of the ancient Way.[89]

Mabuchi and Norinaga

The next link in Atsutane's lineage was between Mabuchi and Norinaga. Before he discussed how Norinaga had received Azumamaro's teachings from Mabuchi, Atsutane had to demonstrate the existence of a master-disciple relationship between Mabuchi and Norinaga. The chief obstacle to such an effort was the sheer number of Mabuchi's disciples in Edo. Whereas Mabuchi was the only major disciple of Azumamaro after 1751, Norinaga was but one of Mabuchi's disciples among many, including Murata Harumi.

Although Norinaga spent his entire life in Matsusaka, he and Mabuchi met face-to-face for the only time in 1765. Two years earlier, Tayasu Munetake (1715–71), Mabuchi's patron, had rewarded Mabuchi for his faithful service with the offer to fund a pilgrimage to the Ise Shrines. On his return journey to Edo, Mabuchi lodged for the night at an inn called the Shinjōya. Once Norinaga learned of the venerable scholar's visit, he quickly proceeded to the inn. Accompanying Mabuchi were the sons of his disciple Murata Harumichi, Harusato and Harumi. Having taken his evening meal, Mabuchi sat down and talked with Norinaga for some time.[90] Although Norinaga was familiar with Mabuchi's research before that time, it was only after this meeting, in 1766, that he formally enrolled in Mabuchi's Edo academy as a disciple. Thus, Atsutane was able to invoke this institutionally sanctioned link between the two as their master-disciple relationship.

Despite Atsutane's insistence that Norinaga was Mabuchi's only true intellectual heir, Norinaga and Mabuchi had profound differences in their views of the ancient Way and classical scholarship. Mabuchi had accepted the idea that ancient Shinto had strong affinities with Daoism; this was simply proof of its congruence with nature. Norinaga vehemently disagreed with his mentor, however.

---

89. Ibid., p. 510.

90. It is not certain if either of the Murata sons were in attendance during this meeting (Uchino, *Edo-ha kokugaku ronkō*, p. 176).

He admitted that his own interpretation of Shinto resembled Daoism. These similarities, however, were only superficial and the result of his close reading of the classical sources.[91] At a deeper level, he argued, one could see that Laozi had abundantly used his own subjective intellect in formulating his ideas of the Way, the assertions of Laozi to the contrary notwithstanding. Thus, Daoism was just as polluted with the *karagokoro* as Confucianism. In Norinaga's estimation, Mabuchi had not completely cleansed himself of the *karagokoro*; Mabuchi's fondness for Daoism was proof of this.[92] While there was a resemblance between Shinto and Daoism for Norinaga, it should not lead to the conclusion that the two were identical, since Shinto had similar resonances with Buddhism and Confucianism. Such similarities were expected, he asserted, and one should be careful not to exaggerate their significance:

In China, there was a man called Laozi who was a very wise person. Teachings that seem to be sound are good only superficially. In truth, they are not [sound]. They are extremely harmful. The true Way is the only one; however, occasionally, when one studies [his teachings], there will be similarities to this true Way. But, the true Way did not develop through the artifice of people. It is a Way that the imperial *kami* created. If one tries to understand what this means, the explanations in which he [Laozi] [claims to] despise artifice naturally resemble and conform [to the true Way]. However, he had merely used his own intellect.[93]

Mabuchi and Norinaga corresponded during the last six years of Mabuchi's life. After their famous meeting in Matsusaka, the two scholars never again met face-to-face and exchanged letters over various scholarly topics. During the early part of this period, Mabuchi had praised Norinaga for his thoughtful questions and careful analysis of classical texts and even confessed his own problems in dealing with the linguistic challenges presented by them.[94] Such praise was meaningful to Norinaga. When he recounted his meeting with Mabuchi in the *Tamakatsuma*, he claimed that Mabuchi had confirmed his interest in the *Kojiki*. According to Norinaga,

---

91. Motoori Norinaga, *Tamakatsuma*, p. 232.
92. Nosco, *Remembering Paradise*, p. 177.
93. Motoori Norinaga, *Tamakatsuma*, p. 232.
94. Terada, *Kamo no Mabuchi*, p. 212.

Mabuchi lamented the fact that he only lived long enough to study the *Man'yōshū*:

> Around the age of thirty, [I (Norinaga)] began to receive the teachings of the Great Man Agatai. [I] was determined to compose a commentary on the *Kojiki*, which [I] related to him [Mabuchi]. To which he replied, "In the beginning, I was also determined to explicate the august texts of the *kami*. But, I first [had to] sever myself completely from the 'Chinese mind,' and to investigate the true heart of antiquity. Attempts to grasp the heart of antiquity are impossible without understanding ancient words. Grasping ancient words means [that one must] explicate the *Man'yō*[*shū*]. [However,] I have grown old and do not have many years left, so I will not be able to fully explain the august texts of the *kami*. But, you are young and have a long life ahead of you. From now on, be mindful [of your studies]. If you work diligently at your studies, you will be able to realize this determination [to comment on the *Kojiki*]."[95]

For Norinaga, this was an undeniable sanction for his work. Mabuchi, he thought, viewed his budding nativist career with hope and optimism.[96]

Despite Norinaga's positive characterization of his relationship with Mabuchi, the elder scholar frequently criticized Norinaga and his work. Mabuchi was especially impatient with his views of classical verse and the *Man'yōshū*, areas that had defined Mabuchi's career. Mabuchi had expressed an interest in research on the *Kojiki*, as Norinaga claimed, but clearly not at the expense of the *Man'yōshū*.[97] The *Man'yōshū* and other classical texts were important linguistic sources for Norinaga and were not themselves significant for the investigation of the ancient Way.[98] Mabuchi was also troubled by Norinaga's stance on classical verse. For Mabuchi the only poems worthy of emulation and study were those in the *Man'yōshū*, since they were the most ancient. Norinaga, however, admired poetic form more than Mabuchi. Norinaga believed that poetry could be—and should be—both elegant and expressive. For this reason, he privileged the styles of the Heian and Kamakura periods over those

---

95. Motoori Norinaga, *Tamakatsuma*, p. 70.
96. Terada, *Kamo no Mabuchi*, p. 209.
97. Nosco, *Remembering Paradise*, p. 175.
98. Koyasu, *Motoori Norinaga*, p. 72.

of the Nara and Asuka (592–701) favored by Mabuchi.[99] In other correspondence with Norinaga, Mabuchi emphasized the practice of versification in the study of poetry; scholars also had to be good poets, according to Mabuchi, who was an accomplished poet himself. Thus, Norinaga submitted his own classical-style verse, perhaps at Mabuchi's request. Mabuchi sharply criticized Norinaga's verse, noting that if he persisted in composing such poor poetry, the two should cease their correspondence. Exasperated, Mabuchi scolded him for not heeding his advice on classical verse: "If you esteem [such poetry], then stop asking about the *Man'yōshū*. [Knowledge of] the *Man'yōshū* will do you no good."[100]

Norinaga acknowledged his intellectual differences with Mabuchi, but he felt no obligation to apologize for them.[101] He claimed that while scholars might accuse him of disloyalty to Mabuchi, his first priority was the clarification of the ancient Way, even at the expense of contradicting Mabuchi's teachings.[102] He admonished his students always to prioritize the Way and to be unafraid of indicating even his own mistakes. He cautioned them that respecting his own teachings, even when they proved false or incorrect, contradicted this fundamental lesson: "The revelation of the failings of one's teacher is highly respectful. If one did not do so, then other scholars would become confused by such [flawed] explanations. . . . Simply respecting one's teacher is to ignore the Way. [I] revere the Way and think of antiquity. [I] intently try to elucidate the Way and to clarify the mind of antiquity."[103] Although Norinaga recognized Mabuchi as his teacher, he never claimed to be Mabuchi's sole, orthodox successor. Atsutane used what was a tenuous teacher-student relationship between the two to make such a claim on Norinaga's behalf.

The final link in the transmission of the wisdom of the ancient Way, according to Atsutane, was the one between himself and Norinaga. Just as Mabuchi had been a disciple of Azumamaro, and

---

99. Nosco, *Remembering Paradise*, p. 181.
100. Quoted in Terada, *Kamo no Mabuchi*, pp. 214–15.
101. Motoori Norinaga, *Tamakatsuma*, p. 72.
102. Ibid., pp. 72–73.
103. Ibid.

Norinaga had been a disciple of Mabuchi, Atsutane asserted that Norinaga was his teacher. The fact that Atsutane had never actually met Norinaga might have undermined the validity of his claim. He tried to overcome this problem in two ways. First, he informed his students that he had received permission to enroll in the Suzunoya from Norinaga himself, just prior to the latter's death in 1801. In the official chronology of Atsutane's life, authored by Kanetane in 1869, the entry for 1801 reads, "In the spring of this year, he read the writings of the Great Man Suzunoya for the first time, and his determination [to pursue] ancient learning was aroused. In the seventh month of that year, his name was entered into the roster at Matsusaka."[104] This story, however, was a blatant fabrication. If it were true, then Atsutane could claim the status of a regular *monjin*, without the appellation of "posthumous" (*botsugo*). He would have gained such a status less than two months before Norinaga died on the twenty-ninth day of the ninth month. Thus, he could claim a personal relationship with Norinaga, even if it was only a brief one and even if he did not meet Norinaga directly. The second strategy, and the one Atsutane used in the *Tamadasuki*, was to present his scholarship as the perpetuation of Norinaga's true teachings.

Atsutane acknowledged that many of his contemporaries in the Edo-ha had an undeniable intellectual pedigree as first- or second-generation students of Mabuchi. As disciples of Mabuchi's scholarship, they were included in the school lineage of the Edo-ha.[105] Thus, they took for granted their intellectual heritage, which was simply founded on their physical proximity to Mabuchi. These connections to Mabuchi implied a spiritual continuity that did not exist, according to Atsutane. Norinaga, a resident of distant Matsusaka, was also a student of Mabuchi. He, therefore, had lacked the close relationship with Mabuchi that his Edo-ha colleagues had had. As Norinaga's work clearly demonstrated, he had truly inherited the wisdom of the ancient Way from Mabuchi: "Of the more than one hundred students of the Great Man Agatai, it was only the Great Man, our teacher [Norinaga], who grasped the right-

---

104. Hirata Kanetane, *Hirata Atsutane nenpu*, p. 662.
105. Hirata Atsutane, *Tamadasuki*, p. 512.

eousness of the learning of the ancient Way. The rest merely composed verse."[106] Norinaga had received these teachings from Mabuchi, who himself had received them from Azumamaro.[107]

In the *Tamadasuki*, Atsutane devoted little time to the discussion of Norinaga's investigation of the ancient Way. Instead, he discussed Norinaga in the context of his own work. Atsutane claimed that he received the teachings of the ancient Way from Norinaga via Hattori Nakatsune, who, he claimed, had apprehended the true meaning of Norinaga's teachings. Just as no one in the Edo-ha understood the true nature of Mabuchi's work, no one in the Norinaga School except Nakatsune had genuinely fathomed the significance of Norinaga's scholarship. As the only true heir to Norinaga, Nakatsune had recognized Atsutane's perpetuation of Norinaga's teachings, which prompted him to designate Atsutane as a kindred heir to Norinaga in 1823. As Atsutane related: "In the sixth year of Bunsei (1823), I [Atsutane] visited Kyoto when Nakatsune was sixty-eight. Since he was in failing health, [he said to me:] 'You have a long future ahead of you. You have somehow received the sacred duty (*miyosashi*) from our Great Man [Norinaga]. Inherit [his teachings from me].' Whereupon he transmitted them to me."[108]

Atsutane ended Book IX with a brief description of the ancient Way, which he claimed Azumamaro had first articulated. As he had argued several years earlier during the *Sandaikō* debate, the essence of the ancient Way was knowledge of the afterlife: "The rule of scholarship on our ancient Way is to search for the meanings of the manifest and of the spirit worlds, to learn them, and to rectify ourselves. . . . Without the help of the *kami* and the ten thousand spirits, we can never fathom the essence of the Way."[109] The ancients, Atsutane argued, had known that knowledge of the supernatural was essential to the comprehension of the blessings of the *kami*. Thus, his scholarship was the culmination of the work begun by Azumamaro and perpetuated by Mabuchi, Norinaga, and Nakatsune. These predecessors had emphasized the importance of

---

106. Ibid.
107. Ibid., p. 519.
108. Ibid., p. 526.
109. Ibid., p. 532.

clarifying the ancient Way, but they never actually described it. Atsutane reserved a place for himself in the *dōtō*, since he was the only nativist to grasp the fundamentally eschatological nature of the ancient Way.

Atsutane's presentation of the *dōtō* in the *Tamadasuki* had one lingering problem, namely, whether or not to include Nakatsune in it. At the beginning of Book IX, he excluded Nakatsune from the lineage of Azumamaro, Mabuchi, and Norinaga. However, in the crucial section describing his own reception of the orthodox transmission of the ancient Way, it was Nakatsune who had performed this important task. At this point, Atsutane was faced with two options. It was clear that he sought to demonstrate his possession of the ancient Way independent of Nakatsune. He could have argued that he had received the ancient Way through the force of his own efforts and devotion, as was the case with Zhu Xi and Yamazaki Ansai in the Confucian tradition. Rather than resort to this Neo-Confucian solution to the problem, he selected the Zen alternative, that is, to somehow demonstrate a direct link to the *dōtō* via Norinaga. This was the main ideological issue that the publication of the *Kiyosōhansho* was to address following the *Tamadasuki*.

Atsutane's Ascendancy

In a letter to a friend, penned by Atsutane in 1807, the account given of his first exposure to Norinaga's scholarship contradicts Kanetane's later, "official" chronology of Atsutane's life.[110] Instead of enrolling in the Suzunoya in the last few weeks of Norinaga's life, Atsutane stated that he had not even heard of Norinaga's name until 1803,[111] two years after the latter's death:

You read my foolish work, the *Kishin[shin]ron*, and I am embarrassed by your praise, which I do not deserve. Regarding your query, I had first heard the name of the venerable man [Norinaga] the year after the year after he passed away [i.e., 1803]. Moreover, although I had already started

---

110. Miki S., *Hirata Atsutane no kenkyū*, pp. 28–44.
111. Muraoka, *Zoku Nihon shisōshi kenkyū*, pp. 262–66.

to read the classics, you can tell that my learning is shallow. I am truly a child of the Way and am [still] learning earnestly.[112]

Kanetane's error, intentional or not, did not attract critical attention until Atsutane's letter was released to the public in 1932. By the 1860s, Atsutane's discipleship under Norinaga had gained general acceptance among nativists, and Meiji scholars subsequently perpetuated the notion of their master-disciple relationship in the modern era.

The myth of Atsutane's tutelage under Norinaga began with another letter. Unlike the 1807 correspondence, this one was widely known among nativists during the early nineteenth century. It was Atsutane's letter to Motoori Haruniwa, dated 1805, in which he requested formal admission to Haruniwa's Matsusaka academy. Around the same time as Atsutane learned of Norinaga's scholarship, he was completing his first scholarly treatise, the *Kamōsho*. Shortly after its completion, he began work on the *Kishinshinron*, which he intended to use as a vehicle for joining Ōhira's academy. Ōhira, annoyed with Atsutane's lack of support for Izumi Makuni in his debate with Murata Harumi in Edo, never responded to Atsutane's request for admission. Thus, Atsutane sent a request to Haruniwa instead. In this letter, he described a dream in which he had met Norinaga. In the dream, Atsutane asserted that he had established a master-disciple relationship (*shide no gokeiyaku*) with Norinaga. He offered his dream as proof of his determination and enthusiasm for nativism:

From my youth, I was focused on the learning of the Way. Under the sway of the Way of the Sages, I fell into futility. For several years, I devoted myself to scholarship. . . . [Eventually,] I disposed of every one of my Chinese writings. I sought out his [Norinaga's] writings and added them to my library. Day and night I read them and discovered with a deep and boundless faith that they were a collective achievement without compare since the beginning of time. Previously, I had only known of his name; so I did not know of any of his disciples here [in Edo]. I asked around and, finally, learned of masters Izumi Kazumaro [Makuni] and Hirano Yoshiki. We became friends and devoted ourselves everyday to

---

112. Atsutane, letter no. 78, 1807, in Watanabe K., *Hirata Atsutane kenkyū*, pp. 807–8.

scholarship. . . . Last spring, incredibly, I saw the old man [Norinaga] in a dream. We established a master-disciple relationship. I wanted to understand [the meaning of] this further, and realized somehow that he had passed away. It was his spirit that had seen into the depths of my heart.[113]

Haruniwa replied to Atsutane and offered him membership in his academy:

Last spring, you met [my father] in your dream and established a master-disciple relationship. I read this in your letter and heard about it from Oda's words of praise [for you]. I also heard other disciples who spoke of your devotion and deep [sense of] righteousness. So, I have decided to grant your request for admission. I have done this because of your letter and the recommendation of Oda. Moreover, I have received the [gift of the] fan and fee in silver that you sent.[114]

With Haruniwa's approval, Atsutane commissioned a painting of the dream that he had mentioned in the letter.[115] To commemorate the painting, he requested some comments from Haruniwa to add to the painting as calligraphy. Haruniwa replied with the following:

In recent years, Hirata Atsutane has become deeply devoted to the Way. He has examined the texts composed by our deceased master [Norinaga] and believes them deeply. He long wondered how he could meet the master, but finally gave up. He was always mindful of the master's words and reminded himself of his [teachings]. Then, at the end of the third month of last year, a person came [to Atsutane] in a dream and told him that the venerable man of the Suzunoya, who had come to [Edo] on an errand, was on his return journey [to Matsusaka]. Atsutane was stunned and rushed to meet him, barely catching up to him in the vicinity of Shinagawa. After speaking with him, [Norinaga] added him to the number of his students. I have now fulfilled [Atsutane's] request, and was very happy to do so.[116]

Haruniwa's response to the dream signified to Atsutane an official recognition of its legitimacy. Haruniwa, however, did not

---

113. Atsutane to Haruniwa, 1805/3/5, reproduced in Miki S., *Hirata Atsutane no kenkyū*, pp. 36–37.
114. Haruniwa to Atsutane, 1805/6/3, reproduced in ibid., p. 37.
115. For a reproduction of this painting, see *Hirata Atsutane ushi toshū*.
116. Haruniwa to Atsutane, reproduced in *Motoori Norinaga zenshū*, vol. 11 (Yoshikawa Kōbunkan, 1938), p. 172.

elaborate on his views of the dream and did not indicate that it was the primary reason for offering Atsutane admission to his academy. As his letter described, he admitted Atsutane on the basis of his dedication to nativism, to which Atsutane's letter and the recommendation of another Edo scholar attested. As for fulfilling Atsutane's request for some additional remarks about the dream, Haruniwa may have merely indulged his new student, which seems to conform to his reputation within the Norinaga School for having an amicable disposition.[117] In any case, Atsutane officially gained membership in the Norinaga School by the middle of 1805. He had the status of one student among *hundreds* of others, divided among the Norinaga School's academies from Kyoto to Edo. The year before his enrollment in the Norinaga School, he had founded his own academy, the Ibukinoya. His admission to Haruniwa's academy formally linked the Ibukinoya to the Norinaga School, and his students were added to its ever-increasing ranks.

Nakatsune's Norito

The second part of Atsutane's discourse of sole, orthodox succession was based on details related in Hattori Nakatsune's *norito* of 1824. Nakatsune sent the *norito* to Atsutane following the latter's visit to Kansai during the previous year, which was a watershed for Atsutane. The purpose of the journey was to present copies of his most important works to the emperor. During his stay in Kyoto, Atsutane paid a visit to the Nudenoya for the first and only time.[118] While in Kyoto, he turned his books over to Mutobe Tokika and his son Yoshika (1806–65), both of whom were Yoshida priests; Yoshika later became his student. The two delivered the items to Emperor Ninkō (1800–1846), and Yoshika later sent word to Atsutane that the emperor, who was duly impressed, had stated: "His exceptional efforts and [scholarly] interests are fine."[119] Atsutane was elated with the news. On his way back to Edo, he visited Ōhira in

---

117. Yamada, *Motoori Haruniwa*, p. 19.
118. For a fuller discussion of Atsutane's journey, see my "Intellectual Polarities and the Development of the Norinaga School 'Field.'"
119. Quoted in Watanabe K., *Hirata Atsutane kenkyū*, p. 79.

Wakayama and passed through Matsusaka with the intention to pay homage to Norinaga at his gravesite. In Matsusaka, he met Haruniwa for the first time, and Haruniwa gave Atsutane directions to the gravesite in Yamamuro, which was a short distance away.

Atsutane finally had the chance to meet Hattori Nakatsune during his stay in Kyoto. As we have seen, Nakatsune's work was the foundation for Atsutane's eschatological research. On the occasion of their meeting, Nakatsune told him about his final conversation with Norinaga. Escorting Norinaga home from a moon-viewing party, he had listened to Norinaga complain about the lack of students pursuing the study of the ancient Way.[120] As Nakatsune related in his *norito* more than twenty years later:

On the evening of the thirteenth day of the ninth month of the first year of Kyōwa [1801], there was a moon-viewing party held at the home of Fuji-no-kakitsu [Motoori Ōhira]. On the return home, [I] accompanied him [Norinaga] and we talked together. [I] thought that [I] should have some time this autumn to devote to the Way, and that I had managed to learn a little about the composition of prose and poetry. To which the Great Man [Norinaga] replied, "No. The composition of prose and poetry is something that you should not do. [Yet] everyone esteems that kind of learning. Consequently, there is absolutely no one who pursues ancient learning in the main. Even if I were to lament what is a sad situation, it seems that this trend will continue into the future. You have ceased to engage in the composition of prose and poetry and have focused instead on the Way of the Gods." There were no disciples who were devoted to this learning; so [Norinaga] prohibited them from studying the composition of poetry and prose. That night, we reached his home. Shortly thereafter, [Norinaga] became ill. The illness grew worse; finally, on the twenty-ninth day of the same month, he died. [I] painfully remembered what [Norinaga] had said to [me] that night and decided that it was absolutely his last wish. Of the five hundred or so disciples of the Great Man, every single one was fond only of literary elegance.[121]

After expressing his profound disappointment with his students, Norinaga had apparently praised Nakatsune for his devotion to the ancient Way, as specifically exemplified by the *Sandaikō*.

---

120. These details are related in Hattori Nakatsune, *Minoda Suigetsu Hattori Nakatsune-ō norito*, pp. 454–72.

121. Ibid., pp. 456–57.

Nakatsune portrayed Norinaga's remarks as clear indications that it was Nakatsune *alone* who pursued the correct scholarly path. The year after Atsutane's journey to Kyoto, he composed his *norito*, which he dedicated to Norinaga's spirit. He reverently informed the deceased leader of the Suzunoya of events since his death, especially the emergence of Atsutane:

> In the tenth year of Bunka [1813], a person named Taira no Atsutane wrote a book called the *Tama no mihashira*, copies of which he sent to Fuji-no-kakitsu and to [me]. It showed that he had received the complete teachings of the Great Man and had perpetuated his august intentions in complete agreement with the *Sandaikō*. [Atsutane's] devotion is truly profound. However, Fuji-no-kakitsu had not yet concurred with Atsutane, and he argued against him. Atsutane responded to [Ōhira] three times. He had researched the august intentions of the Great Man and his interpretations were not even slightly different from [my own]. The august protective spirit of the Great Man had guided [Atsutane], and he finally overcame Ōhira. [My] joy was unending.[122]

As the sole heir to Norinaga's teachings on the ancient Way, Nakatsune claimed that he had formally transmitted Norinaga's orthodox teachings to Atsutane:

> [I] am old and senile now. In the past, [Norinaga] had taught [me]. In accordance with his final wishes, if [I] were to transmit to Atsutane but one or two of his teachings, [Atsutane] has the talent to understand hundreds more. The august teachings of [Norinaga] have thrived and flourished under Atsutane. Since [I] am unlearned and without talent, I can no longer perpetuate [Norinaga's] final intentions. However, [I] gave them to the knowledgeable and talented Atsutane. Since [I] did the best that [I] could to perpetuate [Norinaga's] august intentions, if [I] were to go to Yomi tomorrow, [I] would have no regrets.[123]

Nakatsune designated Atsutane as his own successor. Thus, as the spiritual conduit of Norinaga's teachings, Nakatsune also recognized Atsutane's status as the intellectual heir to Norinaga. Shortly after composing the *norito*, Nakatsune died, leaving Atsutane as the only scholar of the ancient Way.

---

122. Ibid., pp. 461–62.
123. Ibid., p. 470.

Since Atsutane received the *norito* from Nakatsune the year after his journey to Kansai, it was not one of the immediate and tangible successes of the trip. As previously mentioned, the emperor's words of approval were understandably important to Atsutane. They functioned as a kind of imperial sanction for his scholarship, which prompted Mutobe Yoshika to enroll in the Ibukinoya. Although others had enjoyed various other forms of recognition, whether bakufu or domainal, he was the only scholar to receive it from the imperial institution. As a believer in the traditions of lineage formation, especially of Zen Buddhism and Neo-Confucianism, Atsutane also wanted to procure concrete symbols of his status as Norinaga's heir. During his visit to Wakayama, he asked Ōhira for one of Norinaga's prized possessions. Perhaps as a symbol of the cessation of hostilities between the two scholars, Ōhira gave Atsutane a *shaku* (scepter). It was one of three such objects Norinaga had personally crafted. Ōhira informed Atsutane that he and his brother, Haruniwa, were in possession of the other two. Before departing from Matsusaka, Atsutane made a request of Haruniwa. Haruniwa produced a portrait of Norinaga and a set of three of Norinaga's favorite brushes, both of which he gave to Atsutane.[124] Nakatsune sent the *norito* to Atsutane during the early months of the following year. The collection of artifacts together with the *norito* served as the proof of Atsutane's orthodox succession of Norinaga.

The Controversy over the Kiyosōhansho

Unknown to Atsutane, his visit to Kyoto instigated a significant controversy among his colleagues in the Norinaga School. Many of them corresponded with Ōhira, who was their leader, and exchanged letters among themselves. Some condemned Atsutane for his outrageous ideas and unfounded views, arguing that he pursued the sort of scholarship that contradicted Norinaga's teachings, just as Nakatsune had done. Perhaps Atsutane's most ardent foe, Kido Chidate, had the harshest assessment of Atsutane:

For the first time, I heard that he [Atsutane] claimed that he had become a student (*monjin*) [of Norinaga] in a dream. I did not understand this and

---

124. Watanabe K., *Hirata Atsutane kenkyū*, p. 90.

did not know if what came out of his mouth was a lie or the truth. If the Great Man [Norinaga] had truly granted such a request in a dream, then I am certain the he could have said to me in my dream that Hirata was [in fact] his apprentice (*deshi*). I definitely do not consider [Atsutane] to be part of the same [Norinaga] School. . . . Since no one in [our] school believes him, no one approached him ultimately [when he was in Kyoto]. As for meeting him [in person], he is without elegance (*bunga*); so there is no need. [In order to understand] ancient learning [nativism], there are the works of [our] former teacher [Norinaga]. Everyone says that they have read Hirata's views in works like the *Koshichō* and understand [his point of view].[125]

Not all the letters were disparaging of Atsutane, however. Others, most notably Hattori Nakatsune, rallied to his side, and defended his scholarship as consistent with the spirit of Norinaga's teachings.

Ōhira kept these correspondences, as well as copies of his own responses. Several years later, copies of these documents reached Hirata Kanetane (1799–1880), Atsutane's adopted son, who showed them to his father. Kanetane and Atsutane first learned about the negative reaction to Atsutane's stay in Kyoto through these letters. Since they represented two distinct factions within the Norinaga School, one for Atsutane and the other against, Kanetane decided to publish them in 1834 under the title *Kiyosōhansho* (Writings of condemnation and praise). As Kanetane explained:

In this volume are the comments written by the venerable Fuji-no-kakitsu [Motoori Ōhira] of Wakayama and the correspondence of his students concerning my father's visit to Kyoto in the sixth year of Bunsei [1823]. My father and I were [initially] unaware of [the existence of] these [letters]. In the eleventh year of Bunsei [1828], Hatano Yoshio, of our own academy, was shown these documents from Wakayama by Nakayama of the Yoshida [House] in the province of Mikawa. He borrowed them and made copies, which he later showed to me. I then presented them to my father, and the two of us were of the same mind about them. "The venerable Fuji-no-kakitsu is most diligent," my father said, "I shall make my own copies, too." Whereupon he personally copied the documents. Finally, I took out the venerable Hattori's [Nakatsune's] *norito* and recorded some of my own views. I also added the poetic exchanges between my father and the venerable Fuji-no-kakitsu. There was a cache of docu-

---

125. Kido Chidate, *Kido Chidate yori raijō*, 1823/9/18, pp. 383–84.

ments called the "exchange of reports" for its positive and negative assessments written by various people. I later copied these and added them to the collected documents in this volume. One can readily discern at a glance the good and the bad among those represented in this volume. Although it is obvious, the adherents of the Way of learning, even those not in our academy, will certainly [be encouraged] to cooperate among themselves. Even though the negative scholars, like Suehogi, Chidate, and others, are crooked, we must not call them beasts in human disguise. Would that not be shameful? . . . This volume was still without a proper title. So, my father personally entitled it the *Kiyosōhansho*. I then added these prefatory remarks on the fifteenth day of the fifth month of the fifth year of Tenpō [1834].[126]

Haruniwa had died in 1828, and Ōhira had died in 1833; for some, Atsutane was the only prominent member remaining in the Norinaga School. The limited publication of this text (only 300 copies were produced) was an attempt to shed light on the controversy and to bring closure to it. Kanetane hoped that the text would clearly absolve his father of any blame for the Norinaga School's ideological rupture, which he laid at the feet of Kido Chidate, Arakida Suehogi, and others.

Although some of the letters included in the *Kiyosōhansho* address Atsutane and his scholarship in general, many scholars expressed a profound concern with the larger significance of his journey to Kyoto. They understood well that it had a profound symbolic value, especially Atsutane's dealings with the imperial court. Atsutane and Kanetane often traveled to surrounding domains in an effort to recruit new students to the Ibukinoya. The Kyoto trip, however, was not specifically undertaken for such purposes. Instead, Atsutane journeyed to Kyoto with the intention of forging personal ties with his colleagues in Kyoto, Wakayama, and Matsusaka. For this reason, scholars of the Tokugawa period recognized travel for its inherent political and social significance.[127] The sociologist Randall Collins observes that face-to-face contact is an absolutely essential aspect of intellectual life itself. The passion and "emotional energy" that fuels intellectual exchanges result

---

126. Hirata Kanetane, Preface to the *Kiyosōhansho*, *Kiyosōhansho*, pp. 361–64.
127. Omote, "Chi no denpa to shōgeki," p. 139.

from these personal interactions.¹²⁸ The Kansai journey created these conditions for Atsutane and the members of the Norinaga School. It became one of the central themes of the *Kiyosōhansho*.

When Atsutane arrived in Kyoto, he met with Nakatsune, Fujii Takanao, and Kido Chidate, the head of the Nudenoya academy. He asked Nakatsune and Takanao for permission to lecture at the Nudenoya. Nakatsune enthusiastically supported the idea, and Takanao was at least amenable to it. Thus, the two approached Chidate on Atsutane's behalf with the request; Chidate refused, pleading insufficient notice,¹²⁹ even though his personal dislike of Atsutane was well known within the Nudenoya. Embarrassed by Chidate's refusal, Nakatsune suggested that Atsutane lecture at the home of another Nudenoya scholar sympathetic with Atsutane. As we have seen, Chidate later confessed to Ōhira that his skepticism about Atsutane was justified since Atsutane's work lacked "elegance." Moreover, in a criticism reminiscent of the *Sandaikō* debate, he refuted Atsutane's scholarship as contrary to Norinaga's teachings: "His scholarship departs from the axioms of the Great Man. [Atsutane] is full of mountain air [i.e., he is a charlatan]."¹³⁰

In addition to illustrating the antagonism between Atsutane and Chidate, the text also highlights the conflict between Chidate and Nakatsune.¹³¹ This was a confrontation between Atsutane's most visible nemesis and his most vocal supporter. Nakatsune's recognition of Atsutane as Norinaga's legitimate successor represented a direct refutation of Chidate. Chidate privileged poetics over all other forms of nativism, which Nakatsune and Atsutane dismissed as only one aspect of the ancient Way. Chidate and Nakatsune represented the two factions to which the title of the *Kiyosōhansho* referred.

Interestingly, Chidate's letters did not include any direct criticisms of Nakatsune. It is possible that Chidate viewed such an effort as superfluous, since Motoori Ōhira and Uematsu Shigetake had done a thorough job of it several years earlier. Instead, Chidate and Arakida Suehogi attacked Atsutane's dream as the basis for his

---

128. Collins, *The Sociology of Philosophies*, p. 26.
129. Omote, "Chi no denpa to shōgeki," p. 140.
130. Kido Chidate, *Dōjin yori naisho*, 1823/10/4, p. 385.
131. Omote, "Chi no denpa to shōgeki," p. 141.

status as a Norinaga disciple. Chidate tried to make his case to Ōhira in 1823:

> Although the venerable Suigetsu [Nakatsune] has taken care of [Atsutane] [in Kyoto], all others have voiced their extreme disapproval [of Atsutane]. Residents of Kyoto are in the habit of criticizing others; it is [our] custom. So, Atsutane said that a scholar is a scholar even in Kyoto [that is, he dismissed them]. However, his claims that he became a student of the old man [Norinaga] in a dream and such have grown into a great heap of unsubstantiated statements to which I lend no credence.[132]

Suehogi was perhaps even harsher in his assessment:

> [Atsutane] was disappointed that he had not become a student of the Great Man while he was alive. However, he still wanted to claim to be a student. The truth was that such a claim was an invented story. I am sorry to say that people should not recognize such claims. I understood the heart of [our] teacher [Norinaga]. Consequently, it would be an act of deception for me to state that [Atsutane] followed the heart of [our] teacher. [Such a claim] is like trying to ascend to heaven clinging to the beard of the proverbial dragon. Claiming to meet [Norinaga] in a dream and to establish a [teacher-disciple] relationship and such is a baseless claim and very foolish.[133]

These remarks were especially important in the context of 1823. Clearly, both scholars understood the dream's utility as a device by which Atsutane could claim orthodoxy. It was his only direct link to Norinaga. These refutations, however, had the unintended effect of *raising* the importance of the dream in Atsutane's discourse of succession.[134] Atsutane had originally used his dream as a basis for admission into Motoori Haruniwa's academy. As of 1834, with the publication of the *Kiyosōhansho*, it assumed the role of maintaining the continuity of the nativist *dōtō*. In addition, the dream nullified Nakatsune's role in the transmission of orthodoxy. Thus, Kanetane included the *norito* in the *Kiyosōhansho* as the verification of Atsutane's status as Norinaga's successor:

---

132. Kido Chidate, *Dōjin yori naisho*, 1823/10/4, p. 385.

133. Arakida Suehogi, *Arakida Suehogi Masutani-shi Fuji-no-kakitsu-ō azakeru kotoba narabi ni Arakida Hisamori Kitagawa Shingan hyō*, 1823?/11/25, p. 488.

134. Omote argues that Atsutane began to assert the importance of his dream as a legitimation device as early as 1815 ("Chi no denpa to shōgeki," p. 136).

Perhaps the most reverential of the old man's [Nakatsune] bequeathed teachings and his most important achievement was the *norito*. Later, in response to my father's request, it was turned over to him. It has been carefully preserved as an august treasure in our household. However, it was regrettable that we could not show it to others. So, I have copied it without altering even one ideograph and have included it here. Those who want to follow my father and learn about the Way should never neglect it. Recently, someone saw this *norito* and asked, "The *dōtō* of the Great Man Suzunoya's scholarship was transmitted to the venerable Ōhira alone. Thus, it is not possible for others [to have received it]. Given this fact, how can you think this way? Moreover, [Atsutane] falls short of the literary qualities of the capital, which makes [such a claim of succession] difficult to believe." Even though this seems to be the case, it is not. Although it is certain that [Norinaga] transmitted to the venerable Ōhira the scholarship of the capital, he bequeathed his teachings to the venerable Hattori. Some may find this hard to understand. However, it is explained in the Great Man's comments on the *Sandaikō*, in which he professed his confidence.[135]

The text was collected and published by the Hirata family as an account of its rivals in the Norinaga School.[136] As such, it functioned as a kind of internal memo for the Ibukinoya academy. The *Kiyosōhansho* performed an ideological function similar to Atsutane's participation in the *Sandaikō* debate. Whereas the latter focused on the Norinaga School's "L-orthodoxy," which Kanetane referred to as the "scholarship of the capital," the former asserted an "O-orthodoxy," which Kanetane called the "bequeathed teachings" (*yuikyō*).

By 1834, Atsutane's academy had grown to upwards of five hundred students. Kanetane's[137] publication of the *Kiyosōhansho* represented a call for the two factions within the Norinaga School to end their hostilities and cease bickering. Kanetane wanted to unify all

---

135. Hirata Kanetane, *Kiyosōhansho*, pp. 479–80.
136. Omote, "Chi no denpa to shōgeki," p. 141.
137. As Atsutane's son, Kanetane assumed the same role within his academy as that performed by Ōhira in the Norinaga School. Kanetane's role, therefore, was to preserve his father's teachings and avoid the radical intellectual innovation that his father had pursued. Ōhira had also been interested in the preservation of Norinaga's scholarship. Ōhira, however, had earned some repute as a scholar, which generally eluded Kanetane.

nativists under a common banner, the bearer of which was his father, Atsutane. Thus, Naketane claimed the leadership position within the Norinaga School for his father, a position to which the sole possession of the *dōtō* entitled Atsutane. The *Kiyosōhansho* explains Atsutane's ascent within the Norinaga School, which its collected documents proved. Moreover, both of Norinaga's sons were dead by 1834, and no one could assert their privileged legitimacy claims. The *Kiyosōhansho*, when viewed in the larger context of the Norinaga School, was a definitive declaration that Atsutane had inherited the whole of the Kokugaku tradition.

Conclusion

The dream and the *norito* were potent devices crucial to Atsutane's effort to prove his orthodox succession of Norinaga. As we saw in the previous chapter, the scholars who participated in the *Sandaikō* debate struggled over the power to define the boundaries of legitimate membership in the Norinaga School for the first time in its institutional history. The crucial outcome of the debate was the articulation of the School's "L-orthodoxy," which was the philological investigation of classical literature in order to recover the ancient Way. The leading scholars of the Norinaga School assumed that there could only be one true successor, namely, the son of the founder. Since Norinaga had founded the Suzunoya, Motoori Ōhira was his only legitimate successor. The de facto rules of succession were those of the *iemoto* system.

With legitimacy defined in this way, Atsutane found himself relegated to the margins of the Norinaga School. Kido Chidate and the students in his Nudenoya hoped to strip Atsutane of membership entirely. Atsutane had to make a decision. He could accept the debate's outcome and reorient the direction of his scholarship to accommodate this declared orthodoxy; he could also simply leave the Norinaga School entirely and adopt a new scholarly identity. He chose neither of these options. Atsutane decided to reject the views of his critics and claim a position of leadership for himself. Since Ōhira was the acknowledged head of the Norinaga School, Atsutane had to create a new leadership post to occupy. He focused on the ancient Way and argued that literary scholarship and textual study revealed only its minor aspects; his emphasis on eschatology revealed it in all of its fullness and splendor. Atsutane claimed to inherit this wisdom from his eighteenth-century predecessors, as well as from antiquity. He claimed, therefore, the mantle of an "O-orthodoxy," symbolized by the *dōtō*, in which succession was not determined by the *iemoto* system, but by the spiritual relationship of master and apprentice. The Norinaga School was part of a much grander scholarly tradition of nativism. It was the leadership of this tradition that Atsutane claimed for himself.

The trajectory of Atsutane's rise to prominence was the partial result of his conscious efforts coupled with luck and serendipity. The two most important examples of the latter were Nakatsune's *norito* and Atsutane's dream of 1805. Both of these bolstered Atsutane's contention that nativism had its own *dōtō*. Nakatsune's *norito* supported the idea that Atsutane had received Norinaga's true teachings, which had eluded all others in the Norinaga School. For those who accepted the legitimacy of Atsutane's dream of 1805, it was further proof that he had become one of Norinaga's direct disciples. The dream assumed its legitimating potential not solely through Atsutane's efforts, but inadvertently through those of his critics. In letters sent to one another, they raised objections concerning the use of the dream as the grounds for admission into the Norinaga School. Atsutane and Kanetane acquired these letters, which they published along with a copy of Nakatsune's *norito* in 1834. They understood that the dream could play a major role in the nativist *dōtō*, alongside Nakatsune's third-party sanction.

Ōkuni Takamasa formally enshrined Atsutane in the *shiushi* with his *Gakutō benron* (1857):

All people develop. Not only people, but flora and fauna develop, too. Not only the flora and fauna, but mountains, rivers, and the earth all develop. When we look at the teachings of the realm, they, too, develop. The selection of lineages and the return to correctness is the development of Chinese Confucians. The transmission of the lineage and reverence for its founder is the development of the Indian Buddhists. The execution of the lineage and the desire to reach the truth of creation is the development of Western knowledge. From the beginning, the imperial realm [Japan] has had the Great Way. However, there has been no one to guide [us in] it like a true leader. Since antiquity, we have studied the scholarship of foreign lands and did not establish the scholarship of the imperial realm. Consequently, the ancient matters that the early emperors had transmitted have been almost [completely] lost. For this reason, two or three heroes have descended from heaven and studied our ancient practices. They have founded a form of learning that charters our imperial lineage. They are Master Hagura Azumamaro, Master Okabe Mabuchi, Master Motoori Norinaga, and Master Hirata Atsutane.[138]

It is important to remember, however, that Takamasa's recognition of Atsutane was simply a replication of Atsutane's own views, as articulated in the *Tamadasuki*. Moreover, it is clear from Takamasa's text, about which more will be said later in this study, that he had important legitimacy claims of his own, especially when one considers the fact that he was *not* a registered student in the Ibukinoya. For the purposes of the present discussion, however, his recognition of Atsutane was important as an indication of the power and influence of the Hirata School during the bakumatsu period. Thus, Takamasa's observation was a significant index of the dominance of the Hirata School over its rivals. Moreover, the *Gakutō benron* was also significant because of its discussion of the nature of succession in Kokugaku; again, this was nothing original to Takamasa, since it was the articulation of ideas formulated by Atsutane and his followers leading up to 1834.

These views of succession transformed nativism from the narrow preservation of an *iemoto* lineage, as was the case with the Norinaga School, into a full-fledged tradition that transcended it. The drive to broaden the scope of nativism began during Atsutane's lifetime and was completed in the decade following his death. Norinaga had explicitly shunned attempts to expand his academy. Motoori Ōhira, however, oversaw the expansion of the Suzunoya into the Norinaga School, despite Norinaga's reservations. Atsutane, girded by the support of a national following, claimed the leadership of nativism in the aftermath of Ōhira's death. Thus, the nativism of the Norinaga School was finally transformed into Kokugaku.

---

138. Ōkuni Takamasa, *Gakutō benron*, p. 460.

SIX

Forsaking Textualism: Ancient History and the Supernatural

We can divide the first twenty years or so of the nineteenth century into two distinct stages in the development of Atsutane's scholarship. In the initial stage, he wrote the *Shinkishinron* and the *Kamōsho* in order to establish himself as a member of the Norinaga School. The publication of the *Tama no mihashira* represented the second stage of his early career. With this text, Atsutane attempted to shift the focus of the school away from textualism and philology to eschatological matters. This attempt to reorient the school's intellectual direction incurred the collective wrath of its established leadership, who were compelled to attack Atsutane and his scholarship as heterodox.

Rather than recant his controversial interpretations of antiquity, Atsutane chose to remain defiant, convinced that his most vocal critics would never come over to his side. During the mature years of his career, two new trends developed in his scholarship. The first of these was a concern for the peasantry. The members of the Norinaga School privileged the emotional experiences of the ancients as authentic expressions of native culture; these experiences were accurately recorded in the classical texts, which nativists carefully and rigorously analyzed. Atsutane agreed with this assessment, adding that scholars could find vestiges of these emotional expressions in the lives of contemporary commoners. Thus, he turned his attention to the practices of the peasantry, seeing in them a spiritual continuum with their ancient forebears.

At the same time, we must contextualize Atsutane's interests in rural society within the framework of his efforts to earn a livelihood as a professional scholar. As he praised the agricultural labors of the peasantry, he directed his disciples to actively recruit new members from the rural areas of central Japan. The publication of farming manuals facilitated this effort, and they helped to spread the influence of his teachings, as well as generating much-needed income. Atsutane, however, never abandoned his desire to become an officially appointed domainal scholar (*shikan*). His attempt to seek employment as a scholar of the Mito School was perhaps the most important attempt that he undertook. His ultimate rejection by the Mito School indicates how ideologically extreme his scholarship had become, especially his vehement rejection of Confucianism.

The second major trend during the mature phase of Atsutane's scholarship was a fundamental shift in his eschatological interests. His study of the afterlife antedated his enrollment in the Norinaga School; consequently, he attempted to demonstrate the relevance of the afterlife to antiquity in both of his first two scholarly treatises. He insisted that the essence of ancient wisdom concerned the importance of the afterlife to the living; this was where Atsutane departed radically from the majority of the School's members. Moreover, he decided that the crucial evidence needed to explicate the wisdom of the ancients was difficult to glean by an exclusive reliance on the classical sources. Consequently, Atsutane began to investigate the link between the supernatural experiences of commoners and eschatology. He believed that his research into these areas was still a scholarly endeavor, since he retained the framework of Kōshōgaku, the accepted methodology of the Norinaga School.

These two developments in Atsutane's scholarship were related. His valorization of the peasantry as a resource for understanding ancient history broadened the scope of his own academy's membership, laying the foundation for its popularity during the bakumatsu period. In the years leading up to the Meiji period, the number of his rural followers eclipsed that of the registered students of other nativist academies. Even during his lifetime, this increasing popularity allowed him to assert more of his intellectual independence from the Norinaga School. Rather than argue for the relevance of eschatology to antiquity, he pursued investigations into the supernatural by itself, citing evidence that was almost completely nontextual in nature.

Spirits, Ghosts, and Ancient History

Atsutane composed several treatises in the genre of what he called *koshi* (ancient history). The scholarly interest in antiquity, of course, was not new in his time. His contemporaries in Edo, Ban Nobutomo and Oyamada Tomokiyo especially, carefully examined the texts of remote antiquity in order to reconstruct an accurate image of ancient life. Such scholarship had its origins in the *yūsoku kojitsu* (scholarship on the customs of antiquity) of the Muromachi period, evolving into the more rigorous scholarship of Kōshōgaku during the Tokugawa period. Like his colleagues in Edo, Atsutane was also engaged in a careful, textual examination of the past.

Among the most prominent of Atsutane's works on ancient history, the *Koshi seibun* and the *Koshiden* stand as the most significant, and they were both among the texts that Atsutane submitted to Emperor Ninkō in 1823.[1] Drawing inspiration from Norinaga's *Kojiki-den*, he composed his own monumental treatise on antiquity, in 28 *kan*. Unlike Norinaga, he did not limit himself to the explication of one particular classical text. Norinaga had analyzed the *Kojiki* by comparing it with other classical sources like the *Man'yōshū* and the *Wamyōsho*. By deciphering the classical history, the *Kojiki-den* was reminiscent of earlier efforts by Mabuchi and Keichū. Atsutane, however, eschewed the linguistic and philological efforts of his predecessors in favor of a Shinto-centered portrayal of antiquity. Without specific references to particular classical sources, he culled various texts, most notably the *Kojiki* and the *Nihongi*, and fabricated an ancient history written in a style similar to that of the authentic classical histories themselves. Thus, his *Koshiden* functioned as a kind of scripture and as its accompanying exegesis, both of which Atsutane himself authored.

In the *Koshiden*, Atsutane sought to validate his cosmological interpretations with scriptural authority. In the *Tama no mihashira*,

---

1. Watanabe K., *Hirata Atsutane kenkyū*, p. 78.

he had focused specifically on the *kamiyo* chapters of the *Kojiki* and *Nihongi*. In this earlier text, he had demonstrated that the common interpretations of Yomi were false, arguing that it was in fact the moon and not the destination of the soul. Using evidence from an array of classical sources, he had argued that while there was little textual evidence regarding the afterlife, there were subtle references to a hidden realm of souls, which he asserted was the real hereafter. He called this hidden realm the *yūmeikai* and claimed that Ōkuninushi-no-kami dwelled there as its deity. Thus, the souls of the deceased resided in this hidden realm where Ōkuninushi decided their eternal fate after reviewing their earthly conduct. Knowledge of the afterlife, he asserted, was the essential element in apprehending Kokugaku; it was the *hashira* (pillar) that supported scholarship itself. Although he had highlighted the centrality of cosmology and the afterlife in the *Tama no mihashira*, his goal in the genre of ancient history was to minimize its importance in order to blend it into his interpretation of ancient history. His ideas on the hidden realm of souls and spirits were still important to his thought and scholarship in general, but he had to push them into the background of Japanese antiquity in order to ground them scripturally.

The Koshiden

Atsutane composed the prodigious *Koshiden* over a period of more than a decade, beginning the text in 1812 and completing it sometime around 1826. He labored on the *Koshi seibun*, which focused on *kamiyo* specifically, from 1811 to 1818. Kanetane claimed that his father viewed the *Koshiden* as the most important statement of his thought, and he admonished his students in the Ibukinoya to study the text, along with the *Tama no mihashira* and the *Tamadasuki*. Under the direction of Kanetane, the *Koshiden* became the fundamental statement of Hirata Kokugaku; for some, the *Koshiden* was scripture itself.[2] The *Tama no mihashira* represented Atsutane's

---

2. Anne Walthall gives a very detailed description of the activities of the Ina Valley disciples of the Hirata School, one of its main centers of rural support during the bakumatsu period. An important achievement of the Ina Valley disciples was the publication of the *Koshiden*; see Walthall, *The Weak Body of a Useless Woman*, p. 105.

first work on the existence of the hidden realm of spirits, but the *Tamadasuki* elaborated on it and, furthermore, outlined a history of Kokugaku that placed him thoroughly within its orthodox tradition. Thus, modern scholars use these as the fundamental texts of Hirata Kokugaku.

Most of Atsutane's conclusions regarding classical literature in the *Koshiden* were consistent with those of earlier nativists, particularly Mabuchi and Norinaga. Moreover, his statements concerning the *yūmeikai* were identical to those he had made in the *Tama no mihashira*, perhaps because he composed the two in succession. One important element of the *Koshiden* that is conspicuously absent from the *Tama no mihashira*, however, is the association of cosmic creation with the *yūmeikai*. Atsutane attempted not only to place such an idea within the framework of ancient history but also to explain its cosmic and divine significance. His interpretation is important because it was central to the Sōmō no Kokugaku (grassroots Kokugaku) of the bakumatsu period.

As he had done in the *Tama no mihashira*, Atsutane began his ancient history with the creation of the cosmos. The deity Amenominakanushi had existed before creation itself;[3] as the creator deity in Shinto, he was the uncreated Creator.[4] Atsutane made it clear, however, that Amenominakanushi and Kuninotokotachi were separate deities, an interpretation that contradicted a common theological tenet of doctrinal Shinto (1: 100).[5] Shinto theologians viewed Kuninotokotachi as the creator of the world, a function similar to Amenominakanushi's creation of the cosmos. Atsutane insisted that the world and the cosmos were not identical, and he privileged the creation of the latter and thus Amenominakanushi as well.[6]

---

3. Hirata Atsutane, *Koshiden*, p. 91. Subsequent references to this work are cited in the text.

4. While some scholars attribute Atsutane's interpretation of Amenominakanushi as a subtle insertion of Judeo-Christian monotheism into Shinto, it is clear that the notion of an uncreated creator god was neither new nor controversial in his time and appears in the *Kojiki* itself. Moreover, his creator deity had no significant theological function.

5. This was a notion supported by the Watarai house of Ise Shinto.

6. Perhaps the distinction between the universe and the world implicit in Atsutane's theology was the result of his study of Western astronomy; see Chapter 4.

As the creator deity, Amenominakanushi's role in the creation of the cosmos was an indirect one. Instead of creating the entirety of the cosmos himself, he created the two Musubi-no-kami, Takamimusubi and Kamumimusubi, whose union began the chain of creation. Consequently, the two Musubi deities also represented male and female. Thus, Amenominakanushi was less a creator deity than the one who made creation possible by generating the Musubi gods.

The Musubi-no-kami were responsible for the *yorozu no mono* or *banbutsu* (myriad things) via their sexual union (1: 122–23). In addition to the physical contents of the universe, they also created the other "eighty thousand" *kami* who populated it (1: 223). These *kami* became natural phenomena such as mountains, rivers, and waterfalls, which the Japanese still view as manifestations of *kami*; like the "myriad things," their collective creation represented nature. The deities produced during this creation process initiated by the Musubi-no-kami were Izanagi and Izanami, who were responsible for the creation of Japan. Dipping his spear into the brine of creation, Izanagi deposited the muck on the surface of the brine, forming the islands of Japan. Izanagi and Izanami also produced two of the most significant deities in the Shinto pantheon: Amaterasu and Susanō. According to Atsutane, Izanagi was especially important because he created both deities: "After washing the left eye, the name of the *kami* who emerged was Tsuki-sakaki-izu-no-mitama-zukara-mukatsu-hime-no-mikoto, also known as Amaterasu-ō-mikami. . . . After washing his right eye, the *kami* who emerged was Tsukuyomi-no-mikoto, also known as Take-haya-susanō-no-mikoto."[7]

Amaterasu's status as the sun goddess is a fundamental tenet of Shinto even today; her name, in fact, means "to shine in heaven." Atsutane's interpretation of Amaterasu's brother, Susanō, was quite controversial. In Shinto theology since the medieval period, Susanō was known as the storm god and ruler of the seas; he was a *kami* who was responsible for terror and misfortune, owing to the polluted circumstances of his association with Yomi. He repre-

---

7. Hirata Atsutane, *Koshi seibun*, pp. 28–29. Note that there are various accounts of *kamiyo*, including one that describes Susanō as the child of Izanagi and Izanami.

sented darkness and evil in contrast to Amaterasu's shining goodness. Atsutane's account did not depart from this prevailing view: "[Izanagi] said to Amaterasu-ō-mikami, 'You are to rule over Takama-no-hara,' which he then commanded her to do. . . . Thus, [she] received this command, and she took charge of Takama-no-hara. Next, [Izanagi] said to Take-haya-susanō-no-mikoto, 'You are to rule over Ao-una-bara-shio-no-yaoe [the seas].'"[8] Atsutane was not satisfied with this theological contrast. As the opposite of the sun goddess, he reasoned, Susanō was also the god of the moon, Tsukiyomi (or Tsukuyomi)-no-mikoto (3: 359). Atsutane argued that Izanagi banished Susanō to Yomi: "Izanagi-no-mikoto grew very angry [with Susanō] and said [to him], 'Leave this realm. Since you ruled over it, there has been much misfortune.' [Izanagi] told him to take charge of Yoru-no-osu-kuni [in Yomi]."[9] Although he cited philological evidence in various works in support of this contention, the logical contrast seemed to be sufficient for him. By severing the bond between Susanō and the hereafter, he was able to offer a new interpretation of the latter, not as the dank world of the dead but as an unseen realm of spirits that coexisted with the visible realm of the living (3: 178). The term "Yomi" itself, when correctly glossed as "night-seeing," he argued, was another name for the moon. He did not dispute its existence; he only reinterpreted the idea of the afterlife itself. These were all conclusions that he had previously reached in the *Tama no mihashira*.

As previously mentioned, Atsutane referred to the true afterlife as the *yūmeikai*. Since Susanō was the god of the moon, he asserted that Ōkuninushi had to be its primary deity. Ōkuninushi presided over the *kakurigoto* (hidden affairs), which Atsutane argued were identical to Norinaga's *kamigoto* (3: 159). Ōkuninushi's administration of the hidden realm of the afterlife contrasts with the administration of the *utsushigoto* or *arawagoto* (manifest affairs) of the emperor, as the divine descendant of the *kami*:

When Ōkuninushi-no-kami faced the realm [the earth], hefting a large pike, he said to the two deities, "With this pike, I rule [the earth], even

---

8. Ibid., p. 30.
9. Ibid.

now. If Sumemima-no-mikoto [the emperor] were to rule the realm with this pike, there would absolutely be peace. The manifest affairs that I have ruled over, I should now turn over to Sumemima-no-mikoto. I will depart and will rule the hidden affairs."[10]

Thus, the souls of the deceased made the transition from serving the emperor to serving Ōkuninushi in the afterlife. Such a conception of parallel worlds was potentially subversive politically for two reasons. First, it significantly reduced the divine role of Amaterasu in the daily affairs of the people, and it amplified the importance of Ōkuninushi. This was tantamount to heresy, especially among Shinto theologians in Kyoto who served the imperial household. Second, the bakufu had no role in either the visible or hidden realms—that is, neither in the world of the living nor in that of the dead. Atsutane did preserve the sanctity of the emperor, which made his brand of theology palatable to supporters of imperial restoration during the bakumatsu period. In any event, his extreme views, while securing distinction for his scholarship, also alienated significant groups, thereby eliminating any chance for gainful scholarly employment, as we will discuss later.

The Musubi deities not only produced the islands of Japan and their flora and fauna but also created the Japanese people. This was their highest blessing and a cornerstone of Atsutane's work on ancient history. He was careful to note that the progeny of the Musubi-no-kami, Izanagi and Amaterasu, have a more direct role in the governance of the people. For this reason, he argued, scholars of antiquity must understand that, as a fundamental principle, the people must revere Izanagi and Amaterasu in return for their divine blessings and love (1: 222). The *aohitogusa* (the people) have their origins in the eighty thousand *kami* of the Musubi-no-kami (1: 223). The Musubi-no-kami created the people, while Izanagi created the islands of Japan and produced the imperial ancestor and sun goddess Amaterasu. After the creation of the people, Ōkuninushi and the *kami* Sukunabikona blessed them with the means to thrive:

The two *kami* provided the knowledge for curing illness to the people and to the animals. They sought to rectify the evils [brought on by] birds,

---

10. Ibid., p. 68.

beasts, and the insect hordes; [thus,] they provided [the people] with magical incantations. For this reason, the people (*ōmitakara*) have received all of their blessings (*mitamanofuyu*) until now. These were all miraculous signs. Moreover, Sukunabikona-no-kami was the *kami* who first made saké.[11]

In this scheme, he claimed that the people owed their very existence and that of their homeland to *kami* charged with the creation of the cosmos (1: 238–39). The Japanese people ultimately had their origins in the *zōka no kami* (creation gods), namely, the Musubi-no-kami. The study of cosmology, therefore, had a significant religious motivation. It showed Shinto adherents how they were intimately connected to the *kami* of creation.

Atsutane's view of the people revealed an inclination toward peasants and their work. As Confucian scholars had argued for centuries, the ancient sage-king Shennong was responsible for creating the techniques of agriculture in remote antiquity. This innovation, and many more made by other sages and early kings, made human civilization possible. Shennong's historicity was never determined; so it is not surprising that he was also revered as an agricultural deity in China. Atsutane, like the Confucians, located the origin of agriculture in remote antiquity. Instead of an emphasis on technique, which Ogyū Sorai felt was the product of the innovative genius of the ancient sages, Atsutane stressed the blessings of the natural elements—including the soil, water, and favorable weather—essential for the abundant growth of crops, especially rice (1: 289). Japan, he declared, was a nation of rice. Thus, peasants owed both their existence and their livelihoods to the *kami*. This was yet another compelling reason for the peasantry to repay the divine blessings of the *kami*. As a divinely ordained nation of rice, the identity of Japan itself was linked to the peasantry. Although he did not make a direct statement about warriors, artisans, or merchants, the implication was that these non-cultivating classes owed a debt to the peasantry. In the *Koshiden*, he clearly emphasized the relationship between the peasantry and the *kami*. As we will see later, his disciples focused on the implicit hierarchy of the

---

11. Ibid., p. 54.

peasantry over the non-cultivating classes, especially warriors, in formulating an anti-bakufu ideology.

Good and Evil

Atsutane admonished peasants to work diligently at their cultivation as a repayment for the blessings of the *kami* and as a sign of respect for them. Through their diligent work, they also served as loyal subjects of the emperor, the ruler of the "manifest affairs" of the living. Though Atsutane repeatedly instructed the peasantry to work hard, he was aware that the emperor, as ruler of the living world, was incapable of directly overseeing the activities of his subjects. As Norinaga had observed decades earlier, good was not always rewarded and evil not always punished, as the Confucians believed and as was symbolized by the Mandate of Heaven. For Atsutane, the hard work of the peasantry constituted good earthly conduct. He argued that Norinaga's observation was especially applicable to the peasantry. Very often, hard-working peasants suffered hardship, while those who did not directly work the land were rewarded with wealth. For this reason, the creation deities assigned Ōkuninushi to the *yūmeikai*. In his role as overlord, he administered divine justice in the afterlife by assessing the moral quality of the deceased's conduct in life. Therefore, though Norinaga's observations regarding good and evil may hold true in the realm of the living, Ōkuninushi insured that goodness was rewarded and evil punished after death:

> Those who endeavor to act with virtue, when entering the afterlife (*kakuryō*), receive the eternal, sacred reward of the Great *kami* [Ōkuninushi] and are put to use. This is genuine bliss. Those absorbed in arrogance and frivolity, when entering the afterlife, cannot escape the Great *kami*'s sacred punishment and are cast aside. This is a genuine disaster. (3: 175)

Atsutane's reflections on the nature of good and evil were not voluminous, even in such a massive work as the *Koshiden*. Perhaps this was a response to the copious studies of the subject by Confucians, especially Neo-Confucians. For Atsutane, the Musubi-no-kami were pure goodness, as evidenced by their creation of the cosmos. As the descendants of the Musubi-no-kami, the people were endowed with this original goodness, which, following Mabuchi, he called the *magokoro* (3: 172). Thus, it was only natural for peasants to cultivate the land diligently, since this was consistent with the intention of the Musubi-no-kami. The notion of original goodness sounds alarmingly similar to the Neo-Confucian idea of *honzen no sei*. The fundamental difference lies in the conceptualization of evil. While the Neo-Confucians argued that one gradually lost this original goodness, forcing people to engage in rigorous moral training and self-rectification in an effort to regain it, Atsutane located evil in the pernicious influence of *magakami magamono* (evil gods, evil beings). Drawing on prevailing Shinto views of pollution and purity, he argued that such evil spirits were produced by Izanagi's pollution in Yomi (1: 173). Thus, evil spirits deceived peasants into ignoring their natural inclination to work hard. In the afterlife, Ōkuninushi assessed the conduct of souls and decided whether or not the *magokoro* of the *kami* was upheld in life.

Phantom Scholarship

The centrality of spirits in Atsutane's view of evil is not surprising given his deep interest in the afterlife. Although his work on ancient history was important, he was constrained by the nature of the genre and the classical sources at his disposal. He was not as precise with his sources as his colleagues and predecessors; yet the classics still did not present him with enough evidence to prove his eschatological conclusions. He insisted that there was textual evidence to support the existence of spirits, but the reality was that the ancient chroniclers had little to say about such phenomena. Rather than follow Norinaga's precedent and end his investigation once the classical sources were exhausted, he decided to forge ahead, even without textual evidence. He believed that the demonstration of the real existence of spirits was absolutely essential to grasping the ancient Way. Consequently, he abandoned the classical sources in an effort to develop his scholarship on the supernatural and the otherworldly.

There were three distinct stages in the formation of his scholarship. Atsutane's first discourse on the supernatural was the *Shinkishinron* (1805), which he did not publish but did revise for publication under the slightly different title of *Kishinshinron* (1820). The basic ideas of the two texts, however, are essentially the same; they constituted his contribution to the debate on the nature of *kishin* (or *kijin*) that had embroiled Confucian scholars of the previous century. As an ambitious young scholar in 1805, his views of *kishin* echoed elements of the arguments made by the two opposing sides within this Confucian debate. He identified these two groups as the scholars of Song Learning and those of Han Learning. The scholars of the former were mostly associated with Neo-Confucianism, specifically the Daoxue scholarship associated with the Cheng brothers of the Northern Song and Zhu Xi of the Southern Song. The scholars of Han Learning were associated with the brand of scholarship developed during the Former Han dynasty and characterized by a sensitivity to authoritative textual sources. In the Qing dynasty, this brand of scholarship adopted the "evidential" techniques that had their origins in the Ming dynasty. In seventeenth- and eighteenth-century Japan, many prominent scholars identified themselves with the Song tradition of Confucianism, including Hayashi Razan and Yamazaki Ansai. Atsutane criticized these "Song scholars" for their interpretations of *kijin*, and he was especially critical of their disdain for the supernatural. Song Neo-Confucians employed a certain inductive approach to the natural world in their attempt to understand its "principles." They called this approach "the investigation of things and the exhaustion of principle" (Jp. *kakubutsu kyū-ri*). Such a method, Atsutane argued, gave them a false confidence in their ability to know about the world, as well as in the knowledge that they gathered from it. He praised the Neo-Confucians, however, for their recognition of the importance of *kishin* to Confucius. They understood that Confucius was aware of the political and administrative utility of *kishin* for the ruler. Atsutane, however, argued that the methodological self-assurance of the Neo-Confucians did not serve them well in broader matters of the supernatural; they could not possibly know as much as they claimed.

On the other hand, Atsutane's criticisms of the Han Learning scholars were no less harsh. Unfortunately, he did not specifically name any of the scholars he viewed as *kangakusha* (scholars of Han Learning) in the *Shinkishinron*; in later texts, however, he made references to Itō Jinsai, Ogyū Sorai, and Dazai Shundai as representative of this particular Confucian group.[12] Sorai and especially Shundai acknowledged that there was a potential utility in *kishin* as instruments of political control. Neither scholar was particularly interested in the investigation of *kishin* as a matter of the supernatural, and Shundai expressed doubt that such phenomena even existed. Before Shundai, Jinsai had also expressed doubts about the existence of *kishin*, arguing that whether they existed or not, there was no textual evidence to indicate that Confucius made any direct statements about them. Thus, Atsutane critically regarded Han Learning scholars of this kind as "narrow-minded," because they could not believe in something that they could not directly observe:

> In Sorai's *Shariki* it says, "What later Confucians see is mostly inferior to [what] the Buddhists [see]." Just as he said, all Buddhists and those who do not pursue scholarship are not confused by eschatological matters [*yūmei no koto*] or the supernatural [*ayashiki koto*]. However, those who unskillfully pursue Han Learning dismiss [such things] and their minds have become narrow. They try utterly to denounce eschatological matters and the supernatural.[13]

Contrary to Jinsai, he declared that Confucius had acknowledged the existence of *kishin*, but had placed them beyond the grasp of the human intellect.[14] On this account, Atsutane argued that Confucius was correct. Thus, the Neo-Confucians were incorrect in their assumption that they could fathom the supernatural with their flawed methodologies; the Han Learning scholars had erred in their doubts over the existence of *kishin*. Though detailed knowledge of the *kishin*, as sought by the Neo-Confucians, was not possible, the existence of the *kishin* was a matter of faith for Atsutane. On this subject, he agreed with Arai Hakuseki's observations a century earlier:

---

12. Atsutane used this designation for Confucians who used the techniques of evidential learning. John Brownlee pushes the advent of evidential learning further back into the seventeenth century to include Hayashi Razan and the scholars of the Mito domain (*Japanese Historians and the National Myths, 1600–1945*, p. 19). Atsutane placed these scholars in the category of Song Learning.

13. Hirata Atsutane, *Kishinshinron*, pp. 52–53.

14. Ibid., p. 45.

Arai Kinmi [Hakuseki] said that the subject of spirits is truly difficult to discuss. It is not merely difficult to discuss, it is difficult to hear. It is not merely difficult to hear, it is also difficult to believe. The difficulty in belief is due to difficulty in knowing. Thus, after one [sincerely] expresses belief, one will hear well. After one knows [about spirits] well, one will believe [sincerely].[15]

Despite never publishing the *Shinkishinron*, Atsutane expanded his research into the related subject of the afterlife. The *Tama no mihashira* was the result of this work. Unlike his earlier work, the *Tama no mihashira* was his first attempt to investigate eschatology using classical Japanese sources. It represents the second developmental stage in his research. He attempted to resolve the controversy initiated by Hattori Nakatsune concerning the nature of Yomi, supporting Nakatsune's contention that it was the moon since such a position allowed him to completely reconceptualize the afterlife. Atsutane argued for the existence of an unseen realm of spirits ruled by Ōkuninushi.

Perhaps the fundamental difference between the *Tama no mihashira* and the *Shinkishinron* is that the former dealt primarily with the issue of the *tama no yukue*, while the latter dealt with the nature of the *kishin*. Atsutane began his nativist career with an interest in the supernatural and then moved on to the nature of the hereafter. Ten years after completing the *Tama no mihashira*, Atsutane wrote a treatise that dealt with both of these issues. The *Senkyō ibun* is perhaps his most important text focused on phantoms and their world, and it is one of several that he wrote during the 1820s. In this text, which represents the third developmental stage, he attempted to document concrete evidence in support of his contention regarding the existence of the *yūmeikai*; the text also supplied details concerning the spirits and phantoms that resided in this hidden realm. Moreover, this text represented a clear break with the search for scriptural and textual evidence to support his interpretations—the defining methodological approach of scholars in the Norinaga School and one that he himself had used when writing the *Shinkishinron* and the *Tama no mihashira*.

---

15. Ibid., p. 59.

Atsutane learned about the psychic exploits of an Edo shaman, Takayama Torakichi.[16] During the 1820s, Torakichi, though still in his middle teens, made claims about personal encounters with *tengu* (goblins) and *akuma* (demons), the narratives of which fascinated Edo townspeople, Atsutane being no exception. Atsutane heard from nativist colleagues about Torakichi's willingness to meet with those who were curious and to answer their queries about the supernatural realm, so he invited Torakichi to his home in 1822 and convened a series of meetings with him that lasted several months. During these sessions, Atsutane, his students, and his Edo colleagues participated in the questioning of Torakichi. In front of these audiences, Torakichi claimed that years earlier he had met a mountain hermit at a festival who performed feats of magic and divination. Torakichi, who had exhibited mystical powers of his own,[17] approached the hermit and asked him to teach him more about fortunetelling. This meeting initiated a series of encounters between the two that eventually culminated in Torakichi's journey to the hermit's home atop Mount Nandaijō in Hitachi province. It was at this point, Torakichi claimed, that he began his five-year training as a shaman.

Atsutane recorded the details of these meetings and published them as the *Senkyō ibun*, a virtual transcript of his interviews with Torakichi. Most of the questions that Atsutane put to Torakichi dealt with the materiality of the supernatural realm. Torakichi claimed that his teacher, the mountain recluse, had conducted most of his training during Torakichi's visits to the world of spirits and demons. Torakichi's account of the mountain summit seemed to conflict with Atsutane's description of the *yūmeikai*. Torakichi's description conformed to aspects of folk belief in the magical nature of mountains, especially their summits. In the *Tama no mihashira*, Atsutane insisted that gravesites were portals that led to the *yūmeikai*. Apparently, he saw no reason to reconcile his interpretation with Torakichi's account.

Atsutane's interest in the materiality of Torakichi's fantastic realm extended to such mundane matters as the daily life of super-

---

16. Torakichi took the surname Takayama upon joining the Ibukinoya in 1822.
17. Hirata Atsutane, *Senkyō ibun*, p. 362.

natural beings. For instance, he posed a question to Torakichi concerning the nature of food and drink in the other realm. Torakichi informed him that while the food was essentially identical to that of humans, the tea that such phantasmal beings imbibed was quite different.[18] Torakichi nevertheless provided no explanation of the difference. Moreover, in reply to a query concerning recreational pursuits in the other realm, Torakichi replied that while demons and spirits were fond of *go*, they were not familiar with *shōgi*, which, he claimed, did not exist in their world. Again, no explanation was given for such seemingly innocuous disparities between the natural world and that of the supernatural.

Atsutane was interested mostly in the actual beings that populated the spirit realm described by Torakichi. He was especially interested in the sheer variety of creatures that Torakichi claimed to have seen. Torakichi told him that most hermits (*sennin*) who, like his teacher, lived in the mountains, were, in fact, *tengu*.[19] Such beings moved freely between their realm and the human realm; during their frequent visits, however, they had to assume a human disguise. Their preferred mode of travel was flying, and for this purpose they were equipped with wings.[20] Indeed, this was the means that he and his teacher had used in their travels to the distant places they had visited over the course of his five-year training. Not only did *tengu* fly between the two realms, they also used their flying ability to visit foreign lands. On many occasions, Torakichi claimed, he accompanied his teacher on these trips abroad, noting how cosmopolitan his teacher was by virtue of the many languages that he could speak while on such visits.

Torakichi portrayed *tengu* as rather benign creatures, which conflicted with their popular image as malevolent monsters. Perhaps frustrated with such a positive account, Atsutane asked him to describe encounters with frightful creatures, since he was certain that the spirit realm had no shortage of them. Much to Atsutane's relief, Torakichi acknowledged that he had. First of all, he asserted that while many if not most *tengu* were not especially evil, a few

---

18. Ibid., p. 477.
19. Ibid., p. 450.
20. Ibid., p. 517.

were quite diabolical. Commonly, people mistakenly equated all *tengu* with another category of supernatural creature, the *akuma*, which were genuinely demonic in nature. Torakichi insisted that this perception was mistaken.[21] Invoking his more accurate knowledge of the supernatural, he declared that his teacher was not a true *tengu*, but a member of a special group of mortals who had access to the spirit realm; Torakichi himself was such a privileged individual. Much of the mayhem among the living was caused by the pernicious activities of the *akuma*, which attempted to wreak havoc on the earth. Torakichi insisted that the most terrifying creatures in the spirit world were the *yōma* (specters).[22] Unlike the *akuma*, whose origin and nature he never clarified, he described these specters as the corrupted souls of humans condemned to endure divine punishment for their conduct.[23] This description, of course, dovetailed nicely with Atsutane's account of judgment in the afterlife administered by Ōkuninushi, even though Atsutane never specified any precise punishments for evil conduct. In this instance, Torakichi provided him with the crucial details that he had overlooked in his own writings.

Atsutane ended his text with Torakichi's negative views of social elites, especially scholars and wealthy merchants. The rich, Torakichi contended, were disrespectful to the *kami* because they pursued money at the expense of agricultural labor. Instead of working for the benefit of society in compliance with the will of the gods, they were consumed by greed and flagrantly flaunted the tenets of Shinto.[24] Torakichi identified merchant activity with the *madō* (way of evil). Scholars were another example of those who had turned their backs on the gods in the pursuit of book learning instead of divine knowledge. The mysterious phenomena of the supernatural could not be found in the books coveted by scholars. As a result, these scholars were convinced that such matters had no real existence, since they were under the false impression that all of human knowledge was contained in the classics:

---

21. Ibid., pp. 527–28.
22. Ibid., p. 454.
23. Ibid., p. 468.
24. Ibid., p. 568.

All scholarship [*subete gakumon*] has fallen into the way of evil (*madō*), and this is unfortunate. This is because there is nothing redeeming about it. Thus, no one has attained the true principle [of the afterlife]. Most [scholars] pursue mediocre scholarship and are overly proud of their knowledge of numerous books, viewing with contempt those without book knowledge.[25]

Torakichi's views of both merchants and scholars came very close to Atsutane's interpretations in the *Koshiden*. Although Atsutane did not specifically condemn merchants, he did admonish peasants to engage only in subsistence farming as proper repayment for the blessings of the gods. The implication was that activities that fall outside subsistence agriculture did not constitute such a religious devotion. Moreover, Torakichi's views on scholars were also consistent with those of Atsutane in the *Tamadasuki* and the *Kishinshinron*. Although Torakichi did not specify Confucian scholars, his critique was similar to Atsutane's condemnation of them as ignorant of the supernatural, especially those who engaged in Han Learning. Atsutane insisted, like Torakichi, that knowledge of the supernatural took precedence over all forms of scholarship.

Despite Atsutane's harsh words for Confucians and their false knowledge, he did not indicate alternative sources of evidence for the investigation of the supernatural prior to 1820. The *Senkyō ibun* signified his attempt to resolve this issue. Despite posing quite detailed questions about the world of specters and demonic creatures, he never solicited Torakichi's interpretations of the phenomena that he was asked to describe. Atsutane left theology out of his conversations with Torakichi. Perhaps the most important instance of this interpretive lapse concerned the actual identity of Torakichi's supernatural world. He never asked Torakichi if such a world was, in fact, the *yūmeikai* that was so crucial to Atsutane's scholarship. Clearly, his assumption was that the world described by Torakichi and his own interpretation of the "spirit realm" were the same. Thus, he used Torakichi as an authoritative source on the *yūmeikai* by asking him for seemingly vacuous minutiae regarding the nature of the hereafter, such as whether demons were

---

25. Ibid., p. 567. Compare this with Atsutane's own words in the *Tamadasuki*: "The reading of books is not [true] scholarship (*gakumon*)" (p. 573).

homosexual (the answer was "no").[26] He used his interviews with Torakichi to generate empirical data in support of his own theoretical views. In so doing, he attempted to conduct a kind of evidential research of the supernatural, furnishing his work with the kind of detail reminiscent of the antiquarian studies of his contemporaries, Ban Nobutomo and Oyamada Tomokiyo.[27] This was Atsutane's solution for the dilemma that he had articulated in the *Kishinshinron*. Oddly enough, even though he criticized Confucians for their excessive reliance on textual authority, his *Senkyō ibun*, a compilation of detailed information on the afterlife, itself became a textual source.

Atsutane's Search for Employment

When viewed together, the two trends in Atsutane's scholarship—ancient history and evidential research into the supernatural—illuminate themes that influenced the formation of "grassroots" Kokugaku, especially as his disciples developed it during the bakumatsu period. One such theme was the relationship between the people and the *kami*, which he argued was characterized by mutual love and respect. The people owed their existence to the *kami*, a debt they had to repay through their labors in the fields. Without much concern for the non-cultivating classes, Atsutane clearly privileged the peasants as the beneficiaries of this relationship with the divine. A second theme concerned the relationship between the

---

26. Hirata Atsutane, *Senkyō ibun*, p. 535.

27. Atsutane authored three other major evidential studies of the supernatural during the 1820s. He composed the *Kokon yomikō* (1822), which was an analysis of Buddhist *setsuwa*. He used the tales recorded in medieval compilations to discredit Buddhist interpretations of the afterlife. At about the same time, he wrote a treatise on the allegedly true rebirth account of one Katsugorō. Unlike his study of Buddhist *setsuwa*, this later work, called *Katsugorō saisei kibun* (1823), attempted to demonstrate how the idea of rebirth actually conformed to native eschatology. There was no conflict between the two, Atsutane claimed. In the late 1820s, he finished the *Inō bukkai roku*, perhaps the most interesting of these three evidential works on the supernatural. As he had done with the *Katsugorō saisei kibun*, he analyzed the allegedly true account of a man haunted by an assortment of supernatural creatures. He concluded that the hauntings came to an end once the victim of these occurrences manifested his faith in the power of the *kami*.

people and the supernatural. As the example of Torakichi illustrated for Atsutane, commoners themselves possessed knowledge about the divine and the hereafter; firsthand accounts replaced the classics as authoritative sources of eschatological evidence.

Before turning in the next chapter to the issue of how these themes developed in the "grassroots" Kokugaku of Atsutane's successors, we will briefly discuss the latter half of his career in the context of the expansion of the Hirata School.

Agriculturism and Hirata Kokugaku

Atsutane struggled with extreme poverty at various points during his lifetime. He left Akita for Edo around the age of 24. In order to make his living, he became a physician at the urging of the Hirata family, his adoptive family in Edo, where he studied medicine to become a physician in the service of the Itakura of the Matsuyama domain in Shikoku. Like Norinaga had before, he practiced medicine during the day and held scholarly meetings at his home in the evening. At these meetings, he developed his interests in nativism and was determined to pursue his scholarship full-time. Consequently, much of his time was spent seeking the kind of employment that would allow him to devote himself exclusively to scholarship. In the meantime, he and his followers sought ways to generate income for himself and his academy until such employment materialized.

The emerging industry of agricultural manuals served as an important vehicle for the propagation of Hirata Kokugaku in the last two decades of Atsutane's life. During these years, rural scholars studied developments in agricultural techniques and botany in an effort to improve rural productivity. They were known as "agriculturists," and they published their research in *nōsho* (farm manuals). Beginning in the 1820s, some of these scholars approached Atsutane with the idea of combining efforts for the publication of these manuals. In one instance, the agriculturist Konishi Atsuyoshi (1767–1837) visited the Ibukinoya in Edo and consulted with Kanetane over the publication of one such manual in 1826.[28] Atsutane

---

28. Robertson, "Sexy Rice," p. 249.

and Kanetane realized that these manuals could serve as effective tools for the spread of Atsutane's teachings into the countryside. They did this by linking his cosmological ideas, as articulated in the *Tama no mihashira*, to "the existing practice of gender-based seed and plant selection."[29] Atsutane provided theological explanations for botanical phenomena. This was an important opportunity for Atsutane because it gave him access to the peasantry, who might otherwise never be exposed to his teachings.[30] Farm manuals provided him with a wider audience than the traditional (and expensive) publishing industry could otherwise have offered.

As a corollary benefit, the cooperation between Atsutane's academy and these agriculturists enabled him to cover certain debts that he seemed to incur constantly.[31] This benefit seemed only peripheral, since the principal goal was the propagation of Hirata Kokugaku. In fact, the nativist classicism of Norinaga merged with the goals of scholars like Konishi Atsuyoshi to create the foundation of grassroots Kokugaku. The financial benefits of such a collaborative effort between the members of the Ibukinoya and these rural agricultural scholars are undeniable. In view of Atsutane's general financial problems throughout his career, the economic incentive to work with these scholars was perhaps of more immediate importance to him than the rural spread of his scholarship itself. As the social historian Haga Noboru tells us, not only was Atsutane not a farmer, but he knew almost nothing about farming, and his first contact with the countryside came in 1821, at the age of 45.[32] Atsutane and his disciples viewed the countryside as a reservoir of potential new students. Such recruits had to pay a registration fee in order to attain the status of *monjin* and earn an affiliation with the Ibukinoya. It was the collection of such fees that sustained the academy in Edo and helped to support Atsutane's scholarship. Thus, registration fees served as a crucial source of income for Atsutane and his academy. Such rural students, in turn, helped to recruit others, as well as to collect funds for the publica-

---

29. Ibid., p. 239.
30. Ibid., p. 254.
31. Ibid., p. 258.
32. Haga N., *Bakumatsu kokugaku no kenkyū*, p. 223.

tion of Atsutane's texts.³³ The most prominent instance of this effort was the publication during the bakumatsu period of the *Koshiden*, by students from the Ina Valley of Shimōsa province (in what are today parts of Chiba and Ibaraki prefectures).³⁴

The farm manuals published by the Ibukinoya in conjunction with rural scholars were a crucial tool for the recruitment of students and followers into what became the Hirata School,³⁵ whose financial support helped Atsutane pursue scholarship as the professional that he longed to become. Atsutane's rural recruiting efforts were a success and resulted in the creation of the Hirata School, which achieved a prominent political role during the bakumatsu period. It also generated funds for the support of Atsutane's research, though the funds that his school collected did not provide a steady income. Moreover, he still coveted the kind of employment that his nativist predecessors had enjoyed. Azumamaro had worked as a poetry teacher for a short time for Prince Myōhōin. His son, Arimaro, became the tutor to Tayasu Munetake, a position that he eventually resigned in favor of Mabuchi. Norinaga, who Atsutane regarded as his own mentor, had worked for the lord of Kii, Tokugawa Harusada (1728–89), for whom he composed his famous treatise on politics, the *Hihon tamakushige*; Atsutane's contemporary, Ōhira, inherited this position from Norinaga. Most of the successful nativists who preceded Atsutane had enjoyed official patronage in one form or another. He wanted the same kind of employment not only because it meant a steady income, but also because it could provide him the kind of legitimacy that his illustrious nativist predecessors had had. Thus, it is not surprising that he sought such employment at various points during his lifetime. Perhaps the most important instance of his quest for official employment was his attempt to gain a position within the Mito

---

33. In 1833, Atsutane and Kanetane strategized over how to sustain the publication of Atsutane's works using the funds collected in the rural recruitment effort (Haga N., *Yanagita Kunio to Hirata Atsutane*, p. 181).

34. See Walthall, *The Weak Body of a Useless Woman*, p. 105.

35. I use the term Hirata School to signify (1) those students, especially from rural areas, who joined the Ibukinoya but did not reside in Edo; and (2) all of Atsutane's students and disciples following his death.

School. His encounter with Mito scholars also illustrated how fellow nativists of a different ideological persuasion received his scholarship.

The domain of Mito was perhaps the most active supporter of nativism in Tokugawa Japan. In the seventeenth century, Tokugawa Mitsukuni sponsored several projects, the most famous of which was a comprehensive history of Japan, the *Dai Nihonshi*. Moreover, he also sponsored the study of the *Man'yōshū* by Shimokōbe Chōryū, which Keichū later completed. The scholars of the Mito domain continued their nativist activities into the nineteenth century as well, and their school became quite influential nationally.[36] Under the sponsorship of Mito, Aizawa Seishisai and Fujita Tōko conducted research into Japanese antiquity in much the same way as the members of the Norinaga School in Edo, Kyoto, and Matsusaka. Unlike their Kokugaku counterparts outside Mito, they maintained Confucian and Neo-Confucian interpretive frameworks. The investigation of Japanese antiquity by both schools, however, bred a certain curiosity and even mutual respect between the members of both.

Atsutane admired the Mito scholars, and he was especially enamored with the domainal support that they received. In 1834 he initiated contact with Tōko in an attempt to impress him with his knowledge of antiquity:

For some time, I have respectfully studied, at only a rudimentary level, the scholarship of your [historiographical] bureau. I have been endeavoring to do this for decades. The imperial realm is the master realm and the central realm of the gods. Although there is no need to say this again, it is for this reason that, according to the true history [of Japan], there was originally the decrees of the one and only imperial Way. In the classics, there was the ancient Way and such. Concerning these matters, I have elucidated the reality of antiquity and the origins of the ancient Way and

---

36. Bob Wakabayashi observes that there were two distinct stages in the development of the Mito School, the Early and Later Mito Schools. Keichū's study was sponsored by the Early Mito School, whereas Atsutane dealt with the Later Mito School. Wakabayashi observes that most scholars use the blanket term Mito School to refer specifically to the Later Mito (*Anti-Foreignism and Western Learning*, pp. 283–84).

understand [now] their essentials. I have written on this subject of which you are gradually becoming aware.[37]

Atsutane's letter was not simply to express his respects, however; his primary motivation in all his dealings with the Mito School was to become a *shikan*.[38] Twice during the tenth month of 1834, he met with Tōko. During the following month, he confessed his desire to become a *shikan*:

> I have painstakingly conducted research for decades. In the beginning, I had little stamina and few books. At the same time, I did not travel around the provinces. I was ignorant of geographical details and such. Since I was unable to [travel], I was limited to evidential research using only ordinary books. I used as a reference a text on [ancient] ceremonies and [another] on the names of *kami*. However, I know that your research on the ancient Way is first rate. So it is to [someone as] unworthy as I. If you were to make use [of me] and [allow me] to enter your historical bureau, then the scale of my many years of effort will become clear.... I [hope to] receive your notebook and seal. Sometimes, you will want me to stop rambling on. For this, I humbly request [your indulgence].[39]

On the twenty-eighth day of the eleventh month, Tōko submitted a letter to the lord of Mito, Tokugawa Nariaki (1800–1860), on Atsutane's behalf:

> The *kokugakusha* Hirata Taikaku [Atsutane] specializes in Shinto. I know that he has extensively researched Shinto texts. He absolutely desires to join the historiographical bureau. He has written to me to this effect and spoken to me as well. He has not a few mistaken views and doubtful interpretations. However, he earnestly devotes himself to and is knowledgeable of ancient learning, and for this he is exceptional. Gradually, he has produced an enormous corpus of books.... In a similar way, Oyamada Sakan [Tomokiyo] [seeks to] join the bureau. Since you will eliminate [one of them], I [submit that I] started with the investigation of Shinto

---

37. Atsutane to Tōko (no. 136), dated 1834/11, reproduced in Watanabe K., *Hirata Atsutane kenkyū*, p. 899.

38. Kajiyama, "Mitogaku to kokugaku no kankei," p. 37.

39. Atsutane to Tōko (no. 136), dated 1834/11, reproduced in Watanabe K., *Hirata Atsutane kenkyū*, pp. 899–900.

texts [like Atsutane] and have served you in some way. As a matter of course, I leave it to you to make the decision.[40]

We know from personal correspondence between Tōko and other scholars of the Mito School that he admired Atsutane's deep commitment to the scholarly study of antiquity.[41] We can assume, therefore, that Tōko supported his nomination to the daimyo. While he expressed a general admiration for Atsutane, his correspondence also tells us that he still had reservations about Atsutane, which he expressed to Aizawa Seishisai:

> Hirata Taikaku is a strange fellow. I have corresponded with him recently. I am embarrassed by his doubtful and random fabrications. However, his gumption is praiseworthy. If I were to compare him to Matsunoya [Oyamada Tomokiyo] and others, they are [like] bookshop clerks. Sometime ago, you perused [his work].... If you had truly read them, then I must present [Atsutane] for [entrance into the bureau]. He based [one of his works] on the *Sandaikō* and seriously argued a forced interpretation, which stunned me. However, he seeks to elucidate Shinto in the realm. Nowadays, he devotes his days and nights to scholarship, which has yielded works with fascicles that number more than one thousand. This is something that ordinary people [are unable to do]. His strange and mistaken views have been, from the beginning, firmly unshakable. This is unfortunate.[42]

Other Mito scholars did not feel the same way about Atsutane. As Aizawa Seishisai sarcastically observed: "If Hirata Daigaku [*sic*] died and journeyed to the underworld, it would not be such a lamentable thing."[43] These critics had two common complaints. First, they were troubled by his remarks about China and Confucianism.[44] The Mito scholars had not abandoned Confucianism; in fact, their insistence that Japan had inherited the mantle of Chinese culture because of the decline of the Ming dynasty came very close to the views of Ansai during the seventeenth century. This was clearly an instance in which Atsutane's extremely chauvinistic

---

40. Tōko to Tokugawa Nariaki, 1834(?), reproduced in Kajiyama, "Mitogaku to kokugaku no kankei," p. 39.
41. Ibid., p. 51.
42. Tōko to Aizawa Seishisai, dated 1834/3/29, reproduced in ibid., p. 50.
43. Quoted in ibid., p. 51.
44. Ibid., p. 43.

views, although necessary to maintain his position within the Norinaga School, did not serve him well when he attempted to enter the completely different field of the Mito School. It was not, however, the only criticism lodged against him.

At a more practical level, Mito scholars criticized Atsutane because, they insisted, his work was not literary enough. This was a criticism that even Tōko admitted had merit; consequently, his support for Atsutane's nomination was not based on the literary quality of Atsutane's scholarship but on its historical accuracy.[45] Ultimately, Atsutane's nomination for the position was rejected on this basis. Mito scholars observed that while he had prodigious knowledge of Shinto, they needed a scholar more familiar with classical literature; they did not need another Shinto scholar.[46] For Toyoda Tenkō (1805–64), Atsutane's *Koshiden* simply did not qualify as proper classicism: "I originally sympathized with Hirata. [However], the *Koshiden* is something that anyone can do if given a little time to think."[47] Instead of Atsutane, they awarded the position to his colleague, Oyamada Tomokiyo, with whom the letters indicate he was competing. Tomokiyo, of course, was well known in Edo for his evidential investigation of antiquity. He was also a noted scholar of classical literature, frequenting the literary gatherings in Edo attended by the leading literary figures of the time. Apparently, before his appointment as a *shikan* of Mito, Tomokiyo and Atsutane were more than just passive acquaintances.[48] In his memoirs, Tomokiyo briefly referred to Atsutane: "My friend, the venerable Hirata, seeks to transmit the learning of the venerable Motoori. He elucidates ancient books and propagates the Way of the *kami*."[49] Although Tomokiyo recognized Atsutane's skills as a scholar, there appears to have been no intellectual interaction between the two; they may have circulated in the same social groups, but their scholarship remained quite distinct from each other.

---

45. Ibid.
46. Ibid., p. 52.
47. Quoted in ibid., pp. 51–52.
48. Kajiyama, "Mito-han wo meguru Oyamada Tomokiyo to Hirata Atsutane no kōyū," pp. 61–62.
49. Oyamada Tomokiyo, quoted in ibid.

Their mutual interest in the Mito position grew into direct competition around 1832.[50]

Tomokiyo's appointment allows us to make a few observations about Atsutane and his scholarship during following his Kansai journey in 1823. First, even if Tomokiyo's scholarship was more suitable for the Mito School, Tomokiyo began to cultivate a relationship with its members around 1830, a few years before Atsutane. Thus, Atsutane had to overcome at least a two-year head start by Tomokiyo in his effort to impress the members of the Mito School. Second, Atsutane's denial of evidential research in the investigation of classical texts threatened not only his position within the Norinaga School, but it also indicated a conspicuous shortcoming in his own training and resumé. By downplaying such research, he disavowed an important, practical skill of nineteenth-century scholars. Finally, despite his reputation as a nativist, Tomokiyo did not make the kind of radical denunciations of China and Confucianism that characterized Atsutane's scholarship. Tomokiyo was a prominent member of the Edo-ha, which, as we have seen, was formed by Murata Harumi and Katō Chikage. Tomokiyo was a student of Harumi, who in 1803 had described himself as a *jusha* (Confucian), expressing exasperation and confusion over Izumi Makuni's denunciation of China. By rejecting Atsutane and embracing Tomokiyo, the Mito scholars demonstrated how the Edo-ha's intellectual identity and pedigree were acceptable. The selection of Tomokiyo was another indication of the ideological gulf that separated the Norinaga School and the Edo-ha. The exclusively *native* identity advocated by the members of the Norinaga School and Atsutane was alien to the experience of the members of the Edo-ha and of the Mito School, neither of which had made a clean break with Chinese culture or with Confucianism.

Conclusion

After the tumultuous years of Atsutane's early career, a time spent establishing a position for himself within the Norinaga School, he altered the direction of his scholarship following the *Sandaikō* de-

---

50. Ibid., p. 66.

bate. Convinced that the leadership of the Norinaga School was unmoved by his arguments, he decided to chart a distinct course for his academy by emphasizing the lives and experiences of the peasantry.

His work in the genre of ancient history represented a valorization of peasant labor, especially the work of rice cultivation. Atsutane presented a comprehensive view of antiquity by synthesizing passages from various classical sources. Consequently, as he lauded the daily activities of peasants, he rendered antiquity into an accessible form, to save nonscholars from having to master classical literature. His work in ancient history also spared people the trouble of reconciling conflicting accounts of *kamiyo* in the classical sources. His efforts proved popular among the rural population, and students and disciples flocked to his school. The rural appeal of Atsutane's scholarship was in stark contrast with the almost completely urban appeal of the more literary and textually-inclined academies affiliated with the Norinaga School. Atsutane moved his scholarship further away from classicism; by the final years of his life, he turned to divination and calendrical science.[51] As his scholarship lost its resemblance to literary nativism, the popularity of his academy grew in the countryside. His rural success sustained the distinct character of his scholarship, enabling him to maintain a powerful yet, at the same time, polar opposition to the leadership of the Norinaga School.

It may seem like Atsutane's work in ancient history signaled a departure from his earlier research on spirits and the afterlife. This was not the case. Eschatology continued to hold his interest and form the basis of his scholarship and teachings. Rice cultivators, whether living in the present or in antiquity, naturally possessed the correct knowledge and wisdom concerning the hereafter. Thus, the peasants of Atsutane's day had a closer spiritual link to their ancient counterparts than the townsfolk and warriors who actually wielded economic and political power during the Tokugawa period. In his general attempt to portray antiquity in his own synthesized scripture comprehensively, he chose not to foreground eschatological af-

---

51. Tanaka Y., "Kaidai: *Koshi seibun*," pp. 1–2.

fairs in order to make it seem as if they were theological truth, knowing that the textual basis for his assertions was not certain.

At nearly the same time as he composed the prodigious *Koshiden*, Atsutane also labored on a number of other works that specifically dealt with the supernatural. Perhaps the most interesting of these was the *Senkyō ibun*. Despite the fact that the genres of the two texts were separate and distinct, the emphasis on the lives of commoners was one that the two works shared. Atsutane saw the accounts of the shaman Torakichi as authoritative and eschewed the classics esteemed by his colleagues in the Norinaga School. In the *Koshiden*, he validated the wisdom of ancient commoners; in the *Senkyō ibun*, he did the same for contemporary peasants.

The latter work is important for another reason as well. While Atsutane's use of Torakichi's accounts was a significant departure from the literary studies of the Norinaga School, he still sought to maintain his legitimate membership within the school by adhering to the principles of Kōshōgaku. The citation of evidence was a crucial aspect of the orthodox methodology of the Norinaga School. Conclusions substantiated by evidence were the only way to supplant received interpretations, which were shrouded in mystery and transmitted as secret knowledge by scholarly traditions with roots in the Muromachi period. The tacit understanding among the members of the Norinaga School was that evidence had to be textual in nature. Perhaps they reasoned that in the absence of textual evidence, others could not challenge the interpretations upon which their own were based. Torakichi's accounts represented a source of evidence on the supernatural that was anything but textual.

Both texts amply demonstrate that the attacks leveled against Atsutane, especially during the *Sandaikō* debate, did not succeed in coaxing him back into classical literary studies. Far from diluting the distinctive features of his scholarship, Atsutane only deepened and broadened them. He fundamentally transformed the very nature of Kokugaku scholarship. Although he continued to assert his continuity with Azumamaro, Mabuchi, and Norinaga, his evidential investigation of the supernatural in no way resembled the literary and philological efforts of his predecessors. The ideological confrontation between his form of Kokugaku and that of his literary rivals in the Norinaga School carried over into the bakumatsu and Meiji periods. It forced later interpreters of Kokugaku history into seeing an intellectual continuity between Atsutane and his predecessors that was only tenuous at best, leading to a fundamental misunderstanding of his position in the history of Kokugaku.

SEVEN

Bakumatsu Kokugaku and the Hirata School

By cultivating a rural constituency, Atsutane ensured the survival and even prosperity of his school in the decades following his death. By that time, he had molded the Norinaga School into a larger intellectual tradition, an invention that served the goal of self-legitimation. Atsutane did not invent nativism, but he was the chief creative force behind Kokugaku. He acknowledged that there were other sources of native knowledge, but Kokugaku was the only one among them that articulated the true cultural essence of Japan. Thus, he discarded other forms of nativism from inclusion in Kokugaku, either because they were direct threats to his scholarship, which included classical literary studies, or because they did not conform to his narrow ideological definition of Kokugaku, thereby eliminating the Confucian traditions of the Kimon School and the Mito School. The very idea of Kokugaku is perhaps the most significant feature of Atsutane's intellectual legacy. The popularity of his academy and teachings during the bakumatsu period guaranteed that the views of Atsutane and his supporters would determine the intellectual character of Kokugaku.

Atsutane's invention of Kokugaku has endured, but the same cannot be said for many of his teachings. His immediate disciples continued to recruit rural followers; the numbers of Hirata School members increased dramatically during the bakumatsu years (see Table 1), far outpacing the numbers of nativists enrolled in rival

Table 1
Growth of the Hirata School
(number of disciples)

Year	Enrolled disciples
1843*	553
1863	1,330
1868	2,830
1876	4,283

*The year of Atsutane's death.
SOURCE: Adapted from Walthall, *The Weak Body of a Useless Woman*, p. 105.

schools (Table 2). Atsutane's students emphasized certain aspects of his teachings and preached a message that became the ideological foundation for the Hirata School. Influential members suppressed Atsutane's interests in the afterlife and the supernatural in favor of an emphasis on the social and intellectual roles of rural elites, as well as an emphasis on the forms of nonagricultural labor performed by elites. These were distorted interpretations only loosely based on Atsutane's original teachings. This accounts for the popularity of the *Koshiden* during the bakumatsu period, as opposed to any of Atsutane's evidential works on the supernatural or the afterlife.

The Meiji Restoration was the first major factor in the decline of Hirata Kokugaku and the resurgence of literary Kokugaku, associated mostly with Norinaga. This decline was not simply the outcome of an ideological confrontation between rival factions. It occurred with the complicity of the Hirata School's leadership during the Meiji period. Kanetane and the rest of the school's major figures suppressed the less palatable aspects of Atsutane's scholarship in response to the steep decline in the number of enrolled Hirata School members during the early years of Meiji. Kanetane assisted in the dilution of Atsutane's scholarship by reintroducing literary studies and philology into Kokugaku. The classical literary studies of the eighteenth century, which Atsutane had denounced, became prominent once again.

Table 2
Comparison of the Enrollments
of Nativist Academies

Nativist	Enrolled disciples
Eighteenth-century academies	
Kada no Azumamaro	30
Kamo no Mabuchi	128
Motoori Norinaga	491
Nineteenth-century academies	
Fujii Takanao	73
Motoori Haruniwa	418
Hirata Atsutane	562
Motoori Ōhira	1,038*

*Of these, 337 were from Kii-Wakayama.
SOURCE: Adapted from Haga, *Kokugaku no hitobito*, pp. 274–75.

The Birth of Grassroots Kokugaku

Atsutane had designated Kanetane as his adopted son and legal successor following his marriage to Atsutane's daughter Chie in 1824;[1] decades earlier, Norinaga had adopted a son as well. Although both Norinaga and Atsutane were critical of the *iemoto* system because it suppressed innovation in favor of the faithful replication of teachings, both designated their adopted son as their successor. Like Haruniwa, Ōhira continued to pursue Norinaga's classical research, focusing primarily on *kagura*. Kanetane, however, did not independently pursue scholarship, serving mostly in the capacity of Atsutane's personal assistant and secretary.[2] The preparation and editing of Atsutane's manuscripts for publication were among the duties assigned to Kanetane. In addition, he assumed the important task of procuring funds for the publication of Atsutane's main works.[3] Perhaps the most effective fundraising method was to travel to rural villages, deliver some lectures, and then recruit

---

1. Itō, *Kokugakusha no michi*, p. 98.
2. Ibid., p. 99.
3. Ibid., p. 135.

students for the Ibukinoya from those in attendance. The publication of farm manuals proved useful for Kanetane and his father because they familiarized potential students with Atsutane's message before Kanetane would visit, thereby reinforcing the message and enhancing his chances for successful recruitment. Like the publication of farm manuals, the primary motivation for rural recruiting trips by Kanetane and, less often, Atsutane himself was financial.[4]

As a result of Kanetane's efforts, the Hirata School saw a dramatic increase in registered students beginning in 1819.[5] While Haruniwa's Nochi-Suzunoya had experienced an increase in its own enrollment during the first two decades of the nineteenth century, its students were drawn almost entirely from the immediate environs of Matsusaka; the other academies of the Norinaga School also drew urban dwellers. The rural constituency of the Hirata School, therefore, was unusual for Kokugaku at that time.[6] As of 1830, registered students of the Nochi-Suzunoya hailing from Ise province numbered around 200 with an additional 88 from nearby Owari.[7] By contrast, the number of Hirata School members at the time of Atsutane's death in 1843 numbered more than 550 (Table 1).[8]

During the period from roughly 1805 to 1830 (the Kasei period), there were three main schools of Kokugaku. The two most active were the Norinaga and Hirata Schools, each boasting enrollments of several hundred. One other school, however, continued to pursue nativism despite the obscurity that the success of these larger schools created for it. These were students who continued to revere Mabuchi as their founder, nearly fifty years after his death. They constituted the smallest of the three branches of the Mabuchi School, the others being the Edo-ha and the Suzunoya.[9] These adherents of Mabuchi were mostly from Hamamatsu and the province of Tōtōmi. Unlike their colleagues in the Edo-ha, the Hama-

---

4. Haga N., *Bakumatsu kokugaku no kenkyū*, p. 223.
5. Ibid., p. 224.
6. Ibid., p. 225.
7. Ibid.
8. Itō, *Sōmō no kokugaku*, p. 3.
9. Nosco, *Remembering Paradise*, pp. 155–57. Nosco refers to these groups as the *Man'yō*, Edo, and *Shinkokin* (Suzunoya).

matsu students seemed to have maintained a collective institutional identity as a school. In 1818 these students, led by Murata Harukado (a disciple of Norinaga and student of Mabuchi's poetics), resolved to erect a shrine to Mabuchi. Financial difficulties and the great Tenpō famine delayed the construction of the shrine until 1839. It was finally built through the cooperative efforts of the Mabuchi students from Hamamatsu and many members of the Norinaga School from the provinces of Mikawa, Owari, Ise, and Kii.[10] The devotion of these students to Mabuchi, however admirable, was not enough to stem the general decline of their school during the nineteenth century, which appears especially precipitous by comparison with the schools of Norinaga and Atsutane. The decline of the Mabuchi School during this period dramatically highlighted the intellectual dominance of the other two. However, in the struggle for supremacy between the two more popular schools, the Norinaga School gradually lost ground to the Hirata School.

During the Kasei period, the province of Shimōsa was the most significant source for the Hirata School. For example, in 1816, 85 new students entered the rolls of the Hirata School. Of this figure, 44 were from Shimōsa. Two years later, of the 26 that enrolled, 17 were from there.[11] While Shinto priests and samurai were represented among the students who enrolled in the Hirata School during this period, most of the new recruits were peasants, especially those affiliated with the elite classes. The class composition of the Suzunoya was fairly similar to that of the Ibukinoya, with a healthy representation of Shinto priests, samurai, townspeople, and some peasants. Townsmen and peasants constituted the bulk of the Nochi-Suzunoya's students during the Kasei period.[12]

The rural backgrounds of the new recruits into the Hirata School had an important impact on its intellectual trajectory. Villages in Shimōsa produced a number of prominent and active members of the Hirata School. Not only did these students assume roles as recruiters, as Kanetane did, but they were also creative scholars. Among them were rural activists who adhered to the

---

10. Ibid., p. 102.
11. Ibid., p. 3.
12. Haga N., *Bakumatsu kokugaku no kenkyū*, p. 225.

political agendas they had developed prior to joining the Hirata School. Two important examples were Konishi Atsuyoshi and Miyahiro Sadao (1767–1837). Sadao was a particularly important representative of grassroots Kokugaku. His concern for the welfare of peasants struggling against famine and poverty helped reorient the Hirata School toward a more active embrace of the countryside and the peasantry.

Miyahiro Sadao

Sadao was a *nanushi* (village headman) from Shimōsa. He officially joined the Ibukinoya in 1827[13] and was familiar with local Ibukinoya members through his father, Yasumasa, who had joined seven years earlier. Sadao helped Kanetane raise funds and recruit new students from the Shimōsa area. His interest in Atsutane's scholarship is not surprising, considering that Sadao shared a concern for the peasantry.[14] Sadao went so far as to state that only peasants truly possessed the *yamatogokoro* of which Atsutane and Norinaga had spoken.[15] He especially praised rural elites like himself, who were in a unique position vis-à-vis less fortunate villagers. By identifying himself with the rural elite, he appealed to a segment of village society that had the organizational skills and resources necessary to effectively propagate and support Atsutane's scholarship in the countryside and, later, the expansion of the Hirata School.

Sadao formulated his fundamental views of grassroots Kokugaku in the *Kokueki honron* (1831). As the title of the text indicates, his central concern was the issue of the *kokueki* (provincial prosperity); he was especially interested in describing the process by which ru-

---

13. The Hirata School did not have a network of affiliated private academies like the Norinaga School. Members, therefore, continued to enroll directly in the Ibukinoya, even though they did not reside in Edo. Even after Atsutane's death, Kanetane still recruited members as the posthumous disciples of Atsutane, and he never mentored his own. Whereas the Suzunoya was one academy of the Norinaga School, the Ibukinoya signified both Atsutane's Edo academy and the Hirata School as a whole.
14. Itō, *Sōmō no kokugaku*, p. 17.
15. Haga N., *Bakumatsu kokugaku no kenkyū*, p. 248.

ral society could attain such prosperity.[16] Sadao advised villagers to adhere to the will of the gods (*kijin*).[17] Unlike Norinaga, he advocated the use of *oshie* (teachings) as the primary method for shaping the behavior of the peasantry. Norinaga had argued against the use of teachings for inculcating knowledge of the ancient Way, as it was a foreign method favored by Confucians in the instruction of ethical norms that they claimed were already inherent in humanity. The Japanese people, by contrast, naturally behaved according to ethical norms—or at least they had the natural inclination to do so in Norinaga's view:

> If we were to describe the Way [of the Sages], what would it be? It is known variously as benevolence, righteousness, rites, humility, filial piety, loyalty, and so forth. These obnoxious terms were created for the strict edification of the people. . . . In reality, [Japan] has had the Way [since antiquity], even without a word for the Way. Without a word for it, [Japan] has had the Way.[18]

By eliminating the need for Confucian teachings, Norinaga justified philological research for its own sake. Sadao, on the other hand, wanted to restore ethical teachings to Kokugaku in order to assert the leadership role of village elites in rural society. Norinaga's cavalier dismissal of the utility of teachings fell on deaf ears among rural Kokugaku scholars during the Kasei and Tenpō periods.

Sadao asserted that one could not follow both Shinto and Buddhism simultaneously. Indeed, he claimed that throughout Japanese history the people have endured the wrath of the *kami* in protest of the baneful influence of Buddhism; unfortunately for the Japanese people, no one had ever correctly deduced the reasons for the displeasure of the *kami*. The *kami* reacted to the presence of *kegare* (pollution) and wreaked havoc on the people in an effort to purify them of it: "Generally, if one does not follow the august hearts of the *kami*, then, as expected, unfortunate events ensue. Matters that do not follow the august hearts of the *kami* include, as

---

16. Harry Harootunian translates *kokueki* as "regional wealth" (*Things Seen and Unseen*, p. 297).

17. Miyahiro Sadao, *Kokueki honron*, p. 292. Subsequent references to this work are cited in the text.

18. Motoori Norinaga, *Naobi no mitama*, pp. 287–89.

I have explained previously, the practice of infanticide, the worship of the Buddha, and the pollution of fire. The pollution of fire means the consumption of meat" (297). As an example, he cited the various disasters—specifically instances of disease—that were visited upon the ancients during the sixth century. He saw a direct correlation between these disasters and the adoption of Buddhism from Korea. By citing the prohibition in Shinto against Buddhist priests entering the Ise Shrines, he attempted to show that the antagonism between Shinto and Buddhism was ancient and not the result of later doctrinal differences (295–96). Observing Buddhist rituals and worship risked invoking the wrath of the native gods.

Another reason cited by Sadao as a demonstration of the particularly injurious influence of Buddhism was its insistence on the celibacy of the priesthood. The duty of the people, he declared, was to repay the blessings of the gods through prolific procreation. In the hierarchy of organs in the body, the sexual organs were the most important. Procreation itself was not only a gift of the *kami* but also a sacred obligation. As Sadao succinctly stated: "Thus, provincial prosperity, above all, teaches the people of the realm the Way, which is, first of all, to increase the population" (293). The onus to procreate fell especially on men. By taking the tonsure, they acted in direct contradiction to the divine commandment to procreate: "Men are born with a phallus. By the feelings between men and women, children are born, and the people multiply. [Procreation] is a sign that we have received the command of the *kami* and are not to become monks" (295). Japan's stagnant population was proof for Sadao of the malevolent effect of Buddhism on Japanese society.

Sadao did not specifically describe who should teach the peasantry or how they would do so. The implication, however, was that elites like himself had this educational mission. The curriculum would not only include the practical aspects of effective agriculture—a subject that he had addressed in the farm manuals—but also ethics, such as the prohibition against infanticide. Like the institution of the priesthood, the practices of abortion and infanticide (*mabiki*) contradicted the divine obligation to procreate. He was particularly troubled by infanticide because it was a significant impediment to population growth. The *kami* had proclaimed the importance of procreation, he asserted, since they wanted to ensure that the nation's population would perpetually increase. The key to obtaining *kokueki* was not population growth per se but the resultant increase in agricultural output that such an increase would surely generate. The instruction of the peasantry by the village elites was the first step in a process that would ultimately result in increased agricultural productivity.

Sadao's emphasis on the relationship between the *kami* and the peasantry was not new to Atsutane. Atsutane had made the same argument in the *Koshiden*, and we can assume that Sadao's ideas in this instance were a faithful replication of Atsutane's teachings. Sadao's faith in the role of elites as rural educators, however, was original and not an assertion made by Atsutane. Atsutane tacitly supported this idea, since he understood its importance to his rural followers. By linking education to procreation and thus to agricultural productivity, Sadao articulated a new discourse that combined Atsutane's scholarship with the ideals of agriculturists.[19] One could argue that Sadao's discourse, though new within Kokugaku, was highly naive for its facile equation of an increased population with higher rice yields. This may be true; however, as a diligent student of the Hirata School, such naiveté is not likely. Sadao's ideas meshed with Atsutane's to create a more complex social policy. As he stated at the end of the text, the rural education that he envisioned was not limited to reading and writing: "Although tutors certainly can teach boys and girls in childhood how to establish the Way, they do not. The temple instructor is summoned and he makes the children learn only how to read and write, and does not make them study the important Way. . . . Thus, they become adults ignorant of the Way, and there are no techniques for provincial prosperity; [the result] is simply a bad economy" (308). For Sadao, peasants must have the basic skills of literacy so that they can follow the "true Way." This was a reference to Atsutane's teachings, the source of knowledge on the ancient Way. Sadao envisioned a rural society composed not of mere consumers of resources, but of hard-working producers. Elites would instruct them in Shinto, especially in the divine obligation to procreate.

---

19. Harootunian, *Things Seen and Unseen*, p. 297.

Village leaders would also instruct the peasantry in Atsutane's teachings, especially in his insistence on their diligent work. Sadao believed that the combination of the two produced the rural education that would ultimately lead to economic prosperity.

An Alternative Vision of Rural Kokugaku: Suzuki Shigetane

Suzuki Shigetane (1812–63) was another major thinker of grassroots Kokugaku, especially in the years following Atsutane's death. Like Sadao, his ideas helped to transform Kokugaku into more of a political discourse. While Sadao had maintained close ties to both Kanetane and Atsutane, Shigetane expressed his doubts about Atsutane's teachings from quite an early point in his career. He joined the Ibukinoya in 1832 and began his studies as one of its more earnest students. He later described his enthusiasm for Atsutane:

> When I read the works that the Great Man Hirata had written, I found that there were times when his views conflicted with those of the Great Man Motoori. I detested [Atsutane] for his stupidity. [However,] at the right moment, I reread [his works] three or four times. I decided that he had a broad knowledge that [no one] in either China or Japan [had]. Soon after . . . I decided to request that he become my master.[20]

Two years later, perhaps as a result of his initial doubts about Atsutane, he joined the academy of Ōkuni Takamasa as well. Takamasa was a major bakumatsu *kokugakusha* who was later viewed as Atsutane's *dōtō* successor. In 1834, however, he was but one of many students of Kokugaku who were active during the Tenpō era. Shigetane resolved to solidify his status as a member of the Ibukinoya by traveling north to Akita in order to receive Atsutane's teachings in person.[21] Perhaps as a gesture of his devotion, he actively recruited additional members to the Hirata School during his journey.[22] Unfortunately for Shigetane, he arrived just after

---

20. Suzuki Shigetane, quoted in Hoshikawa, *Suzuki Shigetane den*, p. 49.

21. Atsutane was ordered out of Edo and sent back to Akita by the bakufu in 1839 for what they perceived as an anti-bakufu sentiment in his work on calendrical science.

22. Haga N., "Suzuki Shigetane to Hirata-tō," p. 48.

Atsutane's death and was never able to accomplish his goal of a direct transmission of teachings from Atsutane. This may also have had an effect on his later resistance to the Hirata School.

Shigetane's initial doubts about Atsutane were precipitated by his dislike of classical literary studies.[23] Ironically, Atsutane himself had expressed doubts about classicism, leading him to proclaim that the true intent of Norinaga was not the narrow study of prose and poetry, but the broader and more significant clarification of the ancient Way. For Shigetane, Atsutane—his assertions to the contrary notwithstanding—had flirted too closely with literary studies, which fundamentally compromised his teachings. In 1858 Shigetane criticized Atsutane's *Koshi seibun*, a text that Atsutane had considered as one of his major works, as crude and amateurish.[24] Kanetane, as well as Shigetane's own mentor, Takamasa, attempted to intervene and assuage Shigetane's growing impatience with the Hirata School. As Shigetane wryly observed, "[I] do not uphold the usual beliefs of the Hirata School (Hirata-tō)."[25] Their efforts, however, were unsuccessful and he never recanted these statements, which prompted a swift and harsh rebuke by other Hirata School members.

By the bakumatsu period, the Hirata School had grown to several thousand members, and its national prominence had grown as well. Thus, a condemnation of the sort leveled at Shigetane was a gravely serious political matter. By this time, Shigetane no longer viewed himself exclusively as a *kokugakusha*. Rather, he referred to his scholarship as *setchū* (eclectic), a term used by Confucian scholars to designate schools that did not specifically uphold Cheng-Zhu orthodoxy.[26] Five years after Shigetane had ridiculed Atsutane, he was killed under mysterious circumstances. The speculation at the time was that his death was the accidental outcome of an argument; the killer was never found. However, recent scholarship suggests that he was probably assassinated by a member of the Hirata

---

23. Ibid., p. 49.
24. Ibid., p. 54.
25. Suzuki Shigetane, quoted in Hoshikawa, *Suzuki Shigetane den*, p. 58.
26. Haga N., "Suzuki Shigetane to Hirata-tō," p. 76.

School. This view seems plausible, given the climate of political violence during the 1860s. Radical *shishi* (determined samurai), like Sakamoto Ryōma (1835–67), who were committed to imperial restoration, used terror and murder against foreigners and their pro-foreigner allies. As warriors without masters, these radicals justified their acts by invoking the call to political action that the Ming dynasty scholar Wang Yangming had articulated. If Shigetane was killed by a scholar from the Hirata School, then his intractable stance against the rest of its members and his condemnation of Atsutane's scholarship represented the limits of expression within the School. In addition, his "eclectic" scholarship was blasphemous to the more ardent followers of Atsutane's teachings. Thus, Shigetane had tried to occupy different ideological positions within the field of the Hirata School, which only seemed to alienate its other members. For staunch adherents, membership in the field was an all-or-nothing game, a principle that had terrible consequences during the bakumatsu period. Consequently, death was the only instrument of enforcement available to the faithful against one of their own members who had blatantly flouted the field's rules of inclusion.

The Importance of Labor

Shigetane authored the *Yotsugigusa* (1850) as a Kokugaku primer, and he intended to reach a rural audience with it.[27] Like Sadao and Atsutane, he instructed the people to work diligently in order to repay the blessings of the *kami*. As mentioned previously, Atsutane had emphasized the link between agricultural labor and religious practice. Sadao, on the other hand, had afforded a privileged place in rural society for the village elites whom the *kami* had charged with initiating and leading the effort to improve the welfare of poor farmers. Shigetane, however, did not emphasize the leadership role of the elites; neither did he specifically claim that the peasantry had a special relationship with the *kami*. Although he tailored his message for farmers, he admonished members of all classes to adhere to their *shoku* (occupation). He transformed hard work itself into a form of religious observance, even if it was not

---

27. Itō, *Sōmō no kokugaku*, p. 115.

farm labor; such a form of devotion was a link to the *kami* that was accessible to anyone, regardless of class.

Shigetane reiterated Atsutane's teaching that the land was a divine gift to the people.[28] Perhaps as a sign of his political allegiances, he claimed that the people were servants of the emperor, but that they must manifest their servitude by pledging obedience to the directives of their local officials first: "If one were to gradually trace back to the wellspring [of loyalty], it would be the emperor of the realm and the people, the imperial august grandchild. Those who want to serve the imperial court well, should begin with service to their [local] masters (*shujin*). This is the way of servitude for the samurai and the commoners" (235). In some ways, the focus on secular authority resembled the Confucian definition of loyalty; clearly, however, it contradicted Atsutane's emphasis on the emperor. Shigetane argued that people served their samurai superiors best through their diligent work.

In addition to the idea of work as a form of religious practice, he also contended that the conduct of one's mundane affairs was another way to live in harmony with the *kami*:

It says in the classics, "For matters relating to our time, learn from the *kami*; do not learn from the people." It states that, "Since the imperial ancestors created our bodies, master the divine Way (*kannagara no michi*)." The word *kannagara* means to follow the Way of the *kami*, and that the natural state of being is Shinto. Shinto means that as this drifting world is fashioned into a realm of plenitude, there is nothing else to follow. We mundanely practice the ordained virtues of the imperial ancestors without knowing it. (240)

He observed that the concept of *kannagara* signified living in accordance with nature. Thus, human beings could live in this way by the simple performance of their own daily activities. After all, since the *kami* were everywhere, even the most minute and insignificant activity was subject to their scrutiny.

Since Shigetane emphasized all forms of work, not just farm labor, his form of grassroots Kokugaku did not specifically appeal to rural elites. Katsura Takashige (1816–71), his most prominent stu-

---

28. Suzuki Shigetane, *Yotsugigusa*, p. 234. Subsequent references to this work are cited in the text.

dent, rectified this shortcoming. Takashige retained Shigetane's connection between work and religious practice, but he combined it with Sadao's emphasis on the leadership role of rural elites.[29] Despite Takashige's efforts at intellectual reconciliation, Shigetane never returned to the fold of the Hirata School. Thus, he freely used certain elements of Atsutane's scholarship as he invented ideas of his own; this was the reason why he preferred the "eclectic" label to describe his scholarship.

Perhaps Shigetane's rebellious spirit was partially inspired by one of his predecessors in the Ibukinoya, Ikuta Yorozu (1801–38). Yorozu had viewed Atsutane's ideas as an opportunity to advance his own agenda of social reform. He was also very selective in his use of Atsutane's teachings. He had championed a form of social and political activism that was common during the bakumatsu period, yet was too radical for the political climate of the Tenpō era. In fact, his views were so extreme that Atsutane himself denounced Yorozu. The fact that Yorozu's critique of rural society was in some ways validated decades after his death was an indication of the emerging split among Atsutane's followers.

Ikuta Yorozu and Rural Activism

Yorozu was a samurai of the Tatebayashi domain, who was educated in the typical Confucian fashion. During his youth, the influence of the Kimon School was particularly strong, and that of Ansai's disciple Asami Keisai was especially so.[30] In addition to Yorozu's familiarity with Confucianism, he took a personal interest in the scholarship of Mabuchi and Norinaga. Their studies of antiquity intrigued him, since they signified the possibility of recovering the conditions of ancient life.[31] Under the influence of the Hirata School, he began to question the validity of both his Confucian training and his Buddhist beliefs.

Yorozu read Atsutane's works as a young man and was deeply impressed:

---

29. Itō, *Sōmō no kokugaku*, pp. 113–18.
30. Itō, *Kokugakusha no michi*, p. 72.
31. Ibid., p. 83.

The Great Man, our master, does not receive an official stipend; so it is not his responsibility to have to practice the Way in the public realm. Thus, he withdrew [from society] and elucidated the true Way. The broad nobility of his efforts, which established great peace for future generations, includes the composition of the *Koshi seibun*. He produced the correct explanation of the purity of the ancient transmissions and wrote the *Koshichō*. He broadly and fully devoted himself to the true meaning of the ancient Way and composed the *Tama no mihashira*. He produced the ten diagrams and argued for the basis of the soul of ancient learning.[32]

In his estimation, Atsutane's description of Japan's ancient Way was a more accurate conceptualization of the essence of Kokugaku than the literary studies favored by the rest of the Norinaga School, which he viewed as a threat to Atsutane's ideas. He criticized the members of the Norinaga School especially for their preoccupation with the preservation of Norinaga's teachings rather than the pursuit of the ancient Way.[33] Convinced that Atsutane's study of the ancient Way was focused on the lives of ancient commoners, he formally joined the Ibukinoya in 1825. As a member of the Hirata School, he increased his attacks on Confucianism, especially Song Neo-Confucianism.[34] He likened nativist scholarship to the medicine that could cure the ailment of Confucianism: "This . . . is medicine that works quickly. Thus, even though it has a bitter taste, once taken it finally rouses the slumbering followers [of Confucianism] from their drunken stupor in Chinese books."[35] At the same time, he embraced other key areas of Atsutane's scholarship, such as his cosmological views. Yorozu won Atsutane's favor by accepting his eschatology without question:

The human soul does not, of course, dissipate. It dies and then separates from the body. It rests eternally in the spirit realm (*yūmei*), which has all of life's necessities and is no different from this world. The Confucians want to see this spirit realm for themselves, but they cannot. So, it is a ridiculous fabrication [to them]. They do not accept it because they are ob-

---

32. Ikuta Yorozu, *Ryōyaku kuchi ni nigashi*, p. 374.
33. Itō, *Kokugakusha no michi*, p. 88.
34. Ibid., p. 146.
35. Ikuta Yorozu, *Ryōyaku kuchi ni nigashi*, pp. 408–9.

stinate. They cannot fathom at all the division between the supernatural (*yū*) and the natural (*mei*).[36]

His energy as an active recruiter for the Hirata School eventually led to an invitation to stay in Edo with Atsutane. In 1829, Yorozu and his family moved to Edo, residing for a short time with Atsutane and his family. Relations between the two became so close, in fact, that Atsutane considered adopting Yorozu as his successor, in place of Kanetane. Atsutane was concerned with the lack of intellectual originality in Kanetane and was worried that he was perhaps suited only for secretarial work.[37] Kanetane, however, had already married Atsutane's daughter, Chie, which made him a more appropriate heir to the household.

Despite being a favorite of Atsutane, Yorozu grew impatient with the lack of a coherent political agenda within the Ibukinoya. Consequently, he decided to formulate one on his own; unlike his colleagues in the Ibukinoya, he vowed to combine his words with decisive action. His interest in such activism was perhaps the result of his interest in the thought of Wang Yangming. The combination of such a philosophy with his passion for the plight of the peasantry culminated in an open rebellion in 1838. He seized the opportunity to execute his ideas by fomenting and leading an uprising in the province of Echigo. This uprising, however, was poorly planned and quickly suppressed. Faced with impending defeat, Yorozu committed suicide in Kashiwazaki.

Reform and Rebellion

Perhaps the most significant factor that contributed to Yorozu's rebellion was the profound fiscal crisis in his native Tatebayashi domain. He was especially concerned with its potentially devastating impact on the peasantry, so he composed the *Iwa ni musu koke* (1828) as a proposed solution to the crisis. It was one of two works that exemplify his ideas; the other was the *Ryōyaku kuchi ni nigashi* (1826).[38] The former text, however, was not directly related to the

---

36. Ibid., p. 399.
37. Itō, *Kokugakusha no michi*, pp. 188–89.
38. Ibid., p. 140.

ideology of the Hirata School. There were two reasons for this. First, he generally avoided purely theoretical treatises, since he believed that deeds were more important than words. Second, he was a great admirer of Norinaga's *Hihon tamakushige*, the only overtly political treatise written by Norinaga. In Yorozu's eyes, the composition of such a text was an important obligation of conscientious scholars. By 1825, the domainal debt had reached a staggering 250,000 *ryō*. In an effort to deal with it, the daimyo raised the general taxation rate to 40 percent,[39] which squeezed an already impoverished populace. Consequently, Yorozu formulated his solution to the crisis and submitted his unsolicited text to the daimyo.

Yorozu reasoned that the raising of the domain's taxes was an unthinking reaction that resulted from the social chasm between warriors and peasants. Warriors, once cultivators themselves, had been removed from the land to become bureaucrats during the early Tokugawa period. They had lost their physical link to the land and, in the process, lost their empathy with the hardships of peasant life. Yorozu examined Japan's history and noted that the tradition of the *nengu* (annual tribute) had its roots in the epoch prior to the removal of the samurai from the land. In fact, the collection of *nengu* began during the Kamakura shogunate. The samurai class, therefore, had taxed and exploited the peasants for centuries; any reform of the *nengu* had to begin with the samurai class, he concluded.[40] He observed that the taxes that warriors had assessed had grown steadily more onerous over the course of the Sengoku period, culminating in the extreme rates of the Tokugawa era. These rates had become as high as one-third of the total domainal yield in some places: "Nowadays, the annual tribute changes variously according to the land and the supply of [rice] but is about one-third. The source of the decline of the peasantry is absolutely the severity of the annual tribute" (41).

In a move typical of his Kokugaku predecessors, Yorozu asserted that Japanese society had to return to the social conditions of antiquity, a time that he claimed was much more amenable to

---

39. Ibid., p. 154.
40. Ikuta Yorozu, *Iwa ni musu koke*, p. 40. Subsequent references to this work are cited in the text.

the peasantry. Ancient lords had treated their peasants with benevolence; the first step in the resolution of Tatebayashi's crisis, therefore, was to govern the peasantry with the same kind of benevolence. Obviously, the high rates of taxation contravened this idea and actually caused rural suffering and discontent. Thus, benevolent rule had to begin with the relief of the peasantry, including, as he asserted, tax reform.

Yorozu proposed some concrete reforms in order to achieve rural relief. His first proposal was to return the samurai to the land: "If what I have said is true, then we must carry out the precepts of returning [the samurai] to the land (*dochaku*)" (18). Like Sorai before him, he argued that if they were forced to cultivate the land, as they had done in antiquity, then this would restore their empathy with the peasantry. In addition, the samurai would improve their physical strength and endurance as they added their numbers to the ranks of rural cultivators. Thus, returning the samurai to the land would improve the overall agricultural output of the countryside. They would come mostly from Edo, where they served their domains as inconsequential and ineffective bureaucrats in the *sankin-kōtai* system. Such warrior-bureaucrats, he noted, were extremely expensive to maintain in their Edo residences, and every year domains spent large portions of their budgets on their upkeep. Returning them to the countryside, therefore, would produce a net annual budgetary savings of thousands of *ryō* (21). The savings gained by returning warriors to the land could then be applied to reducing the debt, which would allow the domain to drastically reduce its *nengu* taxation. Moreover, the daimyo could use the savings to fund rural granaries for famine relief. He specifically cited the granaries established by Zhu Xi during the Song dynasty as models for such an effort:

From the beginning, the peasants have been the great treasure of the imperial court. For a long time, the court has entrusted them to the shogun and to the daimyo of the realm. Thus, they are the court's truly important custodians. . . . Of course, the precepts by which we can create wealth and prosperity today are, first of all, the Righteousness Granary (*gisō*) and Zhu Xi's Community Granary (*shasō*), both of which are preparations for famine and sources of relief for poor people. This is the best precept. (42)

Both lower taxation and domainal granaries would contribute to the alleviation of peasant suffering.

Like those of Miyahiro Sadao, Yorozu's views may seem extremely naive and unsophisticated. Unfortunately, Sadao and Yorozu suffered from a common weakness in Kokugaku scholarship, which was not the most suitable source of ideas on matters of political economy.[41] Yorozu's struggle to formulate practical economic policies using Kokugaku ideas was admirable but fell short of the level of sophistication achieved by Confucians such as Kaiho Seiryō and Dazai Shundai. Yorozu's thought was atypical within the Ibukinoya, especially in view of Atsutane's repudiation of him shortly following the uprising in Echigo.[42] It is clear that Yorozu incorporated the ideas of Wang Yangming into his agenda for social action, and his notion of political economy, while unusual among scholars in the Hirata School, was itself not original. Perhaps the only link to the ideology of the Hirata School in his thought was the notion of a special relationship that existed between the peasantry and the *kami*. Yorozu's concern for the peasants was one that Atsutane may have shared but did not directly express. However, Yorozu linked his concern for farmers to Atsutane's ideas. In either case, he represented a significant yet influential break from the Hirata School. Unlike Shigetane, who denounced Atsutane, Yorozu believed that he was faithfully serving him. Both scholars, however, strayed away from the central focus of Atsutane's scholarship, namely, eschatology. Harootunian argues that though Yorozu's thought was radically different from that of Atsutane, it did not represent an intellectual break with Atsutane. Instead, Yorozu's ideas signified an important political latency within Atsutane's thought that resurfaced decades after his death.[43] Yorozu's thought was a radical departure from Atsutane's; ironically, it became the ideological foundation of the dominant faction within the Hirata School during the bakumatsu period. Hence, it was they who rendered it into a political discourse.

---

41. Itō, *Kokugakusha no michi*, p. 169.
42. Harootunian, *Things Seen and Unseen*, p. 291.
43. Ibid., p. 277.

Late Bakumatsu and Early Meiji Kokugaku: Ōkuni Takamasa and Yano Gendō

Kanetane guided the expansion of the Ibukinoya during the bakumatsu period. Its enrollment grew from slightly over five hundred in 1843 (the year of Atsutane's death) to several thousand by the early Meiji period (see Table 1). The majority of its registered students were peasants, and many of its most active recruiters came, like Miyahiro Sadao, from elite rural families. It was from these ranks of the ideologically committed that the message of Atsutane's teachings was transformed into one more specifically tailored for a rural audience. Atsutane's primary concerns with the afterlife and classical history were suppressed in favor of admonitions regarding hard work and justifications for social hierarchy in the countryside[44]—the preoccupations associated with grassroots Kokugaku. There were scholars, however, who were aware of this distortion of Atsutane's scholarship, and they attempted to reconcile the ideology of the extremely popular grassroots Kokugaku with what they saw as Atsutane's core teachings. Ōkuni Takamasa (1792–1871) and Yano Gendō (or Harumichi, 1823–87) were two such scholars. Their interpretations of Atsutane's teachings, however, diverged. During the politically turbulent years preceding the Meiji Restoration, the two sought to bring their increasingly disparate forms of Kokugaku together. This cooperation, however, was tenuous, and the sociopolitical state of the Hirata School of the 1860s grew to resemble that of the Norinaga School during the 1820s and 1830s. Consequently, Takamasa and Gendō came to represent opposing poles in the field of the Hirata School. The former claimed to be the *dōtō* successor of Atsutane, while the latter was the undisputed *iemoto* heir. The Hirata School of the 1860s, however, was confronted with a more complex political situation than their earlier nativist counterparts. As imperial restorationists searched for a viable ideology, they created the stakes over which Takamasa and Gendō struggled in their quest to dominate the field.

---

44. For the best study of the relationship between rural elites and Kokugaku, see Fukaya Katsumi, "Bakuhan shihai to mura yakuninsō no kokugaku jūyō," pp. 13–23.

Ōkuni Takamasa

Like most scholars of his day, Takamasa was well acquainted with Confucian scholarship. As a youth, he was deeply fascinated by *kanshi*, an interest that led him to the study of *waka*. Through the recommendation of a family friend, he approached Atsutane as a potential tutor in Japanese poetry. Atsutane was flattered that his name was linked with poetry but confessed to Takamasa that *waka* was not his specialty. Consequently, he recommended that Takamasa enroll in the academy of Murata Harukado, who had a reputation as a scholar steeped in Mabuchi's poetics.[45] Atsutane, however, encouraged him to attend meetings at the Ibukinoya, even though Takamasa never formerly enrolled as one of its students. Despite Atsutane's encouragement and help, Takamasa held little regard for him personally. He later confessed his dislike, blaming it on his preoccupation with Confucianism as a young man.[46]

Takamasa recognized Atsutane's inclusion in the Kokugaku *dōtō*. As Atsutane had done in the *Tamadasuki*, Takamasa argued that his own scholarship demonstrated his possession of the ancient Way, proving that he was the *dōtō* successor to Atsutane:

> I am untalented and cannot compare with the Four Great Men (*shiushi*). However, [some] students, who think of themselves as my children and of me as their father, can revere me as the Fifth Ancestor (*goso*). Even though I myself do not think that this view can be correct, I endeavor to be consistent with the Four Great Men. If this is the case, then one could say such a thing.[47]

He observed that unlike Buddhism and Confucianism—traditions predicated on the replication of teachings—Kokugaku, which he called *kōkoku no gaku* (learning of the imperial realm), was based on the rectification of flaws in received teachings. In this way, Takamasa's explanation of the *dōtō* was diametrically opposed to Atsutane's. Innovation, not blind replication, was the hallmark of the Kokugaku *dōtō*.[48] The orthodox lineage of Neo-Confucianism, he

---

45. Minami, *Kinsei kokugaku to sono shūhen*, p. 7.
46. Ibid., p. 9.
47. Ōkuni Takamasa, *Gakutō benron*, p. 480.
48. Ibid., p. 477.

contended, was the result of Zhu Xi's artificial selection of designated orthodox scholars. Contrarily, the contents of the teachings themselves determined the *dōtō* of Kokugaku, eliminating the arbitrariness of human selection.[49] By describing Kokugaku succession in this manner, Takamasa could simultaneously criticize Atsutane's scholarship and claim to be his successor. Atsutane had similarly criticized Norinaga's interpretation of Yomi while claiming to be the sole heir to his teachings. There was one crucial difference between Atsutane's discussion of the Kokugaku *dōtō* and Takamasa's. Whereas Atsutane went to great lengths to demonstrate his connection to Norinaga, Takamasa did not emphasize his ties to Atsutane. In fact, Takamasa insisted that the *opposition* of the disciple to the master is what distinguished the Kokugaku lineage from others: "Master Motoori destroyed his teacher's explanations and pronounced many new explanations. Master Hirata also destroyed his teacher's explanations and established many new ones. However, each respected his teacher and revered the *kami*, both of which may seem incongruous."[50]

Takamasa reiterated Atsutane's emphasis on the importance of Amenominakanushi in the creation of the universe. Amenominakanushi assumed the crucial role of the uncreated creator deity of the Musubi-no-kami and, as such, did not have a crucial theological role in Atsutane's cosmology. Thus, Takamasa's emphasis on this *kami* was perhaps an indication less of Atsutane's influence than of Suzuki Masayuki's (1837–71).[51] Like Masayuki, Takamasa's emphasis on Amenominakanushi posed a threat to the theological primacy of Amaterasu. Takamasa, however, exceeded Masayuki by

---

49. Ibid., pp. 475–76.
50. Ibid., p. 477.
51. Katsurajima, *Bakumatsu minshū shisō no kenkyū*, p. 111. Like Miyahiro Sadao, Masayuki was an influential scholar from Shimōsa. Unlike Sadao, Masayuki attempted to revise Atsutane's teachings, in addition to pursuing his work on agronomy. Whereas Atsutane had privileged the Musubi-no-kami, Masayuki emphasized a broader theological role for Amenominakanushi, arguing that Amenominakanushi was pure *tamashii* (spirit) and that all other *kami* were merely manifestations of *kokoro* (heart/mind). Masayuki went so far as to deny that Amaterasu was the supreme heavenly deity, a notion that irked supporters of imperial restoration (ibid., p. 113).

arguing that Amenominakanushi was the same deity as the Chinese god Shangdi and was identical to the Judeo-Christian God as well: "The divine spirit called Amenominakanushi in Japan is without a doubt the Deus of the West and the Shangdi, Tiandi, and such of China."⁵² At the same time, whereas most Kokugaku and Shinto scholars viewed Amaterasu and Amenominakanushi as two distinct deities, he conflated them; Amaterasu was simply an aspect of Amenominakanushi: "[Amaterasu] was concealed in the left eye of Izanagi. However, the truth is that [she] is the blessed spirit (*sakimitama*) of Amenominakanushi."⁵³ Therefore, while Suzuki Masayuki alienated supporters of the emperor with his emphasis on Amenominakanushi, Takamasa attempted to win them over by arguing that Amaterasu as Amenominakanushi was the supreme deity of the universe, which included both Asia and the West.

Takamasa upheld Atsutane's teaching that the essence of the ancient Way was rooted in knowledge of a spiritual afterlife: "The world of the living (*ningen sekai*) is manifest; the world of the supernatural (*shingen sekai*) is hidden. It is the same in every country. In the Japanese classics, the facts of the hidden realm are detailed and correct. In foreign countries, they are not."⁵⁴ He also believed that knowledge of the afterlife was revealed in the cosmic origins of the universe as related in the *kamiyo* chapters of the *Kojiki* and *Nihongi*. He called such cosmological knowledge *honkyō* (essential teachings), arguing that it demonstrated that Japan was the center of the universe and that its emperor was a universal sovereign.⁵⁵ He also repeated Atsutane's teaching that Japan was a nation of rice cultivators who had a special relationship with the *kami*.⁵⁶

Takamasa supported some of the contentions of grassroots *kokugakusha* as well, many of whom were his students. Like his student Shigetane, he argued that each occupation had its own theologically legitimate form of work, despite the fact that all

---

52. Ōkuni Takamasa, *Shin shinkōhōron narabi ni furoku*, p. 498.
53. Ibid., p. 511.
54. Ibid., p. 509.
55. Ōkuni Takamasa, *Hongaku kyoyō*, p. 405.
56. Ibid., p. 412.

occupations must ultimately support agriculture.⁵⁷ In the daily performance of one's work, Takamasa emphasized the importance of cooperation and altruism. This was the essence of *reigi* (decorum).⁵⁸ People who performed their work in this way were ultimately rewarded by the *kami*. Those who performed their work selfishly, however, were reprehensible and even diabolical. He extended this idea of altruism to include the relationship between the people and the ruler (*kimi*), although he did not specify whether this was the emperor or the shogun. The ruler must govern the people with benevolence and render them help and aid when needed. It would be contrary to the will of the *kami*, he reasoned, if only the peasants lived up to their part of the relationship via the payment of their taxes, while the ruler ignored his divine obligations, especially during the tough times: "The peasants offer the annual tribute that supports the higher from the lower. The ruler above cannot simply be supported by the lower; he must also support the lower."⁵⁹ Such a notion of mutual political and economic support came close to Yorozu's idea of rural relief. Yorozu, however, had concluded, in a general condemnation of the warrior class, that warriors would never voluntarily cooperate and must be forced to offer such support and assistance. Takamasa was not as critical of the samurai class.

Yano Gendō: Political Activism and Public Education

Yano Gendō was part of a generation of Kokugaku scholars who became active in the years immediately following Atsutane's death. He was an avid follower of Atsutane's teachings and impressed Kanetane with his energy and dedication. Kanetane's admiration of Gendō was such that when Gendō approached him for permission to complete Atsutane's *Koshiden*, Kanetane granted the request.⁶⁰ Gendō began the project in 1877, finishing the final ten books of

---

57. Ibid., p. 432.
58. Ibid., p. 415.
59. Ibid., p. 427.
60. Kobayashi, *Hirata Shintō no kenkyū*, p. 54.

the *Koshiden* by 1884. He became the leader of a small Hirata School faction concerned with investigating the eschatological aspects of Atsutane's teachings; a larger faction focused almost exclusively on Atsutane's texts as religious scripture.[61] Gendō felt that his dedication to spiritual matters made him the only member of the Hirata School who was qualified to finish the *Koshiden*. Kanetane's approval of Gendō's work was an important institutional sanction for Gendō.

Both Kanetane and Gendō developed a close relationship during the bakumatsu and early Meiji. While Takamasa advocated his *dōtō* succession of Atsutane, Gendō viewed him as an outsider who knew little about the essence of Atsutane's teachings. Though Takamasa placed himself in the orthodox lineage of Kokugaku, Gendō's relationship with Kanetane positioned him in direct contact with the *iemoto* lineage of the Hirata School. Despite Takamasa's claims, Gendō also upheld the importance of the *shiushi* lineage for his work:

[The ancients] learned both good and misguided [teachings]. All of the empty teachings and so forth came [to Japan in antiquity]. . . . It took centuries before there were great men who could grasp the fact that there was no [foreign] Way or teachings in antiquity. The age [of that realization] began with the two venerable men, Kada [Azumamaro] and Agatai. Then, the Great Man, Suzunoya, followed by our Great Man, Ibukinoya, appeared. . . . They canvassed even the remotest domains for [knowledge of] ancient conditions and such. . . . Nowadays, according to the explanations of these Great Men, the divine Way takes but a thread and gives back very little [in return]. I think that these are moving words.[62]

For most of the 1860s, the two factions—one led by Kanetane and Gendō; the other by Takamasa—dominated the Hirata School, and their influence extended into the field of doctrinal Shinto. The members of the once dominant Norinaga School could not compete with those of the Hirata School. The members of the two rival factions of the Hirata School enjoyed a level of political influence during bakumatsu that their nativist forebears never had.

---

61. Ibid., p. 66.
62. Yano Gendō, *Tamaboko monogatari*, pp. 542–43.

The members of the Hirata School were able to take advantage of their influence during the early years of Meiji. Since the leaders of the new government viewed the Hirata School as their ideological supporters, they hired many of its members as specialists in Japanese history and Shinto.[63] During these years, Kanetane, Gendō, and Takamasa all joined the government as advisors on matters of religious policy within the revived Jingikan (Bureau of Divinity). In fact, Gendō played a crucial role in the restoration of this institution, considered by nativists to be the highest political organ in antiquity.

As an instructor of Shinto priests of the Yoshida and Shirakawa houses, Gendō began the movement to restore the Jingikan in 1864. With the impending collapse of the bakufu, he argued that the new state would require specialists well versed in knowledge of the imperial institution in order to lead the effort to establish a government founded on the principle of *saisei itchi* (the unity of government and religion) as it had been in antiquity.[64] In addition, he believed that these government officials would be Shinto scholars who would preserve and transmit their specialized knowledge within newly established universities. In order to commemorate the restoration of imperial power, he called for the creation of a *shinden* (new shrine) dedicated to Amenominakanushi and Ōkuninushi—*kami* that were prominent in Atsutane's cosmology—where the worship of the living emperor was to occur.[65] Like many of his bakumatsu contemporaries, he held high hopes for the new state.

With the arrival of the Meiji state in 1868, *kokugakusha* achieved official recognition and legitimacy as scholars of the imperial institution. As a first step in realizing the vision of a new state that united both religious and political spheres, they began their effort to establish a state school dedicated to "the learning of the imperial realm," a broad area of scholarship that encompassed Kokugaku. Although Takamasa supported the idea of using popular education

---

63. For a discussion of Kokugaku and its role in the formation of state Shinto during the Meiji period, see Hardacre, *Shinto and the State*, pp. 16–18.

64. Sakamoto, *Meiji ishin to kokugakusha*, p. 55.

65. Ibid., p. 60.

as a vehicle for spreading the influence of Shinto,[66] Kanetane, his son Nobutane, and Gendō were the primary supporters of the movement to establish a state-supported school of Kokugaku.

The architects of the new Meiji government understood the importance of public education in the success of the Western powers. In 1869 they scrapped most of the educational institutions of the former regime and established their own Kyōdōkyoku (Bureau of Education). Meiji leaders enlisted the aid of specialists deemed qualified to promulgate a new educational policy and philosophy. Many *kokugakusha* were among those chosen to serve in the newly formed Bureau, since they had experience with the private academies of the Tokugawa period.

The ascendance of the Hirata School during bakumatsu, however, altered this trend. As part of Atsutane's effort to marshal the symbolic support of important institutions, he had become a tutor to the Yoshida house; this was one of the important results of his journey to Kyoto. Beginning in the 1830s, priests of the main Shinto rival of the Yoshida, the Shirakawa, also approached Atsutane with a request to establish a similar arrangement. Their affiliation with the Hirata School culminated in the establishment of a *gakuryō* (academic bureau) in Kyoto in 1867. Not to be outdone, priests of the Yoshida approached Kanetane with a proposal to establish their own academy devoted to Shinto and Kokugaku, and they nominated Gendō as its head.[67] Although the members of the Hirata School enjoyed their courtship by the leaders of the Yoshida and the Shirakawa, Kanetane was concerned that rivalry between the two could prove counterproductive in his general effort to rally the members of the Hirata School around Gendō's movement to reestablish the Jingikan. Like Kanetane, Gendō was not interested in the petty rivalry between the Yoshida and the Shirakawa, arguing that any nativist academy founded by the Yoshida would belong to the nation and not be the exclusive possession of the Yoshida.[68]

Although both Kanetane and Gendō cooperated in the effort to expand the influence of the Hirata School, Kanetane realized that

---

66. Ibid., p. 85.
67. Ibid., pp. 180–81.
68. Ibid., p. 183.

Gendō was better suited for politics than he. This is perhaps why Gendō submitted a proposal to the Meiji government that outlined the official position of the Hirata School and favored the first state-supported nativist academy. It was one proposal among many solicited by the government and was ultimately rejected. Gendō and others felt that the new academy should be located in Kyoto, as the traditional capital of Japan and the residence of the emperor; they absolutely opposed Edo—which they associated with the defunct military regime of the Tokugawa—as a potential site.[69] Unfortunately for Gendō and others, the decision was made to reopen Gakushūin in Tokyo, an institution traditionally associated with the education of social elites. Moreover, the Meiji government reopened three important bakufu educational institutions: the Shōheikō (the former Bakufu College), the Kaiseikō, and the Igakkō. These institutions had been founded by the bakufu as training institutions for bureaucrats and physicians (in the case of the Igakkō).

Gendō interpreted these reopenings as part of a larger attempt to suppress the influence of Kokugaku in the curricula of the new educational institutions of Meiji. Indeed, few scholars who were hired to staff Gakushūin were *kokugakusha*; most, in fact, were associated with Kangaku.[70] Meiji Kangaku was not the same as what Atsutane had identified as Han Learning (also "Kangaku") during the Tokugawa period.[71] By early Meiji, it was a term used to signify Chinese learning in general, and this may be one of the reasons why its usage during the Tokugawa period is often misunderstood. Although Neo-Confucianism was associated with the discredited Tokugawa regime, Chinese philosophy experienced a resurgence during the late bakumatsu and early Meiji, as an assertion of Eastern ethics against Western technology. Gendō and oth-

---

69. For a discussion of the early Meiji debate on moving the capital from Kyoto to Tokyo, see Takashi, *Splendid Monarchy*, pp. 34–42.

70. Sakamoto, *Meiji ishin to kokugakusha*, p. 192.

71. The identification of Qing Han Learning with evidential learning was made during the early Meiji period. For many Meiji scholars, evidential learning was one of the few aspects of Confucianism worth adopting because of its latent modernity, one that was not borrowed from the West. Evidential learning was especially useful for scholars who sought to introduce modern historical studies into Japan. See Katsurajima, *Shisōshi no jūkyū seiki*, pp. 273–79.

ers resisted the trend to associate Chinese learning with Japanese culture and history. Unfortunately for him, the reopening of bakufu institutions was a sign that Meiji leaders did not acknowledge his opposition.

Gendō and Kanetane opposed the opening of Gakushūin, arguing that it was too elitist in orientation and its views of Kokugaku were too ideologically distorted. They continued to press the government for an academy with a curriculum that was exclusively nativist. There was another proposal that seemed reasonable to some within the Meiji government. This was to establish a *kōgakuin* (imperial learning institute) that would be dedicated to the study of Kokugaku, military science, Chinese learning, and Western learning.[72] Kanetane, Gendō, and even Takamasa were still opposed to the idea of treating Chinese learning on an equal basis with Kokugaku. Finally, a compromise was reached that established separate institutions for the study of Chinese learning and imperial learning. The three Kokugaku leaders were put in charge of this new institution.

Much like their earlier efforts, the new academy was a total failure; it closed its doors in 1869, less than a year after it opened. The government eventually founded a new educational institution, Tokyo Imperial University, in 1877. The *kokugakusha* initially courted by the government as educational specialists had essentially no influence in its founding.[73] A department of classics, the Kotenkōshūka, was attached to it five years later. However, as was then typical of the efforts of *kokugakusha* to get their scholarship officially recognized, it also closed after just six years.

Early Meiji *kokugakusha* were divided over the intellectual orientation of their proposed academy. Gendō and Kanetane led the faction of scholars maintaining the eighteenth-century emphasis on the analysis of classical texts. Gendō realized that Kokugaku had to retain its scholarly character if it was to appeal to Meiji policymakers; he assumed the responsibility for shaping it into a form that resembled the Kangaku mold. It was mostly through his efforts that the Kotenkōshūka was established at Tokyo Imperial Univer-

---

72. Sakamoto, *Meiji ishin to kokugakusha*, p. 212.
73. Kobayashi, *Hirata Shintō no kenkyū*, p. 75.

sity. The other faction within the Hirata School, however, sought to preserve Atsutane's emphasis on the nontextual aspects of the ancient Way. In the same year that Gendō founded the Kōtenkōshūka, this group of mostly Shinto priests founded Kōggakan University (1882). Kōggakan received government support beginning in 1940 and continues to be one of two universities in Japan that still trains Shinto priests.

The Meiji period was an important and crucial one for the Hirata School. The *kokugakusha*, especially those of the Hirata School, rode the wave of social and political influence generated by the grassroots Kokugaku of the bakumatsu period. By 1868, the Hirata School's enrollment far outdistanced those of any other Kokugaku school. However, beginning in the 1870s, this enrollment began to decline sharply. As Shimazaki Tōson described in *Yōakemae*, supporters of the Hirata School were profoundly disappointed with the social and political order created by the new Meiji government. The leaders of the Hirata School no longer focused their efforts solely on its perpetuation but on educational policy for the government. Ironically, Kanetane and others attained the kind of official appointments that Atsutane had always unsuccessfully sought. Their roles as consultants conferred recognition upon them that bolstered their positions as leaders of the Kokugaku movement, but they were also distracted from the work of sustaining the Hirata School's vitality. The combination of the ascent of a new political order with the powerful intellectual and social position of the Hirata School ultimately dampened the enthusiasm of its members.

As the case of Gendō's support for the Kōtenkōshūka demonstrates, the emphasis within the Hirata School also changed. The grassroots Kokugaku of bakumatsu proved ideologically irrelevant to the Meiji government, losing its appeal to its rural adherents as well. Moreover, the theological aspects of Atsutane's scholarship had to compete with views that emphasized the importance of Amaterasu as the divine ancestor of the emperor. Atsutane's teachings were not the most suitable ideology for supporters of imperial restoration. Sensing the impending irrelevancy of Atsutane's scholarship, Kanetane tried to reassert the literary and textual past of Kokugaku. By attempting to reconceptualize it into a more acceptable form of knowledge, he helped hasten the demise of Atsutane's teachings during the Meiji period. Classical literary studies were, in fact, the form of Kokugaku that Atsutane had most vigorously resisted.

The literary scholar Fujii Sadafumi argues that the modern character of Kokugaku is a product of the Meiji period. He cites two reasons for this. First, it was officially recognized in various ways by the Meiji government, as was just discussed.[74] Lacking such recognition during the Tokugawa period, Kokugaku was never viewed as the intellectual equal of Confucian learning. Second, its recognition during Meiji signified the acknowledgment of both its literary and its religious forms. Kanetane and Gendō were instrumental in this development. As we have seen, the more devoted followers of the Hirata School broke away from its leadership to found Kōgakkan University in protest against the embrace of classical literature. Thus, Gendō and Kanetane remained the leaders of a Hirata School whose popularity was diluted by its emphasis on literature.

In such a weakened intellectual position, the Hirata School became vulnerable to those who advocated literary Kokugaku, especially following the deaths of Kanetane and Gendō. Along with classical literature, the evidential learning of the Tokugawa period also made a comeback during the first two decades of the Meiji period. Literary scholars naturally gravitated toward the combination of the two. Their embrace of literary Kokugaku resulted in a general disdain for the Hirata School as lacking scholarly precision.[75] The scholar who helped lead this effort was Haga Yaichi (1867–1927), whose intellectual lineage included Motoori Uchitō, the son of Ōhira. Haga Yaichi studied philology in Germany following the Sino-Japanese War, returning to Japan with the view that Kokugaku represented the indigenous development of philology.[76] He argued that Japan had its own tradition of philologists like Keichū but lacked the crucial sense of national identity that had developed

---

74. Fujii S., *Edo kokugaku tensei-shi no kenkyū*, p. 40.
75. Haga N., "Bakumatsu henkaku-ki ni okeru kokugakusha no undō to ronri," p. 709.
76. Haga Y., *Nihon no bunkengaku*, p. 1.

in Germany. He was critical of the antiscientific tendencies of Kokugaku,[77] specifically those of the Hirata School, and he flatly rejected grassroots Kokugaku: "Norinaga had very calmly advocated Japanism (*Nihonshugi*) and steadily reached his conclusions; he proceeded in the manner of a scholar. However, Atsutane radically exceeded him. He first advanced a doctrine and then later supported it with evidence. He was a bit daring, like a politician."[78] He and others argued that Kokugaku should be the study of language and literature, but Atsutane was different: "Among Atsutane's works, there are some on literature and language. However, his main concern was Shinto."[79] Consequently, these scholars helped create the fields of Kokugogaku (national language studies) and Kokubungaku (national literature), which they identified collectively as Kokugaku. Hirata Kokugaku was effectively discredited as a legitimate discipline by the end of the nineteenth century.

Conclusion

The members of the Norinaga School enjoyed the dominance of their form of nativism during the early nineteenth century. Atsutane challenged the hegemony not because he himself initially sought such dominance, but because his very position within the Norinaga School was at stake. He sought to form alliances with influential members of the Norinaga School and with priests of Yoshida Shinto in Kyoto, in an attempt to marshal the requisite social capital to bolster his standing. His academy, however, was one among many within the Norinaga School, and his position was therefore marginal during the early years of the nineteenth century.

Rural scholars, however, recognized in Atsutane's scholarship a potential ideology that could both support their agronomic project and also provide a justification for the dominance of rural elites, a group from which most of them came. The combination of agronomy and Atsutane's cosmology resulted in the formation of grass-

---

77. Ibid., p. 8.
78. Haga Y., *Kokugaku-shi gairon*, pp. 85–86.
79. Ibid., p. 83.

roots Kokugaku. Scholars of grassroots Kokugaku provided the foundation for the national expansion of the Hirata School, and many of its most energetic adherents were active in recruiting new members. This was just the first stage, however, in the development of the Hirata School. While central aspects of Atsutane's teachings, such as his concern for the accurate cataloging of supernatural phenomena, were almost entirely ignored by his followers in the bakumatsu period, his other intellectual legacies, most notably the invention of Kokugaku, were retained and transmitted. Thus, the social and political dominance of the Hirata School resulted in the ascendance of Hirata Kokugaku. There were, of course, *kokugakusha* who continued to research the Japanese classics during the bakumatsu period, but the popularity of grassroots Kokugaku eclipsed their efforts.

While Kanetane appreciated the support of the rural members of the Hirata School, he continued to preserve aspects of Atsutane's teachings that were not central to grassroots Kokugaku. Yano Gendō assisted him in this effort by completing Atsutane's *Koshiden*. As the Hirata School grew in prominence during the 1850s, Ōkuni Takamasa argued that Kanetane had lost the Kokugaku *dōtō*, which he believed had come to reside in his own teachings. As the leaders of the Hirata School, all three were brought into the Meiji government as Shinto consultants. Over the course of the first two decades of Meiji, the influence of the Hirata School gradually faded. The supporters of grassroots Kokugaku left the School, and its leadership resigned their government posts. With the importation of Western academic traditions, Hirata Kokugaku was relegated to Japan's traditional past.

EIGHT

Conclusion: Centrality at the Margins

In the present study, we have focused on three interpretive issues. First, we have examined the relationship between the primarily literary form of nativism that typified the eighteenth century and the more religious form dominant during the nineteenth century. The key figures in the articulation of the literary discourse were Kamo no Mabuchi and Motoori Norinaga; Mabuchi emphasized the study of classical poetics and Norinaga favored more narrative genres like classical history and literary tales. The most important nativist of the nineteenth century was Hirata Atsutane, whose scholarship deliberately initiated the transition toward religious knowledge and away from eighteenth-century classicism. He accomplished this transformation in two stages. In the first stage, he attempted to disguise his scholarship as literary in nature and philological in its methodology. This attempt, however, was met with fierce opposition from the entrenched members of the Norinaga School, who dismissed him as an amateur. This failure prompted Atsutane—once he had consolidated and marshaled his own political and social allies both within and outside the School—to dismiss *his* opponents as spiritually misguided; this was the second stage. Thus, the conflict between these two competing forms of nativism was an inherently *social* and *political* struggle over orthodoxy within the Norinaga School. The analysis of Harry Harootunian asserts epistemological commonalities between these two forms of nativism, but the conflict between them reflects a struggle among competing factions within the Norinaga School that was, and continues to be, misunderstood or unacknowledged. The failure to recognize the intellectual implications of this polarity within nativist discourse is the result of significant analytic flaws inhering in the methodological approaches of modern scholars.

A second major issue has been the formation of Kokugaku as a distinct discourse *and* cultural institution during the Tokugawa period. Mabuchi's contribution to this emerging discourse during the eighteenth century was the notion of purging Shinto scholarship of its Confucian elements, namely, its reliance on Neo-Confucian metaphysics. Norinaga extended this critique of Neo-Confucianism by radicalizing Mabuchi's belief in a pure form of Shinto. Norinaga rejected *all* foreign influences on Japanese Shinto, depicting the latter as the cultural essence of Japan. His intellectual and philosophical stance with regard to Neo-Confucianism was inherently xenophobic and culturally intolerant. This was Norinaga's legacy for Kokugaku, and it became a fundamental aspect of its ideology.

The contours of Kokugaku discourse were largely in place by Atsutane's time. His own contributions to that discourse are significant but cannot be understood without reference to the formation of Kokugaku's institutional identity. Modern scholars have conceptualized this identity as "grassroots" Kokugaku. Atsutane's formulation of nativism as a religious discourse was associated with the rural popularization of its message. Atsutane, however, did not initially tailor his scholarship to suit a rural constituency. Certain aspects of it found an attentive audience among village scholars who actively propagated his teachings, resulting in a level of popularity that was unmatched by any other nativist. The obverse of this popularity, however, was the suppression of elements of Atsutane's thought that seemed to baffle his popularizers. The selective reading of his scholarship by his rural supporters was a contributing factor to the historical distortion of Atsutane's scholarship, and one that continues to this day.

The third major focus of this study has been the interpretive problem presented by historical analyses that emphasize an approach that we can call discourse analysis. Such an approach, favored by historians like Harootunian in the United States and Koyasu Nobukuni in Japan, conceptualizes the object of inquiry as fundamentally based on the language used by historical actors. Thus, all human experience is essentially discursive in nature. It is incumbent on the historian to apply to history analytical methodologies specifically formulated to analyze discourse.

As Harootunian and others argue, history, as an artifact of the past, is nothing more than a text, and it must be interpreted as such.[1] Unlike those who favor more traditional approaches to intellectual history, proponents of discourse analysis ignore any causal relationship between the text and its historical conditions of production, dismissing the hermeneutic centrality of the author as an arbitrary attempt to reduce the meaning of a text to one legitimate reading. One of the basic methodological assumptions of the structuralist and post-structuralist frameworks is that authors do not exist outside the texts that they produce. Consequently, authors are not subjects; subjectivity itself does not exist. Post-structuralist philosophers, notably Michel Foucault and Jacques Derrida, agree that the idea of subjectivity's final say on textual interpretation is false because authors cannot and do not possess their own language.[2] What historians have commonly assumed about the relationship between subjects and their utterances is reversed by these philosophers: language possesses, and in the same process constitutes, its enunciator (author). Using such an approach, scholars are free to ignore history as existing "outside" of texts, since it resides *within* them. This view echoes Jacques Derrida's famous line: "There is nothing outside of the text."[3]

As Pierre Bourdieu and Roger Chartier argue, however, there is an alternative to both traditional intellectual history as the history of ideas and the discourse analysis yielded by structuralist, and especially post-structuralist, approaches. They agree with their post-structuralist colleagues that scholars must reject subjectivity as the primary analytic device in the interpretation of texts. They do not,

---

1. Harootunian, *Things Seen and Unseen*, p. 15.
2. For a more elaborate discussion of this issue, especially as it relates to Tokugawa Japan, see Sakai, *Voices of the Past*, pp. 11–18.
3. Derrida, *Of Grammatology*, p. 158.

however, privilege discourse as the primary object of historical investigation either. Existing at a subtextual level, the notion of *practice* introduces an analytic dimension that successfully combines the external reading of the context with the internal reading of the text. The analysis of practice regards the social conditions of textual production as a fundamental counterpart to the actual content of the text itself. The emphasis on practice does not posit an absolute authorial intention as the final reading of a text. Instead, such an approach conceptualizes the text as the locus of its author's struggle in a social space populated by other authors, each competing for particular stakes. These authors are not subjects, as the structuralists and post-structuralists assert, yet they are not mere prisoners of their own language either.

Bourdieu proposes to conceptualize authors as historical *agents*, determined not by an internal subjectivity revealed only to the agents themselves but by a "habitus" that, given enough data, researchers can objectify and quantify.[4] By looking at the struggles of such agents in a particular field, the analyst gains insight into the conditions of textual production that formal texts do not necessarily reveal. Thus, Bourdieu asserts that an approach emphasizing practice yields an interpretation that relies on both the text and a *particular form* of context, without exclusively resorting to authorial intention. The analysis of practice considers an agent's habitus along with the social rules of the particular field within which that agent operated. Thus, agents are not always, if ever, cognizant of their own practice; authorial intention, even if known, does not close the interpretation of a text.

By rejecting any notion of an external reading, scholars who use discourse analysis have no access to the social conditions of textual production. Harootunian claims to focus on the discursive contradictions of Tokugawa scholars in order to avoid the projection of coherence onto the past, but his use of discourse analysis in the writing of history nevertheless depends on highlighting their intellectual continuities, which amounts to just such a historical projection.[5] He rejects the traditional interpretations of Kokugaku per-

---

4. Bourdieu, *In Other Words*, pp. 90–91.
5. Ibid., p. 13.

petuated by Japanese scholars and accepted uncritically by Peter Nosco. These scholars assert that Kokugaku was a distinct intellectual tradition from the moment of its inception in the seventeenth century; they suppress the crucial intellectual differences among the *kokugakusha* in an attempt to preserve the coherence of the discourse. Harootunian seems to be aware of the problems inherent in this view, yet he himself ignores key intellectual contradictions within Kokugaku discourse in order to maintain its status as a distinct discursive phenomenon. A unique Kokugaku discourse did develop, but only very late in the Tokugawa period, and it was subsequently given a long institutional history by Atsutane as a strategy of self-legitimation. By viewing Kokugaku as a discourse, Harootunian uncritically accepts Atsutane's ideological intervention. Atsutane's retrospective projections of continuity, as well as his selective historical amnesia, are forms of practice—informed by his habitus and the field of nativism—that elude both traditional intellectual history and discourse analysis.

☙

Classical literary studies and Shinto scholarship were the main forms of nativism during the Tokugawa period. The tension between the adherents of the two forms continued even after Atsutane's death, and, in some ways, persists to this day. During his lifetime, the more ardent supporters of Atsutane and his academy surpassed the influence of the proponents of literary nativism, mainly the members of the Norinaga School and the Edo-ha. Thus, religious nativism superseded classicism. Missing from modern studies of the Kasei period is an analysis of the mechanisms involved in Atsutane's effort to suppress literary studies. This is an especially vexing problem when one considers that classical literary studies constituted the prevailing form of nativism since the time of Mabuchi in the middle of the eighteenth century. Although the scholars of the Edo-ha and the Norinaga School were rivals, and despite their ideological differences over the broader significance on such endeavors, literary studies were an integral part of each group's identity. The members of the Hirata School enjoyed their dominance over the rest of the Norinaga School until the first decade of the Meiji period, when the former was discredited as a vestige of Japan's premodern past and an impediment to the demands of modernization.

Atsutane's emphasis on eschatological knowledge represented a radical departure from the classical research of the previous century. Such sudden ruptures commonly appear when analyzing the internal formation of discourses, or when tracing the evolution of important ideas. Breaks with the past in the formation of a discourse are an expected occurrence and an indication of the discourse's intellectual dynamism; otherwise, dramatic changes, such as Atsutane's emphasis on knowledge of the afterlife and the supernatural, are relegated to his creativity or brilliance. Studies of Atsutane's role in the history of Kokugaku have relied on the latter explanation; consequently, a satisfactory account of Atsutane's break with the eighteenth century has never emerged.

Bourdieu's emphasis on practice, especially that of historical agents in objective social fields of cultural production, is useful for explaining such abrupt discursive changes. Hence, a sociopolitical analysis of Atsutane and his relationship to other members of the Norinaga School is in order. As we have seen, he occupied an insignificant social position within the expanding Norinaga School at the beginning of the nineteenth century. As a resident of Edo, his marginality was geographical as well, since the Norinaga School itself was based in Matsusaka and Wakayama. Moreover, Edo had a thriving literary culture with scholars and *bunjin* who intermingled in its *shitamachi* districts. The members of the Edo-ha maintained the scholarship of their deceased mentor Mabuchi, as they moved closer to falling under the influence of Edo's most prominent poets and writers. Their fascination with literature eroded their identity as members of the Mabuchi School, an institutional identity that their rivals in the Norinaga School steadfastly maintained. Although Atsutane attended some Edo-ha gatherings, he was an outsider himself, even as a resident of Edo. Indeed, he formally joined the Norinaga School in 1805 and repudiated the Edo-ha in the *Tamadasuki*. Thus, he was a liminal figure in both groups during the early nineteenth century. His decision to join the Norinaga School was a response to feelings of rejection by his colleagues in the Edo-ha. An analysis of Atsutane and his relationship to the

Norinaga School must begin with a discussion of his immediate environment in Edo and his ties with the Edo-ha. Bourdieu's emphasis on practice provides the framework with which to conceptualize this relationship, adding a new dimension to his ultimate rejection of the Edo-ha as well.

Atsutane dismissed the Edo-ha as heterodox because of its exclusive focus on literary studies. He joined the Norinaga School because he felt that it had a more diverse disciplinary approach to nativism. Indeed, as we saw illustrated by the various members of the Norinaga School, his estimation was at least partially correct. However, when he entered the intramural debate in the Norinaga School regarding the orthodoxy of Hattori Nakatsune's *Sandaikō*, he was quickly confronted with the limits of that intellectual tolerance. Atsutane's insistence that the essence of Norinaga's scholarship was not literary but religious and spiritual earned him sharp criticism and calls for his dismissal from the School, especially from its most influential members. Given the dynamics of fields of cultural production, such resistance to his scholarship is not surprising. But modern historians have ignored the fierce resistance to Atsutane's scholarship within the Norinaga School. Not only was such opposition an important aspect of his career, but it is also indispensable in understanding the development of his thought. During his lifetime, Atsutane's distinctive interests were closely tied to his marginal position within the Norinaga School. He produced a discourse that made his scholarship unique, and which, at the same time, solidified his peripheral standing within the School.

There was a link between Atsutane's scholarship and the popularity of the Hirata School during the bakumatsu period. Elements of his scholarship appealed to rural scholars in search of a cosmological framework for their agronomic knowledge. They propagated his teachings in the countryside and attracted the attention of elites who esteemed his general admonition to work diligently in the fields as a form of religious practice. Elements of Atsutane's teachings appealed to them as an ideology that supported their social and political domination of village society, and thus these elites served as the primary tutors for Atsutane's teachings.

Atsutane sought the support of a rural constituency only after he was approached by agriculturists who offered to publish his books and recruit students in exchange for his sanction of their scholarship. He relied on the support of his followers as a form of financial assistance both for his own research efforts and for that of his academy. He wanted to occupy, as his predecessors had, an official and remunerative post as a scholar; the fact that he was never able to secure such a post only augmented the economic importance of his adherents. Moreover, by solidifying his ties with rural society, he was able to amass a following that eclipsed the influence of his Noringa School rivals, who were ensconced in their urban academies. Hence, the nineteenth-century ruralization of nativism was almost entirely attributable to the Hirata School. This movement was a response to the School's rejection by the other scholars of the Norinaga School, who were engaged in classical research. The rural appeal of Atsutane's teachings was *not* the result of a conscious effort by either Atsutane or his immediate disciples to involve villagers in what had been an exclusive pursuit of urban intellectuals. Atsutane did countenance certain transformations of his thought, such as his admonition against nonagricultural labor, by some of his students (like Miyahiro Sadao)—but only *after* he understood the potent financial and social support that rural society could provide. Thus, the ruralization of Kokugaku cannot be understood without reference to Atsutane's position within the Norinaga School.

Nativism Before Atsutane: The Discursive and Institutional Foundations of Kokugaku

Many scholars believe that Azumamaro outlined the fundamental assumptions of Kokugaku in the *Sōgakkōkei*. Based on this view, Japanese researchers, as well as Peter Nosco, assert Azumamaro's role as the founder of Kokugaku. It is unlikely that he actually composed this crucial text, however. It was probably composed around the time of its first publication as a part of Azumamaro's collected works in the 1790s. Moreover, it is not a coincidence that this prevailing view of Kokugaku was advocated by Atsutane. In fact, his outline of the history of Kokugaku in the *Tamadasuki* perhaps originated what became an influential interpretation. This constitutes clear evidence of the persistence and influence of Atsutane's thought since the end of the Tokugawa period.

Atsutane insisted that Azumamaro was the first scholar of Kokugaku. His status as its founder stemmed from his formulation of the Japanese Way (identified by Atsutane as the ancient Way), and the *transmission* of this formulation to Mabuchi. By comparison, Keichū, the scholar revered in an earlier hagiography supported by the members of the Edo-ha, had no understanding of the ancient Way; consequently, he could not pass its wisdom on to anyone. Atsutane advocated the idea of a Kokugaku *dōtō* that did not include Keichū. If Keichū were hailed as the founder of Kokugaku, then Atsutane could not have demonstrated how his own scholarship was the culmination, and even perfection, of the Way. Therefore, he chose Azumamaro over Keichū as the progenitor of the Kokugaku lineage.

In Atsutane's estimation, Azumamaro's disciple and successor, Mabuchi, had applied rigorous textual methods to classical verse in order to demonstrate the existence of the ancient Way. Though Mabuchi had focused his efforts exclusively on classical poetics, Atsutane insisted that Mabuchi had understood that the essence of the ancient Way was not exclusively revealed in the analysis of poetry. Atsutane's contemporary, Murata Harumi, disagreed, asserting that Mabuchi, like Keichū, was concerned only with classical poetics; Harumi argued that Mabuchi never subscribed to the idea of a native Way at all. Thus, Atsutane's interpretation was a direct refutation of Harumi and the entire Edo-ha to which Harumi belonged.

Similar to his dismissal of the members of the Edo-ha from the *dōtō* was Atsutane's criticism of his Norinaga School rivals. Mabuchi had refuted Neo-Confucianism by arguing that Shinto, as Japan's indigenous Way, was nearly identical to Daoism. This was unacceptable to Norinaga, who had rejected Mabuchi's equation of Shinto with Daoism by arguing that the latter was too highly articulated to qualify as the natural essence of Shinto. The need to study nature and to abstract universal principles from it was characteristic of the "Chinese mind." Thus, in his attempt to extend and improve upon Mabuchi's critique of Neo-Confucianism, he was compelled to reject Chinese culture in toto. This was the origin of the cultural chauvinism that characterized nineteenth-century Kokugaku. The call to purge Shinto of its Chinese influences, mistakenly attributed to Azumamaro, was articulated first by Norinaga as a response to Mabuchi.

Although Norinaga formulated the xenophobia that became the foundation of Kokugaku during the nineteenth century, his discourse did not initially foster a self-awareness among nativists that they were part of a distinct intellectual movement. Such an identity began to be discussed in the years immediately following Norinaga's death. The particular incident that inspired this awakening was the debate between Harumi and Izumi Makuni in 1803. As a member of the Norinaga School, Makuni criticized Harumi for his reliance on classical Chinese texts in the interpretation of Japanese texts. In addition, Makuni reiterated Norinaga's earlier criticism, by attacking Harumi's use of Confucian categories and terms, especially the Way of the Sages, in his analysis of antiquity. In what became a famous retort, Harumi declared that his use of such terminology was natural, because, he reasoned, "I am a Confucian."[6]

This debate between the two nativists is significant because it demonstrates the considerable ideological gap between the Norinaga School and the Edo-ha. Harumi's exasperated reply to Makuni and his self-identification as a Confucian scholar indicate that the Mabuchi students in Edo had not made the crucial separation of nativism from Confucianism. Makuni's discourse, wholly derived from Norinaga, represented an anticipation of such a break that Makuni himself did not actually complete. Makuni's refutation of Harumi's stance on Confucianism implied the existence of a certain intellectual coherence for nativism apart from Confucianism and Buddhism. It was the logical development and extension of Norinaga's antiforeign rhetoric. But Makuni was unable to advocate an independent nativist identity since the Norinaga School did not yet have a significant institutional presence outside Matsusaka during the early years of the nineteenth century. We should recall that such an identity was specifically denied by Norinaga because he viewed the establishment of a network of affiliated academies,

---

6. *Meidōsho*, p. 139.

each parroting the teachings of the same master, as a trait of the Chinese mind. However, in the decade following Makuni's death in 1806, such a network of academies began to take shape, and the combination of a nativist discourse with a stronger institutional identity for the Norinaga School contributed to the eventual formation of Kokugaku during the nineteenth century.

The expansion of the Norinaga School began as a direct result of Norinaga's fame during the eighteenth century. As a scholar for the daimyo of Kii, Norinaga wrote his two political treatises and served as tutor on *waka* and classical history. The daimyo's heir invited Ōhira, Norinaga's successor, to serve in his adoptive father's stead. Consequently, Ōhira and his family moved to Wakayama, where he assumed his official post. Such a move meant that he had to abandon Matsusaka and the Suzunoya along with it. In Ōhira's place, and against his father's wishes, Haruniwa, Norinaga's biological son, decided to revive his father's academy. Many of the Suzunoya's most gifted scholars, like Suzuki Akira and Uematsu Arinobu, supported Haruniwa's efforts; the academy reopened as the Nochi-Suzunoya and Haruniwa began to accept his own students.

By 1810 the Norinaga School had two centers, Matsusaka and Wakayama. By 1805 Atsutane had formed his own academy, which he later christened the Ibukinoya. He formally joined Haruniwa's academy the following year, thereby affiliating the Ibukinoya with the Nochi-Suzunoya. Another prominent scholar in Edo, Ban Nobutomo, joined Ōhira's academy around the same time; thus, the Norinaga School had a presence in Edo, even if it was a modest one. Kyoto, however, was a different matter. In 1816 a student of the old Suzunoya, Kido Chidate, formed his own academy in Kyoto, which he called the Nudenoya. Although Chidate was an officially registered student of the Suzunoya, his interest in classical poetry prompted him to establish ties with the Edo-ha as well, even though he never relinquished his identity as a Norinaga disciple. One of his friends, Fujii Takanao, himself a favored disciple of Norinaga, helped establish yet another affiliated academy in Osaka, the Koshibaya, shortly after Chidate founded the Nudenoya. In addition to establishing these academies in Edo, Osaka, and Kyoto, disciples of Norinaga founded an academy in Nagoya (the Meirindō), and disciples throughout Japan, some even in Kyushu, joined the Norinaga School, lecturing and teaching in small groups.

Atsutane identified his Ibukinoya with the expanding Norinaga School in part because of Ōhira's assertion that the School's approach to nativism was versatile and intellectually tolerant. Ōhira denied that an exclusive focus on poetry, as advocated by the members of the Edo-ha, was sufficient for a comprehensive examination of antiquity. Atsutane took Ōhira's observation to heart, hoping that there was room enough in the Norinaga School for his interests in the afterlife. Ōhira sanctioned the intellectual diversity that the geographic expansion of the Norinaga School fostered, and Atsutane hoped to use this tolerance to his advantage.

Atsutane, however, was not welcomed with the warm reception that he had expected. In fact, many of his opponents advocated his dismissal from the Norinaga School entirely. Threatened with ostracism, he reacted to his opponents by going on the offensive. Specifically, he asserted that his vision of nativism was correct, and the scholarship of his opponents was degenerate and self-indulgent. In the *Tama no mihashira*, he argued that his scholarship on spirits and the afterlife was consistent with Norinaga's teachings. With the *Tamadasuki*, published two decades later, his rhetoric sharpened as he claimed that only his scholarship was true to Norinaga's legacy. He effectively turned his rivals' criticisms against them. In assessing the status of his eschatological research within the Norinaga School, he was confronted with two extremes: either he could accept the views of his rivals and leave the School, or he could maintain the validity of his scholarship and claim orthodoxy for himself. Thus, his strategy of self-legitimation was an "all-or-nothing game." Randall Collins observes that some intellectuals face the "strategic choice" either to become "king of the mountain," or to assume the status of a "loyal follower of some successful position."[7] Atsutane's strong convictions eliminated the latter choice as an option. What began as a quest for inclusion in the Norinaga School ended for Atsutane in claims of leadership and orthodoxy.

---

7. Collins, *The Sociology of Philosophies*, p. 40.

By making such claims, Atsutane was forced to define the precise meaning of orthodoxy. He repeated Norinaga's assertions that Shinto constituted a Way of its own that was *not* derivative of either Buddhism or Confucianism. He defined Japan's indigenous Way as simply the ancient Way. The key difference with Norinaga was that Atsutane specifically identified the ancient Way with eschatology and the supernatural. Moreover, he incorporated the ancient Way into the first orthodox lineage for Kokugaku. He argued that Azumamaro was the first to articulate this ancient Way, transmitting it to Mabuchi, who in turn transmitted it to Norinaga. Atsutane claimed that he himself received the teachings of the Way from Norinaga in a dream, which established him as the fourth saint of the lineage. In addition, he identified certain classical texts such as the *Kojiki* and *Nihongi* as scriptural sources for the revelation of the ancient Way. With his orthodox lineage, he combined the discursive framework articulated by Norinaga with the institutional expansion of the Norinaga School led by Ōhira. Atsutane transformed eighteenth-century nativism into nineteenth-century Kokugaku by "establishing or symbolizing social cohesion" in the invention of a new tradition.[8]

The Analysis of Kokugaku: Discourse and Practice

In the present study, we have problematized the view that Kokugaku was an ideologically and institutionally coherent phenomenon from its putative origins in the seventeenth century. This is not to assert that a movement called Kokugaku never existed. In a sense, the Kokugaku of the seventeenth and eighteenth centuries was but the shadow of an ideological projection back from the nineteenth century. Its existence was as spectral as the wraiths that Atsutane pursued to prove the ancient Way. Atsutane's phantom scholarship resulted from an imperative to demonstrate the validity of his teachings. The writing of the history of Kokugaku and its retrospective projection onto the past were forms of practice that are crucial to the interpretation of Atsutane's scholarship. Bourdieu's theory of fields focuses on what he calls the social conditions

---

8. Hobsbawm and Ranger, *The Invention of Tradition*, p. 9.

of cultural production. Atsutane's ideological efforts are evidence of the social conditions particular to him. Historians and literary scholars have not analyzed this aspect of his career as it related to his intellectual production. It is for this reason that received interpretations of Kokugaku do not recognize the crucial role of competition and struggle in the development of his scholarship.

Bourdieu observes that the creation of polar oppositions within a certain "universe" of cultural producers generates competition over the power to determine legitimate membership within it; such dynamism and energy make the "universe" into a field.[9] Fields of cultural production are characterized by a limited autonomy from external forces and operate by their own social rules. The members of the field are agents (not subjects) with an awareness of their relative autonomy. Atsutane's religious scholarship created the irreconcilable opposition to native classicism that transformed the Norinaga School into a field. Norinaga's cultural chauvinism, coupled with the expansion of the Suzunoya into the Norinaga School by Ōhira, formed the critical foundation for this transformation. Atsutane's self-legitimation efforts eventually spawned his assertions of orthodoxy and succession, a development that completed the invention of Kokugaku.

ଓ

Atsutane's vision of nativism as Kokugaku underwent some changes after the end of the Tokugawa period. Since Atsutane's death, the aspects of his scholarship that were the most important to him have been gradually distorted or suppressed. His followers during the bakumatsu period emphasized the relevance of his teachings to rural society. During Meiji, when the Hirata School was all but abandoned by its rural supporters, Kanetane even advocated the merits of classical literature. Atsutane was concerned primarily with the investigation of the ancient Way, the knowledge of which was primarily eschatological. A unique form of evidential learning that was not applied to the classics was the methodology for demonstrating the validity of his assertions. Although it is not the goal of the present study to deny the sincerity of his

---

9. Bourdieu, *The Rules of Art*, p. 193.

beliefs, his role in the systemization of Kokugaku was not the result of a deliberate plan. As the tradition most commonly associated with the articulation of Japanese cultural identity, Kokugaku was more an accident of history than the inevitable historical culmination of a national spirit.

EPILOGUE
Twentieth-Century Ethnology and Nationalism

Although this study ends during the mid-Meiji period, it is appropriate to provide at least a brief outline of the development of scholarship on Atsutane and Kokugaku during the twentieth century. Specifically, I hope to show how the association of Kokugaku and ultra-nationalism developed and to illustrate its consequences in the postwar period. I will also discuss the status of research on Atsutane in the contemporary Japanese academy.

The general decline of interest in the Hirata School and the founding of language and literary studies on eighteenth-century nativism lasted from the late Meiji period until the beginning of the Showa period. Early Showa scholars utilized Tokugawa classical research in an effort to formulate a set of Japanese ethical values in opposition to those of an increasingly demonized West.[1] This effort supported the rising power of reactionary political groups and the military. Scholars felt that the nativists of the eighteenth and nineteenth centuries were attuned to the *yamatogokoro*. After 1930, Hirata Atsutane was increasingly identified as one of its most representative Tokugawa figures.

Perhaps the most important scholars to use Atsutane's teachings in the articulation of unique Japanese values were those of the new Minzokugaku ("learning of the folk," or, in other words, ethnol-

---

1. John Dower demonstrates that the image of a demon was commonly used during the Pacific War to depict Westerners, especially Americans (*War Without Mercy*, p. 244).

ogy). Yanagita Kunio (1875–1962) was the first to conceptualize the idea of Japanese ethnology with the publication of *Tōno monogatari*.[2] He focused his scholarship on the rural folk he first met when doing field research for the Meiji government during the late nineteenth century. Like Atsutane, whom he credited as a pioneer in the field,[3] he took an avid interest in folk customs, especially those related to the "concealed" world.[4] Yanagita's interest in the supernatural world was part of a broader effort to identify cultural commonalities among rural communities in Meiji Japan.[5] By representing village life, Yanagita thought that he could identify unique cultural features among various rural groups. He agreed with Atsutane's use of rural informants as sources of data on the hidden realm of spirits,[6] but he thought that Atsutane's method was ultimately unscientific and unsuitable for a modern investigation of rural society.[7] Marilyn Ivy, however, observes that despite Yanagita's efforts to achieve scientific precision, his ultimate goal was the expression of an experience that defied conventional representation.[8] Spirits and ghosts were perfect objects to convey this experience via "naturalized direct representation." Thus, he sought to discover a new brand of literary writing "which (for Yanagita) says more when it says less and thus writes what cannot be said."[9]

The literary impulse was perhaps more deeply felt by Yanagita's junior in the ethnographic project, Orikuchi Shinobu (1887–1953). Orikuchi thought that Yanagita was obsessed with scientific precision. Thus, in an effort to establish his own intellectual position, he advocated a form of ethnology that relied on literary sources.[10] Despite Ivy's assertion that Yanagita's ethnology was also fundamentally literary, it is clear that Orikuchi was more overtly determined to introduce a concern for native literature to ethnology.

---

2. Ivy, *Discourses of the Vanishing*, p. 79.
3. Yanagita, "Senso no hanashi," p. 257.
4. Ivy, *Discourses of the Vanishing*, p. 80.
5. Harootunian, *Things Seen and Unseen*, p. 418.
6. Haga N., *Yanagita Kunio to Hirata Atsutane*, p. 211.
7. Harootunian, *Things Seen and Unseen*, p. 423.
8. Ivy, *Discourses of the Vanishing*, p. 80.
9. Ibid., pp. 80–81.
10. Harootunian, *Things Seen and Unseen*, p. 423.

With the increased attention on Atsutane among ethnologists, he was faced with the challenge of linking Atsutane's teachings to literature.

Orikuchi acknowledged the literary roots of Tokugawa Kokugaku. A common misperception, he argued, was that the investigation of classical texts was the sole purpose of early modern nativists. Orikuchi asserted, as Atsutane too had argued in the *Tamadasuki*, that classical research was the means to a greater end.[11] The *kokugakusha* undertook scholarship in order to understand the experiences of the common people.[12] Their scholarship, unlike that of the Confucians, had a purpose, which was to extol the virtues of rural life.

For Orikuchi, scholars of the Meiji period had fundamentally transformed Kokugaku from the proto-ethnology of Atsutane into antiquarianism or even "nativism" (*kuni no gakumon*).[13] He attributed this unfortunate development to Haga Yaichi, yet Orikuchi did not condemn him for it. Rather, it was a historical inevitability; Haga reacted to the trends of his time. Unfortunately, Orikuchi observed, Meiji scholars had lost sight of the raison d'être of the Hirata School, which was the investigation of the *Nihon seishin* (Japanese spirit).[14] Atsutane was the most important of all the Tokugawa scholars because of his concern for the national spirit.[15] Orikuchi championed Atsutane's scholarship, claiming that it most closely approximated the ethnographic concerns of Yanagita. By investigating the supernatural, Atsutane demonstrated his empathy for rural folk, and he treated seriously the ethical considerations inherent in their customs and traditions.[16]

Despite Orikuchi's emphasis on the importance of Atsutane's teachings for the development of Yanagita's scholarship, he admitted that the literary foundation of Kokugaku was important and was unwilling to discard it completely. He asserted that the pre-

---

11. Orikuchi, "Kokugaku no kōfuku," p. 312.
12. Ibid., p. 315.
13. Orikuchi, "Hirata kokugaku no dentō," p. 321.
14. Ibid.
15. Ibid., p. 323.
16. Ibid., p. 349.

vailing image of Kokugaku during the first half of the twentieth century was associated almost exclusively with Atsutane and the grassroots movement of the bakumatsu period. Just as early Meiji Kokugaku scholars reasserted the centrality of classical literature, the standpoint in Orikuchi's day was too heavily slanted toward Kokugaku's Shinto side. In Orikuchi's estimation, the correct view was one that incorporated both the literary and the religious aspects of Kokugaku. Thus, Atsutane should be studied alongside the two greatest literary Kokugaku scholars, Mabuchi and Norinaga.[17]

The recombination of Atsutane's scholarship with literary Kokugaku resulted in what Orikuchi called Shinkokugaku (new Kokugaku), which was identical to Yanagita's concept of Minzokugaku. Yanagita had used the concept of Shinkokugaku in his own work, but he did not insist on the inclusion of Norinaga and Mabuchi, as Orikuchi did. Orikuchi was faced with the same dilemma as Kanetane during the Meiji period, namely, the reconciliation of the two distinct forms of Kokugaku. Kanetane had diluted Atsutane's scholarship with literature in order to make it more acceptable to Meiji leaders. This ultimately led to Haga Yaichi's studies of literary Kokugaku during the 1890s. Some forty years later, Orikuchi and Yanagita brought Kokugaku back into the forefront of scholarly discourse. Orikuchi, clearly emphasizing the role of rural folk in Atsutane's research, nevertheless sought to strengthen its significance by bonding it to classical literature. Yanagita viewed Atsutane's research as a naive and primitive form of proto-science, but this preoccupation with science troubled Orikuchi. By invoking classical research, he tried to weaken Yanagita's emphasis on science as he supported the centrality of Kokugaku. The result, however, was a contrived link between classical literature and Atsutane's teachings, one that had already collapsed during the Meiji period, as well as during Atsutane's lifetime.

The Shinkokugaku advocated by Yanagita and Orikuchi was part of a general proliferation of nationalist ideologies during the 1920s and 1930s. The scholarship of Yanagita and Orikuchi appealed to reactionary groups and radical elements within the mili-

---

17. Orikuchi, "Kokugaku to kokubungaku to," p. 292.

tary because of its emphasis on the search for cultural uniqueness and a national essence. The infatuation with nationalism, however, was not limited to the extreme right. Scholars and writers traditionally associated with the left, such as the Romantics, were also drawn to the nationalistic message of the Shinkokugaku scholars.[18] Nationalism seeped into nearly every layer of the prewar and wartime Japanese intellectual community, reaching even the philosophical discourse of scholars like Kuki Shūzō (1888–1941). Kuki and others viewed themselves "as self-appointed guardians of cultural authenticity."[19] Kuki focused his study of Edo culture on the Kasei period. His idea of the unique cultural experience of the Japanese was the urban flair of Edo residents of this time. Perhaps not coincidentally, the Kasei era was also the formative period of the Ibukinoya. Due to the intellectual embrace of nationalism by many intellectuals during the 1930s and 1940s, the assertions of Yanagita and Orikuchi were not shocking. The strong association of nationalism with Kokugaku, and with Atsutane in particular, had a profound impact on postwar Kokugaku scholarship.

൙

The history of Kokugaku from the Meiji period until the present has undergone interesting changes. In fact, the supporters of religious Kokugaku and those of literary Kokugaku have been engaged in a struggle for dominance in the academy during the twentieth century.[20] In the years immediately following World War II, there were only a few studies of Kokugaku that emerged in Japan. One of these was Maruyama Masao's *Nihon seiji shisōshi kenkyū* (1952). Maruyama argued that Norinaga succeeded Ogyū Sorai as the dominant intellectual of Tokugawa Japan. By linking Norinaga to the indigenous development of modernity, he weakened the association of Kokugaku with wartime nationalism. He made almost no mention of Atsutane in his study, which allowed Atsutane's connection to ultranationalism to endure.

---

18. Miki Y., "Shinkokugaku to sensō sekinin no mondai," p. 66.
19. Pincus, *Authenticating Culture in Japan*, p. 102.
20. Koyasu suggested this idea to me in 1996.

Koyasu Nobukuni, however, questioned Maruyama's search for modernity in the Tokugawa period. With the publication of Koyasu's *Norinaga to Atsutane no sekai* (1977), Atsutane's significance in the formation of a discourse that was critical of modernity came into focus. Koyasu argues that Atsutane, unlike Norinaga, left the link between politics and ethics intact. By resolving the inherent ethical irrationality of Norinaga's thought, Atsutane formulated a set of ethical values derived from Shinto. Such a discursive revolution, Koyasu argues, was a major achievement of Atsutane that was unnoticed by postwar scholars still reeling from Japan's wartime defeat.

Koyasu's study of Atsutane, however, has had only a limited impact on the Japanese academy. Twenty years later, Maita Katsuyasu, a descendant of Atsutane, argued for a reappraisal of Atsutane and his scholarship. Unlike Koyasu, Maita contended that scholars must bracket Atsutane's career as a Kokugaku scholar and broaden their research to encompass the varied intellectual and spiritual interests that he held during his lifetime.[21] Nineteenth-century studies of Kokugaku distorted Atsutane's historical importance, as a result of the ideological confrontation between the members of the Hirata School and their nativist rivals. Postwar histories of Kokugaku, reacting against militarism and wartime nationalism, have suffered from a general reluctance to analyze Hirata Atsutane. The aggregate result has been a paucity of postwar studies of either Kokugaku or of Atsutane. Although the calls made by Koyasu and Maita for a new look at Atsutane's life and scholarship are somewhat divergent, they both recognize a lacuna in the secondary literature. This study is an attempt to fill that void in the scholarship. Instead of a project that either emphasizes Atsutane's discursive significance or asserts his non-nativist interests, a truly historical appraisal of Atsutane's career can reveal the formative origins of Kokugaku itself.

---

21. Maita, "Yomigaeru karisuma, Hirata Atsutane," p. 435.

Reference Matter

Character List

This list includes the names of major figures mentioned in the text and selected terms.

Aizawa Seishisai　会沢正志斎
Arakida Hisaoyu　荒木田久老
Arakida Suehogi　荒木田末寿
Asami Keisai　浅見絅斎

Ban Nobutomo　伴信友

Cheng Hao　程灝
Cheng Yi　程頤
Chieko　千枝子

Dazai Shundai　太宰春台
Dōjō　堂上

Edo-ha　江戸派

Fujii Takanao　藤井高尚
Fuji-no-kakitsu　藤垣内
Fujita Tōko　藤田東湖
Fujitani Mitsue　富士谷御杖
Fujitani Nariakira　富士谷成章

Haga Yaichi　芳賀矢一
Hatano Yoshio　羽田野敬雄
Hattori Nakatsune　服部中庸
Hattori Nankaku　服部南郭
Hirata Atsutane　平田篤胤

Hirata Kanetane　平田鉄胤
Hun (*kon*)　魂

Ibukinoya　気吹舎
Ikuta Yorozu　生田万
Imibe Hironari　斎部広成
Inishie manabi　古学
Itō Jinsai　伊藤仁斎

Jindai moji　神代文字

Kada no Arimaro　荷田在満
Kada no Azumamaro　荷田春満
Kada no Nobuna　荷田信名
Kakubutsu kyūri　格物窮理
Kamiyo　神代
Kamo no Mabuchi　賀茂真淵
Kangaku　漢学
Kasei　化政
Katō Chikage　加藤千蔭
Katō Enao　加藤枝直
Katō Umaki　加藤宇万伎
Katsugorō　勝五郎
Katsura Takashige　桂誉重
Kido Chidate　城戸千盾
Kokugaku　国学
Konishi Atsuyoshi　小西篤好

Koshibaya 小柴屋
Kōshōgaku 考証学
Kuki Shūzō 九鬼周造
Kunshi 君子

Maita Katsuyasu 米田勝安
Matsudaira Sadanobu 松平定信
Matsunoya 松屋
Matsusaka 松坂
Meirindō 明倫堂
Minzokugaku 民俗学
Miyahiro Sadao 宮負定雄
Miyake Kiyoshi 三宅清
Mono no aware 物の哀れ
Motoori Arisato 本居有郷
Motoori Haruniwa 本居春庭
Motoori Norinaga 本居宣長
Motoori Ōhira 本居大平
Motoori Uchitō 本居内遠
Murata Harukado 村田春門
Murata Harumi 村田春海
Murata Harumichi 村田春道
Murata Harusato 村田春郷
Mutobe Tokika 六人部節香
Mutobe Yoshika 六人部是香
Myōhōin 妙法院

Ninkō 仁孝
Nochi-Suzunoya 後鈴屋
Nudenoya 鐸屋

Ogyū Sorai 荻生徂徠
Orikuchi Shinobu 折口信夫
Oyamada Tomokiyo 小山田与清

Po (*paku*) 魄

Rangaku 蘭学

Sakamoto Ryōma 坂本竜馬
Santetsu 三哲
Santō Kyōden 山東京伝
Shikitei Sanba 式亭三馬

Shimazu Nariakira 島津斉彬
Shimizu Hamaomi 清水浜臣
Shimokōbe Chōryū 下河辺長流
Shimōsa 下総
Shinkokugaku 新国学
Shiushi 四大人
Shōnin 小人
Sōmō no kokugaku 草莽の国学
Sugawara no Michizane 菅原道真
Suzuki Akira 鈴木朗
Suzuki Masayuki 鈴木雅之
Suzuki Shigetane 鈴木重胤
Suzunoya 鈴屋

Tachibana Moribe 橘守部
Takayama Torakichi 高山寅吉
Takizawa Bakin 滝沢馬琴
Tayasu Munetake 田安宗武
Tōjō Gimon 東条義門
Tokugawa Harusada 徳川治貞
Tokugawa Harutomi 徳川治寳
Tokugawa Mitsukuni 徳川光圀
Tokugawa Nariaki 徳川斉昭
Tokugawa Yoshimune 徳川吉宗
Tokugawa Yoshinao 徳川義直
Toyoda Tenkō 豊田天功

Ueda Akinari 上田秋成
Uematsu Arinobu 植松有信
Uematsu Shigetake 植松茂岳

Wakayama 和歌山
Watarai Nobuyoshi 度会延佳

Yamazaki Ansai 山崎闇斎
Yanagita Kunio 柳田国男
Yano Gendō 矢野玄道
Yūmeikai 幽冥界
Yushima 湯島
Yūsoku kojitsu 有識故実

Zhou Dunyi 周敦頤
Zhu Xi 朱熹

Works Cited

Unless otherwise noted, all places of publication in Japan are Tokyo.

Abe Akio. "Keichū, Azumamaro, Mabuchi." NST 39. 1972.
Arakida Suehogi. *Arakida Suehogi (Masutani-shi) Fuji-no-kakitsu-ō azakeru kotoba narabi ni Arakida Hisamori Kitagawa Shingan hyō*. In *Kiyosōhansho*. SHAZ (supp.), vol. 5.
Backus, Robert. "The Kansei Prohibition of Heterodoxy and Its Effects on Education." *Harvard Journal of Asiatic Studies* 39, 1 (1979): 55–106.
Ban Nobutomo. *Shinji sanben*. In *Ban Nobutomo zenshū*, vol. 2.
Ban Nobutomo zenshū. 5 vols. Perikansha, 1977.
Bol, Peter. *"This Culture of Ours": Intellectual Transitions in T'ang and Sung China*. Stanford: Stanford University Press, 1992.
Brownlee, John. *Japanese Historians and the National Myths, 1600–1945: The Age of the Gods and the Emperor Jinmu*. Vancouver: University of British Columbia Press, 1997.
Bourdieu, Pierre. *In Other Words: Essays Towards a Reflexive Sociology*. Stanford: Stanford University Press, 1990.
———. *The Rules of Art: Genesis and Structure of the Literary Field*. Stanford: Stanford University Press, 1996.
Bourdieu, Pierre, and Loïc Wacquant. *An Invitation to Reflexive Sociology*. Chicago: University of Chicago Press, 1992.
Chartier, Roger. *On the Edge of the Cliff: History, Language, and Practices*. Baltimore: Johns Hopkins University Press, 1997.
Collins, Randall. *The Sociology of Philosophies: A Global Theory of Intellectual Change*. Cambridge, Mass.: Belknap Press, 1998.
Dai Nihon shisō zenshū kankōkai (DNSZ). 18 vols. 1931–35.
Dazai Shundai. *Bendōsho*. DNSZ, vol. 7.
———. *Bendōsho*. *Kogaku-ha*, gekan. Dai Nihon bunko jukyō-hen. Dai Nihon Bunko Kankōkai, 1938.

Derrida, Jacques. *Of Grammatology*. Baltimore: Johns Hopkins University Press, 1976.
Devine, Richard. "Hirata Atsutane and Christian Sources." *Monumenta Nipponica* 36, 1 (1981): 37–54.
Dower, John. *War Without Mercy: Race and Power in the Pacific War*. New York: Pantheon Books, 1986.
Elman, Benjamin. *From Philosophy to Philology: Intellectual and Social Aspects of Change in Late Imperial China*. Cambridge, Mass.: Council on East Asian Studies, Harvard University, 1984.
———. "Ming Politics and Confucian Classicism: The Duke of Chou Serves King Ch'eng." In *The International Conference on Ming Dynasty Classical Studies*, pp. 93–144. Nankang, Taiwan: Institute of Chinese Literature and Philosophy, Academia Sinica, 1996.
Foucault, Michel. *The Archaeology of Knowledge and the Discourse on Language*. Trans. A. M. Sheridan Smith. New York: Pantheon Books, 1972.
Fujii Fusako. "Fujii Takanao to Nudenoya: kōki kokugaku no ichidanmen." *Kokugo kokubun* 46, 12 (1975): 1–19.
Fujii Sadafumi. *Kokugaku tensei-shi no kenkyū*. Yoshikawa Kōbunkan, 1987.
Fujii Takanao. *Mitsu no shirube*. In NZT, series 1, vol. 22.
Fujitani, Takashi. *Splendid Monarchy: Power and Pageantry in Modern Japan*. Berkeley: University of California Press, 1998.
Fukaya Katsumi. "Bakuhan shihai to mura yakuninsō no kokugaku jūyō." *Shikan*, no. 91 (1975): 13–23.
Haga Noboru. "Bakumatsu henkaku-ki ni okeru kokugakusha no undō to ronri." NST 51. 1971.
———. *Bakumatsu kokugaku no kenkyū*. Kyōiku Shuppan Sentā, 1980.
———. "Edo ni okeru Edo kabun-ha to Hirata Atsutane." *Edo no geinō to bunka*. Ed. Nishiyama Matsunosuke. Yoshikawa Kōbunkan, 1985.
———. *Kokugaku no hitobito: sono kōdō to shisō*. Nihonjin no kōdō to shisō, no. 42. Hyōronsha, 1975.
———. "Motoori Norinaga no shisō keisei: Kyōto yūgaku jidai wo chūshin toshite." *Kikan Nihon shisō-shi*, no. 8 (1978): 69–88.
———. "Suzuki Shigetane to Hirata-tō: Suzuki Shigetane ansatsu jiken no haikai." *Rekishi jinrui* 5 (1978): 45–86.
———. *Yanagita Kunio to Hirata Atsutane*. Kōseisha, 1997.
Haga Yaichi. *Kokugaku-shi gairon*. Kokugo Denshūjo, 1900.
———. *Nihon no bunkengaku*. Toyamabō, 1928.
Hagura Nobuya, Maita Katsuyasu, and Sakurai Katsunoshin. *Shintō kokugaku to Shōwa jidai*. Kokumin Seishin Kenshū Saidan, 1988.
Hardacre, Helen. *Shintō and the State, 1868–1988*. Princeton: Princeton University Press, 1989.

Harootunian, Harry. *Things Seen and Unseen: Discourse and Ideology in Tokugawa Nativism*. Chicago: University of Chicago Press, 1988.
Hattori Nakatsune. *Minoda Suigetsu Hattori Nakatsune-ō norito*. In *Kiyosōhansho*. SHAZ (supp.), vol. 5.
——. *Sandaikō*. In NST 50.
Hayashi Razan. *Shintō denju*. In NST 39.
Higuchi Kōzo. "Watarai Nobuyoshi to kinsei shintō no seiritsu." *Edo no shisō*, 1 (1996): 118–35.
Hirata Atsutane. *Ibukinoya hisso*. In SHAZ, vol. 15.
——. *Inō bukkai roku*. In SHAZ, vol. 9.
——. *Kadō tai'i*. In SHAZ, vol. 15.
——. *Kamōsho*. In SHAZ, vol. 15.
——. *Katsugorō saisei kibun*. In SHAZ, vol. 9.
——. *Kishinshinron*. In SHAZ, vol. 9.
——. *Kokon yōmikō*. In SHAZ, vol. 9.
——. *Koshiden*. In SHAZ, vol. 1.
——. *Koshi seibun*. In SHAZ, vol. 1.
——. *Sandaikō-benben*. In SHAZ, vol. 7.
——. *Senkyō ibun*. In SHAZ, vol. 9.
——. *Tamadasuki*. In SHAZ, vol. 6.
——. *Tama no mihashira*. In NST 50.
——. *Tensetsu-benben*. In SHAZ, vol. 7.
Hirata Atsutane, Ban Nobutomo, Ōkuni Takamasa. *Nihon shisō taikei* [NST] 50. Ed. Tahara Tsuguo, Saeki Arikiyo, and Haga Noboru. Iwanami, 1973.
Hirata Atsutane ushi toshū. Akita: Iyataka Jinja, 1993.
Hirata Kanetane. *Hirata Atsutane nenpu*. In NST 50.
Hirata Kanetane, ed. *Kiyosōhansho*. In SHAZ (supp.), vol. 5.
Hisamatsu Sen'ichi. "Bunkengaku-teki kenkyū to kōshōgaku: Ban Nobutomo wo chūshin toshite." In *Ban Nobutomo zenshū*, bekkan. Perikansha, 1979.
——. *Keichū*. Jinbutsu sōsho, no. 110. Yoshikawa Kōbunkan, 1963.
——. "*Man'yō daishoki* no seikaku to ichi." KZ, vol. 1. 1973.
Hobsbawm, Eric, and Terence Ranger, eds. *The Invention of Tradition*. Cambridge, Eng.: Cambridge University Press, 1983.
Hoshikawa Kiyotami. *Suzuki Shigetane den*. Kotodama Shobō, 1943.
Ikuta Yorozu. *Iwa ni musu koke*. In NST 51.
——. *Ryōyaku kuchi ni nigashi*. In *Ikuta Yorozu zenshū*, vol. 1.
Ikuta Yorozu zenshū. 4 vols. Shintaiyōsha, 1944.
Inoue Yutaka. *Kamo no Mabuchi no gyōseki to monryū*. Kazama Shobō, 1966.
Itō Tasaburō. *Kokugakusha no michi*. Shintaiyōsha, 1944.

———. *Sōmō no kokugaku*. Masago Shobō, 1966.
Ivy, Marilyn. *Discourses of the Vanishing: Modernity, Phantasm, Japan*. Chicago: University of Chicago Press, 1995.
Izumi Makuni. *Meidōsho*. In NST 51.
Kada no Azumamaro. *Sōgakkōkei*. In NST 39.
Kajiyama Takao. "Mitogaku to kokugaku no kankei: Hirata Atsutane no Mito-han shikan undō wo megutte." *Geirin* 39, 3 (1990): 35–55.
———. "Mito-han wo meguru Oyamada Tomokiyo to Hirata Atsutane no kōyū." *Geirin* 44, 1 (1995): 55–71.
Kamo no Mabuchi. *Go'ikō*. In NST 39.
———. *Inishie-buri*. In KKNMZ, shisō-hen.
———. *Ka'ikō*. In KKNMZ, shisō-hen.
———. *Kokuikō*. In NST 39.
———. *Manabi no agetsurai*. In KKNMZ, shisō-hen.
———. *Niimanabi*. In NST 39.
Katsurajima Nobuhiro. *Bakumatsu minshū shisō no kenkyū: bakumatsu kokugaku to minshū shūkyō*. Bunrikaku, 1992.
———. *Shisō-shi no jūkyū seiki: 'tasha' toshite no Tokugawa Nihon*. Perikansha, 1999.
Keichū. *Man'yō daishoki no sōshaku*. In KZ, vol. 1.
Keichū zenshū (KZ). 16 vols. Ed. Hisamatsu Sen'ichi, Tsukishima Hiroshi, et al. Iwanami, 1973.
Kido Chidate. *Dōjin yori naisho*. 1823/10/4. In *Kiyosōhansho*. SHAZ (supp.), vol. 5.
———. *Kido Chidate dōjin yori raijō*. 1823/9/18. In *Kiyosōhansho*. SHAZ (supp.), vol. 5.
———. *Manabi no hiromichi*. In *Kokumin dōtoku sōsho*, vol. 3.
———. *Shimimuro zakki*. In NZT, series 1, vol. 2.
Kinsei bungei sōsho. Kokusho Kankōkai, 1912.
Kinsei shintōron zenki kokugaku. NST 39. Ed. Abe Akio and Taira Shigemichi. Iwanami, 1972.
Kiyohara Sadao. *Kokugaku hattatsu-shi*. Kokusho Kankōkai, 1981.
Kobayashi Kenzo. *Hirata Shinto no kenkyū*. Osaka: Koshintō Senpyōkyō Honchō, 1975.
Kōhon Kamo no Mabuchi zenshū (KKNMZ). Shisō-hen. 2 vols. Comp. Yamamoto Yutaka. Kobundō, 1942.
Kokugaku undō no shisō. NST 51. Ed. Haga Noboru and Matsumoto Sannosuke. Iwanami, 1971.
Kokumin dōtoku sōsho. 3 vols. Ed. Arima Sukemasa and Kurokawa Masamichi. Hakubunkan, 1911–12.
Koyasu Nobukuni. *Motoori Norinaga*. Iwanami, 1992.
———. *Motoori Norinaga mondai to wa nani ka*. Seidosha, 1995.

———. *Norinaga to Atsutane no sekai*. Chūkōsōsho, 1977.
Kudō Shinjirō. *Fujii Takanao to Matsunoya-ha*. Kazama Shobō, 1986.
Maita Katsuyasu. "Yomigaeru karisuma, Hirata Atsutane." Interview by Aramata Hiroshi. *Shōsetsu subaru* 11, 1 (1997): 432–41.
Maruyama Masao. "Orthodoxy and Legitimacy in the Kimon School." Pt. 1. Trans. Barry Steben. *Sino-Japanese Studies* 8, 2 (1996): 6–49.
———. *Studies in the Intellectual History of Tokugawa Japan*. Trans. Mikiso Hane. Princeton: Princeton University Press, 1974.
Matsumoto Shigeru. *Motoori Norinaga, 1730–1801*. Cambridge, Mass.: Harvard University Press, 1970.
Matsuura Mitsunobu. "Ōkuni Takamasa ni okeru kokugaku shitaijin-kan no keisei katei." *Nihon shisō-shi gaku* 17 (1985): 52–62.
McNally, Mark. "Intellectual Polarities and the Development of the Norinaga School 'Field:' Hirata Atsutane and the Nudenoya, 1823–1834." *Early Modern Japan* 9, 2 (1999): 19–29.
Miki Shōtarō. *Hirata Atsutane no kenkyū*. Kyoto: Shintōshi Gakkai, 1969.
———. "Hirata Atsutane no tenchi kaibyaku-setsu: toku ni Norinaga, Nakatsune to no kankei ni oite." *Kōgakkan daigaku kiyo*, 2 (1964): 133–65.
Miki Yasutaka. "Shinkokugaku to sensō sekinin no mondai." *Nihon bungaku* 7, 1 (1958): 63–72.
Minami Kenji. *Kinsei kokugaku to sono shūhen*. Miyai Shoten, 1992.
Miyahiro Sadao. *Kokueki honron*. In NST 51.
Miyake Kiyoshi. *Kada no Azumamaro*. Unebi Shobō, 1932.
———. *Kada no Azumamaro no kotengaku*, vol. 1. Urawa-shi: Miyake Kiyoshi, 1981.
Mori Senzo. "Murata Harumi iji." *Kokugakusha kenkyū*. Hokkai Shuppansha, 1943.
Morita Yasunosuke. *Ban Nobutomo no shisō*. Perikansha, 1979.
Motohashi Hiroko. "Kasei Tempo-ki ni okeru Keihan no kokugaku no ichi-danmen: Nudenoya to Koshibaya ni tsuite." *Wayō kokubun kenkyū* 16/17 (1981): 91–108.
Motoori Haruniwa. *Kotoba narabi ni uta*. In *Kiyosōhansho*. SHAZ (supp.), vol. 5.
———. *Kotoba no kayoichi*. In *Motoori Ōhira, Motoori Haruniwa zenshū*. *Motoori Norinaga zenshū*. Yoshikawa Kōbunkan, 1938.
Motoori Norinaga. *Isonokami no sasamegoto*. In MNS.
———. *Kojiki-den*. In MNZ, vol. 9.
———. *Michi to iu koto no ron*. In MNZ, vol. 14.
———. *Naobi no mitama*. In NNS.
———. *Sandaikō wo yomite shirie ni shiruseru*. In NST 50.
———. *Shibun yōryo*. In MNS.
———. *Tamakatsuma*. In NST 40.

———. *Tamakushige*. In MNZ, vol. 8.
———. *Uiyamabumi*. In NST 40.
Motoori Norinaga. NST 40. Ed. Yoshikawa Kōjirō et al. Iwanami, 1975.
Motoori Norinaga shū (MNS). Shinchōsha, 1983.
Motoori Norinaga shū (NNS). Nihon no shisō, no. 15. Chikuma Shobō, 1969.
Motoori Norinaga zenshū. 13 vols. Comp. Motoori Toyokai and Motoori Seizo. Yoshikawa Kōbunkan, 1937–38.
Motoori Norinaga zenshū (MNZ). 20 vols. Comp. Ōno Susumu and Ōkubo Tadashi. Chikuma Shobō, 1968–75.
Motoori Ōhira. *Fuji-no-kakitsu-ō chinjōbun*. In *Kiyosōhansho*. SHAZ (supp.), vol. 5.
———. *Fuji-no-kakitsu shōsoku*. In *Nihon geirin sōsho*, vol. 9.
———. *Kogakuyō*. In *Kokumin dōtoku sōsho*, vol. 2.
———. *Kogakuyō*. In *Nihon kokusui zensho*, vol. 13. Ed. Endō Takayoshi. Nihon Kokusui Kankōkai.
———. *Sandaikō-ben*. Unpublished manuscript. Sōgō Toshokan, Tokyo University.
Muraoka Tsunetsugu. *Nihon shisō-shi kenkyū*. 4 vols. Iwanami, 1930–39.
———. *Zoku Nihon shisō-shi kenkyū*. Iwanami, 1975.
Murata Harumi. *Utagatari*. In *Nihon kagaku zensho*, vol. 12. Hakubunkan.
———. *Wagaku taigai*. In NST 39.
Najita, Tetsuo, ed. *Readings in Tokugawa Thought*. Select Papers, vol. 9. Chicago: Center for East Asian Studies, University of Chicago, 1994.
Nakai, Kate Wildman. *Shogunal Politics: Arai Hakuseki and the Premises of Tokugawa Rule*. Cambridge, Mass.: Council on East Asian Studies, Harvard University, 1988.
Nakamura Kazumoto. *Motoori-ha kokugaku no tenkai*. Osankaku, 1993.
Ng, Wai-ming. *The "I Ching" in Tokugawa Thought and Culture*. Honolulu: University of Hawaii Press and the Association for Asian Studies, 2000.
Nihon geirin sōsho. 12 vols. Rokugōkan, 1927–29.
Nihon kagaku zensho. 12 vols. Ed. Sasaki Hirotsuna and Sasaki Nobutsuna. Hakubunkan, 1890–91.
Nihon kokusui zensho. 24 vols. Nihon Kokusui Kankōkai, 1915–18.
Nihon zuihitsu taisei (NZT). Series 1. 23 vols. Yoshikawa Kōbunkan, 1975–76.
Nihon zuihitsu taisei (NZT). Series 3. 24 vols. Yoshikawa Kōbunkan, 1976–78.
Nishikawa Masatami. "*Sandaikō* no seiritsu ni tsuite." *Kogakkan daigaku kiyō* 10 (1972): 193–211.

Nishiyama Matsunosuke. *Edo Culture: Daily Life and Diversions in Urban Japan, 1600–1868.* Trans. Gerald Groemer. Honolulu: University of Hawai'i Press, 1997.

———. *Iemoto no kenkyū.* Azekura Shobō, 1959.

Nosco, Peter. *Remembering Paradise: Nativism and Nostalgia in Eighteenth-Century Japan.* Cambridge, Mass.: Council of East Asian Studies, Harvard University, 1990.

———. "Nature, Invention, and National Learning: The *Kokka hachiron* Controversy, 1742–46." *Harvard Journal of Asiatic Studies* 41, 1 (1981): 75–91.

———. "Keichū (1640–1701): Forerunner of National Learning." *Asian Thought and Society* 5, 1 (1980): 237–52.

Ogasawara Haruo. *Kokuju ronsō no kenkyū.* Perikansha, 1988.

Okino Iwasaburō. *Hirata Atsutane to sono jidai.* Koseikaku, 1943.

Ōkuni Takamasa. *Gakutō benron.* In NST 50.

———. *Hongaku kyoyō.* In NST 50.

———. *Shin shinkōhōron narabi ni furoku.* In NST 50.

Omote Tomoyuki. "Chi no denpa to shōgeki: Hirata Atsutane to 'Kiyosōhansho.'" *Edo no shisō* 5 (1996): 134–149.

———. "Hito no kangaete shirubeki wa tada me no mae no oyobu kagiri: kokugaku-teki tenchi seiseizu to kindai." *Nihon gakuhō* 15 (1996): 1–16.

———. "Katareru 'kamiyo' to 'utsushi': *Sandaikō* ni okeru 'katari' no kōzō tenkan." *Nihon gakuho* 12 (1993): 69–83.

Ooms, Herman. *Charismatic Bureaucrat: A Political Biography of Matsudaira Sadanobu, 1758–1829.* Chicago: University of Chicago Press, 1976.

———. *Tokugawa Ideology: Early Constructs, 1570–1680.* Princeton: Princeton University Press, 1985.

Orikuchi Shinobu. "Hirata kokugaku no dentō." OSZ, vol. 20.

———. "Kokugaku no kōfuku." OSZ, vol. 20.

———. "Kokugaku to kokubungaku to." OSZ, vol. 20.

Orikuchi Shinobu zenshū (OSZ). 32 vols. Chūōkōronsha, 1976.

Oyamada Tomokiyo. *Yōshorō nikki.* In *Kinsei bungei sōsho.*

Ozawa Masao. "*Sandaikō* wo meguru ronsō." *Kokugo to kokubungaku* 20, 5 (1943): 465–76.

Pincus, Leslie. *Authenticating Culture in Japan: Kuki Shūzo and the Rise of National Aesthetics.* Berkeley: University of California Press, 1996.

Robertson, Jennifer. "Sexy Rice: Plant Gender, Farm Manuals, and Grass-Roots Nativism." *Monumenta Nipponica* 39, 3 (1984): 233–60.

Rubinger, Richard. *Private Academies of Tokugawa Japan.* Princeton: Princeton University Press, 1982.

Ryūkō. *Santetsu shōden.* Unpublished manuscript. National Diet Library, Tokyo.

Sakai, Naoki. *Voices of the Past: The Status of Language in Eighteenth-Century Japanese Discourse.* Ithaca: Cornell University Press, 1992.
Sakamoto Koremaru. *Meiji ishin to kokugakusha.* Ōmeidō, 1993.
Saussure, Ferdinand de. *General Course in Linguistics.* La Salle, Ill.: Open Court, 1993.
Sawai Keiichi. "Jūhasseiki Nihon ni okeru 'ninshikiron' no tankyū: Sorai, Norinaga no gengo chitsujokan." In *Edo bunka no hen'yō: jūhasseiki Nihon no keiken,* ed. Shimonaka Hiroshi, pp. 203-45. Heibonsha, 1994.
Seeley, Christopher. *A History of Writing in Japan.* Honolulu: University of Hawaii Press, 2000.
Seidensticker, Edward. *Low City, High City: Tokyo, 1867-1923.* Cambridge, Mass.: Harvard University Press, 1991.
Shimizu Hamaomi. *Sazanami hitsuwa.* In NZT, series 1, vol. 7.
Shinshū Hirata Atsutane zenshū (SHAZ). 21 vols. Meichō Shuppan, 1976- .
Shiryūgoto. In NZT, series 3, vol. 11.
Sources of Japanese Tradition, vol. 2. Comp. Ryusaku Tsunoda, Wm. Theodore de Bary, and Donald Keene. New York: Columbia University Press, 1958.
Suzuki Akira. *Sandaikō Suzuki Akira setsu.* Microform copy of an unpublished manuscript. Nihon Bungaku Kenkyū Shiryōkan, Tokyo.
Suzuki Shigetane. *Yotsugigusa.* In NST 51.
Taira Shigemichi. "Kinsei no shintō shisō." NST 39. 1972.
Tanaka Kōji. "Edo-ha to iu genshō: Murata Harumi to Motoori Norinaga to no gaku-teki kankei wo megutte." *Kokugo to kokubungaku* 74 (1997): 29-43.
———. "Murata Harumi no Wagaku-ron: 'Yamato damashii' no kaishaku wo megutte." *Nihon bungaku* 47 (1998): 30-39.
Tanaka Yoshito. *Hirata Atsutane no tetsugaku.* Meiji Shōin, 1944.
———. "Kaidai: *Koshi seibun.*" SHAZ, vol. 1.
Teeuwen, Mark. "Poetry, Sake, and Acrimony: Arakida Hisaoyu and the Kokugaku Movement." *Monumenta Nipponica* 52, 3 (1997): 295-325.
Terada Yasumasa. *Kamo no Mabuchi: shōgai to gyōseki.* Hamamatsu: Hamamatsu Shiseki Chōsa Kenshōkai, 1979.
Tillman, Hoyt C. *Confucian Discourse and Chu Hsi's Ascendency.* Honolulu: University of Hawai'i Press, 1992.
Tucker, John Allen. "Chen Beixi, Lu Xiangshan, and Early Tokugawa (1600-1867) Philosophical Lexicography." *Philosophy East & West* 43, 4 (1993): 683-713.
———. "Ghosts and Spirits in Tokugawa Japan: The Confucian Views of Itō Jinsai." *Japanese Religions* 21, 2 (1996): 229-51.
Uchino Gorō. *Edo-ha kokugaku ronkō.* Sōrinsha, 1979.

―――. "Hirata-ha to Edo-ha no gakushi-teki tei-i: Atsutane no 'Tamadasuki' wo chūshin ni." *Kokugakuin zasshi* 24, 11 (1973): 12–24.

―――. "Norinaga gakutō no keishō: Norinaga botsugo no Suzumon to Atsutane no tachiba." *Nihon bungaku ronkyū* 25, 18 (1966): 12–27.

―――. "Norinaga to Atsutane: sono shisō kankei wo meguru mondai." *Kokugakuin zasshi* 66, 12 (1965): 1–17.

―――. *Shinkokugakuron no tenkai*. Sōrinsha, 1983.

Ueda Kenji. "Kada no Azumamaro no shingaku." 3 pts. *Kokugakuin zasshi* 80, 12 (1979): 1–12; 81, 1 (1980): 131–47; 81, 2 (1980): 54–67.

Uematsu Shigetaka. *Tensetsu-ben*. In *Uematsu Shigetaka*.

Uematsu Shigeru. *Uematsu Shigetaka*. Nagoya: Aichi-ken Kyōdo Shiryō Kankōkai, 1982.

Wakabayashi, Bob. *Anti-foreignism and Western Learning: The "New Theses" of 1825*. Cambridge, Mass.: Council on East Asian Studies, Harvard University, 1986.

Walthall, Anne. *The Weak Body of a Useless Woman: Matsuo Taseko and the Meiji Restoration*. Chicago: University of Chicago Press, 1998.

Watanabe Hiroshi. "'Michi' to 'miyabi': Norinaga-gaku to 'kagakuha' kokugaku no seiji shisō-shiteki kenkyū." 4 pts. *Kokka gakkai zasshi* 87 (1974): 477–561, 647–721; 88 (1975): 238–68, 295–366.

Watanabe Kinzo. *Hirata Atsutane kenkyū*. Rokko Shobō, 1943.

Watanabe Shōichi. "Motoori Norinaga no 'kami no michi' to 'hito no michi': sono kōzō to seikaku ni tsuite." *Kikan Nihon shisō-shi* 8 (1978): 89–105.

Watarai Nobuyoshi. *Yōfukuki*. In NST 39.

Wilson, Thomas. *Genealogy of the Way: The Construction of the Confucian Tradition in Late Imperial China*. Stanford: Stanford University Press, 1995.

Yamada Kanzo. *Motoori Haruniwa*. Matsusaka: Motoori Norinaga Kinenkan, 1983.

Yanagita Kunio. "Senso no hanashi." In *Yanagita Kunio shū*.

Yanagita Kunio shū. Kindai Nihon shisō taikei, vol. 14. Ed. Tsurumi Kazuko. Chikuma Shobō, 1975.

Yano Gendō. *Tamaboko monogatari*. In *Kokumin dōtoku sōsho*, vol. 1.

Yasunishi Katsu. *Oyamada Tomokiyo no sōken*. Yokohama: Sometani, 1990.

Index

Afterlife, 10, 12, 86, 88, 163, 180, 182, 210, 228, 231, 247, 253; and the *Sandaikō* debate, 96, 100, 108, 111, 116–28 *passim*; and ancient history, 185, 186, 188, 206; and phantom scholarship, 189, 192, 195, 196, 197*n*. *See also* Ancient Way; Cosmology; Eschatology; *Tama no yukue*; *Yūmei*
Agatai, 143, 145, 147, 160, 162, 233. *See also* Kamo no Mabuchi
Age of the Gods, 121, 141. *See also* Kamiyo
Agriculturist, 198, 199, 217, 249
Aizawa Seishisai, 201, 203
Amaterasu, 151; and the *Sandaikō*, 107–12 *passim*, 117, 121, 125; and ancient history, 184, 185, 186; theological centrality of, 230, 231, 238
Amenominakanushi-no-kami, 120*n*, 183, 184, 230, 231, 234
Ancient Learning, 38*n*, 153, 202; name for Kokugaku, 1*n*, 82, 83, 104, 124, 146, 148, 162, 168, 171, 223. *See also* Kogaku; Kokugaku; Kōshōgaku; Philology
Ancient Way, 9, 10, 33, 42, 52–57 *passim*, 63, 77, 82, 83, 95, 101, 123, 202, 215, 217, 223; Ban Nobutomo's view, 66, 67, 68; Hirata Atsutane's view, 126, 133, 134, 147, 148, 149, 152–69 *passim*, 173, 176, 189, 201, 219, 231, 238, 250, 254, 255. *See also* Afterlife; Eschatology; Supernatural
Ansai School, 80, 132, 136. *See also* Kimon School; Suika Shinto
Antiquarianism, 61, 259. *See also* Yūsokugaku
Arai Hakuseki, 86, 191, 192
Arakida Hisaoyu, 56
Arakida Suehogi, 172, 173
Artifice, 103, 104, 159
Asami Keisai, 80, 98*n*, 222
Ashiwake Obune, 27
Astronomy/astronomical, 12, 99, 109, 111, 115, 120, 183*n*. *See also* Cosmology; *Sandaikō*
Azumamaro School, 16*n*

Backus, Robert, 39*n*
Bakufu, 16*n*, 234, 236, 237; and Kokugaku, 134, 154, 170, 186, 188, 218*n*
Ban Nobutomo, 23*n*, 27, 67*n*, 88, 94, 127*n*; the *kōshōgakusha*, 51, 66, 67, 197

Bendōsho, 38, 39, 77, 78
Book of Changes, 41, 58n, 79
Bourdieu, Pierre, xiii, xiv, 8n, 12, 65n, 244–48 *passim*, 254, 255
Brownlee, John, 191n
Buddhism, 31–34 *passim*, 34n, 76, 91, 142, 170; as a foreign creed, 39, 41, 52, 53, 57, 59, 75, 113, 115, 152, 159, 215, 216, 229, 251, 254
Bunjin, 24, 25, 26, 63, 66, 247

Calendrical science, 206, 218n
Chan, 132–36 *passim*. See also Zen
Chartier, Roger, 9n, 244
Chen Beixi, 38n, 42n
Cheng Hao, 133
Cheng Yi, 133
Cheng-Zhu, 38n, 39n, 219. See also Daoxue; Dōgaku; Song Confucianism; Song Learning
Chie/Chieko (Atsutane's daughter), 211, 224
Christianity, 120n
Collins, Randall, 7, 8, 172, 253
Confucianism, 38n, 84, 139, 190, 222, 236, 236n, 251; intellectual dominance of, 2, 12, 23, 40n; as a foreign creed, 32–41 *passim*, 52, 53, 57, 58, 59, 75–78 *passim*, 103, 113, 115, 159, 180, 203, 205, 223, 229, 243, 250, 254; and orthodox succession, 132, 133n, 134, 137, 138, 147–52 *passim*, 170. See also Dōgaku; Jugaku; Kangaku; Kōshōgaku
Confucius, 36, 36n, 84–88 *passim*, 132, 149, 190, 191
Cosmology/cosmological, 92, 94, 150, 151, 199, 223, 240, 248; and the *kami*, 230, 231, 234; and the *Koshiden*, 181, 182, 187; and the *Sandaikō* debate, 97, 98, 99, 105, 106, 106n, 112, 115, 122. See also Eschatology
Cultural chauvinism, 13, 251, 255

Daoism, 33, 36, 40, 40n, 41, 158, 159, 250
Daotong, 132, 133, 149. See also Dōtō
Daoxue, 37n, 98n, 137, 190. See also Dōgaku; Song Confucianism; Song Learning
Dazai Shundai, 38–41 *passim*, 77–81 *passim*, 87, 88, 146, 191, 227
Derrida, Jacques, xiv, 102n, 244
Devine, Richard, 120n
Divination, 36n, 193, 206
Dōgaku, 37n. See also Jugaku; Kangaku; Kogaku; Kōshōgaku
Dōjō School, 144, 144n
Domainal scholar, 180
Domainal schools, 23, 39n, 54, 55
Dōtō: Atsutane's view of, 12, 139, 147, 164, 174–77 *passim*, 250; as orthodox succession, 132, 133, 134, 137, 138, 151; Ōkuni Takamasa's view of, 218, 228, 229, 230, 233, 241. See also Orthodoxy; Santetsu; Shiushi
Duke of Zhou, 36, 36n, 149

Eclectics, 39n, 219, 220, 222
Edo Faction, 1n, 9. See also Edo-ha; Mabuchi School
Edo-ha, 9, 10, 11, 14, 15, 16, 16n, 22–27 *passim*, 35, 51, 52, 53, 61–71 *passim*, 77–84 *passim*, 90–95 *passim*, 205, 212, 246–53 *passim*; and Kido Chidate, 56, 57, 59n; and the *Santetsu*, 144, 146, 147; and Hirata Atsutane, 155, 156, 157, 162, 163. See also Mabuchi School; *and individual scholars by name*

Elman, Benjamin, viii, 22n, 36n
Engishiki, 43
Episteme, 6, 7. See also Foucault, Michel; Post-structuralist
Eschatology/eschatological, 10, 12, 85, 164, 168, 177–81 passim, 206, 247, 253, 254, 255; Bakumatsu Kokugaku, 223, 227, 233; and the Sandaikō debate, 97, 116, 122, 123, 126, 130; and the supernatural, 189, 191, 192, 197n, 198. See also Afterlife; Yūmei
Ethnology, 258, 259
Evidential/evidentialism, 10, 12, 52, 98n, 104n, 115, 126, 202–7 passim; supernatural and, 197, 197n, 210
Evidential Learning, 191n, 236n, 239, 255; and the Edo-ha, 22, 23, 51; and the Norinaga School, 66, 104n, 132. See also Kaozhengxue; Kōshōgaku

Farm manuals, 198, 199, 200, 212, 216
Field of cultural production, 12. See also Bourdieu, Pierre
Five Phases, 58, 103
Foucault, Michel, xiv, 6, 244. See also Episteme; Post-structuralist
Four Books, 37n, 40n
Fujii Sadafumi, 239
Fujii Takanao, xiv, 43, 55, 56, 60, 60n, 66, 211, 252
Fuji-no-kakitsu, 96n, 123, 168, 169, 171. See also Motoori Ōhira
Fujitani Mitsue, 45
Fujitani Nariakira, 45
Fujita Tōko, 201

Gakutō benron, 177, 178
Genji monogatari, 27, 28, 31, 32, 34, 43, 60, 62, 69

Gesakusha, 23
Grassroot Kokugaku, 183, 221, 228, 231, 238, 240, 241; and Hirata Atsutane, 199, 211, 214. See also Sōmō no kokugaku

Haga Noboru, 22, 23, 25, 157, 199
Hagura, 153, 178
Hagura Nobuya, 154n
Hankō, 39n
Han Learning, 36n, 37, 37n, 190, 191, 236, 236n. See also Kangaku; Sorai School
Hanxue, 37n. See also Kangaku
Harootunian, Harry, xiii, 5–8 passim, 21, 32n, 52n, 215n, 227, 242–46 passim
Hattori Nakatsune, xiv, 52n, 54, 164, 167–77 passim; and the Sandaikō debate, 97–100 passim, 104–31 passim, 163, 192, 248. See also Norito; Sandaikō
Hattori Nankaku, 38, 38n, 146
Hayashi Razan, 77, 151, 190, 191n
Hiden, 138
Hirata Atsutane, xiii, xiv, 1n, 2, 5–9 passim, 11–15 passim, 36n, 57, 61, 70, 80, 85–89 passim, 95, 179–210 passim, 227–43 passim, 246–56 passim; and nationalism, 3, 8, 257, 259–62 passim; and Grassroots Kokugaku, 4, 13, 211–14 passim, 217–24 passim; and the Norinaga School, 10, 44, 55, 64–69 passim, 96n, 97, 98n, 122n; and the Edo-ha, 27, 60n, 78, 81–84 passim, 92–94 passim; and Motoori Ōhira, 51, 52n, 79, 90, 91, 127n, 128, 129; and the Sandaikō debate, 96–101 passim, 109, 116–30 passim; and the dōtō, 131–39 passim, 143–49 passim, 152–58

passim, 161–78 *passim*. *See also* Hirata School; Ibukinoya
Hirata Kanetane, 162, 164, 165, 171–77 *passim*, 182, 198, 199, 200*n*, 210–14 *passim*, 218, 219, 224; Bakumatsu/Meiji Kokugaku, 228, 232–41 *passim*, 255, 260
Hirata School, 44*n*, 178, 182*n*; and Grassroots Kokugaku, 198, 200, 200*n*; and Bakumatsu/Meiji Kokugaku, 209–14 *passim*, 217–28 *passim*, 233–41 *passim*, 246, 248, 249, 255, 257, 259, 262. *See also* Hirata Atsutane; Ibukinoya
Hisamatsu Sen'ichi, 23, 24
Honzen no sei, 150

Ibukinoya, 1*n*, 56, 170, 172, 178, 182, 193*n*, 198–200 *passim*, 212–14 *passim*, 218, 222, 223, 224, 227, 233, 252, 261; and the Norinaga School, 96*n*, 167, 175, 253. *See also* Hirata Atsutane; Hirata School
Ibukinoya hisso, 82
Iemoto, 137, 138, 147, 176, 177, 178, 211, 228, 233. *See also* Dōtō
Ikuta Yōrozu, 222–27 *passim*, 232
Imperial August Grandchild, 110, 118, 151, 221. *See also* Ninigi-no-mikoto
Imperial regalia, 67, 68
Inagake Shigeo, 45. *See also* Motoori Ōhira
Inishie manabi, 1*n*. *See also* Kogaku
Investigation of things and exhaustion of principle, 86, 190
Ise monogatari, 27, 43, 60, 69
Ise Shinto, 39, 136, 183*n*
Isonokami no sazamegoto, 45

Itō Jinsai, 18, 38*n*, 88, 88*n*, 104, 104*n*, 146, 150, 191
Ivy, Marilyn, 258
Iwa ni musu koke, 224
Izanagi-no-mikoto, 110, 184, 184*n*, 185, 186, 189, 231
Izanami-no-mikoto, 108, 109, 110, 119, 184, 184*n*
Izumi Makuni, 66, 148, 157, 165, 205, 251, 252; and the *Meidōsho* debate, 69–83 *passim*, 90, 91

Jindai moji, 89
Jugaku, 35
Jukyō-ji, 49*n*

Kada no Azumamaro, 12, 14, 47, 75, 94, 200, 211, 251; and the *dōtō*, 134, 138, 139, 144–58 *passim*, 161, 163, 164, 178, 207, 233, 249, 250, 254; the Edo scholar, 16, 17, 24–28 *passim*, 93
Kada no Arimaro, 16, 17, 27, 145, 148, 152, 155, 156, 200
Kada no Nobuna, 16, 17, 155
Kadō, 30, 53, 59
Kadō tai'i, 82
Kagura, 51, 60, 211
Kagura shinshaku, 51
Kaiho Seiryō, 227
Kakubutsu kyūri, 86, 190
Kami, 19, 41, 42, 76, 79, 80, 85–91 *passim*, 133, 148, 159, 160, 163, 184–89 *passim*, 195, 197, 197*n*, 202, 204; and Grassroots Kokugaku, 215, 216, 217, 220, 221, 227, 230–34 *passim*; and the *Sandaikō* debate, 105, 109, 114, 118, 125. *See also individual* kami *by name*
Kami no michi, 34*n*, 41. *See also* Shendao; Shinto

Kamiyo, 231; Norinaga's view of, 101, 104, 105; Nakatsune's view of, 109, 111, 112; and the *Sandaikō* debate, 116, 120, 130, 131; Atsutane's view of, 182, 184*n*, 206

Kamo no Mabuchi, 2, 3, 9, 12, 36*n*, 38, 39, 40, 56, 60, 65, 72, 82, 83, 93, 181, 189, 200, 211, 212, 213, 222, 229, 242, 243, 246; and the *dōtō*, 14, 143–49 *passim*, 155–64 *passim*, 178, 207, 250, 254; and the Edo-ha, 15, 16, 17, 21–27 *passim*, 57, 59*n*, 63, 70, 93, 247; and Motoori Norinaga, 29–34 *passim*, 43, 45, 58, 67, 69, 96, 104, 138, 183, 251, 260; the scholarship of, 18–21 *passim*, 28, 40*n*, 41, 46, 47, 59, 62, 73–77 *passim*, 103*n*, 141

Kamōsho, 78–84 *passim*, 91, 92, 94, 165, 179

Kamumimusubi, 184

Kanbungaku, 35

Kangaku, 35, 37, 37*n*, 54, 236, 237. See also Dōgaku; Jugaku; Kōshōgaku

Kanzen chōaku, 28, 31, 32

Kaozhengxue, 22, 71. See also Evidential Learning; Kōshōgaku

Kara, 34*n*

Karagokoro, 34–37 *passim*, 102, 103, 115, 157, 159

Kasei period, 212, 213, 215, 246, 261

Katō Chikage, 15, 17, 21, 60, 92, 146, 205

Katō Enao, 15, 17, 18

Katō Umaki, 26

Katsura Takashige, 221, 222

Kaya, 34*n*

Keichū, 12, 17, 18, 19, 27, 28, 29, 46, 82, 104, 138–49 *passim*, 181, 201, 201*n*, 239; and the *dōtō*, 138–49 *passim*, 156, 250

Kido Chidate, xiv, 43, 55–63 *passim*, 66, 68, 148, 170–76 *passim*, 252

Kijin, 39, 190, 215. See also kishin

Kikkawa Koretaru, 136, 151

Kimon School, 98*n*, 136, 137, 209, 222

Kishin, 80, 84–88 *passim*, 190, 191, 192

Kishinshinron, 83, 86, 91, 122, 165, 190, 196, 197. See also Shinkishinron

Kiyosōhansho, xiv, 131, 164, 170–76 *passim*

Kodō, 9, 33

Kōgakkan University, 3, 239

Kogaku, 1*n*, 83, 124, 153. See also Inishie manabi

Kogakuyō, 52, 52*n*

Kojiki, 59, 71, 82, 140, 181, 182, 183*n*, 231, 254; and Norinaga, 15, 33, 43, 44, 51, 159, 160; and the *Sandaikō* debate, 97, 100–111 *passim*, 115–21 *passim*, 129

Kojiki-den, 15, 44, 73, 181; and the *Sandaikō* debate, 97, 101–9 *passim*, 113, 116, 125, 128

Kokinshū, 18, 27, 43, 47, 61, 83

Kokka hachiron, 145

Kokueki honron, 214

Kokugaku, xiii, xiv, 1, 1*n*, 23, 33, 43, 44*n*, 54, 55, 66, 92, 96–100 *passim*, 144, 182, 201, 207, 208, 229–43 *passim*, 251, 252, 257–62 *passim*; Atsutane's invention of, 81, 82, 131, 132, 138, 139, 147, 149, 152–56 *passim*, 176, 178, 183, 250, 254, 256; and the Hirata School, 198, 199, 209, 210, 212, 215–20 *passim*, 223–28 *passim*; secondary schol-

arship on, 2–16 *passim*, 246, 247, 249, 255. *See also* Edo-ha; Hirata School; Norinaga School
Kokugakuin University, 3
Kokuikō, 36n, 38, 39, 40n, 74
Konishi Atsuyoshi, 198, 199, 214
Koshibaya, 59, 60, 96n, 252
Koshiden, 204; and the Hirata School, 200, 210, 217, 232, 233, 241; validation of commoners, 181–83 *passim*, 187, 188, 196, 207
Koshi seibun, 181, 182, 219, 223
Kōshōgaku, 22n; and the Edo-ha, 22, 23, 68, 71, 74, 181; and the Norinaga School, 52, 62, 67, 72, 90, 100, 104, 104n, 112, 113, 116, 124, 129, 180, 207. *See also* Dōgaku; Jugaku; Kangaku
Kōshōgakusha, 51, 67. *See also* Ban Nobutomo; Oyamada Tomokiyo
Kotoba no yachimata, 46, 48
Kotodama, 19
Koyasu Nobukuni, xiii, 3, 4, 244, 262
Kuki Shūzō, 261
Kumazawa Banzan, 77

Laozi, 40, 40n, 159
Later Suzunoya, 48. *See also* Nochi-Suzunoya
Li Tong, 133
Lu Xiangshan, 38n

Mabuchi School, 1n, 26, 45, 213; and the Edo-ha, 48, 56, 60, 247
Magokoro, 17, 21, 34, 34n, 40n, 42, 141, 189
Maita Katsuyasu, 152n, 154n, 262
Manabi no hiromichi, 57
Mandate of Heaven, 58, 80, 188
Man'yōgaku, 82

Man'yōshū, 43, 47, 62, 102n, 121, 139–45 *passim*, 201; and the Edo-ha, 15, 24, 48; and Kamo no Mabuchi, 17, 18, 22, 27, 28, 29, 83, 156, 160, 161; and Motoori Norinaga, 43, 61, 181
Maruyama Masao, 2, 38n, 98n, 261, 262
Masurao/masuraogokoro, 18, 157
Matsudaira Sadanobu, 16n, 21, 39n
Matsumoto Shigeru, 5n, 34n
Matsunoya, 60, 60n, 203
Matsusaka: and Motoori Norinaga, 15, 43, 45, 49, 49n, 74, 96, 158, 159, 166; and the Norinaga School, 11, 14, 14n, 44n, 48, 50, 54, 55, 61–66 *passim*, 69, 90, 96n, 162, 165, 168, 170, 172, 201, 212, 247, 251, 252
Meidōsho, 52, 69, 70, 73, 78, 81, 157
Meiji period, 1, 2n, 13, 49n, 97, 165, 180, 208, 210, 228, 233–41 *passim*, 246, 255–61 *passim*
Meiji Restoration, 210, 228
Meirindō, 96n, 253
Mencius, 132, 133, 137, 149
Michi, 41
Miki Shōtarō, 100, 104, 120n
Mimana, 34n
Ming dynasty, 25, 37–40 *passim*, 71, 71n, 104n, 134, 190, 203, 220
Minzokugaku, 257, 260
Mito School, 180, 201n, 202, 203, 204, 205, 209. *See also individual scholars by name*
Miyahiro Sadao, 214–22 *passim*, 227, 228, 230n, 249
Miyake Kiyoshi, 153, 154
Monjin, 96, 162, 170, 199
Mono no aware, 28, 30, 31, 32, 32n, 34, 58, 62
Motoori Arisato, 50

Motoori Haruniwa, 15, 43–45 *passim*, 49*n*, 55, 68, 96*n*, 212, 252; the scholarship of, 46, 47, 48, 60, 63; and Motoori Ōhira, 49, 50, 211; and Hirata Atsutane, 66, 79, 81, 83, 89, 91, 94, 165–74 *passim*

Motoori no Miya, 49*n*

Motoori Norinaga, 1*n*, 2–10 *passim*, 14*n*, 15, 26, 27*n*, 32*n*, 34*n*70, 34*n*72, 42–45 *passim*, 48–72 *passim*, 75–78 *passim*, 83, 85, 90, 91, 97–99 *passim*, 113, 116, 122–30 *passim*, 141–47 *passim*, 150, 175*n*, 198, 199, 210–15 *passim*, 222, 223, 225, 240, 242, 252, 253, 255, 260, 261, 262; and the *dōtō*, 12, 14, 131, 138, 139, 144, 148, 149, 164; and Kamo no Mabuchi, 27, 40*n*, 158–63 *passim*; the scholarship of, 28–38 *passim*, 41, 42, 46, 59, 59*n*, 61, 73, 74, 80, 96, 100–114 *passim*, 118, 119, 121, 181, 189, 243, 250, 251; and Hirata Atsutane, 163–78 *passim*, 183, 185, 188, 200, 207, 219, 230, 248, 254. *See also* Norinaga School; Suzunoya

Motoori Ōhira, 15, 104*n*, 122, 138, 200, 211, 239, 252–55 *passim*; and the Norinaga School, 43–63 *passim*, 66–71 *passim*, 112–17 *passim*, 123–30 *passim*; and Hirata Atsutane, 79, 83, 88–94 *passim*, 97, 122*n*, 157, 165–78 *passim*

Motoori Uchitō, 50, 239

Muraoka Tsunetsugu, 120*n*

Murasaki Shikibu, 31, 34

Murata Harukado, 56, 68, 213, 229

Murata Harumi, 143–48 *passim*, 155, 158; and the Edo-ha, 15, 17, 21–24 *passim*, 56, 63, 205; and the Norinaga School, 66, 69–81 *passim*, 84, 90–94 *passim*, 157, 165, 250, 251; the scholarship of, 40*n*, 47, 48

Murata Harumichi, 15, 16, 17, 74, 158

Murata Harusato, 17, 158

Muro Kyūsō, 87

Musubi-no-kami, 184, 186, 188, 190, 230, 230*n*

Mutobe Tokika, 167

Mutobe Yoshika, 167, 170

Myōraku-ji, 49*n*

Nakamura Kazumoto, 91

Nanga, 25

Naobi no mitama, 38

Nationalism/nationalist, 2, 3, 257, 260, 261, 262

Nativism/nativist, xiii, xiv, 1–5 *passim*, 9–12 *passim*, 36*n*, 211, 257, 259; of the Edo-ha, 23–27 *passim*, 74–78 *passim*, 93, 143–46 *passim*; of the Norinaga School, 33, 35, 43, 44, 47, 49, 52–72 *passim*, 81–89 *passim*, 91, 94, 97, 99, 100, 104, 115, 122, 124, 126, 132–39 *passim*, 148, 149, 150, 157, 160, 164–80 *passim*, 183, 192, 193, 198–201 *passim*, 205, 206, 209, 212, 228, 233–37 *passim*, 240, 242, 243, 246–55 *passim*, 262. *See also* Kokugaku

Neo-Confucianism, 36–39 *passim*, 151, 190, 223, 236, 243, 250; and orthodox succession, 132, 133*n*, 134, 137, 147, 149, 170, 229. *See also* Daoxue; Dōgaku; Jugaku; Song Confucianism; Song Learning

Ng, Wai-ming, 58*n*, 71*n*

Nihongi, 59, 67, 71, 76, 79, 139, 140, 145, 150, 181, 231, 254; and the

Sandaikō debate, 101, 102, 103, 119, 182
Nijō School, 45, 46
Ninigi-no-mikoto, 110, 118, 121
Ninkō, 167, 181
Nishikawa Masatami, 99, 100, 109
Nochi-Suzunoya, 11, 48, 96*n*, 212, 213, 252. *See also* Motoori Haruniwa; Norinaga School
Norinaga School, 1*n*, 27, 44, 44*n*, 48–60 *passim*, 63–69 *passim*, 79, 167, 201, 212, 213, 214*n*, 228, 233, 240, 243, 246; and Hirata Atsutane, 8–15 *passim*, 88–98 *passim*, 101, 112, 115, 116, 117, 122–26 *passim*, 129–32 *passim*, 139, 148, 163, 170, 172, 175–80 *passim*, 192, 204–9 *passim*, 223, 242, 247–55 *passim*; and the Edo-ha, 35, 70, 71, 72, 77, 78, 81. *See also* Motoori Norinaga; Suzunoya; *and individual scholars and academies by name*
Norinaga to Atsutane no sekai, xiii, 262
Norito, 62, 131, 132, 148, 167–71 *passim*, 174–77 *passim*
Nosco, Peter, 5–8 *passim*, 140, 152*n*, 212*n*, 246, 249
Nōsho, 198
Nudenoya, 55–61 *passim*, 96*n*, 167, 173, 176, 252

Ogyū Sorai, 104, 146, 150, 187, 226; and nativism, 2, 18, 36–42 *passim*, 104*n*, 191, 261; and *kishin*, 77, 80, 86, 87, 88
Ōkuninushi-no-kami, 110, 121, 182, 185, 186, 188, 189, 192, 195, 234
Ōkuni Takamasa, 144, 177, 178, 218, 219, 228–34 *passim*, 237, 241

Omote Tomoyuki, 99, 106
Ooms, Herman, xiii
Orikuchi Shinobu, 258, 259, 260, 261
Orthodox lineage, 12, 131, 138, 139, 143, 156, 229, 233, 254. *See also Daotong*; *Dōtō*
Orthodoxy, 8, 39*n*, 147, 219; and the Norinaga School, 10, 57, 97, 98, 98*n*, 112, 124, 130–37 *passim*, 174–77 *passim*, 242, 248, 253, 254, 255. *See also Daotong*; *Dōtō*; Orthodox lineage
Oyamada Tomokiyo, xiv, 23–26 *passim*, 60*n*, 93, 181, 197, 202–5 *passim*; and Kōshōgaku, 51, 52, 66, 90
Ozawa Masao, 99

Peasantry, 179, 180, 187, 188, 199, 206, 214–20 *passim*, 224–27 *passim*
Philology/philological, 37*n*, 210, 239; and Hirata Atsutane, 10, 12, 82, 93–97 *passim*, 100–104 *passim*, 108, 109, 113–19 *passim*, 122, 123, 126–30 *passim*, 179, 181, 185, 207, 242; and nativism, 17, 18, 22–27 *passim*, 33, 46, 57, 58, 63, 141, 145, 146, 150, 152, 176, 215. *See also* Kogaku; Kōshōgaku
Post-structuralist, 244, 245. *See also* Derrida, Jacques; Foucault, Michel
Practice (Bourdieu's theory of), xiv, 7, 9, 9*n*, 245–48 *passim*, 254. *See also* Bourdieu, Pierre; Field of cultural production
Prasad, Sajja A., 5*n*
Private academies, 43, 44, 55, 129, 214*n*, 235

Qing dynasty, 37n, 71, 71n, 104n, 106n, 190, 236n

Rangaku, 57, 59, 99, 113, 116, 127
Rubinger, Richard, 43, 44, 44n
Ryōbu Shintō, 33, 136
Ryōnogige, 70, 71
Ryōyaku kuchi ni nigashi, 224
Ryūkō, 143, 143n

Sakai, Naoki, 140n
Sakashira, 103
Samurai, 39n, 136, 220; and nativism, 16, 54, 213, 221, 222, 225, 226, 232
Sandaikō, 52n, 97–100 passim, 105, 106, 107, 112–15 passim; and Hirata Atsutane, 116–28 passim, 131, 163, 168, 169, 173, 175, 176, 203, 205, 207, 248
Sandaikō-ben, 112, 112n, 115, 117, 126, 127, 127n
Sandaikō-benben, 127, 130
Sandaikō Suzuki Akira setsu, 112
Sanskrit, 19, 20, 141, 142
Santetsu, 143–47 passim. See also *Dōtō; and individual scholars by name*
Santetsu shōden, 143, 143n
Santō Kyōden, 25
Satsuma, 55
Saussure, Ferdinand de, 19
Sawai Keiichi, 102n
Sazanami hitsuwa, 143, 146
Secret teachings, 45, 136. See also Hiden; Secret transmissions
Secret transmissions, 45, 151. See also Hiden; Secret teachings
Seidensticker, Edward, 93n
Senkyō ibun, 192, 193, 196, 197, 207
Shaku, 170
Shakyamuni, 75

Shendao, 39, 41, 76, 79, 80. See also Shinto
Shijuku, 55
Shikan, 180, 202, 204
Shikitei Sanba, 25
Shimazaki Tōson, 238
Shimazu Nariakira, 55
Shimimuro zakki, 56
Shimizu Hamaomi, 56, 60, 77, 143, 146
Shimokōbe Chōryū, 146, 201
Shimosa, 200, 213, 214, 230n
Shinjoya, 158
Shinkishinron, 79–84 passim, 90–94 passim, 96, 130, 179, 189, 190, 192. See also *Kishinshinron*
Shinkokinshū, 27, 43, 47, 145
Shinkokugaku, 260, 261
Shinto/Shintoism, 1n, 132, 136, 137, 154n, 260; and nativism, 2, 3, 6, 16, 17, 23, 29, 33–41 passim, 51–63 passim, 76, 91, 115, 122, 139, 145, 149, 150, 151, 156, 158, 159, 243, 246, 250, 251; and Hirata Atsutane, 9, 10, 78, 79, 80, 84, 86, 122, 127, 131, 181–89 passim, 195, 202, 203, 204, 254, 262; and the Hirata School, 213–18 passim, 221, 231–35 passim, 238, 240, 241
Shitaijin, 30. See also *Dōtō; Shiushi*
Shitamachi, 24, 92, 93, 247
Shiushi, 14, 143, 144, 148, 154n, 177, 229, 233. See also *Dōtō*
Showa, 1, 257
Six Classics, 37, 37n, 40n
Sociology of knowledge, xiv
Sociology of Philosophies, The, 7
Sōgakkōkei, 138, 149, 152, 153, 154, 249
Sōmō no kokugaku, 183
Song Confucianism, 12, 37, 37n, 132, 133, 190, 223. See also Cheng-Zhu;

Daoxue; Dōgaku; Jugaku; Song Learning
Song Learning, 37, 37*n*, 190, 191*n*. *See also* Cheng-Zhu; Daoxue; Dōgaku; Song Confucianism
Sorai School, 36, 37, 38, 38*n*, 78, 146
Soul, destination of, 114, 115, 119, 121, 124, 182. *See also* Tama no yukue
Spirit realm, 120, 121, 122, 128, 194, 195, 196, 223. *See also* Yomi; Yūmei
Structuralist, 244, 245. *See also* Bourdieu, Pierre; Saussure, Ferdinand de
Sugawara no Michizane, 133, 149
Suika Shinto, 38, 136, 137
Sumemima, 110. *See also* Ninigi-no-mikoto
Supernatural, 12, 80, 85, 123, 163, 189–98 *passim*, 210, 224, 231, 247, 254, 258, 259; and commoner experiences, 180, 181, 193–98 *passim*, 207, 241. *See also* Afterlife; Eschatology
Susanō-no-mikoto, 108, 109, 114, 116, 117, 121, 184, 184*n*, 185
Suzuki Akira, 48, 55, 112–17 *passim*, 124, 125, 126, 129, 252
Suzuki Masayuki, 230, 230*n*, 231
Suzuki Shigetane, 218, 219, 220, 221, 222, 227, 231
Suzunoya, 98*n*, 104*n*, 143, 166, 175, 233; and the Norinaga School, 14*n*, 43–45 *passim*, 48, 49, 52–56 *passim*, 60, 63, 105, 106, 112, 138, 162, 164, 169, 176, 178, 212–14 *passim*, 252, 255. *See also* Motoori Norinaga

Tachibana Moribe, 62
Taisho, 1
Takama-no-hara, 100, 106, 107, 111, 113, 114, 117, 118, 185
Takamimusubi, 184
Takizawa Bakin, 25
Tamadasuki, 182, 196, 196*n*, 249, 259; and the *dōtō*, 14, 131, 132, 139, 143, 143*n*, 144, 148, 162, 163, 164, 178, 183, 229, 253; and the *Meidōsho* debate, 69, 70, 81
Tamakatsuma, 73, 159
Tama no mihashira, 52*n*, 84, 93, 120*n*, 169, 199, 223; and the afterlife, 109, 116, 121–27 *passim*, 130, 179–85 *passim*, 192, 193, 253
Tama no yukue, 119, 124, 192
Tanaka Yoshito, 123
Tang dynasty, 34*n*, 73, 132–36 *passim*, 140, 142
Taoyame, 18
Tayasu Munetake, 16, 16*n*, 158, 200
Teeuwen, Mark, 77*n*
Tengu, 193, 194, 195
Teniwoha, 46, 47
Tensetsu-ben, 124, 126
Tensetsu-benben, 128, 129, 130
Things Seen and Unseen, xiii
Tiantai, 134, 135, 136
Tokugawa Harusada, 200
Tokugawa Harutomi, 49, 50, 51
Tokugawa Ieyasu, 133, 149
Tokugawa Mitsukuni, 133, 149, 201
Tokugawa Nariaki, 202
Tokugawa period, 71*n*, 93*n*, 236, 239; and Kokugaku/nativism, xiii, xiv, 1–7 *passim*, 10, 14, 22, 25, 30, 37, 64, 87, 97, 133–46 *passim*, 149–53 *passim*, 172, 181, 201, 206, 225, 235, 243–46 *passim*, 250, 255–62 *passim*
Tokugawa Yoshinao, 133, 149
Tōjō Gimon, 46
Tōno monogatari, 258

Index

Torakichi, 193–98 *passim*, 207
Toyoda Tenkō, 204
Tsuki-yomi-no-mikoto, 108, 109, 114, 117
Tucker, John, 38*n*, 42*n*, 88*n*

Uchino Gorō, 9, 10, 24, 92, 93, 123, 143–46 *passim*
Ueda Akinari, 26
Uematsu Arinobu, 48, 90, 90*n*, 252
Uematsu Shigetake, xiv, 55, 114, 124–30 *passim*, 173
Ultranationalism, 261
Utagatari, 69, 143, 146

Wagaku, 1*n*, 23, 33, 35, 72, 78, 84, 153. See also Kokugaku; Nativism
Waka, 40, 40*n*, 139, 229; and the Edo-ha, 21, 26, 67, 92; and Motoori Norinaga, 28, 29, 30, 252; and the Norinaga School, 43–49 *passim*, 53, 56–62 *passim*, 70–75 *passim*; and Hirata Atsutane, 81, 82, 83
Wakabayashi, Bob, 20*n*
Walthall, Anne, 182*n*
Wang Yangming, 220, 224, 227
Watanabe Shōichi, 34*n*
Watarai Nobuyoshi, 136, 151
Way of the Gods, 41, 42, 168. See also Shendao; Shinto
Way of Poetry, 30, 53, 146. See also Kadō
Way of the Sages, 33, 38–42 *passim*, 76, 79, 80, 165, 251
Wen, 40, 41
Wenren, 25. See also Bunjin
Wilson, Thomas, 135

Yamagata Bantō, 86, 88
Yamamuro/Yamamuroyama, 49, 49*n*, 168
Yamanote, 24, 92, 93
Yamatogokoro, 74, 143, 157, 214, 257
Yamazaki Ansai, 58, 80, 87, 151, 190, 203, 222; and the *dōtō*, 98*n*, 132, 136, 137, 164
Yanagita Kunio, 258–61 *passim*
Yano Gendō, 228, 232, 241
Yin and Yang, 58, 103
Yōakemae, 238
Yomi, 105, 108–26 *passim*, 169, 182, 184, 185, 189, 192, 230. See also Afterlife; Eschatology; *Sandaikō*; *Yūmei*
Yoshida, 9, 38, 136, 167, 171, 234, 235, 240
Yoshimune, 16, 152, 154
Yōshorō nikki, 23
Yotsugigusa, 220
Yūmei/Yūmeikai, 128, 223; and Hirata Atsutane, 120, 121, 182, 183, 185, 188, 191, 192, 193, 196
Yushima, 24, 93
Yūsokugaku/*yūsoku kojitsu*, 17, 61, 181

Zen, 132, 137, 138, 164, 170
Zhou Dunyi, 133, 134, 149
Zhou dynasty, 36
Zhu Xi, 37*n*, 38*n*, 226; and *kishin*, 86, 87, 190; and the *dōtō*, 133, 134, 137, 149, 164, 230. See also Cheng-Zhu; Daoxue; Dōgaku; Jugaku; Song Confucianism; Song Learning
Ziyi, 38*n*

Harvard East Asian Monographs
(* out-of-print)

*1. Liang Fang-chung, *The Single-Whip Method of Taxation in China*
*2. Harold C. Hinton, *The Grain Tribute System of China, 1845–1911*
3. Ellsworth C. Carlson, *The Kaiping Mines, 1877–1912*
*4. Chao Kuo-chün, *Agrarian Policies of Mainland China: A Documentary Study, 1949–1956*
*5. Edgar Snow, *Random Notes on Red China, 1936–1945*
*6. Edwin George Beal, Jr., *The Origin of Likin, 1835–1864*
7. Chao Kuo-chün, *Economic Planning and Organization in Mainland China: A Documentary Study, 1949–1957*
*8. John K. Fairbank, *Ching Documents: An Introductory Syllabus*
*9. Helen Yin and Yi-chang Yin, *Economic Statistics of Mainland China, 1949–1957*
*10. Wolfgang Franke, *The Reform and Abolition of the Traditional Chinese Examination System*
11. Albert Feuerwerker and S. Cheng, *Chinese Communist Studies of Modern Chinese History*
12. C. John Stanley, *Late Ching Finance: Hu Kuang-yung as an Innovator*
13. S. M. Meng, *The Tsungli Yamen: Its Organization and Functions*
*14. Ssu-yü Teng, *Historiography of the Taiping Rebellion*
15. Chun-Jo Liu, *Controversies in Modern Chinese Intellectual History: An Analytic Bibliography of Periodical Articles, Mainly of the May Fourth and Post-May Fourth Era*
*16. Edward J. M. Rhoads, *The Chinese Red Army, 1927–1963: An Annotated Bibliography*
17. Andrew J. Nathan, *A History of the China International Famine Relief Commission*
*18. Frank H. H. King (ed.) and Prescott Clarke, *A Research Guide to China-Coast Newspapers, 1822–1911*

Harvard East Asian Monographs

   19. Ellis Joffe, *Party and Army: Professionalism and Political Control in the Chinese Officer Corps, 1949–1964*

*20. Toshio G. Tsukahira, *Feudal Control in Tokugawa Japan: The Sankin Kōtai System*

   21. Kwang-Ching Liu, ed., *American Missionaries in China: Papers from Harvard Seminars*

   22. George Moseley, *A Sino-Soviet Cultural Frontier: The Ili Kazakh Autonomous Chou*

   23. Carl F. Nathan, *Plague Prevention and Politics in Manchuria, 1910–1931*

*24. Adrian Arthur Bennett, *John Fryer: The Introduction of Western Science and Technology into Nineteenth-Century China*

   25. Donald J. Friedman, *The Road from Isolation: The Campaign of the American Committee for Non-Participation in Japanese Aggression, 1938–1941*

*26. Edward LeFevour, *Western Enterprise in Late Ching China: A Selective Survey of Jardine, Matheson and Company's Operations, 1842–1895*

   27. Charles Neuhauser, *Third World Politics: China and the Afro-Asian People's Solidarity Organization, 1957–1967*

   28. Kungtu C. Sun, assisted by Ralph W. Huenemann, *The Economic Development of Manchuria in the First Half of the Twentieth Century*

*29. Shahid Javed Burki, *A Study of Chinese Communes, 1965*

   30. John Carter Vincent, *The Extraterritorial System in China: Final Phase*

   31. Madeleine Chi, *China Diplomacy, 1914–1918*

*32. Clifton Jackson Phillips, *Protestant America and the Pagan World: The First Half Century of the American Board of Commissioners for Foreign Missions, 1810–1860*

   33. James Pusey, *Wu Han: Attacking the Present Through the Past*

   34. Ying-wan Cheng, *Postal Communication in China and Its Modernization, 1860–1896*

   35. Tuvia Blumenthal, *Saving in Postwar Japan*

   36. Peter Frost, *The Bakumatsu Currency Crisis*

   37. Stephen C. Lockwood, *Augustine Heard and Company, 1858–1862*

   38. Robert R. Campbell, *James Duncan Campbell: A Memoir by His Son*

   39. Jerome Alan Cohen, ed., *The Dynamics of China's Foreign Relations*

   40. V. V. Vishnyakova-Akimova, *Two Years in Revolutionary China, 1925–1927*, trans. Steven L. Levine

*41. Meron Medzini, *French Policy in Japan During the Closing Years of the Tokugawa Regime*

   42. Ezra Vogel, Margie Sargent, Vivienne B. Shue, Thomas Jay Mathews, and Deborah S. Davis, *The Cultural Revolution in the Provinces*

*43. Sidney A. Forsythe, *An American Missionary Community in China, 1895–1905*

Harvard East Asian Monographs

*44. Benjamin I. Schwartz, ed., *Reflections on the May Fourth Movement.: A Symposium*

*45. Ching Young Choe, *The Rule of the Taewŏngun, 1864–1873: Restoration in Yi Korea*

46. W. P. J. Hall, *A Bibliographical Guide to Japanese Research on the Chinese Economy, 1958–1970*

47. Jack J. Gerson, *Horatio Nelson Lay and Sino-British Relations, 1854–1864*

48. Paul Richard Bohr, *Famine and the Missionary: Timothy Richard as Relief Administrator and Advocate of National Reform*

49. Endymion Wilkinson, *The History of Imperial China: A Research Guide*

50. Britten Dean, *China and Great Britain: The Diplomacy of Commercial Relations, 1860–1864*

51. Ellsworth C. Carlson, *The Foochow Missionaries, 1847–1880*

52. Yeh-chien Wang, *An Estimate of the Land-Tax Collection in China, 1753 and 1908*

53. Richard M. Pfeffer, *Understanding Business Contracts in China, 1949–1963*

54. Han-sheng Chuan and Richard Kraus, *Mid-Ching Rice Markets and Trade: An Essay in Price History*

55. Ranbir Vohra, *Lao She and the Chinese Revolution*

56. Liang-lin Hsiao, *China's Foreign Trade Statistics, 1864–1949*

*57. Lee-hsia Hsu Ting, *Government Control of the Press in Modern China, 1900–1949*

58. Edward W. Wagner, *The Literati Purges: Political Conflict in Early Yi Korea*

*59. Joungwon A. Kim, *Divided Korea: The Politics of Development, 1945–1972*

*60. Noriko Kamachi, John K. Fairbank, and Chūzō Ichiko, *Japanese Studies of Modern China Since 1953: A Bibliographical Guide to Historical and Social-Science Research on the Nineteenth and Twentieth Centuries, Supplementary Volume for 1953–1969*

61. Donald A. Gibbs and Yun-chen Li, *A Bibliography of Studies and Translations of Modern Chinese Literature, 1918–1942*

62. Robert H. Silin, *Leadership and Values: The Organization of Large-Scale Taiwanese Enterprises*

63. David Pong, *A Critical Guide to the Kwangtung Provincial Archives Deposited at the Public Record Office of London*

*64. Fred W. Drake, *China Charts the World: Hsu Chi-yü and His Geography of 1848*

*65. William A. Brown and Urgrunge Onon, trans. and annots., *History of the Mongolian People's Republic*

66. Edward L. Farmer, *Early Ming Government: The Evolution of Dual Capitals*

Harvard East Asian Monographs

*67. Ralph C. Croizier, *Koxinga and Chinese Nationalism: History, Myth, and the Hero*
*68. William J. Tyler, trans., *The Psychological World of Natsume Sōseki*, by Doi Takeo
69. Eric Widmer, *The Russian Ecclesiastical Mission in Peking During the Eighteenth Century*
*70. Charlton M. Lewis, *Prologue to the Chinese Revolution: The Transformation of Ideas and Institutions in Hunan Province, 1891–1907*
71. Preston Torbert, *The Ching Imperial Household Department: A Study of Its Organization and Principal Functions, 1662–1796*
72. Paul A. Cohen and John E. Schrecker, eds., *Reform in Nineteenth-Century China*
73. Jon Sigurdson, *Rural Industrialism in China*
74. Kang Chao, *The Development of Cotton Textile Production in China*
75. Valentin Rabe, *The Home Base of American China Missions, 1880–1920*
*76. Sarasin Viraphol, *Tribute and Profit: Sino-Siamese Trade, 1652–1853*
77. Ch'i-ch'ing Hsiao, *The Military Establishment of the Yuan Dynasty*
78. Meishi Tsai, *Contemporary Chinese Novels and Short Stories, 1949–1974: An Annotated Bibliography*
*79. Wellington K. K. Chan, *Merchants, Mandarins and Modern Enterprise in Late Ching China*
80. Endymion Wilkinson, *Landlord and Labor in Late Imperial China: Case Studies from Shandong by Jing Su and Luo Lun*
*81. Barry Keenan, *The Dewey Experiment in China: Educational Reform and Political Power in the Early Republic*
*82. George A. Hayden, *Crime and Punishment in Medieval Chinese Drama: Three Judge Pao Plays*
*83. Sang-Chul Suh, *Growth and Structural Changes in the Korean Economy, 1910–1940*
84. J. W. Dower, *Empire and Aftermath: Yoshida Shigeru and the Japanese Experience, 1878–1954*
85. Martin Collcutt, *Five Mountains: The Rinzai Zen Monastic Institution in Medieval Japan*
86. Kwang Suk Kim and Michael Roemer, *Growth and Structural Transformation*
87. Anne O. Krueger, *The Developmental Role of the Foreign Sector and Aid*
*88. Edwin S. Mills and Byung-Nak Song, *Urbanization and Urban Problems*
89. Sung Hwan Ban, Pal Yong Moon, and Dwight H. Perkins, *Rural Development*
*90. Noel F. McGinn, Donald R. Snodgrass, Yung Bong Kim, Shin-Bok Kim, and Quee-Young Kim, *Education and Development in Korea*

Harvard East Asian Monographs

91. Leroy P. Jones and II SaKong, *Government, Business, and Entrepreneurship in Economic Development: The Korean Case*
92. Edward S. Mason, Dwight H. Perkins, Kwang Suk Kim, David C. Cole, Mahn Je Kim et al., *The Economic and Social Modernization of the Republic of Korea*
93. Robert Repetto, Tai Hwan Kwon, Son-Ung Kim, Dae Young Kim, John E. Sloboda, and Peter J. Donaldson, *Economic Development, Population Policy, and Demographic Transition in the Republic of Korea*
94. Parks M. Coble, Jr., *The Shanghai Capitalists and the Nationalist Government, 1927–1937*
95. Noriko Kamachi, *Reform in China: Huang Tsun-hsien and the Japanese Model*
96. Richard Wich, *Sino-Soviet Crisis Politics: A Study of Political Change and Communication*
97. Lillian M. Li, *China's Silk Trade: Traditional Industry in the Modern World, 1842–1937*
98. R. David Arkush, *Fei Xiaotong and Sociology in Revolutionary China*
*99. Kenneth Alan Grossberg, *Japan's Renaissance: The Politics of the Muromachi Bakufu*
100. James Reeve Pusey, *China and Charles Darwin*
101. Hoyt Cleveland Tillman, *Utilitarian Confucianism: Chen Liang's Challenge to Chu Hsi*
102. Thomas A. Stanley, *Ōsugi Sakae, Anarchist in Taishō Japan: The Creativity of the Ego*
103. Jonathan K. Ocko, *Bureaucratic Reform in Provincial China: Ting Jih-ch'ang in Restoration Kiangsu, 1867–1870*
104. James Reed, *The Missionary Mind and American East Asia Policy, 1911–1915*
105. Neil L. Waters, *Japan's Local Pragmatists: The Transition from Bakumatsu to Meiji in the Kawasaki Region*
106. David C. Cole and Yung Chul Park, *Financial Development in Korea, 1945–1978*
107. Roy Bahl, Chuk Kyo Kim, and Chong Kee Park, *Public Finances During the Korean Modernization Process*
108. William D. Wray, *Mitsubishi and the N.Y.K, 1870–1914: Business Strategy in the Japanese Shipping Industry*
109. Ralph William Huenemann, *The Dragon and the Iron Horse: The Economics of Railroads in China, 1876–1937*
110. Benjamin A. Elman, *From Philosophy to Philology: Intellectual and Social Aspects of Change in Late Imperial China*
111. Jane Kate Leonard, *Wei Yüan and China's Rediscovery of the Maritime World*

Harvard East Asian Monographs

112. Luke S. K. Kwong, *A Mosaic of the Hundred Days: Personalities, Politics, and Ideas of 1898*
113. John E. Wills, Jr., *Embassies and Illusions: Dutch and Portuguese Envoys to K'ang-hsi, 1666–1687*
114. Joshua A. Fogel, *Politics and Sinology: The Case of Naitō Konan (1866–1934)*
*115. Jeffrey C. Kinkley, ed., *After Mao: Chinese Literature and Society, 1978–1981*
116. C. Andrew Gerstle, *Circles of Fantasy: Convention in the Plays of Chikamatsu*
117. Andrew Gordon, *The Evolution of Labor Relations in Japan: Heavy Industry, 1853–1955*
*118. Daniel K. Gardner, *Chu Hsi and the "Ta Hsueh": Neo-Confucian Reflection on the Confucian Canon*
119. Christine Guth Kanda, *Shinzō: Hachiman Imagery and Its Development*
*120. Robert Borgen, *Sugawara no Michizane and the Early Heian Court*
121. Chang-tai Hung, *Going to the People: Chinese Intellectual and Folk Literature, 1918–1937*
*122. Michael A. Cusumano, *The Japanese Automobile Industry: Technology and Management at Nissan and Toyota*
123. Richard von Glahn, *The Country of Streams and Grottoes: Expansion, Settlement, and the Civilizing of the Sichuan Frontier in Song Times*
124. Steven D. Carter, *The Road to Komatsubara: A Classical Reading of the Renga Hyakuin*
125. Katherine F. Bruner, John K. Fairbank, and Richard T. Smith, *Entering China's Service: Robert Hart's Journals, 1854–1863*
126. Bob Tadashi Wakabayashi, *Anti-Foreignism and Western Learning in Early-Modern Japan: The "New Theses" of 1825*
127. Atsuko Hirai, *Individualism and Socialism: The Life and Thought of Kawai Eijirō (1891–1944)*
128. Ellen Widmer, *The Margins of Utopia: "Shui-hu hou-chuan" and the Literature of Ming Loyalism*
129. R. Kent Guy, *The Emperor's Four Treasuries: Scholars and the State in the Late Chien-lung Era*
130. Peter C. Perdue, *Exhausting the Earth: State and Peasant in Hunan, 1500–1850*
131. Susan Chan Egan, *A Latterday Confucian: Reminiscences of William Hung (1893–1980)*
132. James T. C. Liu, *China Turning Inward: Intellectual-Political Changes in the Early Twelfth Century*
133. Paul A. Cohen, *Between Tradition and Modernity: Wang T'ao and Reform in Late Ching China*

Harvard East Asian Monographs

134. Kate Wildman Nakai, *Shogunal Politics: Arai Hakuseki and the Premises of Tokugawa Rule*
135. Parks M. Coble, *Facing Japan: Chinese Politics and Japanese Imperialism, 1931–1937*
136. Jon L. Saari, *Legacies of Childhood: Growing Up Chinese in a Time of Crisis, 1890–1920*
137. Susan Downing Videen, *Tales of Heichū*
138. Heinz Morioka and Miyoko Sasaki, *Rakugo: The Popular Narrative Art of Japan*
139. Joshua A. Fogel, *Nakae Ushikichi in China: The Mourning of Spirit*
140. Alexander Barton Woodside, *Vietnam and the Chinese Model.: A Comparative Study of Vietnamese and Chinese Government in the First Half of the Nineteenth Century*
141. George Elision, *Deus Destroyed: The Image of Christianity in Early Modern Japan*
142. William D. Wray, ed., *Managing Industrial Enterprise: Cases from Japan's Prewar Experience*
143. T'ung-tsu Ch'ü, *Local Government in China Under the Ching*
144. Marie Anchordoguy, *Computers, Inc.: Japan's Challenge to IBM*
145. Barbara Molony, *Technology and Investment: The Prewar Japanese Chemical Industry*
146. Mary Elizabeth Berry, *Hideyoshi*
147. Laura E. Hein, *Fueling Growth: The Energy Revolution and Economic Policy in Postwar Japan*
148. Wen-hsin Yeh, *The Alienated Academy: Culture and Politics in Republican China, 1919–1937*
149. Dru C. Gladney, *Muslim Chinese: Ethnic Nationalism in the People's Republic*
150. Merle Goldman and Paul A. Cohen, eds., *Ideas Across Cultures: Essays on Chinese Thought in Honor of Benjamin L Schwartz*
151. James M. Polachek, *The Inner Opium War*
152. Gail Lee Bernstein, *Japanese Marxist: A Portrait of Kawakami Hajime, 1879–1946*
153. Lloyd E. Eastman, *The Abortive Revolution: China Under Nationalist Rule, 1927–1937*
154. Mark Mason, *American Multinationals and Japan: The Political Economy of Japanese Capital Controls, 1899–1980*
155. Richard J. Smith, John K. Fairbank, and Katherine F. Bruner, *Robert Hart and China's Early Modernization: His Journals, 1863–1866*
156. George J. Tanabe, Jr., *Myōe the Dreamkeeper: Fantasy and Knowledge in Kamakura Buddhism*
157. William Wayne Farris, *Heavenly Warriors: The Evolution of Japan's Military, 500–1300*

Harvard East Asian Monographs

158. Yu-ming Shaw, *An American Missionary in China: John Leighton Stuart and Chinese-American Relations*
159. James B. Palais, *Politics and Policy in Traditional Korea*
160. Douglas Reynolds, *China, 1898–1912: The Xinzheng Revolution and Japan*
161. Roger R. Thompson, *China's Local Councils in the Age of Constitutional Reform, 1898–1911*
162. William Johnston, *The Modern Epidemic: History of Tuberculosis in Japan*
163. Constantine Nomikos Vaporis, *Breaking Barriers: Travel and the State in Early Modern Japan*
164. Irmela Hijiya-Kirschnereit, *Rituals of Self-Revelation: Shishōsetsu as Literary Genre and Socio-Cultural Phenomenon*
165. James C. Baxter, *The Meiji Unification Through the Lens of Ishikawa Prefecture*
166. Thomas R. H. Havens, *Architects of Affluence: The Tsutsumi Family and the Seibu-Saison Enterprises in Twentieth-Century Japan*
167. Anthony Hood Chambers, *The Secret Window: Ideal Worlds in Tanizaki's Fiction*
168. Steven J. Ericson, *The Sound of the Whistle: Railroads and the State in Meiji Japan*
169. Andrew Edmund Goble, *Kenmu: Go-Daigo's Revolution*
170. Denise Potrzeba Lett, *In Pursuit of Status: The Making of South Korea's "New" Urban Middle Class*
171. Mimi Hall Yiengpruksawan, *Hiraizumi: Buddhist Art and Regional Politics in Twelfth-Century Japan*
172. Charles Shirō Inouye, *The Similitude of Blossoms: A Critical Biography of Izumi Kyōka (1873–1939), Japanese Novelist and Playwright*
173. Aviad E. Raz, *Riding the Black Ship: Japan and Tokyo Disneyland*
174. Deborah J. Milly, *Poverty, Equality, and Growth: The Politics of Economic Need in Postwar Japan*
175. See Heng Teow, *Japan's Cultural Policy Toward China, 1918–1931: A Comparative Perspective*
176. Michael A. Fuller, *An Introduction to Literary Chinese*
177. Frederick R. Dickinson, *War and National Reinvention: Japan in the Great War, 1914–1919*
178. John Solt, *Shredding the Tapestry of Meaning: The Poetry and Poetics of Kitasono Katue (1902–1978)*
179. Edward Pratt, *Japan's Protoindustrial Elite: The Economic Foundations of the Gōnō*
180. Atsuko Sakaki, *Recontextualizing Texts: Narrative Performance in Modern Japanese Fiction*
181. Soon-Won Park, *Colonial Industrialization and Labor in Korea: The Onoda Cement Factory*

Harvard East Asian Monographs

182. JaHyun Kim Haboush and Martina Deuchler, *Culture and the State in Late Chosŏn Korea*
183. John W. Chaffee, *Branches of Heaven: A History of the Imperial Clan of Sung China*
184. Gi-Wook Shin and Michael Robinson, eds., *Colonial Modernity in Korea*
185. Nam-lin Hur, *Prayer and Play in Late Tokugawa Japan: Asakusa Sensōji and Edo Society*
186. Kristin Stapleton, *Civilizing Chengdu: Chinese Urban Reform, 1895–1937*
187. Hyung Il Pai, *Constructing "Korean" Origins: A Critical Review of Archaeology, Historiography, and Racial Myth in Korean State-Formation Theories*
188. Brian D. Ruppert, *Jewel in the Ashes: Buddha Relics and Power in Early Medieval Japan*
189. Susan Daruvala, *Zhou Zuoren and an Alternative Chinese Response to Modernity*
190. James Z. Lee, *The Political Economy of a Frontier: Southwest China, 1250–1850*
191. Kerry Smith, *A Time of Crisis: Japan, the Great Depression, and Rural Revitalization*
192. Michael Lewis, *Becoming Apart: National Power and Local Politics in Toyama, 1868–1945*
193. William C. Kirby, Man-houng Lin, James Chin Shih, and David A. Pietz, eds., *State and Economy in Republican China: A Handbook for Scholars*
194. Timothy S. George, *Minamata: Pollution and the Struggle for Democracy in Postwar Japan*
195. Billy K. L. So, *Prosperity, Region, and Institutions in Maritime China: The South Fukien Pattern, 946–1368*
196. Yoshihisa Tak Matsusaka, *The Making of Japanese Manchuria, 1904–1932*
197. Maram Epstein, *Competing Discourses: Orthodoxy, Authenticity, and Engendered Meanings in Late Imperial Chinese Fiction*
198. Curtis J. Milhaupt, J. Mark Ramseyer, and Michael K. Young, eds. and comps., *Japanese Law in Context: Readings in Society, the Economy, and Politics*
199. Haruo Iguchi, *Unfinished Business: Ayukawa Yoshisuke and U.S.-Japan Relations, 1937–1952*
200. Scott Pearce, Audrey Spiro, and Patricia Ebrey, *Culture and Power in the Reconstitution of the Chinese Realm, 200–600*
201. Terry Kawashima, *Writing Margins: The Textual Construction of Gender in Heian and Kamakura Japan*
202. Martin W. Huang, *Desire and Fictional Narrative in Late Imperial China*
203. Robert S. Ross and Jiang Changbin, eds., *Re-examining the Cold War: U.S.-China Diplomacy, 1954–1973*

Harvard East Asian Monographs

204. Guanhua Wang, *In Search of Justice: The 1905–1906 Chinese Anti-American Boycott*
205. David Schaberg, *A Patterned Past: Form and Thought in Early Chinese Historiography*
206. Christine Yano, *Tears of Longing: Nostalgia and the Nation in Japanese Popular Song*
207. Milena Doleželová-Velingerová and Oldřich Král, with Graham Sanders, eds., *The Appropriation of Cultural Capital: China's May Fourth Project*
208. Robert N. Huey, *The Making of 'Shinkokinshū'*
209. Lee Butler, *Emperor and Aristocracy in Japan, 1467–1680: Resilience and Renewal*
210. Suzanne Ogden, *Inklings of Democracy in China*
211. Kenneth J. Ruoff, *The People's Emperor: Democracy and the Japanese Monarchy, 1945–1995*
212. Haun Saussy, *Great Walls of Discourse and Other Adventures in Cultural China*
213. Aviad E. Raz, *Emotions at Work: Normative Control, Organizations, and Culture in Japan and America*
214. Rebecca E. Karl and Peter Zarrow, eds., *Rethinking the 1898 Reform Period: Political and Cultural Change in Late Qing China*
215. Kevin O'Rourke, *The Book of Korean Shijo*
216. Ezra F. Vogel, ed., *The Golden Age of the U.S.-China-Japan Triangle, 1972–1989*
217. Thomas A Wilson, ed., *On Sacred Grounds: Culture, Society, Politics, and the Formation of the Cult of Confucius*
218. Donald S. Sutton, *Steps of Perfection: Exorcistic Performers and Chinese Religion in Twentieth-Century Taiwan*
219. Daqing Yang, *Technology of Empire: Telecommunications and Japanese Imperialism, 1930–1945*
220. Qianshen Bai, *Fu Shan's World: The Transformation of Chinese Calligraphy in the Seventeenth Century*
221. Paul Jakov Smith and Richard von Glahn, eds., *The Song-Yuan-Ming Transition in Chinese History*
222. Rania Huntington, *Alien Kind: Foxes and Late Imperial Chinese Narrative*
223. Jordan Sand, *House and Home in Modern Japan: Architecture, Domestic Space, and Bourgeois Culture, 1880–1930*
224. Karl Gerth, *China Made: Consumer Culture and the Creation of the Nation*
225. Xiaoshan Yang, *Metamorphosis of the Private Sphere: Gardens and Objects in Tang-Song Poetry*
226. Barbara Mittler, *A Newspaper for China? Power, Identity, and Change in Shanghai's News Media, 1872–1912*

Harvard East Asian Monographs

227. Joyce A. Madancy, *The Troublesome Legacy of Commissioner Lin: The Opium Trade and Opium Suppression in Fujian Province, 1820s to 1920s*
228. John Makeham, *Transmitters and Creators: Chinese Commentators and Commentaries on the Analects*
229. Elisabeth Köll, *From Cotton Mill to Business Empire: The Emergence of Regional Enterprises in Modern China*
230. Emma Teng, *Taiwan's Imagined Geography: Chinese Colonial Travel Writing and Pictures, 1683–1895*
231. Wilt Idema and Beata Grant, *The Red Brush: Writing Women of Imperial China*
232. Eric C. Rath, *The Ethos of Noh: Actors and Their Art*
233. Elizabeth J. Remick, *Building Local States: China During the Republican and Post-Mao Eras*
234. Lynn Struve, ed., *The Qing Formation in World-Historical Time*
235. D. Max Moerman, *Localizing Paradise: Kumano Pilgrimage and the Religious Landscape of Premodern Japan*
236. Antonia Finnane, *Speaking of Yangzhou: A Chinese City, 1550–1850*
237. Brian Platt, *Burning and Building: Schooling and State Formation in Japan, 1750–1890*
238. Gail Bernstein, Andrew Gordon, and Kate Wildman Nakai, eds., *Public Spheres, Private Lives in Modern Japan, 1600–1950: Essays in Honor of Albert Craig*
239. Wu Hung and Katherine R. Tsiang, *Body and Face in Chinese Visual Culture*
240. Stephen Dodd, *Writing Home: Representations of the Native Place in Modern Japanese Literature*
241. David Anthony Bello, *Opium and the Limits of Empire: Drug Prohibition in the Chinese Interior, 1729–1850*
242. Hosea Hirata, *Discourses of Seduction: History, Evil, Desire, and Modern Japanese Literature*
243. Kyung Moon Hwang, *Beyond Birth: Social Status in the Emergence of Modern Korea*
244. Brian R. Dott, *Identity Reflections: Pilgrimages to Mount Tai in Late Imperial China*
245. Mark McNally, *Proving the Way: Conflict and Practice in the History of Japanese Nativism*